Bankers, Bureaucrats, and Central Bank Politics

Most studies of the political economy of money focus on the *laws* protecting central banks from government interference; this book turns to the overlooked *people* who actually make monetary policy decisions. Using formal theory and statistical evidence from dozens of central banks across the developed and developing worlds, this book shows that monetary policy agents are not all the same. Molded by specific professional and sectoral backgrounds and driven by career concerns, central bankers with different career trajectories choose predictably different monetary policies. These differences undermine the widespread belief that central bank independence is a neutral solution for macroeconomic management. Instead, through careful appointment and retention of central bankers, partisan governments can and do influence monetary policy – preserving a political trade-off between inflation and real economic performance, even in an age of legally independent central banks.

Christopher Adolph is Assistant Professor of Political Science and Adjunct Assistant Professor of Statistics at the University of Washington, Seattle, where he is also a core faculty member of the Center for Statistics and the Social Sciences. He is a former Robert Wood Johnson Scholar in Health Policy Research and won the American Political Science Association's Mancur Olson Award for best dissertation in political economy. His research on comparative political economy and quantitative methods has appeared in *American Political Science Review*, *Political Analysis*, *Social Science & Medicine*, and other academic journals.

Cambridge Series in Comparative Politics

Other Books in the Series

Ben W. Ansell, *From the Ballot to the Blackboard: The Redistributive Political Economy of Education*
Leonardo R. Arriola, *Multiethnic Coalitions in Africa: Business Financing of Opposition Election Campaigns*
David Austen-Smith, Jeffry A. Frieden, Miriam A. Golden, Karl Ove Moene, and Adam Przeworski, eds., *Selected Works of Michael Wallerstein: The Political Economy of Inequality, Unions, and Social Democracy*
Andy Baker, *The Market and the Masses in Latin America: Policy Reform and Consumption in Liberalizing Economies*
Lisa Baldez, *Why Women Protest: Women's Movements in Chile*
Stefano Bartolini, *The Political Mobilization of the European Left, 1860–1980: The Class Cleavage*

(*continued after "About the type, figures, and data"*)

Bankers, Bureaucrats, and Central Bank Politics

THE MYTH OF NEUTRALITY

Christopher Adolph
University of Washington, Seattle

CAMBRIDGE
UNIVERSITY PRESS

32 Avenue of the Americas, New York NY 10013-2473, USA

Cambridge University Press is part of the University of Cambridge.

It furthers the University's mission by disseminating knowledge in the pursuit of education, learning and research at the highest international levels of excellence.

www.cambridge.org
Information on this title: www.cambridge.org/9781107567092

First published 2013
First paperback edition 2015
Grateful acknowledgement is made to
the BBC, Antony Jay, and Jonathan Lynn for permission
to reproduce selections from *Yes Minister* © BBC 1980, 1982.

A catalogue record for this publication is available from the British Library

Library of Congress Cataloguing in Publication data

Adolph, Christopher, 1976–
Bankers, bureaucrats, and central bank politics : the myth of neutrality / Christopher Adolph.
p. cm. – (Cambridge studies in comparative politics)
Includes bibliographic references and index.
ISBN 978-1-107-03261-3 (hardback)
1. Monetary policy. 2. Banks and banking, Central – Political aspects. 3. Bureaucracy. I. Title. II. Series.
HG230.3.A36 2012
332.1/1 – dc22 2012027612

ISBN 978-1-107-03261-3 Hardback
ISBN 978-1-107-56709-2 Paperback

For Erika

Sir DESMOND *Glazebrook, Chairman of Bartlett's Bank*: Like I say, it's up to my board. Could go either way, quite frankly, could go either way.

Sir HUMPHREY *Appleby, Permanent Undersecretary for the Department of Administrative Affairs*: I see.

DESMOND: Incidentally, to change the subject completely, you remember the new Ministry Co-Partnership Commission.... The chairmanship hasn't been filled yet? Because should one be offered...

HUMPHREY: I can tell you that your name is on the short list.... There has to be some reason to appoint you, you see. What about the advisory committee of dental establishments? Know anything about teeth?

DESMOND: I'm a banker.

HUMPHREY: How about the Dumping at Sea Representations Panel? Where do you live, near the sea?

DESMOND: Knightsbridge. Just behind Harrod's.

HUMPHREY: Not near enough... Meat Marketing Board – know anything about meat?

DESMOND: I eat it.

HUMPHREY: My dear chap, what *do* you know about?

DESMOND: Nothing, really. I'm a banker.

HUMPHREY: There must be some minority group you can represent.

DESMOND: Bankers?

"Jobs for the Boys," *Yes Minister*

CONTENTS

FIGURES

TABLES

BOXES

ABBREVIATIONS

CBCC	Central Banker Career Conservatism
CBCD	Central Banker Conservatism in Developing Countries
CBI	Central Bank Independence
CBNA	Central Bank Nonaccommodation
CWB	Centralization of Wage Bargaining
ECB	European Central Bank
ERM	Exchange Rate Mechanism
FOMC	Federal Open Market Committee
FSE	Financial Sector Employment
FSS	Financial Sector Score
GDP	Gross Domestic Product
IMF	International Monetary Fund
IMI	Inflation Mitigating Institutions
MPA	Monetary Policy Autonomy
OECD	Organization for Economic Cooperation and Development
PCoG	Partisan Center of Gravity
RPCF	Ratio-Preserving Counterfactual
TARP	Troubled Asset Relief Program

ACKNOWLEDGEMENTS

Although I did not know it at the time, this book began when I was assigned to lead a discussion of dueling articles written by my comparative political economy professors. Because the articles came to sharply distinct conclusions, I could not retreat behind praise. Figuring out which perspective I found more persuasive was difficult: the papers' setup was fairly similar, and their disagreement somewhat puzzling. Both noted that the standard model of monetary policy making assumed central banks preside over perfectly competitive labor markets; both argued that varying degrees of wage bargaining coordination made this assumption problematic; both showed that labor unions and central banks strategically interact in different ways across the rich industrialized countries so often studied by comparative political economists. The trouble was, my mentors disagreed about the real economic outcomes this strategic interaction produces.

As I cast about for an intelligent comment that might lead to consensus, I noticed that while my professors' theoretical models and their intellectual predecessors assumed central bankers' policy preferences vary, all their empirical strategies ignored preferences and focused instead on measuring differences in central bank charters, especially how much legal authority central bankers had. To my surprise, this simplifying assumption ran right through the history of economic study of monetary policy. As far as the monetary policy literature was concerned, central bankers might in theory be more or less concerned with inflation or unemployment, but in practice they were surely all inflation hawks, and the only thing that mattered was how much power or "independence" central bankers enjoyed.

Then came an uncomfortable thought for a first-year graduate student signed up for the institutionalist school of political economy. Many institutionalist models explain variation in policy outcomes based on the interaction of political actors' preferences with the rules and structure of the organizations they inhabit. While the relationship among political actors is often more or less adversarial (as in legislatures or elections), in many cases actors exist within a hierarchy (such as a bureaucracy or party) where a principal assigns an agent to carry out a task. Loud proclamations and public votes usually reveal the preferences of adversarial political actors, who also generally serve as principals to bureaucratic agents. Therefore, it might seem that the political economist's job is to develop a deep understanding of how institutions help pick the winning principals and then bind agents to obey them. But what if bureaucratic agents have a chance to shift things towards their own prefered outcomes? Granting central bankers independence creates exactly that opportunity for bureaucratic agents, putting the onus on political economists to measure agent preferences. There lay the cornerstone of a massive project, for bureaucratic agents keep much lower profiles than their elected political masters. Mindful that markets watch their every move, central bankers are particularly reticient: discovering systematic correlates of their preferences would not be easy.

Happily, an important clue to central bankers' behavior lay in plain sight: their career trajectories. As I assembled personal information about these secretive officials, I found again and again that the places central bankers spent their formative working years strongly predicted their choices as central bankers. In the end, this key piece of information helped explain many aspects of monetary policy making: the policies made and their economic effects; the officials chosen to make monetary policy decisions and the length of time they held on to that power. But gathering complete biographies of the hundreds of officials who made monetary policy across many decades and countries was a daunting task. The book you hold – either as a slab of paper or a bundle of electrons – is built on a foundation of thousands of separately collected pieces of biographical information and thousands of lines of computer code sifting through those data.

None of it could exist without the help of dozens of people over the course of a decade.

First, I gratefully acknowledge the aid of central bank staff members who kindly helped identify and provide biographical information about the past leaders of their institutions. As is fitting for a student of monetary policy, I am indebted to many banks, including the Banco Central de la República Argentina, Reserve Bank of Australia, Oesterreichische Nationalbank (National Bank of Austria), Central Bank of Barbados, Banque Nationale de Belgique (National Bank of Belgium), Bulgarian National Bank, Bank of Canada, Banco Central de Chile, Hrvatska narodna banka (Croatian National Bank), Central

Bank of Cyprus, Česká národní banka (Czech National Bank), Danmarks Nationalbank (National Bank of Denmark), Bank of England, Eesti Pank (Bank of Estonia), Suomen Pankki (Bank of Finland), Banque de France, Deutsche Bundesbank (Germany), Central Bank of Ireland, Bank of Israel, Banca d'Italia (Bank of Italy), Bank of Jamaica, Central Bank of Jordan, National Bank of Kazakhstan, Central Bank of Kuwait, Latvijas Banka (Bank of Latvia), Central Bank of Lesotho, Lietuvos Bankas (Bank of Lithuania), Maldives Monetary Authority, Banco de México, De Nederlandsche Bank (Bank of the Netherlands), Bank of the Netherland Antilles (now Central Bank of Curaçao and Saint Maarten), Reserve Bank of New Zealand, Norges Bank (Bank of Norway), Bangko Sentral ng Pilipinas (Central Bank of the Philippines), Narodowy Bank Polski (National Bank of Poland), Banco de Portugal, Banca Națională României (National Bank of Romania), Central Bank of the Russian Federation, Faletupe Tutotonu o Samoa (Central Bank of Samoa), Banka Slovenije (Bank of Slovenia), South African Reserve Bank, Banco de España (Bank of Spain), Sveriges Riksbank (Bank of Sweden), Swiss National Bank, Bank of Thailand, National Reserve Bank of Tonga, Central Bank of Trinidad and Tobago, Bank of Uganda, and Banco Central de Venezuela. Although none of these institutions is responsible for the conduct or conclusions of this study, without their aid I would have been seeking buried data without a map.

Of course, a map is no use if you cannot read it. I thank my friend and colleague Christian Brunelli for excellent translations of Japanese sources, and I thank Dean Hunt of Shoenhof's for meticulously deciphering the mysterious undocumented abbreviations of Swedish biographical dictionaries. I gratefully acknowledge the research assistance of Isik Ozel, who helped finalize the careers database, and Aaron Erlich and Brad Epperly, who shared their expertise on the related bureaucratic delegation problems of administering elections and justice, respectively. I have also been the beneficiary of thousands of hours of other scholars' labor. Tom Cusack, Rob Franzese, Torben Iversen, and Sylvia Maxfield kindly shared data, and I thank Henry Chappell and Pierre Siklos for providing invaluable resources through their websites.

During my time in graduate school, Jim Alt, Peter Hall, and Michael Hiscox all helped shape this work; without their guidance, the final product would be less persuasive and less coherent. Gary King showed me that social scientists can tailor their statistical methods to their research problems and find ways to visually explain even the most complex models. In a project devoted to uncovering preferences and associations that few are eager to advertise, both lessons were crucial. Most of all, I am grateful to Torben Iversen, whose work inspired this book and whose confident support help me question basic assumptions of the literature. My colleagues at the University of Washington have encouraged and supported my research in many ways, and I am grateful for their feedback and suggestions. Peter May, Aseem Prakash, Thomas Richardson, Kate Stovel, Mike Ward, and Erik Wibbels have all given vital support and suggestions. Margaret Levi pushed me to think broadly about the implications of my research, shared her deep knowledge of political economy and publishing, and is, as always, an invaluable mentor and friend.

Many other colleagues have offered useful suggestions and comments over the long development of this project. I am grateful to all who participated in a workshop on my manuscript sponsored by the University of Washington's Center for Comparative Historical Analysis of Organizations and States (CHAOS) and Cambridge University Press, as well as those who offered comments in seminars at Harvard University, Yale University, the University of Washington, New York University, Pennsylvania State University, Rice University, and Cornell University, and at the annual meetings of the Midwest Political Science Association, the American Political Science Association, and the Society for Political Methodology. I am especially grateful to John Ahlquist, Bill Bernhard, Christian Brunelli, Bill Clark, Rob Franzese, John Freeman, Elisabeth Ivarsflaten, Alex Kuo, Adam Przeworksi, Ken Scheve, Ken Shepsle, David Stassavge, Endre Tvinnereim, Christopher Way, and several anonymous reviewers for stimulating comments and helpful suggestions. Naturally, I am solely responsible for oversights and errors that remain.

Many institutions have made this book possible. I could not have completed this research without the generosity of the National Science Foundation; the Center for Basic Research in the Social Sciences (now the Institute for Quantitative Social Science) and the Multidisciplinary Program in Inequality and Social Policy, both of Harvard University; the Department of Political Science and the Center for Statistics and the Social Sciences, both at the University of Washington, Seattle; the Robert Wood Johnson Scholars in Health Policy Research Program; and the University of Michigan School of Public Health. At Cambridge University Press, Lew Bateman, Shaun Vigil, and Mark Fox, along with Adrian Pereira of Aptara, helped make the transition from manuscript to book as smooth as possible and gave me the freedom to present social science in a format that is simultaneously visual, mathematical, and narrative.

I could never have finished this book without the faith of my family and friends. My parents and grandparents have my deepest gratitude for their support and love. My brother Brian lent his drafting skills to help produce the visual representation of career paths shown in the first chapter, and my grandmother Beanie – a late-blooming political activist and a natural social scientist – insisted on reading the full manuscript, pencil in hand. Many friends listened patiently as I told them more about central banks than they ever expected (or, I suspect, wanted) to learn; my thanks and apologies go especially to Salma Bakht, Maria Goff, Stephanie Jaros, Ryan Krech, Piret Loone, Victor Shih, and Aimee Vafaie. I owe a special debt of gratitude to Rob Fannion, who read almost every draft of this work. In countless conversations over the years, I've benefited from Rob's brilliant and wide-ranging knowledge of political economy, politics, and current events; his persistent skepticism of conventional wisdom; and his determination that I cast my argument in as wide a context as possible. Without Rob's insight, patient counsel, and friendship, this project would have been much less than it is.

Finally, Erika Steiskal gave more to this book than I can ever repay. Erika didn't just patiently endure a distracted partner whose mind was lost in the pages of a manuscript – though endure she did – she selflessly offered to help make this book better. For a month, the two of us spent our evenings watching *Yes Minister* (surely the most enjoyable introduction to the study of bureaucracy that exists) and revising graphics together. Erika's expertise in illustration and graphic design touched literally every visual display within these pages. Better still, her original artwork gave this book a cover I can only hope it deserves. Erika's love, faith, patience, and support made this book a reality. I am eternally grateful to her.

CHRISTOPHER ADOLPH
SEPTEMBER 2012

1

AGENTS, INSTITUTIONS, AND THE POLITICAL ECONOMY OF PERFORMANCE

> We know more about abstract agents dealing with abstract principals than we do about real bureaucrats dealing with real politicians.
>
> James March

This book introduces a new approach to the politics of money focused on the decisive role played by central bankers themselves. There is a surprisingly large gap between what we know about the behavior of ideal central bankers, and how *real* central bankers make crucial decisions about interest rates, inflation, unemployment, and economic growth. To understand how monetary policy really works, I offer practical means of measuring, explaining, and predicting central bankers' preferences and the effects of those preferences on economic outcomes.

I argue that patrons, or "shadow principals" in the financial sector and partisan governments, shape the beliefs and career incentives of bureaucratic agents otherwise legally insulated from outside pressure. This claim is simple but has important implications. Focusing on developed countries between the end of Bretton Woods and the birth of the euro, with sidetrips to developing countries and earlier periods, I show that career theories of central banker behavior explain substantial differences in interest rate decisions, inflation rates, and in some cases, real economic performance, especially in countries with independent central banks.

The concept of shadow principals lets us revisit the role of outside pressures on monetary policy. The political influence of banks is now a critical public issue in many industrial democracies. From the sober assessment of MIT economist Simon Johnson, who argues the six largest American banks are a dangerous "oligarchy" threatening public welfare, the economy, and democracy itself (Johnson and Kwak, 2010, 221), to Matt Taibbi's furious diatribes against Goldman Sachs, the "great vampire squid wrapped around the face of humanity," condemnation of the political activities of the financial sector has reached a pitch not heard in a century.[1] Populist fury against the combination of bank bailouts and public austerity has brought down governments in Iceland, Ireland, Spain, and Greece. Disapproval of state favoritism toward banks and bankers is perhaps the only thing the American left and right can publicly agree on. Arguably, no sector of the ecomomy is more responsible for the economic crisis that began in 2008, yet no other sector has emerged more profitably, or with greater leverage over policy in the United States and Europe.

Solving the problem of overpowered banks depends on understanding the origins of their political influence. Is financial sector influence on politics a new phenomenon dating back just to the deregulation of American banks in the 1990s? Is it the result of the massive increase in financial sector concentration over the last decade, likely to recede (as some argue) if the largest banks are broken up? Would new, legally independent regulatory agencies be sufficient to restore the balance of power between public regulators and banks? By focusing on the making of monetary policy, the central mission of supposedly autonomous central banks, I cast doubt on the idea that heavy financial sector influence on economic policy is new, operating through new channels, or solvable through institutional reform alone. We have only underestimated outside influence on policy because of the masking role of a supposedly perfect form of political independence, embodied by the modern central bank. Once we recognize the systematic ability of private banks to influence central bankers' future careers, the enduring basis of private banks' ability to shape the policies set by central banks – from interest rates to bailouts – becomes clear.

To gain a deeper understanding of the politics of central banking, I take a broadly comparative approach to monetary policy, centered on agents. Central bankers' ranks are much larger than the handful of celebrities – Greenspan, Volcker, Trichet, Bernanke – who make monthly rounds in the headlines. We can learn much more about monetary policy if we cast our nets wide enough to include the hundreds of monetary policy board members who have collectively set the interest rates of dozens of economies over the last half century. Though my focus is on individual decision makers, I do not tell a story of personalities.

1 Matt Taibbi, 2010, "The Great American Bubble Machine," *Rolling Stone*, April 5.

Instead, I trace the patterns and incentives underlying central bankers' policy preferences and behavior using the ideas and tools of modern political economy, and emphasizing the political and institutional context in which central bankers operate.

But the arguments I make about the policy preferences of central bankers have implications beyond monetary policy and should inform the wider debate on delegation and institutions in political economy. I offer not only a theory of how bureaucratic agents' preferences and behavior can be understood through career effects, but also tools of quantitative measurement and statistical analysis designed to efficiently catalog bureaucrats' career experiences and assess the effects of those careers in a wide variety of bureaucratic contexts. If models and measures of bureaucratic preference can shed new light even on monetary technocrats, there is little doubt the same techniques will reveal new insights about regulators and policy implementers in all corners of the state.

Interests and Institutions in Comparative Political Economy

Comparative political economy is the study of what happens when political and economic actors with different interests interact within different institutional contexts.[2] The political economy of performance, an important subfield within comparative political economy, is interested in how the interactions of institutions and preferences shape economic outcomes. But the balance between these two variables has tilted firmly to institutions, with scholars paying less attention to individuals' preferences, some attention to large groups such as political parties, industrial sectors, or economic classes, and a great deal of attention to the rules of the political games that individuals and groups play.

By focusing on long-overlooked organizing features of the social world, the institutionalist turn in comparative political economy has yielded impressive advances. Earlier economic and sociological analyses glossed over variation in

2 The actors of interest are individuals and organizations (formally constituted groups) of individuals. *Institutions* are formal and informal rules defining permitted interactions among individuals and organizations (North, 1990). Recursively, these include the rules that constrain the interaction of individuals within organizations. *Interests* are the preferences of actors over policies, induced by their underlying preferences over economic and political outcomes and their *ideas* about the causal relationships among them (Hall, 1989; Blythe, 2002). If we can take for granted that actors with the same preferences share the same economic ideas, descriptions of interest can even subsume ideas, at least within a shared context. For the most part, I talk only of interests and institutions, leaving economic ideas in the background.

institutional context and its effects on incentives and behavior. These perspectives struggled to explain differences in political economic outcomes across cases with congruent economic conditions, societal demands, and endowments of technology and capital. In contrast, institutional theories offered powerful new explanations of diverse long-standing problems.[3] If the new institutionalism has opened up new ways of seeing politics, it has also – unintentionally and unnecessarily – created new blindspots. Most often lamented is the weakness of institutional explanations of change, but the most important may be the tendency to under-study the agency and interests of actors operating within the constraints of rules. Human actors working within institutions play an indispensable role, and their preferences and strategies are inextricably linked with the outcomes institutional scholars study. Their interests shape the content of policy from everyday decisions on budgets and regulations to the extraordinary questions raised by social revolutions and institutional design. But the role of agents is often submerged, especially in empirical tests of institutional theories.

Agent preferences can flow *from* institutions, a phenomenon contemporary institutionalists are well prepared to study (North, 1990; Knight, 1992; Zysman, 1994; Acemoglu, Johnson, and Robinson, 2004). But the relationship between interests and institutions is not always so one-sided. At other times, preferences shape institutions – either suddenly, when institutions are made from scratch, or gradually, through the layering of changes on top of existing institutions.[4] Most often, however, preferences and institutions persist independently, jointly determining policy outcomes. To comprehend cases in which

3 Institutional theories help explain why, despite similar natural endowments, some nations develop and others do not (North, 1990; Acemoglu, Johnson, and Robinson, 2004); why different economies have "failed" to converge on the neoliberal model (Hall and Soskice, 2001; Hollingsworth and Boyer, 1997); why public policy changes rapidly in some polities, and remains frozen in others (Tsebelis, 2002); why some governments exercise more oversight than others (Huber and Shipan, 2002); why labor market systems evolved differently across the industrialized world (Swenson, 1991; Thelen, 2004); whether and how governments manipulate the economy for electoral gain (Clark and Hallerberg, 2000); and on and on. Casting our net beyond political economy, institutionalism has helped explain why social unrest only rarely culminates in social revolution (Skocpol, 1979); how the modern state develops from the legacies of past institutions (Skowronek, 1982; Ertman, 1997); and how legislatures resolve the fundamental ambiguities of majority rule (Shepsle and Weingast, 1981; Laver and Shepsle, 1996), among many other examples.

4 Thelen (2004) calls this layering process "conversion." An example can be found in the development of the Federal Reserve from its birth in 1913 to its divorce from the

agent preferences are at least partially exogenous, we need to shine a spotlight on the agents themselves.

For a concrete example of the successes and limitations of current institutionalist practice, I consider one of the most famous, accepted, and influential topics of institutionalist scholarship, the independent central bank. After the Great Inflation of the 1970s, economists on the hunt for general explanations and solutions for this persistent problem found an attractive explanation in the concept of time inconsistency. Elected governments, even if they understand that easy money is no free lunch, are tempted to occasionally stimulate the economy through unexpected jolts to the money supply. Unless this temptation is banished, inflation will be permanently higher (Kydland and Prescott, 1977). Later authors suggested the problem could be resolved by passing on responsibility for monetary policy to an agent with credible anti-inflation preferences, so long as that agent's independence from the elected government was legally guaranteed (Barro and Gordon, 1983; Rogoff, 1985). When still more studies found that central bank independence (CBI) was correlated with low inflation, countries the world over jumped on the CBI bandwagon (Grilli, Masciandaro, and Tabellini, 1991; Cukierman, Webb, and Neyapti, 1992; Alesina and Summers, 1993; Maxfield, 1997). Although it remains an open question whether the low inflation of the 1990s was a result of higher CBI, the appearance of success was enough to convince twelve members of the European Union to create the über-independent European Central Bank (McNamara, 1998). But institutional independence is not the the whole story of monetary policy, and central bank independence brought not the "end of history" for central banks, but a new set of questions.

The CBI literature exemplifies the popular principal–agent model of delegation.[5] Many problems in politics are intrinsically dilemmas of delegation, in which a political executive (the principal) must choose a bureaucrat (the agent) to carry out her agenda. Granting discretion to an agent entails two dangers for the principal, both of which hinge on the agent's informational advantages over her. First, there is the *moral hazard* that an agent might secretly benefit at the expense of the principal. Second, there is the possibility that by *adverse selection*, the principal has unwittingly chosen an agent with dissonant policy preferences

Treasury in 1951; Meltzer (2003) claims the cumulative change rendered the institution unrecognizable to its founders.

5 For reviews of the application of principal–agent models to bureaucratic delegation, see Bendor, Glazer, and Hammond (2001) and Meier and Krause (2003*b*). For a rigorous introduction to the logic of these models, see Laffont and Martimort (2002).

who will implement a policy at odds with the principal's agenda. The principal–agent framework highlights the importance of the interests of principal and agent, on one hand, and of the institutions of agent selection, monitoring, and enforcement on the other. Elegant theoretical and empirical work tackles the question of how political principals monitor, discipline, constrain, oversee, or otherwise control the bureaucracy (McCubbins, Noll, and Weingast, 1987; Epstein and O'Halloran, 1999; Huber and Shipan, 2002).

But there is something missing from this literature. Regarding principal–agent relationships, and especially monetary delegation, James March (1997) hits the bullseye when he laments that "[w]e know more about abstract agents dealing with abstract principals than we do about real bureaucrats dealing with real politicians." The modern approach to the bureaucracy devotes the lion's share of attention to legislatures and executives, often treating the bureaucracy and its preferences as a "black box," and in the case of central banks, a *deus ex machina*.[6] Studies of principal–agent relationships usually focus on what principals want and the enforcement mechanisms they use to discipline agents, but spend little time finding out what agents desire. Yet how can we understand what constraints achieve if we do not know what they are constraining?

Agents, Institutions, and Change

Treating the bureaucracy as a black box fosters dangerous habits. If we never peek in the box, we might assume its contents never change. Static thinking impoverishes the stock of explanations for change, limiting political agency to rare "critical junctures," crises when the rules of the game can be rewritten. During those periods, actors design new institutions to systematically advantage themselves in the future (Knight, 1992; Katznelson, 2003; Thelen, 2004). But if agents can pack their preferences into institutions, the temptation arises to treat institutions as sufficient statistics of the political system. We end up with punctuated equilibrium theories that overwork the few available explanations and

6 Meier and Krause (2003*a*) identify inattention to bureaucrats as the key failing of the bureaucracy literature. They applaud the growing "theoretical and empirical understanding of the motivation, incentives, and tactics employed by political institutions to mold bureaucracy," but warn that in failing to "reserve a place for the bureaucracy at the table ... we get a portrait of bureaucracy that is neither bureaucracy centered nor institutionally balanced."

overlook gradual changes during periods of apparent equilibrium.[7] In particular, people seem simply redundant to explanations of outcomes during settled times.

But agents, groups, and even social forces come and go. Pierson (2004) takes punctuated equilibrium theories to task for assuming an impossible degree of actor continuity. Even if the rules governing a specific bureaucracy were put in place to serve a particular policy goal held by a particular faction, many years and shocks to the political system later, new actors inhabiting or interacting with the bureaucracy may employ the same institutions to unanticipated ends (Pierson, 2004; Thelen, 2004).[8] As the agents of a bureaucratic organization change over time – because of elections, retirement, recruitment, and career shuffling – the original purpose of an agency can be buried or even subverted without any alteration of its governing charter.

Political economists are beginning to recognize that the actors inside bureaucracy are neither timeless nor inert. At the same time, institutionalists are breaking free of the punctuated equilibrium setup to consider ways in which actors – including principals, agents, and outsiders – chafe at institutional constraints. As Streeck and Thelen (2005) put it,

> Political institutions are not only periodically contested; they are also the object of ongoing skirmishes as actors try to achieve advantage by interpreting or redirecting institutions in pursuit of their goals, or by subverting or circumventing rules that clash with their interests.... [T]he aim must be to understand ... the way actors cultivate change from within the context of existing opportunities and constraints – working around elements they cannot change while attempting to harness and utilize others in novel ways.

As an effort to re-evaluate the interplay of structure and preference in policy making, this book falls neatly within Streeck and Thelen's agenda. In particular, I discuss various ways in which the *interaction* of institutions and successive generations of agents influences policy outcomes. Doing so uncovers an underappreciated answer to a commonly perceived limitation of institutional theories

7 The punctuated equilibrium metaphor originates in evolutionary biology (Eldredge and Gould, 1972), and is subject to similar critiques there (Dawkins, 1986).

8 An American example: the laborers and farmers who fought for the 1890 Sherman Act – a policy change allowing the courts to restrain industrial monopolists – were doubtless chagrined when conservative judges later used the same law to curtail union activities (Letwin, 1981).

	Country A		Country B	
	Period 1	Period 2	Period 1	Period 2
Institution	○	○	□	□
Agent	+	−	+	−
Outcome	⊕	⊖	■	■

Figure I.1. *How static institutions cause change through agent replacement.* In some cases, an institution (○) gives agents the autonomy to affect outcomes, such that the final outcome is a synthesis of agent preferences (+ or −) and institutional effects (yielding ⊕ or ⊖). Other institutions (□) constrain agents to produce the same outcome (■) regardless of agent preferences.

of policy, the difficulty of explaining change. Whereas institutions often provide explanations – even too many explanations – of cross-sectional variation, it seems at first impossible that static institutions could "explain" variation in outcomes over time. But if actors and their preferences are changing over time, and interacting with static institutions, those institutions can matter. In fact, studying interactions can add a necessary dose of gradualism to the punctuated equilibrium models so common in comparative political economy.

Figure I.1 provides a simple representation. Two countries (A and B) studied over two periods (1 and 2) have different time-invariant policy making institutions (○ and □, respectively). In period 1, type + agents set policy under each country's institutional rule, and in period 2, type − agents take over. The figure illustrates an example where the effects of institutions are felt through the change in agents over time: institution ○ allows agents to change the policy outcome, whereas institution □ does not. From a comparative perspective, it would be misleading to say that either agents or institutions alone caused the outcomes to differ. What matters is their joint effect, which can be discerned even though the institutions are static.[9] In Chapter 6, I exploit this logic to im-

9 One methodological upshot is that the interaction of agent preferences and static institutions offers political economists working with panel data the chance to escape the dilemma posed by fixed effects specifications. Including fixed effects in a panel data model protects estimates of the effects of time-varying covariates from confounding by omitted time-invariant variables. However, the same protection does not extend to any time invariant institutions for which we might want parameter estimates. Even if these parameters are backed out of the model, our estimates of them will still be subject to confounding by any of the myriad omitted static features of the units stud-

prove our understanding of the effects of mostly static institutions when run by different agents.

Many institutionalists concede their theories explain continuity far better than change (DiMaggio and Powell, 1991; Orren and Skowronek, 1994). As Thelen (1999) emphasizes, change in an institutionalized world must come from exogenous shocks – shocks which either so disorder politics that real institutional reconfiguration is possible, or which institutions withstand and mediate in unique ways. Exogenous shocks might include technological change or (in North's (1990) deceptively modest phrase) changes in relative prices. Orren and Skowronek (1994) add the insight that exogenous shocks can also come from the collision of different institutional streams.[10]

I emphasize a different kind of shock – the turnover of agents within institutions. New agents transform institutions and policies from the inside out. Change can happen suddenly, when a new regime installs its own elite civil servants, or it can also occur gradually, when the training, socialization, and career interests of bureaucrats shifts over years and generations. Therefore, even the routine replacement of personnel provides insights into the process of change between critical institutional events.

Bringing Bureaucrats Back In

Ironically, just as some political economists were relegating the study of real actors to the backseat in favor of institutions and ideal representations of actors, strands of research in other fields of political science, notably the study of legislatures and courts, moved in the opposite direction. Understanding the motivations and preferences of political actors is now a core component of the American politics research agenda, as the large literature surrounding ideal point estimation shows. Extending its reach into the study of courts and Supreme Court

ied. Agent-institution interaction terms, on the other hand, can be estimated without omitted variable bias in a fixed effects panel model. The analyst can simply control for both the time-varying agent preferences and their interaction with institutions, which is always time varying. Note that if fixed effects are used, the institution itself must be omitted from the specification, as this base term is already incorporated in the fixed effect.

10 Acemoglu, Johnson, and Robinson's (2002) "reversal of fortune" is a world-shaping example.

Justices, this literature resists the puzzling tendency to assume some political actors are different: not economically rational beings but selfless wise men.[11]

Central bankers are the most important political actors still veiled by the myth of bureaucratic impartiality. The myth has many sources, including fawning accounts of central bankers as oracles (Woodward, 2000), but it draws sustenance from economists' eagerness to treat monetary policy as a purely technical problem with an optimal solution, downplaying or dismissing its distributive consequences. Not least, the myth of neutrality persists because central bankers have every reason to feed it – it is always easier to be considered above politics, whether or not one has a political agenda (Kettl, 1986).

Like legislators, executives, judges, and other bureaucrats, central bankers are political agents with their own interests and plans. As with any question of bureaucratic decision-making, to comprehend monetary policy choices we must know the goals of the central bankers themselves. Of course, we also need to know something about the institutions central bankers inhabit, the constraints they operate under, and the governments that appoint them. But it is not sufficient to know these things: an understanding of policy delegation that ignores agents' preferences will be flawed, with rare exceptions.

What do bureaucrats want? A simple typology of motivations helps work through the myriad answers political scientists, sociologists, and economists have offered to this question.[12] The catalog is incomplete, but it helps fix the reasons bureaucrats might work or shirk, and the ends to which they direct their efforts.

Table 1.1 classifies eight material and non-material bureaucratic motives. Perhaps the oldest view of state officials supposes the rewards of office come from the power of office to set policy. On this view, bureaucratic agents can be political players. Recognizing that battles over regulation and distribution have winners and losers, these bureacratic agents gain ego-rents from picking the winners.[13] A second, rarer politicized bureaucrat seeks power itself. Their num-

11 The seminal work on Congress is Poole and Rosenthal (1997). For the study of judges' preferences, see Segal and Cover (1989); Segal and Spaeth (1993, 2002); Martin and Quinn (2002); and Epstein and Knight (1998). Although most central banks provide no record of their members' voting behavior, the Federal Reserve does, and several attempts have been made to tease preference information out of these data (Chang, 2003; Chappell, McGregor, and Vermilyea, 2004*a*); see Chapter 4.

12 See also Downs (1967), Wilson (1991), Brehm and Gates (1999), and Golden (2000) for overviews.

13 Examples of models that assume bureaucrats are policy seekers are too numerous to name. It should be said that many of these studies use "policy" as an implied short-hand

Table 1.1. *A typology of bureaucrats' motivations.*

Type of reward	
Material	**Non-material**
Rents, bribes, and perks: Budget maximizers and other narrowly self-interest actors (Downs, 1967; Niskanen, 1971)	Intrinsic motivation: Public servants who believe "the job is its own reward" (Desi, 1971)
Career concerns: Forward-looking rent-seekers trying to win jobs inside or outside the bureaucracy (Bernstein, 1955; Stigler, 1971)	**Technocratic rewards:** Skilled, "neutral" bureaucrats satisfied by getting things "right" (Weber, 1946).
Political power: Innovators and kingdom-builders who remake politics from inside the bureaucracy in pursuit of agenda-setting power (Carpenter, 2001)	**Policy preference:** Ideologically-driven true believers who receive "policy rents" when their preferences are enacted (Downs, 1967)
	Socialization: Careerists who adopt their organization's or profession's preferences as their own; "Where you stand..." (Kaufman, 1960; Allison, 1969)
	Democratic ethic: Public servants who set aside personal views to faithfully implement the elected government's wishes (Finer, 1941; Golden, 2000)

All categories help explain bureaucratic effort; goals in bold are likely to influence the direction of central bankers policy preferences as well. For each motive, I list seminal or exemplary works.

bers include policy innovators who initiate policy change, rather than waiting on a political principal's commands, and kingdom builders who aspire to grow their departments into formidable political players. These bureaucrats aim not simply for larger paychecks and cushier offices, but for a place at the agenda-setting table (Carpenter, 2001).

Most bureaucrats likely find motivation in smaller rewards, such as job satisfaction (Desi, 1971; Frey, 1997; Brehm and Gates, 1999). For overworked and underpaid street-level bureaucrats such as teachers and social workers, these "intrinsic motivations" are surely the most important. Even elite central bankers no doubt feel a thrill working on interesting and important policy decisions (Meyer, 2004). If one psychological motivation is the joy of doing the job, another is the joy of doing it "right" – the psychological salary of the technocrat. This motivation is most closely associated with Max Weber (1946), who observed the rise of routinized, impersonal, seemingly objective bureaucratic organizations and contrasted their meritocratic selection processes with the inefficient favoritism of patronage politics. In Weber's view, the modern state requires neutrally competent experts: administrators whose personality types (and supportive insulating institutions) can be counted on to produce "correct" or "sound" policies. A strictly Weberian view of the bureaucracy seems naïvely functionalist today, but Weber's ideas still lurk behind many discussion of bureaucracy, and especially influence thinking about central banks.

Starting in the 1960s and 1970s, some economists broke free of the Weberian spell. They disputed every element of neutral competence. Arrow (1951) dealt the notion of a single "correct policy" or well-defined "public interest" a death blow. And if bureaucrats cannot be neutral, perhaps they are instead self-interested; focused not on gaining competence, but on extracting rents. But which rents, and how to maximize them? One can discern two different, albeit related, visions of *homo economicus bureaucratus*. The first subspecies, associated with public choice, seeks rents, bribes, and perks *right now*. Following Niskanen (1971), a common shortcut is to suppose that selfish bureaucratic agents mainly act to maximize their bureaus' budgets, on the assumption that larger budgets enhance job security, comfort, and the scope for corruption. An alternative view, growing out of capture theory, holds that bureaucrats seek support from the very industries they regulate: either political support within the state

for mechanisms of career rewards or socialization, which I treat as distinct motivations below.

or, as I discuss at greater length in the following, post-civil service career rewards (Bernstein, 1955; Stigler, 1971; Peltzman, 1976; Cohen, 1986).

Some motivations can be described best as sociological. Foremost of these is socialization, a cultural phenomenon in which an organization passes on to its members shared norms. Crucially, these norms may include ideas about the proper goals of policy (Kaufman, 1960; Allison, 1969; Meier and Nigro, 1976; Wilson, 1991; Brehm and Gates, 1999, among many others). Socialization underlies the aphorism "where you stand is where you sit" (Miles, 1978), and is a mainstay of the public administration literature.[14] Finally, some bureaucrats act on a democratic ethic, seeking to enforce the shared norms of the entire polity, not just the culture of a particular profession or organization. Like Weberian bureaucrats and socialized agents, these civil servants are motivated primarily by their sense of what is right. Yet they draw their direction not from technical know-how or agency-norms, but from the democratically elected government – even when the government's agenda goes against deeply held beliefs (see Golden 2000 and works cited therein).

Three observations help apply the typology to central bankers. First, most studies of bureaucratic behavior focus on the problem of shirking, but high effort is a given among elite bureaucrats like central bankers – only the purpose of that effort is uncertain. As Brehm and Gates (1999) put it, there has been too much emphasis on moral hazard, and not enough attention to adverse selection. Accordingly, we focus on those motives that seem likely to cause a divergence between the goals of elite bureaucrats and the aims of their principals. With this insight, we can whittle down the relevant portions of Table 1.1. Intrinsic motivations probably do not intrude on the policy leaning of central bankers, and we do not consider them further. Neither do we devote time to democratic responsiveness: given the state of monetary theory, there are no bureaucrats *less* likely to espouse this ethic than central bankers. Budget maximization is likewise irrelevant for money-creating agencies so rich they give funds back to the government.[15] Finally, the pursuit of power – especially the preservation of legal independence – surely does motivate central bankers, but probably does not

14 See Golden (2000) for an extensive bibliography.

15 For a study of "budget-maximizing" central bankers, see Toma (1982). However, there is little recent work on monetary policy in this vein. Because central banks usually have a (large) excess of cash to remit to the central government, the budget-maximizing bureaucrat of public choice analysis has little explanatory power, unless one makes hard-to-justify assumptions (such as that central banks can keep only a small, constant proportion of their excess revenues).

make one central banker more conservative than another, so I will not explore it here.[16]

That leaves four motives: technocracy, careers, policy, and socialization. Oddly, given their views on other actors, many economists studying central banks have assumed central bankers are the last remaining neutrally competent technocrats. It is not clear whether this jarring inconsistency is a genuine oversight, or a less forgivable reluctance to apply standard economic assumptions to officials who are often part of the economics community. Either way, I treat the neutral, Weberian central-banker–technocrat as a sort of null hypothesis for this study. Against this view, I emphasize the remaining three alternatives, especially career concerns and socialized preferences.

Of course, there is no single cause of all central banker behavior, any more than there is one correct theory of bureaucratic motivation. The behavior of most bureaucrats flow from a mixture of motives. For example, Golden (2000) argues many liberal federal bureaucrats acquiesced in Ronald Reagan's deregulatory efforts because they considered it their duty to implement the elected government's wishes, even when the government's agenda undermined their lives' work. But Golden also shows that career incentives and threats played a crucial role. Bureaucrats with strong exit options, including Justice Department attorneys, could and did resist the Reaganites. Bureaucrats whose skills and specialization offered few options outside the bureaucracy, such as auto safety engineers and nutrition program specialists, complied more readily. Reagan's management of the latter group rested heavily on career reprisals: recalcitrant bureaucrats were fired, transferred to the hinterlands, demoted, or stripped of authority. This pairing of principled and self-interested motives repeats throughout this book.

Finally, we should beware overidentifying agents with their organizations. Even the most selfish rent-seeker has other interests besides extracting material rewards from the budget. Bureaucrats' other objectives – job security, career advancement, outside employment – may conflict with the interests of the agency as a whole. Likewise, even bureaucrats who act primarily on socialized preferences may have been socialized not by the current agency, but earlier in their lives at other agencies or in school. For central bankers, whose budgets are effectively limitless and whose formative experiences lie mostly outside the

16 Interested readers should see Goodman (1992), who argues central bankers build up and maintain autonomy by cultivating expertise and social networks (especially in the financial sector) and by producing good economic outcomes – the same variables Carpenter (2001) identifies as underlying bureaucratic autonomy.

central bank, we must look past narrow conceptions of budget maximization and single-agency socialization, to broader economic and sociological motives: *career incentives* and *career socialization*.

A Career Paths Approach to Bureaucrats' Preferences

Although the underlying policy preferences of bureaucrats are difficult to reliably measure, many of the influences on those preferences are bound up in the agents' observable career paths. Career paths tell us where agents have been, and where they are likely to go. Sometimes agents follow the path of the classic revolving door bureaucrat-lobbyist, swinging back and forth from regulator to regulated industry.[17] Sometimes agents rise ever upwards in the government; they may be in one ministry today, but tomorrow move sideways to keep their careers on a fast track upwards. Along the way, agents pick up knowledge and ideas about policy. An agent who leaves the coal industry to become a regulator may bring along stronger convictions about the limits of government intervention and a finer sensitivity to the costs of regulation than a environmental scientist in the same regulatory agency. I call the process by which career backgrounds shape policy ideas *career socialization*. Career paths influence preferences by a second, often complementary mechanism: agents' desire to move their careers forward. The prospect of career advancement – whether within the organization or laterally to another organization – creates a *career incentive* for an agent to please not only his direct superiors, but anyone who might give him a step up.

The schematic in Figure 1.2 shows career paths typical of central bankers. Most monetary policy makers start their careers outside the central bank, often in other parts of the government bureaucracy or in the private financial sector. Eventually, they are appointed to the central bank's policy board. But after a short while (on average, about five years), they leave the central bank, often returning to careers in government or finance. The diagram highlights an important point: agencies and agents are not coterminous. Instead, agents' careers intersect with various organizations over time. Looking backward, we note that central bankers may bring social connections and socialized policy preferences with them from prior careers in finance or government. But central bankers

17 Career transitions from regulator to regulated industry (or consultant to regulated industry) are extremely common in the United States. Eckert (1981) studied a sample in which 66 percent of independent commissioners made the jump to the private sector; Heyes (2003) and Spiller (1990) cite figures in the same range.

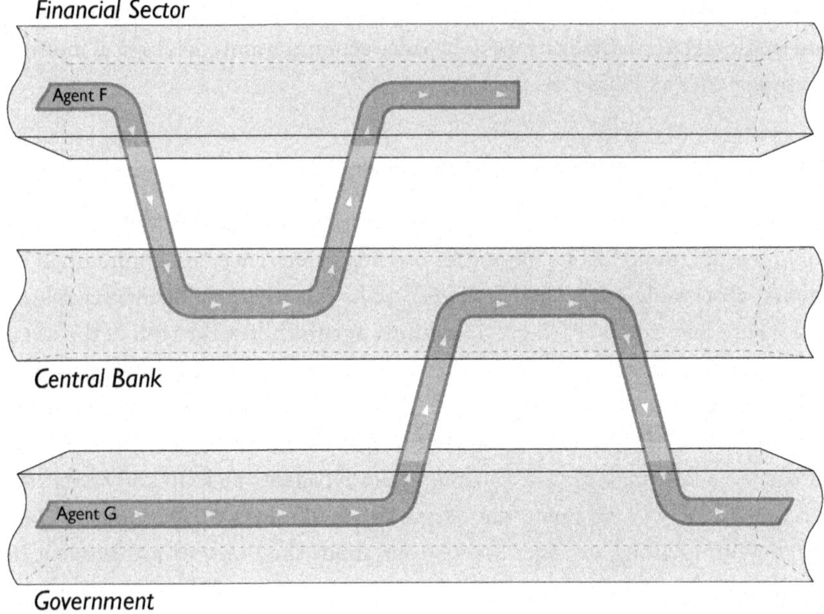

Figure 1.2. *Career paths and institutional contexts.*

may also look forward. Anticipating a return to the old organization, they may choose policies that make the reunion as welcome and lucrative as possible. As Schneider (1993) says, where you stand is not simply a matter of where you sit, but where you have sat, and hope to sit in the future.[18]

To get a better grip on career incentives, consider their implications for principal–agent models. Most scholars invoke the principal–agent framework to

18 Many theoretical investigations of regulation employ the metaphor of a revolving door (Bernstein, 1955; Stigler, 1971; Peltzman, 1976; Spiller, 1990; Makkai and Braithwaite, 1992; Laffont and Tirole, 1993; Brezis and Weiss, 1997). Most theorists view the revolving door as a means by which regulated industries gain lenient treatment in exchange for promising career rents to self-interested regulators. Against the conventional view, a few authors argue that revolving doors may be efficiency-enhancing checks on extractive regulation (Che, 1995; Salant, 1995), or alternatively, run by manipulative bureaucrats who create red tape in order to make their knowledge of it valuable to future private employers (Brezis, Paroush, and Weiss, 2002; Heyes, 2003). Empirical work on revolving doors is less common, but see Gormley (1979), Eckert (1981), Cohen (1986), and Brezis, Paroush, and Weiss (2002).

describe legally contracted or codified lines of responsibility between a superior and an inferior member of the same organization. Political science applications typically assume that a single principal (a representative voter or an executive) commands a single subordinate (the executive again, or a bureaucratic agent). To the extent career concerns are a factor in such models, they only spur agents to signal competence (thus mitigating moral hazard). The possibility of signalling or influencing agent preferences is less often explored.[19] Some models allow multiple principals whose preferences are aggregated formally by some decision rule (such as studies of delegation by governments with divided power).[20] Still, these models retain two limitations: the principals include only legally-empowered superiors, and the agent has little influence on which principal ends up on top.

Often, however, bureaucrats respond to pressures or inducements from outside the formal chain of authority. I introduce the term *shadow principal* to describe patrons who set implicit contracts with bureaucratic agents to implement policies that the shadow principal desires. Although the payoff to the agent could be a literal bribe, for the most part I focus on career inducements. Thus a firm with an interest in a specific policy might offer, perhaps only implicitly, a desirable job in exchange for the implementation of that policy. Alternatively, the shadow principal may be the governing party, acting outside the usual civil service institutions and making it known that future political appointments depend on loyalty to the party's interests. There need not be a single shadow principal in any one policy area; instead, there may be several, all competing to capture the services of bureaucratic agents.

Only in models lacking shadow principals is it possible to imagine that agents' legal independence from the government guarantees bureaucratic autonomy. By creating a back channel to the personal fortunes of agents, shadow principals and career rewards short-circuit legal autonomy. Autonomy degenerates into capture, or with multiple shadow principals, competitive capture. Because the shadow principals may include party organizations, it is not clear *a priori* whether career incentives favor private or public principals; that will depend on the agent's preferences and the shadow principals' capacities, as we see in Chapter 2. For now, the important point is that true agent autonomy may be much rarer than usually assumed.

19 See Hölmstrom (1999), Gibbons and Murphy (1992), and Soskice, Bates, and Epstein (1992). See also Alesina and Tabellini (2007), who admit the possibility of multiple principals offering career rewards but assume the principals reward only competence.
20 For applications to central banking see Morris (2000) and Chang (2003).

Career effects on preferences are easier to observe than underlying tastes for policy but still require careful measurement to detect. How do we collect evidence of career effects, including socialization and career incentives? The most persuasive evidence would be admissions from officials that career concerns or socialization influenced their policy decisions. Unfortunately, most officials are loathe to confess ulterior motivations and can easily insist on a high-minded concern for the general good, in either the Weberian technocratic or democratic ethics variants. Agents who have been granted a measure of independence by law are especially likely to attribute their decisions to impartial wisdom and expertise, as these claims are often essential to protecting that independence.

Direct tests of career hypotheses are seldom possible, as shown by an infamous episode from the controversial American presidential election of 2000. Al Gore and George W. Bush both needed Florida's electoral votes to capture the presidency, but the count in Florida was a virtual tie, complicated by a flawed punch-card system that left many votes miscounted or ignored (Imai and King, 2004). Florida Secretary of State Katherine Harris, the state official charged with conducting the election, enjoyed the legal authority to decide whether to allow a recount. In a deeply controversial decision, she refused one. Harris was not only Secretary of State, but also Bush's campaign chairwoman in Florida. Two years later, when she ran unopposed in the Republican primary for a safe, open House seat, critics suspected a career-for-policy deal had been struck. Circumstantial evidence favors this view. Prior to the 2000 election, Harris was a minor politician, unable to prevent her own party from eliminating the office she held; what else could explain her reversal of fortune? But proving a career *quid pro quo* in a particular case is usually impossible. If a deal was struck, even tacitly, Harris has every reason to deny it.[21]

Still, one might wonder whether the Republican Party, having gotten what it wanted in 2000, had any need to come through with a 2002 House seat for Harris, a radioactive figure who reminded both Democrats and Republicans of a traumatic time. In game-theoretic terms, are career-for-policy bargains subgame perfect? Seen as a one-shot game, they are certainly not. But as part of repeated interactions between a principal and a *series* of agents, they are quite sustainable (Fudenberg, Kreps, and Maskin, 1990). Indeed, an iterated version of

21 See "Katherine Harris's decision," *Washington Post*, November 16, 2000, A27; Michael Kinsley, "The Secretary's discretion," *Washington Post*, November 24, 2000, A43; Corry Reiss, "Her image as the spoiler of the 2000 election pays off with GOP donors," *Lakeland (Florida) Ledger*, February 1, 2002, B7; and Rachel LaCorte, "Katherine Harris heads to Congress after easy victory," *Associated Press*, November 6, 2002.

the careers-for-policy game helps explain a paradox: givers and receivers of career favors must deny that career-bargains even exist to stay within the bounds of the law and public approval, yet there nevertheless must be a conventional wisdom that such trades do happen if principals and agents are to easily arrange them.

Reputation makes career deals stick because giving rewards is an investment in future favors from *other agents*. We need look no further than the next iteration of the election-administration game played by the Republican Party and state Secretaries of State. Repaying Harris sent a signal to election officials that their cooperation would be similarly rewarded, and election officials in other states got the message. Ohio Secretary of State Kenneth Blackwell, a Republican, aggressively administered the 2004 presidential election in his pivotal state. He promised to deny provisional ballots cast in the wrong precinct and at one point even threatened to invalidate absentee ballots not printed on the proper weight of card stock. His mismanagement of voting machines was blamed for six-hour-long lines at many heavily Democratic polling places. These efforts earned Blackwell widespread criticism as the "new Katherine Harris," for Blackwell, like Harris, was Bush's statewide campaign chair. Rather than deny the comparison, Blackwell welcomed it, telling *Newsweek* two weeks before the election that "[t]he last time I checked, Katherine Harris wasn't in a soup line, she's in Congress."[22]

Many central bankers would understandably resent comparisons with Harris and Blackwell, but acting on career incentives does not necessarily imply corruption as it is usually understood. Actors following career incentives may not be fully conscious of their ulterior motives. They might not even consider other career or policy paths as options, and they may pay little attention to the merits of policy options unfavored by their shadow principals. By limiting the range of "legitimate" policy options, socialization within a career track may soothe the consciences of officials who are aware of career pressures on their

22 See Weston Kosova, "A clean count?" *Newsweek*, October 18, 2004; Catherine Candinsky, "Blackwell ends paper chase," *The Columbus Dispatch*, September 29, 2004; and David S. Bernstein, "Questioning Ohio," *Portland Phoenix*, November 12, 2004. Blackwell clearly aspired to higher office, and was the 2006 Republican gubernatorial candidate in Ohio, losing by 24 points in a bad year for Republicans; see "Ohio's Blackwell used to spotlight," *CNN Inside Politics,* November 3, 2004, http://www.cnn.com/2004/ALLPOLITICS/11/03/ohio.blackwell/, and Ian Urbina, "In the race for Ohio governor, all sides agree on a need for change," *New York Times,* April 21, 2006.

policy decisions. Still, most career-motivated central bankers claiming to make disinterested policy choices probably do believe their own pronouncements because they have been socialized to associate the course of action favored by their shadow principals with the public interest. Central bankers need not even be aware that as a group their backgrounds, views, or preferences vary over time and space – an illusion of consensus I suspect many central bankers share.

For all these reasons, simply asking central bankers how they make decisions is unlikely to resolve the questions posed in this book. I have encountered people inside central banks and outside who insist that the typical central banker is the very model of a modern neutral bureaucrat. I also have spoken with insiders and outsiders who believe career backgrounds shape central bankers' monetary policy preferences. If testing the career socialization hypothesis with first-hand accounts is hard, confirming the career incentives hypothesis is well-nigh impossible. Ken Blackwell's statement is unusually candid, politically unwise, cocky, and revealing. But few officials – least of all habitually guarded central bankers – will hint that they hope to be rewarded for their policy choices with a career step.[23] The difficulty of studying motives forces us to indirect means, and we will rely on large comparative datasets that reveal something about average career effects, even if we cannot be certain of career effects in particular cases. If this book were a courtroom drama, we would be building a case based on a preponderance of circumstantial evidence, not a smoking gun.

Central Banks and Short-Run Economic Performance

On the role of central banks in the political economy of performance, I emphasize three key questions, the focus, respectively, of the three parts of this book:

1. Who chooses interest rates? Inflation performance depends on more than central bank independence, as an example shows. In Denmark, inflation hovered around 4 percent in the latter half of the 1980s, and about 2 percent in the early 1990s (see Figure 1.3). There appears to be a sharp difference between the two periods. Why? It cannot be institutions; they did not change. The Danish central bank was quite independent, but no more so in the early 1990s than in the

23 Even central bankers occasionally lose their composure. To a group of state legislators complaining about the burden of high interest rates on farmers, Paul Volcker once said "Look, your constituents are unhappy, mine aren't" (Greider, 1987, 676). But who did Volcker see as his constituents? Banks? The president? Congress? "The people"?

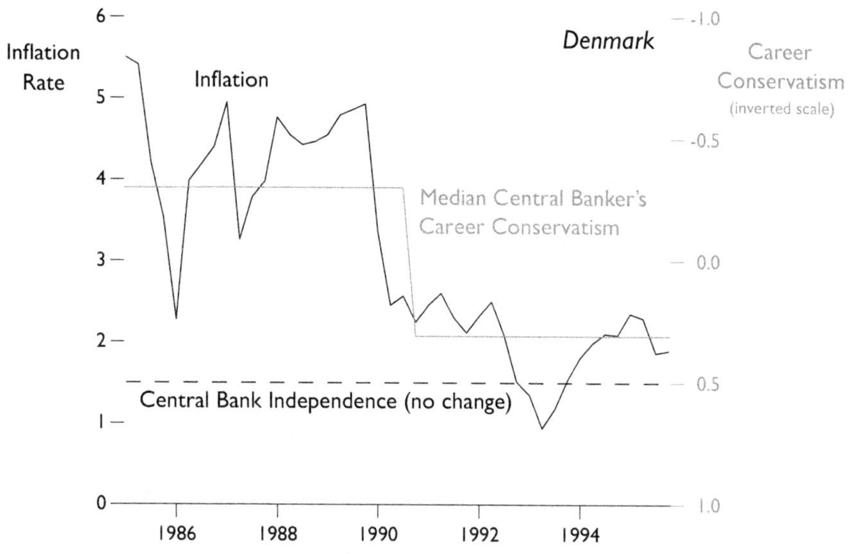

Figure 1.3. *The limits of institutional explanations of inflation: an example.* I plot inflation performance (left scale) against central bank independence (a constant) and the career conservatism of the median member of the central bank policy board (right scale) for Denmark, 1985–1996 (quarterly data). Independence and conservatism are plotted on an inverted scale to align changes in these variables with the corresponding change in inflation (more of either independence or conservatism is thought to lower inflation). Over this period, inflation fell, but as there was no institutional change, the explanation of this change in outcomes falls to preferences – which did grow more conservative at the crucial time.

1980s (Cukierman, Webb, and Neyapti, 1992; Maxfield, 1997). Nor was there any contemporaneous shift in the partisan composition of government (Cusack and Engelhardt, 2002). One thing that did change was the composition of the policy board. In the late 1980s, the median member of the board was a former bureaucrat. In the early 1990s, it was a former private banker. If we accept provisionally that bankers are more conservative than bureaucrats, perhaps the difference was not a change in rules, but a change in interests – in the bias against inflation – of the central bankers themselves.

I do not wish to push this example too far. A deeper examination would surely produce rival explanations and confounding variables. Nor have I yet clarified precisely how career backgrounds affect central bankers' policy preferences. For now, the Danish example suggests there is a gap in our understanding of central banks and monetary policy and a set of variables that may patch it. In Chapter 2, I develop the theory underlying career effects in monetary policy, and in the chapters following, I test the career approach to inflation on a large comparative dataset with proper controls for myriad alternative hypotheses. To preview the punchline of these chapters, I find that all else equal, a one standard deviation increase in central banker conservatism – as measured by career backgrounds – leads to a point and a half decline in inflation in industrial democracies and a single point decline in developing countries.

On this evidence, career-based central banker conservatism appears to be at least as important a determinant of monetary policy outcomes as central bank independence. In fact, as I show in the fifth and sixth chapters, central banker conservatism is what makes central bank independence an effective defense against inflation in the first place. Again, a sketch of the findings helps prepare the argument. In developed countries, the inflation-suppressing effect of independence is more than half again as strong under conservatives as it is under liberal central bankers, while raising central banker conservatism has almost five times the inflation-suppressing effect under an independent central bank as it does under a dependent one. In developing countries, increasing the independence of central bankers who have low career conservatism does nothing to control inflation, but increasing the conservatism of independent central bankers can cut the inflation rate by as much as two-thirds. The preferences and autonomy of central bankers are reinforcing and interdependent. Without taking both into account, we cannot understand the contribution of either to policy outcomes.

2. What context surrounds the choice? Recent work in political economy identifies three institutions that shape short-run economic performance: central banks, wage bargaining systems, and partisan governments. If each institution works in isolation, we could hold wage bargaining institutions and partisan governments constant, and make *ceteris paribus* conclusions about the role of central banks and central bankers. However, the effects of each institution depend on the others, so we cannot revise our view of central banks' economic impact without revisiting these interactions.

Figure 1.4 illustrates three pairwise interactions among central banks, wage bargainers, and partisan governments, which I take up in turn. First is the strategic interaction of wage- and price-setters. According to an important body of work (Iversen, 1998*a*, 1999; Hall and Franzese, 1998; Cukierman and Lippi,

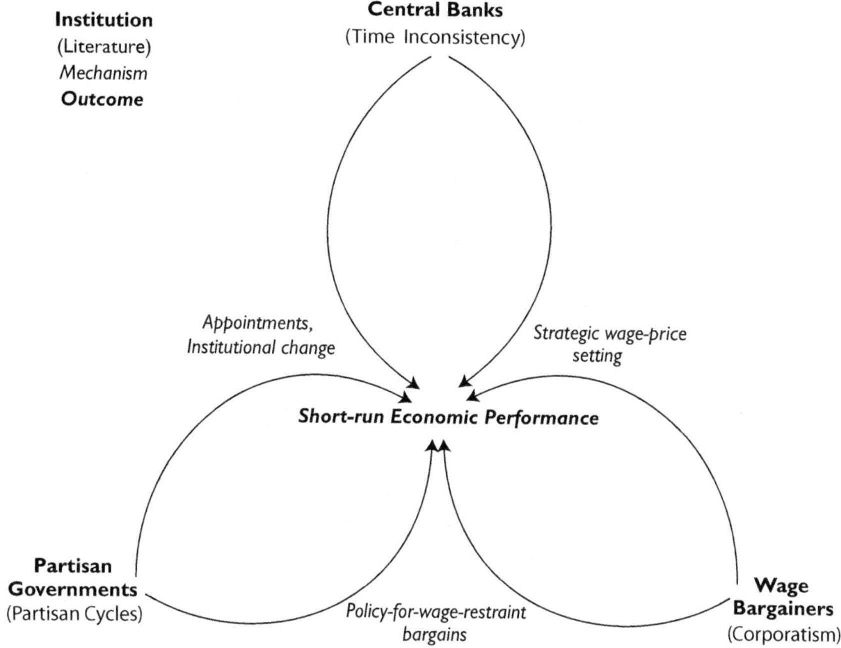

Figure 1.4. *The interactive political economy of performance.* The schematic depicts three separate literatures (in parentheses) tracing the influence of three institutions (in bold) on short-run economic performance. Although these literatures developed in isolation, their borders have recently blurred. As the schematic suggests, the effect of each institution on the economy may depend on the other two, through the processes labelled in italics.

1999), monetary policy has real economic effects when wage bargainers have some wage-setting power. The central question of this literature is whether – and at what cost in unemployment – central banks can persuade or force unions to accept non-inflationary wage contracts. To date, empirical tests of this question have been impoverished by the lack of measures of central bank conservatism, which I remedy in Chapter 6. The real-world implications are potentially quite large: I find that in either highly decentralized labor markets like the United States, or in highly centralized labor markets like Sweden, increasing the career conservatism of central bankers can raise unemployment by two points or more, suggesting a return of the inflation–unemployment trade-off. However, this trade-off does not apply everywhere: in moderately centralized labor markets like Germany there appears to be no unemployment effect of central bank conservatism.

But even as unions are interacting with central banks, they may also be playing a similar game with partisan governments, trading wage restraint for social policy gains. I consider this additional interaction in Chapter 7 and find that these bargains may be most attractive in moderately centralized economies, setting up the possibility of partisan cycles in which left-wing parties generate unemployment rates as much as two points lower than under the right.

3. Who chooses the chooser? Ideal democratic politics consists of a loop of public demands, policy delegation, and political responsibility. In the monetary policy arena, central bankers' preferences have a significant effect on short-run economic performance. Taking a step back in the loop, central bankers are themselves appointed by governments, who may purposefully choose types of central bankers that share the government's economic priorities. Of course, the chain of causation runs back still further: governments are elected by voters, who vote in part based on economic performance, which results in part from the actions of the central bank, and so on. In Chapter 8, I tie the central bank into the political economy of performance by exploring not only the link leading from the central bank to economic outcomes, but also the link leading back from the bank to the appointing governments. I show that right-leaning governments tend to select central bankers with more conservative career backgrounds than left governments.[24] In Chapter 9, I complete the link from monetary policy agents to democratic accountability by revealing how central bankers' tenures in office depend not only on career histories, but on their performance on the specific economic goals of elected partisan government.

Conventional wisdom holds that interest rates are the province of neutral technocrats – citizens should pay little attention to monetary policy, trusting independent experts to make the "right" decisions. Because there is no such thing as

24 Systematic appointment need not make agent discretion a mere epiphenomenon. Carpenter (2001) and Skocpol (1995) persuasively argue that bureaucratic behavior is not reducible to legislative preferences. The idea that agents' actions are sufficiently summarized by principals' preferences leads, *reductio ad absurdum*, to the conclusion that to understand any facet of policy making, we need only study citizens' preferences. Voters, interest groups, executives, and legislators all influence bureaucrats but of course do not completely control them.

a neutral agent, the conventional wisdom is wrong. Through its effects on the economy, monetary policy matters for all citizens. Moreover, because the parties in government help determine the types of central bankers in office, central banker conservatism and thus monetary policy itself is ultimately the product of voters' choices, *especially* in countries with independent central banks. In order to make informed choices with real economic consequences, voters need and deserve an explanation of the politics of monetary policy.

Plan of the Book

I argue we should change the way we think about central bank politics to emphasize bureaucratic agents and their preferences. This book is mainly devoted to testing this new approach – it takes a heavy dose of evidence to support heterodox views of a well-established literature. I reexamine the findings of numerous studies of monetary policy over the last three decades to show that our understanding would be different had we paid proper attention to agents from the start. There is a great deal of ground to cover and many lessons to be learned from the extensive literatures on central bank independence, monetary reaction functions, and institutional effects on monetary policy. At times, the reader may feel inundated by robustness checks and methodological details, but all these tests contribute to one aim: understanding and documenting the transmission of policy preferences from career backgrounds and shadow principals through agents to outcomes.

A guide to the remainder of the book follows (see also Box 1.1 on the use of visual displays). Chapters 2 and 3 are foundational, laying out the theory of career effects and presenting a framework for testing that theory:

Chapter 2 *Career theories of monetary policy*	Presents career socialization and incentives hypotheses for central banker behavior; formalizes them in a standard monetary policy game.
Chapter 3 *Testing career theories of inflation*	Develops measures of career backgrounds; explores career data for industrialized countries; tests for career effects on inflation.

Each of the subsequent chapters adds a different twist to the basic approach of Chapters 2 and 3; readers can peruse these in any order, or read only chapters of particular interest:

Box 1.1. Guides to the Graphics

This book uses graphics to make complex formal and statistical models approachable and informative. Most of these graphics exploit techniques widely used in the visual display of quantitative information, but some are less well known. As it would do no good to replace obscure mathematics with equally obscure pictures, whenever a new style of graphic is introduced a box like this one guides readers on its uses and interpretation.

Chapter 4 *Careers and the policy process*	Tests for effects of career types on declarations of interest rate preference, monetary policy votes, and interest rates.
Chapter 5 *Inflation in developing countries*	Presents hypotheses for career effects in developing countries; explores developing country career data; tests for career effects on inflation.
Chapter 6 *Using independence*	Explores the interactive effects of career conservatism, independence, and wage bargaining centralization on inflation and unemployment.
Chapter 7 *Parties, unions and central banks*	Expands the interaction of central banks and labor unions to include partisan governments; tests for unemployment-reducing social policy bargains.
Chapter 8 *Central banker appointment*	Investigates the decision to appoint central bankers of different career types; tests for partisan effects on central banker appointment.
Chapter 9 *Central banker tenure*	Considers the effects of career types, economic performance, elections, and partisan economic goals on the length of central banker tenures.

In Chapter 10, I consider this book's implications for the Great Recession in the United States, the darkening future of the euro, and the development of an agent-centered approach to political economy.

2

CAREER THEORIES OF MONETARY POLICY

Where you stand depends on where you sit.

Rufus E. Miles, Jr.

When the economy begins to stall, central bankers must decide when to turn from inflation fighting to demand management. Recent global downturns have lasted longer than those of the mid-twentieth century, suggesting central banks have been too conservative, prioritizing phantom inflation fears in the face of global recession or even deflation. The dilemma of inflation-prevention versus recession-fighting raises questions not only about the balance between central bank's independence and their accountability to the public, but also about the beliefs and interests of people working within them. Which kinds of central bankers are conservative, and which are not?

Unfortunately, the political economy literature remains ill-positioned to address this question because scholars normally conflate central bank conservatism and central bank independence. This confusion of preferences and institutions arises from the unsupported assumptions that independent central bankers are naturally conservative and that government meddling is the only source of loose monetary policy. Rather than ground a large and influential literature in untested assumptions, we should disentangle our understanding of monetary preferences and institutions. To succeed, we need a theory and measure of central bank conservatism to complement existing work on central bank independence.

Understanding central bankers' monetary policy preferences begins with central bankers' career paths and career concerns. A central banker's career background may influence his personal beliefs about the ideal tradeoff between inflation and output stability, while at the same time providing the basis for an exchange: future careers for the central banker; policy influence for the shadow principal providing the central banker's next job. Therefore, financial sector veterans may serve as more conservative monetary agents than generalist bureaucrats not only because former bankers are socially conditioned to care more about inflation vis-à-vis output, but also because former bankers are more interested in, and suitable for, high-level financial jobs offered by financial sector firms seeking conservative monetary policy.[1] On the other hand, career bureaucrats are less likely to be obsessed with inflation-fighting for its own sake, and more likely to be interested in tacit promises of higher political office in exchange for accommodating monetary policy. In both cases, the career trajectories of monetary policy agents before and after the central bank shape their monetary policy conservatism.

In this chapter, I place the career argument in the context of research on central banks. I develop two strands of the argument: one based on career socialization and the other on career incentives mechanisms. Finally, I show that career effects of both kinds can be embedded in the standard game theoretic model of monetary policy (Rogoff, 1985), allowing outside principals leverage over monetary policy even when the central bank is legally independent.

Do We Really Need to Study Central Bank Conservatism?

For decades, the problem of time inconsistency has dominated the study of monetary policy. Starting with the assumption that elected governments are always tempted by expansionary monetary policy, scholars in this tradition use the logic of rational expectations to argue that democratic control of monetary

1 For expositional convenience, I use the terms "bank" and "financial firm" interchangably throughout the text. In a broadly comparative work there is little to be gained by drawing a sharp distinction between these terms. To be sure, under the Glass-Steagall Act, which held sway in the United States from 1933 to 1999, American law distinguished commerical banks holding deposits and making loans to individuals and businesses from investment banks participating in securities markets. However, this separation did not exist in most European countries over this period and no longer exists in the United States. Moreover, because the theory of career effects developed here works on the basis of socialization and human capital developed within the financial sector, distinctions between types of private financial firms may be a second-order concern. Of primary importance is whether a central banker has socialized in a milieu that considers inflation anathema and whether a central banker has the human and social capital to flourish in a private financial firm of whatever type.

policy makes inflation permanently higher without long-term economic benefits (Kydland and Prescott, 1977; Barro and Gordon, 1983).[2] An influential series of models suggests a credibly conservative and independent monetary agent can ameliorate this inflationary bias (Rogoff, 1985; Lohmann, 1992). Scholars have measured and policy makers have implemented central bank independence, but the other half of the formula – central bank conservatism – has been ignored in comparative research.

Autonomy is the ability to act on one's preferences and tells us nothing about the content of those preferences. Yet early studies set the precedent of treating CBI as a sufficient measure of both autonomy and conservatism (Grilli, Masciandaro, and Tabellini, 1991; Alesina and Summers, 1993; Cukierman, Webb, and Neyapti, 1992), and dozens of published works that rely in some way on CBI have followed this example. This modeling choice is an oversimplification. It cannot be justified by the explanatory power of central bank independence taken alone, as even the best CBI measures fail to explain inflation performance in models with plausible controls (Campillo and Miron, 1997) or in developing countries generally (Cukierman, Webb, and Neyapti, 1992). Moreover, the same theories that argue a tougher stance by the central bank will reduce inflation also predict sharper swings in the employment rate, a result no empirical study finds. The simplest explanation for this disconnect is that CBI is an incomplete measure of nonaccommodation, which, when properly measured, would produce evidence of real consequences for conservative monetary policies. Unsurprisingly, efforts to disaggregate CBI into separate measures of independence and conservatism fail to find any added effect of statutory injunctions to pursue price stability (Berger, de Haan, and Eijffinger [2001] review the evidence).

2 Some scholars and central bankers question whether these famous inflation bias results apply to modern central banks, suggesting that they have given up the quest to raise employment above its natural rate (McCallum, 1995; Blinder, 1998). But Cukierman and Gerlach (2003) show that inflation bias persists even if McCallum and Blinder are right about central bankers' newfound wisdom, provided central bankers place any weight on stabilizing unemployment at the natural rate are uncertain about the future state of the economy and asymmetrically concerned about positive and negative output gaps. As Cukierman and Gerlach note, these assumptions seem easily satisfied by experience. Nor should we give up on the traditional Barro-Gordon perspective too quickly; as Persson and Tabellini (2000) point out, the inflation bias can be felt not just when a central bank actively indulges in expansionary policy: faced with a high inflation, a central bank lacking credible conservatism cannot (and thus perhaps will not) disinflate without causing recession.

A single oversight lies behind all these puzzles: policy preferences run deeper than unenforceable commands, and only an approach focused on central bankers themselves will uncover the roots of their behavior. Except for studies of partisan appointment, however, the central bankers themselves have been ignored.[3] Perhaps stereotypes of conservative, financial-sector-trained central bankers led many scholars to assume that these agents (and hence central bank conservatism itself) are invariant across time and space. But the stereotype is misleading: central bankers hail from a variety of careers of which private finance is not even the most common, and these differing backgrounds form the basis for a measure of central bank conservatism.

A tendency to accord central bankers with remarkable self-restraint may also contribute to the neglect of their preferences. This faith – implicit in studies that presume legal declarations of policy objectives will be followed as a matter of course – is paradoxical for a literature founded on the inability of the government to faithfully execute the long-term interests of its own constituents. Constitutional directives to the central bank to pursue low inflation merely relocate the time inconsistency problem – the government has no more incentive to enforce such commands than it has to resist inflationary policies in the first place (McCallum, 1995). Further, once the government gives an independent central bank an official policy goal, it is unclear what the government could do in the short-run to police or clarify the mission of a wayward central bank, short of changing the law to remove the central bank's independence. It is the very nature of agent independence to give the principal as little power to enforce as to override.

Contrast this murky delegation problem with the optimistic view of Alan Blinder, an economist and former Vice Chairman of the Fed, that central bankers (and political agents generally) check their preferences at the central bank's door:

> It is not necessary to find a "truly conservative" central banker whose personal value of the parameter α [the amount of output the central banker is willing to sacrifice to lower inflation] is excessive; you can simply direct the central bank to behave *as if* α were

3 Several authors have examined the effect of partisanship in the appointment of central bankers, particularly in the United States (Chappell, Havrilesky, and McGregor, 1993), but also in Germany (Berger and Woitek, 2001). These studies generally find that more conservative parties appoint central bankers who pursue more hawkish monetary policy. See Chapter 8.

> higher. In either case, central bankers set aside their own personal beliefs about what is best for society (α or k [the ideal inflation rate]) and adopt instead parameter values that lead them to "do their duty."

Blinder concedes that "*Homo economicus* may not behave this way. But responsible people, put in positions of authority, do" (Blinder, 1997, 14).

Even though Blinder served on the FOMC, his claims ring hollow. First, compared with their political principals, central bankers enjoy better access to economic data and can draw on specialized staff studying monetary policy questions. A political principal facing dozens of policy problems may not even be aware that agents are implementing policies the principal would oppose if he knew more (Peters, 1981; Weir and Beetham, 1999). Second, it is hard to see how Blinder's "responsible central banker" can escape the unconscious biases that follow each agent's unique experience, knowledge, and interests. Can any independent agent really modify the "preference function in his head" on command?

The temptation to follow one's policy instincts is hard to escape, especially when the legal strictures on central bankers tend to leave substantial wiggle-room. Blinder himself laments the lack of discussion and consensus on targets and weights by the FOMC, suggesting that unenforceable directives to central bankers do not really bind decisions (Blinder, 1997, 5). When the law does not say precisely how much the central banker should resist inflation or what inflation rate they should target, there is no reason to expect all central bankers will interpret – or want to interpret – the law in the same way. Of course, agents who use the law to rationalize their pre-existing policy preferences are not constrained, but shielded from accountability.[4]

4 This critique of purely legal arrangements that purport to "solve" the monetary delegation problem also applies to the concept of inflation targeting (Svensson, 1997), adopted by several countries – the United Kingdom, Canada, Spain, Australia, Finland, New Zealand, and the ECB – throughout the 1990s and 2000s. Many economists and central bankers consider legally enshrining an inflation goal a crucial step towards central bank accountability. Essentially all inflation targeting countries follow a "flexible" inflation target in which the central bank accepts deviations from the target to some degree (or for some period) to minimize output variability (Siklos, 2002; Cukierman, 2002). However, this degree of flexibility (that is, the weight of the tradeoff between inflation and output stabilization) is never dictated, policed, or even publicized, nor is the output target ever explicitly set (Cukierman, 2002). Finally, the mechanism by which a government would enforce the inflation goal is usually either unclear, untested, or dif-

Because central bankers are neither homogenous nor truly straightjacketed, their own preferences are likely to show up in policy. And monetary policy matters: most economists agree it has real effects in the short run, so central bankers always have to consider the tradeoff between inflation control and maintaining stable economic output.[5] In this context, any presumption that there is a single "right" level of inflation-aversion begs the political question: "Right for whose interests?" Because the tradeoff between inflation and economic stability has distributional consequences, governments, political parties, and private actors differ in their preferred inflation hawkishness. To this list of political actors, we must add the central bankers themselves. For all the attention paid to grants of discretion to central bankers, what central bankers do with discretionary power is woefully undertheorized. It is time to ask how central bankers' preferences vary, whether their preferences are influenced by other actors, and what effect those preferences have on economic outcomes.

Career and Policy Choices of Bureaucrats

The effects of career incentives on public officials are often asserted in scholarly and journalistic accounts but have seldom received systematic attention. It is therefore worth reviewing how career paths influence policy, what options exist for civil servants to advance their private or political careers, and how opportunity structures vary across countries.

Political actors' career ambitions vary; some simply want to stay in place, others desire to rise to higher office within a given sector or organization, and

---

ficult to impose. Indeed, per McCallum's critique of CBI, governments may not even wish to punish central banks that fail to quickly return to the target inflation level. In this context, a central banker who officially enjoys only instrument independence (in the Debelle and Fischer [1994] sense) could exploit weak oversight and information advantages to establish *de facto* goal independence, at least in the short run. Even central bankers with (partially) assigned goals retain substantial monetary policy flexibility, and the preferences of individual central bankers still matter under inflation targeting regimes.

5 Walsh (2003, Chapter 1) is a good place to start on the short run tradeoff between output and price stability. The popular Taylor Rule approximation of monetary policy decisions is one embodiment of this dilemma, and empirical work accepting this framework suggests that central bankers' preference differ and matter. For example, Judd and Rudebusch (1998) find different behavior under Fed Chairmen Greenspan, Volcker, and Burns by estimating separate Taylor-rule-like reaction functions for each Chair's tenure.

still others plan to rotate between two sectors, ratcheting higher with each turn. American politics is replete with examples of all three career trajectories. Since Mayhew (1974), political scientists' understanding of Congressional behavior has centered on legislators' overriding need to preserve their careers through re-election. Since Schlesinger (1966), scholars have recognized that many legislators seek to rise above their offices; from the state house to the U.S. House, from the U.S. House to the Senate, and so on. In each case, legislators' policy preferences result from the career incentives created by the electorate – and sometimes even the prospective electorate of a new office (Carey, 1994, 1996; Rothenberg and Sanders, 2000).[6] By contrast, the executive branch is often described as a revolving door for "in-and-outers," officials who are first employees of regulated sectors, then regulators themselves, and finally lobbyists or leaders for the regulated once more (Heclo, 1988; Donahue, 2003).

In recent years, the revolving door has been more evident among financial regulators than in any other corner of the American bureaucracy. Table 2.1 collects the career paths of just a handful of key public officials with authority over financial issues and contrasts with them a pair of nonfinancial actors who have circulated through the private and public sectors. In every case, these officials appeared to many observers to make policy choices based on their career experiences and career ambitions; some even helped create their final private sector jobs through their own deregulatory actions as public officials.[7] Against

6 Diermeier, Keane, and Merlo (2005) expand the career concerns of members of Congress to include their post-Congressional careers and find that expected private-sector salaries play a large role in Congressional retirement decisions.

7 *Dick Cheney:* Critics link Halliburton's no-bid contract to rebuild Iraqi oil fields with Cheney's years at Halliburton and large retirement bonus (David Lazarus, "Conflict of interest for vice president?" *San Francisco Chronicle*, Nov. 3, 2002, G1). At a minimum, the Office of the Vice President was asked to approve Halliburton's contracts, an unusual procedure (Joshua Chaffrin, "Cheney's office 'briefed on Pentagon deal,'" *Financial Times*, Jun. 14, 2004). To some observers, the whole of Cheney's career – through two presidential administrations and his interregnum as CEO – revolves around defense department favors to Halliburton; in Cheney's five years there, the company received \$2.3 billion in federal contracts, up from \$1.2 billion in the previous five years (Robert Bryce, "Cheney's Multi-Million Dollar Revolving Door," *Mother Jones* News Wire, August 2, 2000, Knut Royce and Nathaniel Heller, "Cheney Led Halliburton To Feast at Federal Trough," Center for Public Integrity, accessed July 24, 2003).
Meredith Attwell Baker: The daughter-in-law of former Secretary of State James Baker, Meredith Attwell Baker worked as an attorney in the telecommunications industry until joining the Commerce Department in 2004. Barack Obama appointed Baker to a Republican seat in the Federal Communications Commission in 2009 She voted to

Table 2.1. *Recent examples of the revolving door in American politics.*

Public official	Revolving door	Policies favorable to shadow principal
Finance		
Wendy Gramm[a]	Commodity Futures Trading Comm. $\xrightarrow{1993}$ Enron	Exempted OTC derivatives from regulation
Frank Newman[a]	Bank of America $\xrightarrow{1993}$ Treasury $\xrightarrow{1995}$ Bankers Trust	Blocked derivatives regulation
Phil Gramm	US Senate $\xrightarrow{2002}$ UBS Warburg	Glass-Steagall repeal; blocked derivates regulation; weakened SEC
William Rainer[a]	CFTC $\xrightarrow{1993}$ OneChicago futures exchange	Lifted ban on single-stock futures
Robert Rubin	Goldman Sachs $\xrightarrow{1993}$ Treasury $\xrightarrow{1999}$ Citibank	Financial sector deregulation
Neel Kashkari	Goldman Sachs $\xrightarrow{2006}$ Treasury $\xrightarrow{2009}$ PIMCO	Administered Troubled Asset Relief Program
Other policy areas		
Dick Cheney	Defense $\xrightarrow{1995}$ Halliburton $\xrightarrow{2000}$ Vice President	Defense contracts to Halliburton
Meredith A. Baker	Telecoms $\xrightarrow{2004}$ Commerce & FCC $\xrightarrow{2011}$ Comcast	Approved Comcast-NBC merger

[a] These officials helped create their final private sector jobs through their own deregulatory acts as public officials.
Sources: Johnson and Kwak (2010) and others; see note 7.

this conventional wisdom, these officials have generally – and self-interestedly – denied that career-incentives shaped their policy choices. And that is the way most studies of the revolving door leave the issue: suspicious career movements versus pious denials, and perhaps the occasional knowing admission that "everyone does it." But even some insiders admit that as banking compensation has soared out of sight, U.S. regulatory agencies have become "barely disguised employment agencies, as staff increasingly [focus] on making themselves attractive hires to the firms they were supposed to be regulating" (Ferguson and Johnson, 2010, 21). The closest thing we have to a smoking gun comes from Neil Barofsky, former Special Inspector General to the Troubled Asset Relief Program (TARP). Barofsky begins his memoir by recounting a private conservation with TARP director Herbert Allison, who wonders at length why a "young man" whose job "won't last forever" would risk his career by using the formal independence of his office to publicize abuse and regulatory capture in the massive bailout scheme – only to suggest a softer "tone" might still bolster his prospects on Wall Street or in government (Barofsky, 2012, xii–xiv).

Career paths matter in other countries besides the United States. Reviewing the comparative evidence, Schneider (1993) argues that where a bureaucrat stands depends not only on where he sits, but on where he *has sat* and *will sit*. In many countries, senior bureaucrats often rise to the top of the civil service only to jump to a lucrative private sector job. Known as *pantouflage* in France, this pattern is also found in Denmark, Japan, the Netherlands, and Spain (Rouban, 1999; Schneider, 1993; Jensen and Knudson, 1999; van der Meer and Raadschelders, 1999; Alvarez de Cienfuegos, 1999). On the other hand, *pantouflage* was historically limited or forbidden in Belgium and Sweden – intensifying competition for the next rung on the civil service ladder (Brans and Hondeghem, 1999; Dargie and Locke, 1999; Pierre and Ehn, 1999). Britain, too, historically limited the movement of public officials into the private sector, but increasing use of private contractors and consultants has created not only a revolving door, but future career rewards for civil servants who take a turn in the private sector (David-Barrett, 2011).

This competition provides partisan governments leverage over agencies – promotion to the top of the civil service has grown more politicized in Britain

allow the controversial Comcast-NBC merger four months before joining Comcast as a lobbyist (Hayley Tsukayama, 2011, "FCC commissioner Meredith Baker to join Comcast-NBC," *Washington Post*, May 12).

Finally, see www.opensecrets.org/revolving/ for a database of thousands of cases of American public officials taking private jobs in regulated industries.

and Germany, just as it has long been in most other European democracies (Peters, 1997; Mayntz and Derlien, 1989; Dowding, 1995; Page and Wright, 1999). Likewise, though many consider it the paradigmatic case of bureaucratic dominance, even Japan provides examples of political principals manipulating bureaucrats' careers to ensure that policy meets the government's needs. Loyal Japanese bureaucrats are often rewarded with private or political posts: thanks to the support of the ruling party, from 1949 to 1980 the lower house of the Diet contained, on average, 51 former bureaucrats, including 10 from the Ministry of Finance. Bureaucrats rarely ran for the opposition (Naka 1980, quoted in Ramseyer and Rosenbluth 1993; Kim 1988). Disloyal bureaucrats face the blacklist.[8]

The use of career rewards and punishments to affect policy implementation has implications for the study of delegation that are not fully appreciated. Most of the vast delegation literature focuses on formal, legal means of monitoring and control (see Bendor, Glazer, and Hammond 2001 for a review). Initial pessimism that political agents cannot be controlled – because formal avenues are often cumbersome and seldom used – has given way to tentative optimism that some principals manage agents effectively without frequent recourse to formal sanctions (Huber and Shipan, 2002). The "fire-alarm" argument holds that an effective principal need not be an active overseer, but instead can rely on a combination of credible sanctions and sporadic, perhaps even third-party, monitoring (Weingast and Moran, 1983; McCubbins and Schwartz, 1984). But principals may also control agents through extra-legal mechanisms: rewards and punishments that require neither hearings nor legislation. Where available and effective, informal methods may even be preferred by both principals and agents, as they allow bureaucrats to maintain an aura of independence. Contingent career rewards are the very epitome of these informal controls.

Career mechanisms for bureaucratic control also open the playing field to groups outside the government. Tracing career incentives thus gives us theo-

8 Ramseyer and Rosenbluth (1993) document many career mechanisms by which the governing Liberal Democratic Party manipulates Japanese bureaucrats, including threats of dismissal and control over promotion within the bureaucracy. Most important, elite bureaucrats' wages are kept below market to ensure obedience to the government, which has the legal right to grant or deny lucrative private and public jobs. Top civil servants retire early to avail themselves of these career rewards, a process known as *amakudari*, or "descent from heaven" (Koh, 1989). By showing that political principals can control seemingly independent expert agents using career incentives, Ramseyer and Rosenbluth turned the notion of Japanese bureaucratic dominance on its head.

retical and empirical leverage over the case of an agent serving several masters. Scholarly work on delegation by multiple principals tackles situations where the roles and powers of the principals are clearly defined (Epstein and O'Halloran, 1996, 1999; Morris, 2000). But many political principals, such as interest groups and firms, lack a formal role in policy making and implementation, yet still exert influence by informal means. Career rewards may be among the most potent tools these shadow principals possess for manipulating bureaucrats.

Career Incentives for Monetary Policy Making

The application of career incentives to monetary policy delegation is not entirely new. The same paper that first popularized the "independence plus conservatism" solution alludes to career-based central bank conservatism (Rogoff, 1985), a notion seconded by Lohmann (1992) and Stiglitz (2002, 19). Central bankers are often veterans of the financial sector, the argument goes, and the promise of future career rewards renders the financial sector a shadow principal of the central bank, encouraging conservative monetary policy.[9] The idea that financial sector experience makes central bankers more inflation-averse also appears in the literature on the Federal Reserve. For example, Havrilesky and Gildea (1991*a*) find that years spent in the financial sector predicts Federal Open Market Committee (FOMC) members' dissents in favor of tightness, while Woolley (1984) and Belden (1989) link regional bank presidents' greater conservatism to their careers in private banking. In the United States, several former FOMC members attributed quitting the Fed to the gap between public and private sector salaries.[10] The evidence for career-concerned central bankers grows when one notes from 1950 to 2000, the median Fed Governor chose to serve

9 For examples of the argument that central bankers tend to be scions of the financial sector, see Bowles and White (1994) and Padayachee (2000). Posen (1995) takes the argument further, claiming CBI is irrelevant – only financial sector influence matters. However, his proxies of financial sector opposition (a lack of universal banking, banking regulation by the central bank, and the presence of federalism and party fractionalization), although reflective to an extent of financial sector interests, say little about financial sector influence *per se* and may pick up spurious correlation from alternative sources of central bank independence (federalism, for instance; see Lohmann, 1998*a*,*b*; Treisman, 2000). The argument itself remains provocative, but without stronger evidence, we should not dismiss central bank institutions and officials as epiphenomenal.

10 Governor Robert C. Holland protested he could not pay his children's tuition bills on a Fed Governor's salary. Another governor, Jeffrey M. Bucher, lamented the "financial

only 5.2 years out of a guaranteed fourteen year term, and many Governors reenter the private sector on leaving the Fed. However, the career incentives argument has not been extended across countries or career types.[11]

Recognizing that central bankers are as likely to be career bureaucrats as financial sector types opens a new front for the career-incentives approach. Just as a former private banker, hoping to secure a better private banking job later, bears private banks' preferences in mind when setting monetary policy, so must a bureaucrat or politician with ministerial ambitions accommodate the government's election-driven desire for economic stability. Career concerns loom large for a bureaucrat serving a stint at the central bank because governing parties exercise significant control over the appointment of senior civil servants and subcabinet ministers, even where the civil service is nominally neutral.

For both bankers and bureaucrats, the human capital, social networks, and preferences acquired over a career point to the likely shadow principals at work behind the scenes. To the extent that monetary policy makers are either "government" or "financial" types who feel pressured by these sectors to be doves or hawks, the careers of central bankers constitute an observable measure of conservatism in central banks. Because governments have an electoral incentive to keep the economy stable, while banks tend to be particularly concerned with inflation, my basic prediction is simple: *central bankers with career backgrounds in the financial sector should be more anti-inflation than central bankers who are career bureaucrats.*

Former finance ministry officials and former central bank staff (that is, those who worked in the central bank below the monetary policy making level) comprise a possible exception to this hypothesis. Given their expertise and opportunities to make connections with banking sector officials, these bureaucrats are more likely to have developed their own views on monetary policy and are arguably better equipped to plunge into the financial sector than other bureaucrats. Chapter 3 shows these officials also have different career patterns from other bureaucrats who find themselves on central bank boards. Therefore, I distinguish finance ministry and central bank experience from other types of government experience, holding out the possibility that their career incentives may be quite different.

---

penalty" he paid to leave the private sector for the Fed. Both men served only three years before returning to private employment (Katz, 1992).

11 Chappell, Havrilesky, and McGregor (1995) find that years of bureaucratic service among FOMC members correlates with dissenting votes for easy money, although they do not link this to career concerns.

Career socialization and monetary policy

There is an another interpretation of the correlation between financial sector experience and central bank conservatism: rather than career incentives, perhaps long experience in private banking engenders conservative ideas about inflation and monetary policy. At least three different mechanisms could produce pre-existing preferences for hawkish monetary policy: (1) bankers may be *socialized* to believe that inflation-fighting is the primary purpose of monetary policy, (2) wealthy private bankers' *material interests* may induce anti-inflation feeling,[12] and (3) conservatives with anti-inflation views may *self-select* into financial careers.

Of the three possibilities, socialization requires the most explanation. The literature offers two reasons to suspect central bankers' approaches to policy problems are influenced by prior work experience, and that the monetary policy convictions of career-based peer groups influence central bankers.[13] First, we know that workplaces shape attitudes, as widely found by organization theorists (van Maanen and Schein, 1979; Hambrick and Mason, 1984; Gunz and Jalland, 1996) and public administration scholars (Kaufman, 1960; Meier and Nigro, 1976; Wilson, 1991). Experiments show that industry background and past functional roles within organizations influence executive decision-making (Dearborn and Simon, 1958; Beyer, Chattopadhyay, George, Glick, ogilvie, and Pugliese, 1997; Melone, 1994; Hitt and Tyler, 1991) and in particular which data decision-makers perceive as relevant (Rosman, Lubatkin, and O'Neill, 1994). There is no reason to suspect that banking is an exception. On the contrary, Ho's (2009) ethnography of Wall Street investment banks

12 See Scheve (2002, 2004) for cross-national evidence that asset wealth leads to anti-inflation attitudes and Burden (2007) for evidence that policy makers consider their material interests in passing laws.

13 Some speculate central bankers might someday form (Kapstein, 1992), or perhaps already constitute (Johnson, 2002), a cohesive community collectively puzzling through policy choices; this perspective would relocate the socialization process within the central banking community itself. The argument of this book is not premised on the existence of a policy community of central bankers, though it would jibe with the notion of several distinct communities (financiers, bureaucrats, and economists) intersecting the world of central banking. In particular, the growing cooperation among central bankers and academic economists on monetary policy research has struck several observers (McCallum, 1999), but as the data presented in the next chapter show, economists remain a minority among central bank leaders, and comprehensive explanations of central banker behavior will need to reach beyond the economics community.

describes an intense work environment that comprehensively reshapes employees' attitudes, values, and economic ideas, including views on the desirability of a flexible, churning labor market.

Second, we have reason to suspect early workplace socialization grounds the political beliefs of elite and activist actors. Students of political elites noticed in the 1970s that career socialization had pervasive, lingering effects on the behavior of policy makers (Putnam, 1976). Meier and Nigro (1976) found that agency membership, more so than economic class, explained bureaucrats' political beliefs, and one scholar of comparative elites went so far as to assert that "[v]alue-socialization is not parental, or even based on early political experience, but apparently takes place from working in a given field or institutional setting" (Barton, 1973, 242, quoted in Putnam, 1976). More recently, using the example of labor unions, Levi (2005) and Ahlquist and Levi (2013) argue that under the right institutional conditions, an organization's leaders can mold the preferences of members to create new communal political goals and values, in effect making workers into activists. In their telling, founding leaders of the International Longshore and Warehouse Union created an organization capable of broadening wage-seeking members' motives and actions to include altruistic support for social policy reform, even in distant contexts.

For a more elite example of career socialization, consider American Supreme Court justices. Long viewed as wise arbiters of legal precedent, justices have turned out to be political beings whose policy preferences systematically influence their decisions – Segal and Spaeth (1993) built the coffin for the so-called legal theory, and *Bush v. Gore* hammered the nails. In part, justices owe their policy preferences to their career tracks. For example, justices with prosecutorial experience are more conservative on civil liberties decisions, controlling for the judge's partisanship and appointing president's ideology (Tate and Handberg, 1991). Because Supreme Court justices generally lack career concerns, this seems to follow socialization (and perhaps some self-selection), with the experience, training, and environment of prosecutors imparting conservative policy beliefs.

Applied to financial-sector-trained central bankers, the socialization argument is similar: a history of work within a sector that fears inflation and considers the struggle against it the only acceptable monetary stance should shape a central banker's attitudes on monetary policy.[14] According to the socialization

14 Private bankers have a long-standing reputation for conservatism on inflation, though I am unaware of any systematic surveys of their attitudes. In the United States, members

hypothesis, *central bankers with career backgrounds in the financial sector should be more anti-inflation than other central bankers*. Note that in the case of central bankers, we expect career socialization and career incentives to be reinforcing.

The socialization hypothesis holds that past career experience determines preferences over policy itself, whereas the career-incentives hypothesis sees in policy choices a means to a private end. Both perspectives are theories about the effects of career paths, and to the extent that either or both mechanisms act on central bankers, career variables are an important antecedent of monetary policy.

Career Models of Monetary Policy Delegation

So far, I have laid out two mechanisms by which careers may influence or reflect central banker preferences over monetary policy: career socialization and career incentives. Formalizing these arguments helps clarify the assumptions needed to support them. Just as important, the implications of formal models of career effects show how the theoretical implications of these mechanisms differ, so that we can sharpen our empirical tests in later chapters.

I discuss four models, including two simple models of where central bankers get their initial preferences over policy and two variations on career incentives. The simplest model is (1) *self-selection* into careers based on prior preferences over monetary policy. On the other hand, preferences over monetary policy may develop over the course of a career, leading to (2) *career socialization*. Career incentives work differently depending on whether shadow principals benefit from hiring central bankers whose career agendas lie in that principal's sector. In this case, central bankers with a given career type (usually finance or government) seeking further advancement in that career may send costly (3) *policy signals* to the shadow principal to indicate that they are loyal agents – the right type to hire back into the sector. On the other hand, if hiring is always costly for shadow principals, implicit (4) *career-for-policy bargains* would still let central bankers exploit their official roles for career advancement in a desired sector.

---

of Congress and the Federal Reserve believe that "[i]f one's goal is to minimize inflation ... a sure way to achieve that goal is to have private bankers – who are among the world's fiercest inflation hawks – appoint the regional bank presidents" (S. Greenhouse, "Showdown: The populist versus the Fed," *New York Times*, October 12, 1993, D1). In many cases, banks' fear of inflation surely has a rational basis. For example, Santoni (1986) provides evidence that the stock prices of banks react negatively to unanticipated inflation, as might be expected of net holders of nominal assets.

These four perspectives on career effects in monetary policy form a menu of mechanisms for career-based policy. The self-selection and socialized preference mechanisms both lead to decision theoretic models in which the central banker simply sets his ideal monetary policy given preferences already established when he arrives at the central bank. On the other hand, the career incentives models are strategic games involving the central banker and one or more shadow principals.

I present formalizations of all four models of career-based monetary policy in the Theory Appendix to this chapter. Here, I focus on the testable implications of these theories, as shown through comparative statics drawn from the equilibrium states of the models. To keep mathematical notation to a minimum, I use graphical tools, especially *image plots*, to explore the comparative statics of the more complex career incentives models (see Box 2.1).

The simplest way career backgrounds could reveal the monetary policy preferences of central bankers is if inflation hawks are more likely to enter the financial sector in the first place. Suppose that young people with a stronger than average desire for monetary gains relative to other career motivations are drawn to careers in the banking sector. Suppose further that they tend to acquire larger than average wealth over their careers there. The combination of materialist preferences and nominal wealth should make these individuals more inflation-averse than the average person. So if some of these private bankers later become monetary policy authorities, and are representative of the wealth and materialism in the population of bankers, there would follow a self-selection of privately motivated inflation-hawks into the subset of central bankers hailing from the financial sector. *Self-selection* forms our first model of career effects in monetary policy delegation. Its explication requires nothing more than a decision theoretic model (see the Theory Appendix at the end of this chapter). The predictions of the model are equally simple: Central bankers with backgrounds in the financial sector should have higher aversion to inflation (in terms of our model's parameters, higher χ) than other central bankers and set relatively more conservative monetary policy.

But suppose preferences over monetary policy – a topic few people consider at a young age – develop throughout the course of private bankers' careers due to exposure to the beliefs and preferences of others in the financial sector. This would lead private bankers to become more conservative on monetary policy the longer they work in the banking sector, creating not just a correlation but a causal relationship between financial sector careers and anti-inflation preferences (high χ_i; see the Theory Appendix to this chapter). This is

Box 2.1. Image Plots for Comparative Statics

Formal models can sharpen the implications of theory, but only if the presentation of the model is clear and accessible. This is most easily done by describing how the equilibrium outcome of the model shifts when one varies the model's parameters. Comparative statics of this kind are easy to follow for simple models with few parameters, but grow harder to summarize as the number of parameters grows. In other words, a model with many parameters involves many dimensions, and is therefore challenging to represent visually.

Figures 2.1 to 2.4 use image plots to get around this "curse of dimensionality." An image plot displays a different value, shown as a color, for every point in a two-dimensional space and so convey information more densely than any other style of plot. These plots borrow their design from the phase diagrams used in physics to show how temperature and pressure interactively determine when a substance is solid, liquid, or gaseous.

Each plot shows the consequences of freely varying two different parameters on the outcome of the game, holding all other parameters constant. Because we have more than two parameters to vary, we work through a series of plots letting different pairs of parameters vary while holding other combinations of parameters constant (Adolph, 2003). A useful way to read these plots is to choose subtantively interesting combinations of parameters, and then look up what equilibrium conditions the model predicts for that case. In this way, readers can interrogate the model about any substantively interesting counterfactual without recourse to a calculator.

Model 2, the *socialization* model of career effects on monetary policy. As in the self-selection model, no more than the standard decision-theoretic approach to monetary policy is needed, and the predictions of this model closely mirror the self-selection model.

Our third model, and the first to include career incentives, is a signaling game in which the central banker must decide whether to set a more conservative monetary policy than he personally prefers in order to send a costly signal to financial firms that he is the "type" of agent they would like to hire. I denote this hirable type as θ, and denote central bankers who make less attractive financial sector hires as non-θ types. Dividing central bankers into these types reflects the idea that central bankers who successfully deliver the financial sector's ideal policy may be signaling a characteristic desirable in senior banking staff, such as

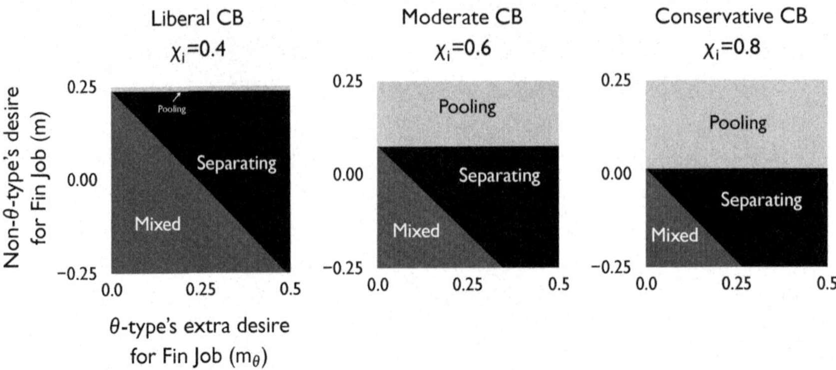

Figure 2.1. *Separating equilibria in the monetary policy game.* Regions indicate whether a pooling, partial pooling (mixed), or separating equilibrium obtains given varying central banker preferences. For all plots, I assume that $m_F^{\theta} = 0.1$, $m_F^{\sim\theta} = 0.1$, $\chi_F = 0.9$, $P(\theta) = 0.5$, $\widehat{y}_i = \widehat{y}_F = \widehat{y}_G = 0.2$, and $\sigma_z = 1$. See the Theory Appendix for parameter definitions.

loyalty to the banking sector or a specific bank, belief in conservative monetary principals, or concern for investors returns. Alternatively, placing an esteemed central banker on a bank's board may signal clients of the bank's clout or resources, but this benefit may be attenuated if the former central banker is associated with failed or inflationary policies or is not widely regarded as having financial expertise.

The signaling game predicts the conditions under which central bankers separate into two groups: a θ group setting conservative policy to send a "hiring request" to the financial sector, and a non-θ group ignoring the financial sector and implementing the central banker's own ideal monetary policy, as dictated by the parameter χ. As in all our models, higher χ implies more conservative innate preferences. Equilibria where these groups cleanly separate are known as "separating" equilibia, cases where they only partially separate are known as "mixed" or "partial pooling," and conditions under which central banker signals are totally unreliable indicators of type are "pooling" equilibria. The signaling game suggests monetary policy is coopted by financial sector agents if real-world conditions approximate the conditions for separating equilibria and to a lesser extent, partial pooling equilibria.

To understand these conditions, we turn first to Figure 2.1, where partial pooling is marked as "mixed." Strict separation of types through signaling depends entirely on central banker characteristics. There are two conditions that must hold for separation to occur:

First, central bankers of different types must strongly (through high m_θ) and uniquely (through low m) prefer corresponding future careers to the degree that these factors outweigh their concern for policy per se. To see this in Figure 2.1, consider first the liberal central banker descibed by the leftmost plot. In this plot, points to the northeast, which correspond to a sharp distinction in the preferences of θ and non-θ types over financial jobs, are separating. In the western part of the plot, where the types are similar in their preferences over financial jobs, or in the southern part of the plot, where neither type actually wants financial jobs, we see partial pooling.

Second, separation by type depends on the interaction of a central banker's policy and job preferences. For conservative central bankers, the cost of a signal is naturally smaller because their preferred policy is already close to the financial sector's ideal. In this case, signals are very sharp just so long as only θ types want financial sector jobs (that is, if $m \leq 0$ and $m_\theta > 0$). To see this in the plot at the right of Figure 2.1, notice that nearly the entire lower half of the plot, in which non-θ types do not want financial jobs, is in separating equilibrium. But if both types want financial sector jobs, every central banker gives the financial sector the same signal, and type does not predict differences in policy. For liberal central bankers, signals are more costly and thus more credible. This holds even if both types have some desire for financial jobs, just as long as θ types want those jobs more.

Figure 2.1 suggests central banker types separate – and financial sector job seekers set more conservative monetary policy than other central bankers – when θ types want financial sector jobs more than other central bankers do and care more about these jobs than they do about policy. That is, if Alan Blinder is wrong, and central bankers really are ordinary mortals subject to their private desires, we expect the signaling game to give private banks leverage over monetary policy when their type of central banker is in office.

But suppose Blinder is right, and central bankers are selfless angels and not selfish agents. Even then, for liberal and moderate central bankers who care more about policy than financial sector jobs, there remains the possibility of partial pooling so long as the types still differ in how much they want to work for the financial sector. Under certain conditions, this partial pooling can approximate complete separation by type and thus also sustain type-based monetary policy.

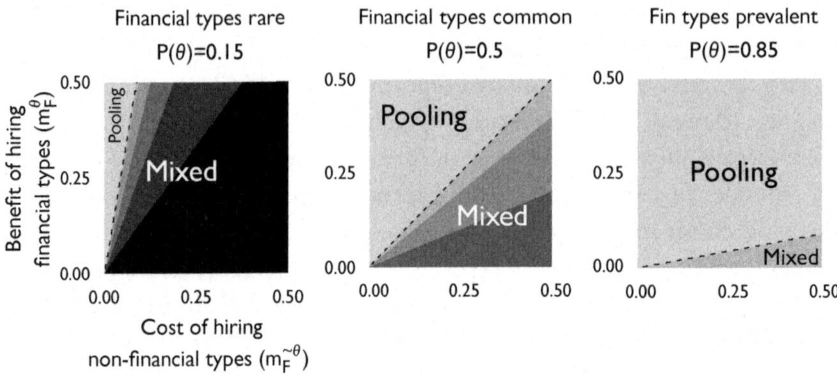

Figure 2.2. *Pooling equilibria in the monetary policy signaling game.* The dotted line shows whether a pooling or partial pooling (mixed) equilibrium obtains given varying financial firm preferences. The shading of the regions indicates the probability that a central banker sends a type appropriate signal. Darker regions indicate probabilities approaching 1, which is the pure separating equilibrium. For all plots, I assume that m = 0.05, $m_\theta = 0.05$, $\chi_i = 0.6$, $\chi_F = 0.9$, $\widehat{y}_i = \widehat{y}_F = \widehat{y}_G = 0.2$, and $\sigma_z = 1$. See the Theory Appendix for parameter definitions.

The conditions for weak pooling depend on the characteristics of financial firms and the overall distribution of types among central bankers. Partial pooling approximates separation when financial firms strongly prefer to avoid non-θ types, and when genuine θ types are relatively less common, making false signals less credible. To see this graphically, we zoom in on the triangular "mixed" region from the center plot of Figure 2.1 and consider in Figure 2.2 the degree to which signaling separates types. We hold fixed central banker preferences and vary instead the cost of hiring non-θ types, the benefit of hiring θ types, and the prevelance of θ types in the central banker population.

To distinguish the degree of separation in the mixed equilibrium, we calculate the probability that a central banker drawn at random signals according to type.[15] As the fraction of central bankers signaling according to type approaches one, we enter an approximately separating equilibirum (indicated by darker shades in Figure 2.2); as it approaches zero, we enter an approximately pooling one (indicated by lighter shades). Overall, Figure 2.2 suggests that within a mixed equilibrium reached because central bankers are relatively more con-

15 In terms of the model parameters, this probability is $P(\text{signal}|\theta) \times P(\theta) + [1 - P(\text{signal}| \sim \theta)] \times [1 - P(\theta)]$.

cerned with policy than careers, successful career signaling still occurs if the benefit to the financial firm of hiring θ types is not "too great" (which would lead to even higher salaries and encourage false signals by non-θ types), or if θ types are rare. The prediction that partial pooling approximates full separation when financial types are uncommon is important, as financial careers are less common backgrounds for central bankers than conventionally assumed.

Conversely, the finding that liberal θ types are *most* likely to separate from their liberal non-θ peers supports the importance of type – and by extension the career backgrounds correlated with type – in determining monetary policy. In theory, central banker career type can overwhelm personal belief about monetary policy.

Model 3 suggests that within the standard model of monetary policy, adding future career concerns leads under plausible conditions to the subversion of monetary policy by jobseekers sending signals to the financial sector. A key assumption, however, is that financial firms actually want to hire former central bankers, especially θ types.[16] What if granting a share of the profits to former central bankers is instead costly to financial firms?

Even if financial firms must pay a price to secure their desired monetary policy from central bankers, it may still be worth their while to cultivate potential allies in the central bank. In our fourth and final model, we consider the possibility that *both* the financial sector (F) and the government in office (G) act as shadow principals offering future lucrative or prestigious positions to central bankers who support monetary policy aligned with the respective patron's ideals. Offering these jobs imposes a cost on shadow principals, just as relinquishing control of policy exacts a cost from central bankers; nonetheless, under a wide range of conditions, bargains may be reached between a shadow patron and the central banker. The bargain reached need not be explicit.

Our notion of central banker type is now broader in two ways. First, we distinguish θ types, who want financial sector jobs, from τ types, who want additional elite positions in government. Second, the intensity of the central banker's desire for these jobs is now given by θ and τ, which are continuously varying indicators of type. Thus, these types are not mutually exclusive: a central banker could be open to just one, both, or neither avenue of promotion. As before, χ_i indicates a central banker's own policy preferences, while χ_F indi-

16 Other key assumptions are that θ types tend to be former financial sector employees, that θ types more strongly prefer financial jobs than non-θ types, and that θ types are not systematically less conservative than non-θ types. If we accept the first of these, the latter two assumptions seem uncontroversial.

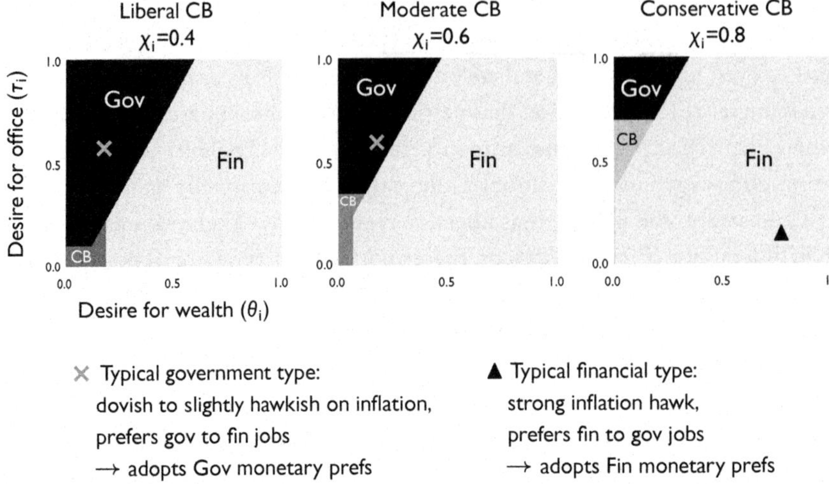

Figure 2.3. *Who sets monetary policy? Monetary policy according to central banker preferences.* Shaded regions indicate whose monetary preferences the central banker adopts as the indicated parameters of the model are varied; this is also the sector in which the central banker will work in the next period. Fin indicates the financial sector, Gov the government, and CB the central banker's own preferences. The lighter the region, the more conservative the policy implemented. In the final plot, a thin, barely visible stripe extends down along the vertical axis to the origin from the CB region (because a central banker with no career concerns always implements his own policy preferences). Typical outcomes for government types (×) and financial types (▲) are marked. For all plots, I assume that $\chi_F = 0.9$, $\chi_G = 0.3$, $\theta_F = \tau_G = 0.25$, $\widehat{y}_i = \widehat{y}_F = \widehat{y}_G = 0.2$, $\delta_i = 0.95$, and $\sigma_z = 1$. See the Theory Appendix for parameter definitions.

cates the financial sector's more conservative preferred policy and χ_G the government's more liberal ideal.

The Theory Appendix develops a game theoretic treatment of this bargaining game; here I focus only on its implications. The easiest way to understand the empirical implications of job-for-policy trades is to compare equilibria that result when different types of central bankers act as the agent. To illustrate comparative statics, I map out the parameter space according to the policy the central banker adopts given his personally preferred policy, the financial sector's prefered policy, and the government's. These diagrams demonstrate that agents with preferences typical of a financial careerist implement the financial sector's preferred policy, and vice versa for government types.

First, we explore the effects of different central banker preferences on the monetary policy outcome, holding fixed the preferences of the financial sector and government. Figure 2.3 shows which sector wins the monetary policy auction given central bankers with varied tastes for policy, political office, and private banking positions. To understand the intuition of the results, it helps to begin with the middle panel, depicting the case of a central banker with moderate monetary policy preferences. We see that if the central banker cares more about winning a government post (has higher τ_i), the government tends to prevail in monetary policy, but if the monetary agent cares more about financial sector rewards (has higher θ_i), private banks win. Finally, if the banker cares little for either kind of reward, then he follows his own policy preferences and receives no post–central-bank rewards from either shadow principal.

Looking from left to right across the panels shows what happens when we consider the range of central banker inflation preferences. Four patterns emerge:

First, regardless of the central banker's preference over policy, the right career incentives can make any monetary policy outcome possible. Regardless of whether the central banker is liberal or conservative on inflation, the corner cases in each plot are always the same: an agent who wants office but not wealth always sides with government, an agent who wants wealth but not office with the financial sector, and an agent who cares for neither implements his own preferred policy.

Second, career incentives and central banker's inflation preferences interact. Bargains with a shadow principal become easier when the agent's monetary policy preferences are close to the principal's ideal policy. Therefore, a conservative central banker must strongly prefer government advancement over financial sector jobs if he is to make a career deal with the government, while a wider range of liberal or moderate central bankers would accept the government's offer.

Third, over the range of central bank preferences shown, opportunistic central bankers equally and substantially attracted to private and government posts always side with the financial sector, which offers a bigger reward *ceteris paribus*. This follows from assuming monetary policy affects the level and variance of inflation, but only the variance of output. Thus, unless the economy fluctuates wildly (σ_z is large), the financial sector stands to win or lose more by intervening in monetary policy that the government, and is willing to pay more for policy as a result. Alternative economic models that allow monetary policy to affect

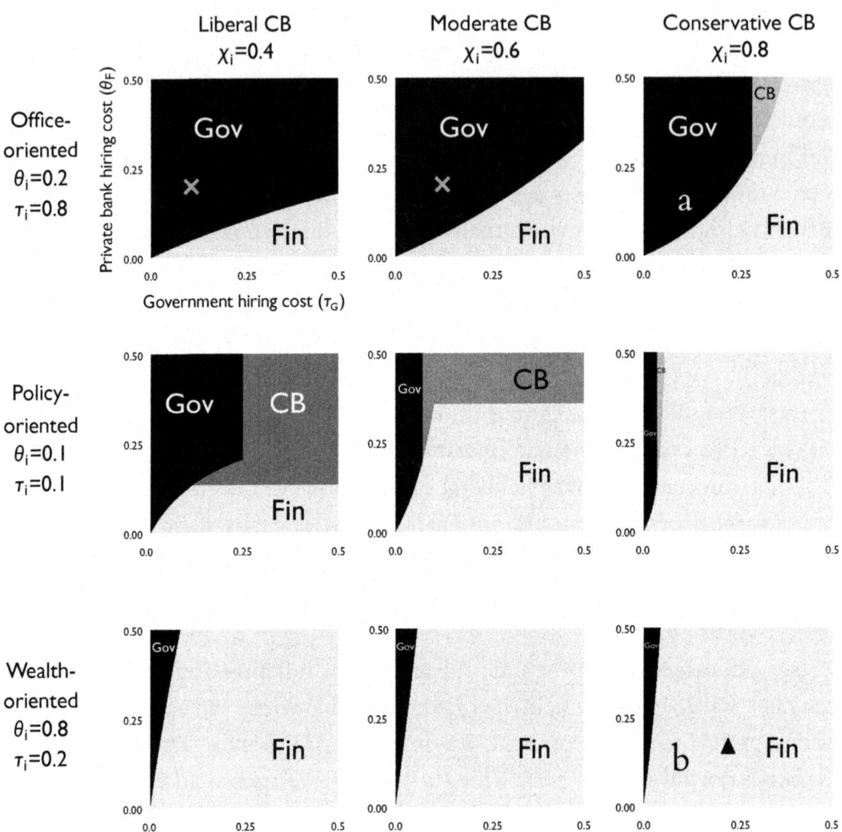

× Typical government type:
dovish to slightly hawkish on inflation,
prefers gov to fin jobs,
more easily employed in Gov
→ adopts Gov monetary prefs

▲ Typical financial type:
strong inflation hawk,
prefers fin to gov jobs,
more easily employed in Fin
→ adopts Fin monetary prefs

Figure 2.4. *Who sets monetary policy? Monetary policy according to career-bargain costs (facing page).* Shaded regions show whose monetary preferences the central banker uses, according to the model, as the indicated parameters are varied; this is also the sector in which the central banker will work in the next period. Fin indicates the financial sector, Gov the government, and CB the central banker's own preferences. The darker the region, the less conservative the policy implemented. Typical outcomes for government types (×) and financial types (▲) are shown. Also demonstrated is that for otherwise identical conservative agents, different career goals can produce different policy outcomes (contrast "a" and "b"). For all plots, $\chi_F = 0.9$, $\chi_G = 0.3$, $\widehat{y}_i = \widehat{y}_F = \widehat{y}_G = 0.2$, $\delta_i = 0.95$, and $\sigma_z = 1$. See the Theory Appendix for parameter definitions.

the average level of unemployment as well as the variance would, of course, change this result (see Chapters 6 and 7 for models of this kind).

Finally, central bankers are truly independent only when their career concerns are minimal.

Together, these patterns suggest that "financial type" central bankers – who prefer financial sector jobs and espouse hawkish inflation views – consummate career-for-policy bargains with the financial sector, while "government types" – who prefer government posts and have inflation preferences ranging from dovish to slightly hawkish – accede to government demands in order to advance their careers.

Figure 2.4 shows how the hiring costs of government and private banks affect their ability to influence monetary decisions across the range of central banker types. As before the columns of plots correspond to the policy preferences of the central banker. But now the rows of plots reflect whether the agent is office-, policy-, or wealth-seeking, while the axes show the cost of hiring for the financial sector (on the vertical axis) and government (on the horizontal axis). Hiring costs encompass a range of concerns, including the central banker's potential productivity in a sector (based on human capital and accumulated social networks) and the size of the organization across which the costs and benefits of the bargain are spread. Lower hiring costs make job-for-policy bargains easier to consummate.

Each plot demonstrates that all else equal, agents who can be hired cheaply by one sector but dearly by another sides with the cost-saving sector. Where costs are closer to equality, the agent's preferences usually tip the scales. The exception is when strong career preferences are reinforced by congruent policy biases (such as liberalism combined with office-orientation or conservatism with wealth-orientation), in which case agent preferences tend to overwhelm all but the largest disparities in hiring costs (as in the top left and bottom right plots).

To the extent that financial types are more easily rehired by the financial sector and government types by the government, these comparative statics reinforce the impression that adopted monetary policies hold true to central bankers' types. But consider for moment an appointee who does not exactly conform to type: suppose the government appoints a career bureaucrat with political aspirations but conservative inflation preferences. This government is following Rogoff's recommendation to appoint a "more conservative" central banker, but the agent's career concerns undermine his independence from the government. When in economic trouble, the government can employ career leverage to get around the central bank's nominal independence. As the upper-right plot shows, this kind of agent sides with government in the more likely case that government job offers are less costly than financial ones (this central banker is marked "a"). In contrast, a conservative financial type strikes a career bargain with the financial sector, as the central banker labelled "b" in the bottom right plot shows. Thus, even with a legally independent central bank, central bankers who prefer financial sector jobs produce more conservative policies than those who prefer government jobs.

Finally, two simple implications of the model should be noted. First, if the central banker has zero concern for political office or private jobs, then he always implements his preferred policy. To the extent that central bankers' policy preferences reflect career socialization, then financial types still adopt conservative monetary policy. Note, however, from the middle row of Figure 2.4 that even a modicum of career concerns might be enough to shift policy decisions. Second, even for central bankers with career concerns, all careers come to an end. Central bankers approaching retirement have less concern for job-policy bargains and can be expected to implement their own preferred policies.[17]

A key assumption in the model is that both the financial sector and the government are indefinitely-lived unitary actors. Though financial sector firms might foresee indefinite lives, they are not generally unified in behavior or interests. Any given firm could hope to free-ride on another firm's efforts to buy monetary policy influence through job offers. There are several ways this prob-

17 This conclusion could be undermined to the extent jobs are really just vehicles for lump-sum payments – bribery is a danger no matter the age of the policy maker.

lem could be solved. First, because banks are playing a repeated game with each other, cooperation around a number of equilibria in the job-for-policy game may arise through the threat of future defection. To consider just one of the many possibilities, banks may focus on the equilibrium in which each bank offers a job-for-policy bargain to all of its former employees on their appointment to the central bank. Second, even without cooperation, the largest bank may be big enough to offer some level of job-for-policy bargains, though perhaps with suboptimal $\tilde{m}$ – that is, the largest bank may be an Olsonian "privileged group." Although these explanations are speculative, the following chapters provide evidence from many directions that actual monetary policy practice is consistent with financial sector influence through career paths, in a fashion not unlike the financial bailouts that took place across the United States and Europe following 2008. As with any study of unrevealed – and unflattering – intentions, one must at some point turn from theory to the observable evidence of informal arrangements.

Which model is the right one? Ultimately, this is an empirical question. Each model captures a different mechanism by which central bankers could make monetary policy, and there is no logical reason to disallow any one of these models or even any combination of them. But the models do have differing strengths and weaknesses.

The strength of the self-selection and socialization models is their simplicity: unlike the game theoretic models, they do not depend on a multitude of parameters or assumptions about the course of play. Of the two, career socialization seems the more powerful because monetary policy is a subject few give any thought before adulthood. Spending years or decades in a sector deeply affected by monetary policy – be it finance or elected national government – could easily overwrite preferences derived from general economic conservatism.

Turning to models of career concerns, the signaling model largely avoids collective action and time consistency problems, both of which could undermine the bargains in the fourth model. On the other hand, the bargaining perspective has a certain plausibility. Surely a large financial firm would relish the chance to influence monetary policy at the cost of a rich contract to a former central banker or two? And surely a central banker aiming for the cabinet feels pressure to provide for the government's economic needs? To dismiss such bargains before even examining the evidence flies in the face of most conventional wisdom about how private interests lobby for public policy.

Empirical Implications of the Models

All four models predict monetary policy are made according to central banker type, which I argue is well proxied by central banker career paths. But what are the distinctive implications of the models? What kind of evidence would validate one model over the others? The following five possibilities stand out.

Age effects. It is reasonable to assume that socialization effects accumulate with time: five years in the financial sector should have greater impact on preferences than one year; twenty years a greater effect than five. In other words, socialization effects should increase with age, while career incentives should be most important for the young.

Publicity effects. Career signals and bargains should be easier to achieve when central bankers can credibly communicate their conservatism. This occurs in countries with not-too-delayed reporting of monetary policy votes and in countries with a unitary monetary policy maker. If career incentives exist, they should make career effects stronger in these cases.

Successful career rewards. Career effects, whether based on signals or bargains, should lead to more post-bank jobs when the principal receives its desired policy. That is, producing lower inflation should help financial sector veterans on the central bank get back into a private bank; high growth should help former bureaucrats step up into high government positions. Neither follows from socialization alone.

Tenure effects. Shadow principals making bargains with central bankers are in no hurry to see their expensive agents leave the bank. Once that happens, the principal must either strike a costly new bargain or lose control of policy. On the other hand, shadow principals primarily interested in detecting through policy signals those central bankers who would make good hires should be more eager to scoop up their finds. This suggests central banker tenures should be higher under bargaining than signaling, all else equal.

Ideological consistency. If the financial sector makes everyone regardless of preexisting ideology hawkish on inflation, it would be reasonable, if not strictly necessary, to see a lower correlation between monetary policy preferences and general ideology among financial sector veterans than among the general public. On the other hand, if the financial sector merely attracts conservatives, there should be a similar degree of ideological consistency in each population.

We bear these distinct predictions in mind when we turn to the question of *why* career effects exist.

Broader Implications for the Study of Bureaucracy

This chapter developed four models of monetary policy making. The first two are simple decision theoretic accounts of monetary policy that presume central banker preferences arise from early life or career socialization. The third and fourth models are more intricate and build on the standard Barro-Gordon framework by allowing the monetary agent to consider the future of his career as well as his ideal policy when setting the inflation rate. This "career concerns" approach is novel to monetary policy but is similar in spirit to models used to study managerial labor markets.[18] Career concerns models like these have much to offer political science, particularly in the area of delegation. Ambitious policy makers care not only about the policy discretion or rents they can extract today, but also about their ability to advance to more prestigious, powerful, or lucrative posts tomorrow. Legally defined principals can exploit career anxiety to reward or punish their agents: compliance wins a plum appointment, shirking a cold shoulder. But shadow principals can play the game, too. An organization (such as a party, interest group, firm, or rival bureaucracy) possessing no present contractual relationship with the agent could still hold out a future appointment that beats the formal principal's offer; in exchange, the shadow principal receives a better policy today. In this way, varied prospective principals can exert pressure on the agent, whose career path links institutions lacking any formal connection. If today's central banker is tomorrow's private banker, today's monetary policy – and regulatory policy – may belong to the banks as well.

18 Hölmstrom (1999) introduced this approach, which ordinarily focuses on encouraging effort or skills acquisition rather than issues of policy discretion. Career concerns models assume a principal–agent problem (monitoring of effort is imperfect) which is at least partly resolved by the agent's concern for future employability – in his current firm or elsewhere – which in turn depends on observable outputs from his labors (for an example involving CEOs, see Gibbons and Murphy, 1992). Tirole (1994) suggests that because public sector actors accrue less monetary compensation than private managers (especially in the sense of receiving only a small share of their marginal product), career concerns loom at least as large in government agencies as in the private sector.

Theory Appendix to Chapter 2

I show formally that central bank careers and career concerns can influence monetary policy decisions and through them economic outcomes such as the level of inflation and the variance in unemployment. Combined with the theory appendices to Chapters 7 and 8, these models suggest partisan governments should have preferences over the career types of the central bankers they appoint.

We consider four models. In the first, the self-selection of wealth-seekers into the financial sector ensures financial sector veterans in the central bank are more concerned with inflation control than other central bankers, simply to protect their own assets. In the second, financial sector experience socializes inflation-hawkishness. In the third, certain types of central bankers use monetary policy decisions to send costly signals to financial sector firms that they would be good future hires for elite positions. Finally, in the fourth model, central bankers can make informal future-job-for-policy bargains with shadow principals in the financial sector or government.

Economic Assumptions

Throughout the four models, assumptions about the economy itself remain fixed and mirror the well-known models of Barro and Gordon (1983), Rogoff (1985), and Lohmann (1992). I assume the economy follows a Lucas supply function given by

$$y = \pi - w + z, \tag{2.1}$$

where y is economic output, π is inflation, w is the wage level, and z is a Normally distributed shock with mean zero and standard deviation σ_z. The labor market is characterized by price-takers who accept $w = \mathrm{E}(\pi)$. If the monetary authority has quadratic utility over inflation π and output y, with ideal output $\hat{y}$ and ideal inflation of zero,

$$U = -(1 - \chi)(y - \hat{y})^2 - \chi\pi^2, \tag{2.2}$$

then monetary policy is subject to an inflationary bias inversely related to the policy maker's conservatism χ. In turn, equilibrium output is unaffected by money on average, but the variance in output in response to shocks grows with the conservatism of the monetary agent:

$$\pi^{\star} = (1 - \chi)\left(\frac{\hat{y}}{\chi} - z\right), \quad y^{\star} = \chi z. \tag{2.3}$$

This sets up a tradeoff between the level (and variance) of inflation and the variance of the real economy, over which different policy makers may have different preferences, governed by χ, $\hat{y}$, and σ_z. Note that if governments could credibly commit to a conservative monetary policy (one based on a high χ), they would enjoy lower inflation and the same output on average. But governments may be hard pressed to keep their commitments when a deviation from the rule could keep them in power, a contingency other actors anticipate. This is the time inconsistency problem that led Rogoff to suggest delegation to a conservative, independent central banker. Of course, because conservatism comes at the price of greater economic instability, governments do not want an ultraconservative central banker, either. All else equal, different governments prefer agents more conservative than themselves.

Model 1: Self-Selection

The simplest career model we could build on these economic assumptions holds that a unitary central banker agent, *i*, to whom the government delegates both monetary authority and the legal independence to set monetary policy as he wishes has more conservative monetary policy preferences if he hails from the financial sector.

The central banker loses utility from both poor real economic performance and high inflation, as previously assumed:

$$U_i = -(1 - \chi_i)(y - \hat{y}_i)^2 - \chi_i \pi_2^2. \tag{2.4}$$

The monetary conservatism of this agent – his relative concern for inflation compared to growth – is simply χ_i. We assume that χ_i is a function of past career type, with financial types having higher χ_i than the average central banker.

In this model, the correlation between monetary conservatism and career is simple self-selection: if more conservative people enter the financial sector in the first place – perhaps because of a greater desire for monetary gains relative to other career rewards – then we might expect those people to have more conservative preferences over monetary policy, not least because of their likely greater nominal asset holdings. As there are no other players in this model, decision theory offers a simple result: financial types, being more conservative, set a lower $\pi_i^\star$ than other types, leading to lower inflation and higher variance in real output.

Model 2: Career Socialization

Assume the central banker still follows the utility function given in equation 2.5, but suppose the origin of central banker preferences χ_i changes. What if preferences over monetary policy, a topic few people consider at a young age, develop instead throughout the course of the career? Exposure to the beliefs and preferences of others in the financial sector may lead agents to become more conservative as they spend more time there. This creates not just a correlation but a causal relationship between financial sector careers and anti-inflation preferences (high χ_i). The same result as in Model 1 holds, but with a different story of preference origin.

It is crucial to underscore that this result is not an implication of independence alone, but of independence plus conservative preferences; by explaining where those preferences originate and how they may vary, the socialization hypothesis is a crucial adjunct to the basic monetary policy model.

Model 3: Policy Signals

Models of career incentives add more players – shadow principals – and strategic interaction to the simple models already introduced. First, we consider a model in which some central bankers use costly policy signals to tell shadow principals in the financial sector whether they are the type of central banker, θ, financial firms like to hire. Let $P(\theta)$ denote the probability that a central banker is a θ type.

To build this model, we need to first expand the utility function of central bankers to include future career rewards. Let m represent the benefit all central bankers receive from a subsequent financial sector job, and let m_θ be the added benefit of financial sector jobs for a special type of central banker, θ. To simplify notation, we adopt the convention that $f_a(\chi_b)$ represents the utility gained to agent a from setting monetary policy according to the preferences of actor b. This leads to the following utility function for the central banker:

$$\begin{aligned} U_i &= m + m_\theta - (1-\chi_i)(y-\hat{y}_i)^2 - \chi_i \pi_2^2 \\ &= m + m_\theta + f_i(\chi^\star). \end{aligned} \qquad (2.5)$$

We assume that central bankers from the financial sector tend to be θ types, and that $m_\theta > 0$, so that the agents the financial sector prefers to hire also are more interested in financial sector jobs than other agents.

For this model, we consider only one other actor, a financial sector firm, F. This shadow principal would like to hire former central bankers to serve in high-level positions in the private banking sector, but only if they are also θ types. (Perhaps non-θ types cannot be as trusted to have the interests of financial firms at heart or are less likely to have relevant skills.) The financial sector also benefits from low inflation. Let $m_F^\theta > 0$ be the benefit to the financial firm of hiring a θ type, let $m_F^{\sim\theta} > 0$ be the cost to the financial firm of hiring a non-θ type, and let $f_F(\chi^\star)$ be the utility F receives from the policy actually implemented. This leads to the utility function

$$\begin{aligned} U_F &= m_F^\theta - m_F^{\sim\theta} - (1 - \chi_F)(y - \hat{y}_F)^2 - \chi_F \pi^2 \\ &= m_F^\theta - m_F^{\sim\theta} + f_F(\chi^\star). \end{aligned} \tag{2.6}$$

Whether a central banker is really a θ type is unknown to F, creating an opportunity for central banker i to send a costly signal through policy. To send this signal, the central banker does not set his own ideal policy, but the ideal policy of the financial sector as implied by χ_F. If i really is a θ type, the added benefit of a financial job, $m + m_\theta$, may compensate the central banker for deviating from his ideal policy. The sequence of play, outlined in extensive form in Figure 2.5, is as follows: first, nature determines the type of the central banker; second, the central banker, who is aware of his type, chooses whether to set his ideal policy or to signal by setting the financial firm's ideal policy; third, the firm, aware of the signal but not i's type, decides whether to hire the central banker.

If the signaling process separates θ and non-θ types, and if these types correlate with previous careers, then we should expect to see financial sector "types" setting very conservative monetary policy and receiving financial sector jobs later. In the signaling game, this arrangement is not a bargain but a result of rational search by financial firms for their preferred senior staff, combined with career seeking by central bankers.

Like other signaling games, whether signaling successfully separates types in equilibrium depends on whether the non-θ types choose to falsely signal that they are θ types to get a financial sector reward as well. We can distinguish three equilibria: a separating equilibirum in which all θ types, and only θ types, set conservative policy to signal the financial sector; a pooling equilibrium in

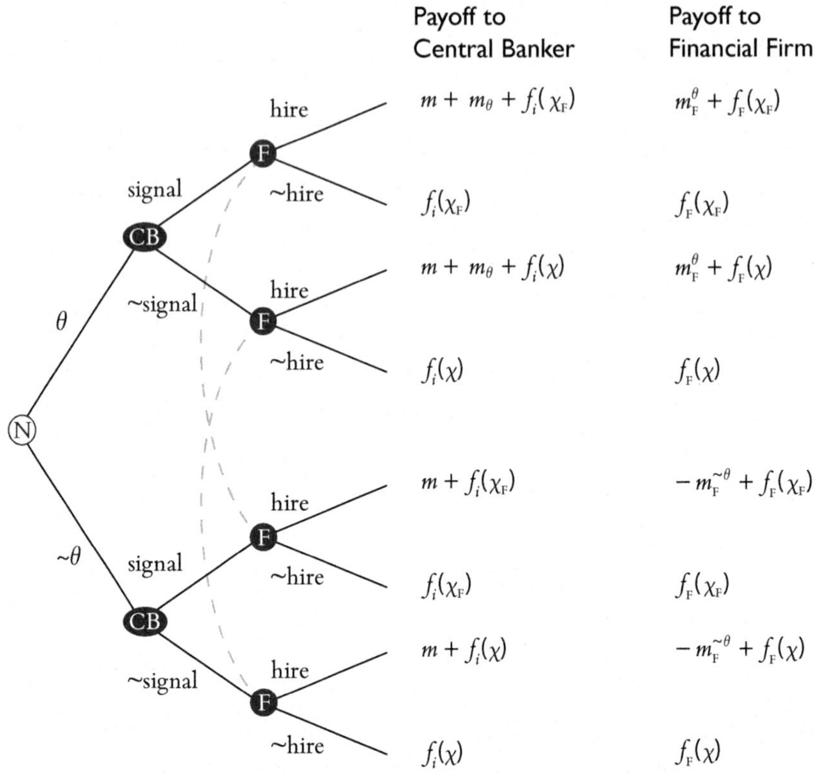

Figure 2.5. *Monetary policy as a signaling game.* The first column of payoffs are to the central banker, *i*; the second column are the payoffs to the financial firm, F. Note that *i* but not F knows the type of *i*, so that for F, each node in the lower branch of the game shares an information set with the corresponding node in the upper branch.

which all (or none) send a signal, regardless of type; and a partial pooling equilibrium, in which some fraction of each type signals, perhaps approximating full separation. Which equilibrium occurs depends on the parameters of the players' utility functions.

A separating equilibrium arises if θ types prefer to be hired, given the cost of a signal and a guarantee of success, while non-θ types find the cost of signaling too high, even if the signal is guaranteed to succeed. Formally, these conditions are

$$m + m_\theta + f_i(\chi_F) \quad > \quad f_i(\chi) \tag{2.7}$$
$$m + f_i(\chi_F) \quad < \quad f_i(\chi) \tag{2.8}$$

and can be confirmed by inspection of the extensive form.

Otherwise, a pooling equilibrium can occur in two distinct cases. First, if $f_i(\chi_i) > m + m_\theta + f_i(\chi_F)$, then even θ types prefer to implement their ideal policies rather than signal, and thus no central bankers signal. Second, all central bankers signal when F prefers to offer jobs to all central bankers who signal and the rewards to signaling outweigh the costs for all central bankers. This occurs when $m + f_i(\chi_F) > f_i(\chi_i)$ *and* the probability of a random draw from the pool of central bankers yields a θ type with sufficient probability to pay for the cost of unlucky draws, which in this game is

$$P(\theta) > \frac{m_F^{\sim\theta}}{m_F^\theta + m_F^{\sim\theta}}. \tag{2.9}$$

For the derivation, see the section "Signaling equilibria" later in this appendix.

If none of the preceding conditions obtain, then F and i will play mixed strategies. Some fraction of central bankers signal, and some fraction of the time, F hires signalers. In this equilibrium, central bankers of each type choose to signal with a probability just high enough to make them indifferent between the outcome of signaling and non-signaling. Likewise, the financial firm F chooses to reward signals at a probability that balances the expected payoffs to hiring and not hiring former central bankers. Under these conditions, we can use Bayes rule to deduce the probability that a central banker of each type will signal, as well as the probability firms will hire signalers and non-signalers, given the parameters of the model.

First, we find the probability a firm hires given a signal to be

$$P(\text{hire}|\text{signal}) = \frac{f_i(\chi) - f_i(\chi_F)}{m} + P(\text{hire}|\text{no signal}); \tag{2.10}$$

for the derivation, see the section "Signaling equilibria" later in this appendix. If we are willing to assume the firm does not hire unless it sees a signal, this simplifies to

$$P(\text{hire}|\text{signal}) = \frac{f_i(\chi) - f_i(\chi_F)}{m}, \tag{2.11}$$

which is increasing in the costliness of the signal, and decreasing in the benefit of financial jobs to central bankers.

Because we are interested in the relevance of signaling to predicting policy choice by central bankers, the key result is the probability of signaling on the part of non-financial types. When this probability is low, central banker career types should be a strong indicator of monetary policy behavior:

$$\mathrm{P}(\text{signal}|\text{CB is not } \theta \text{ type}) = \frac{m_{\mathrm{F}}^{\theta}\mathrm{P}(\text{signal}|\theta)\mathrm{P}(\theta)}{m_{\mathrm{F}}^{\sim\theta}\left[1-\mathrm{P}(\theta)\right]}. \tag{2.12}$$

For the derivation, see the section "Signaling equilibria" later in this appendix. If we are willing to assume that all true θ types signal, this simplifies to

$$\mathrm{P}(\text{signal}|\text{CB is not } \theta \text{ type}) = \frac{m_{\mathrm{F}}^{\theta}}{m_{\mathrm{F}}^{\sim\theta}} \times \frac{\mathrm{P}(\theta)}{1-\mathrm{P}(\theta)}, \tag{2.13}$$

which says that false signals are rare when the benefit of θ hires to F is low but positive, and θ types are themselves somewhat rare. False signals are frequent when non-θ's can hide in a forest of θ types, or when the cost of hiring a non-θ type is low.

I discuss the derivation of these equilibria in the next section, and investigate the testable implications of this model in the main text using comparative statics.

Signaling Equilibria

To find the pooling equilibria, note that all types of central banker signal if the financial firm always responds to a signal with a hire and all central bankers desire such jobs. The firm always hires if and only if the returns to hiring, given the population of central bankers, exceed the returns to not hiring. This condition is

$$\mathrm{P}(\sim\theta)[f_{\mathrm{F}}(\chi_{\mathrm{F}}) - m_{\mathrm{F}}^{\sim\theta}] + [1-\mathrm{P}(\sim\theta)][f_{\mathrm{F}}(\chi_{\mathrm{F}}) + m_{\mathrm{F}}^{\theta}] > f_{\mathrm{F}}(\chi_{\mathrm{F}}), \tag{2.14}$$

which can be verified from the extensive form. This simplifies to

$$\mathrm{P}(\sim\theta) > \frac{m_{\mathrm{F}}^{\theta}}{m_{\mathrm{F}}^{\theta} + m_{\mathrm{F}}^{\sim\theta}}, \tag{2.15}$$

which is the condition for pooling given in equation 2.9.

In the partial pooling equilibrium, the firm is indifferent between responding to signals and non-response. Letting equation 2.15 hold with equality, conditional on the signal, this requires that the probability a central banker is a non-θ type given that he signals to be

$$P(\sim \theta|\text{signal}) = \frac{m_F^{\theta}}{m_F^{\theta} + m_F^{\sim\theta}}. \tag{2.16}$$

Substituting the above into Bayes rule, we can determine the probability that a non-θ type signals:

$$P(\sim \theta|\text{signal}) = \frac{P(\text{signal}| \sim \theta)\,[1 - P(\theta)]}{P(\text{signal}| \sim \theta)\,[1 - P(\theta)] + P(\text{signal}|\theta)P(\theta)}, \tag{2.17}$$

which simplifies to equation 2.12.

We can determine the probability that a signal leads to a hire, P(hire|signal), in like fashion. First note that for a non-θ type to play a mixed strategy, he must be indifferent to being hired by the firm. That is,

$$P(\text{hire}|\text{signal})\,[m + f_i(\chi_F)] + P(\text{no hire}|\text{signal})\,f_i(\chi_F) =$$

$$P(\text{hire}|\text{no signal})\,[m + f_i(\chi_i)] + P(\text{no hire}|\text{no signal})\,f_i(\chi_i), \tag{2.18}$$

which can be verified from the extensive form. This simplifies to equation 2.10 above. ■

Model 4: Job-for-Policy Bargains

In Model 4, we assume that shadow principals pay a cost when offering jobs to central bankers. This eliminates the signaling game previously considered, but opens up a new possibility: implicit bargaining between central bankers and shadow principals.

Once again, central banking agents come in different "types," but now they care to varying degrees about three payoffs: policy, wealth (a proxy for financial sector jobs), and political officeholding (a proxy for government posts). We also assume these types suggest different forms of human and social capital which make them more or less suitable for other kinds of future employment.

Play now occurs between permanent or infinitely-lived principals and a series of agents indexed by i who each enjoy a three period career. Period $0i$ is always spent outside the central bank in either the financial sector or government.

The government appoints the central banker to set monetary policy in period $1i$ and gives him legal independence to set monetary policy as he wishes, including making unwritten and legally unenforceable arrangements to exchange monetary policy influence today for career favors tomorrow. In the last period of his career, period $2i$, a central banker may either take a job outside the bank or continue as monetary policy agent.

In this model, central bankers derive utility over the last two periods of their careers from four sources: from the policy outcomes they select (π and y) and possibly from either wealth-enhancing private sector jobs (m) or powerful government positions (r). The relevant portions of the ith central banker's utility function are

$$U_i = \underbrace{-(1-\chi_i)(y_1-\hat{y}_i)^2 - \chi_i\pi_1^2}_{\text{current policy}} + \delta_i\Big[\underbrace{-(1-\chi_i)(y_2-\hat{y}_i)^2 - \chi_i\pi_2^2}_{\text{future policy}} + \underbrace{\theta_i m + \tau_i r}_{\text{future jobs}}\Big]. \quad (2.19)$$

Depending on the value of χ_i, θ_i, τ_i, and δ_i, a central banker may be mainly concerned with *policy*, *wealth*, or rents from political *office*, and with respect to policy may be either *conservative* or *liberal*. Note that θ_i and τ_i are now continuous parameters, so an infinite range of job-seeking "types" are possible.

I assume that the central banker makes his final choice of π by calculating the value of χ^* which, when plugged into equation 2.3, will maximize his utility according to equation 2.19, taking into consideration both career side-payments (m or r) and his own true policy preference (χ_i). In other words, the prize in this game is the policy parameter χ^* ultimately chosen by the central banker, which in turn yields π^* and y^* according to equation 2.3.

There are two other players in the game, the financial sector (F) and the government (G), both of which are treated as indefinitely-lived unitary actors (that is, they do not change over the course of the game). Each receives utility from policy and loses utility by doling out positions, which incurs an opportunity cost. F and G have no legal role in setting π but may make promises of m or r to the agent in exchange for the chance to choose the equilibrium level of χ and thus π. Their utility functions are similar:

$$U_F = \sum_{\forall t} \delta_F^{t-1}\left[-(1-\chi_F)(y_t-\hat{y}_F)^2 - \chi_F\pi_t^2 - \theta_F m_t\right], \quad (2.20)$$

$$U_G = \sum_{\forall t} \delta_G^{t-1} \left[-(1-\chi_G)(y_t - \hat{y}_G)^2 - \chi_G \pi_t^2 - \tau_G r_t \right]. \qquad (2.21)$$

I assume $\chi_F > \chi_i > \chi_G$ to focus on the interesting and likely case in which (1) tension exists between the government's monetary preferences and those of the more conservative financial sector, (2) the government attempts to stave off the temptations of monetary policy through delegation to a more conservative, legally independent central banker, but (3) this banker is still not as conservative as the financial sector desires.

Play of the Game

The game takes place over an indefinite number of periods with each central banker serving at most two periods. To understand the policies and career tracks supportable in equilibrium, it is necessary to consider the play of the game over the latter two periods of a central banker's career (see Figure 2.6):

Period 1*i*

- F offers CB_i a job in Period $2i$ worth $\tilde{m}$ in exchange for CB_i's promise to set policy according to χ_F in Period $1i$.
- Simultaneously, G offers a job in Period $2i$ worth $\tilde{r}$ in exchange for CB_i's promise to set policy according to χ_G in Period $1i$.
- Subsequently, CB_i chooses a policy tradeoff $\chi^\star \in \{\chi_i, \chi_F, \chi_G\}$. Policy choices result in same-period economic outcomes, $\pi_{1i}^\star$ and $y_{1i}^\star$.

Period 2*i*

- F and G decide whether to make good on their offers, choosing $m^\star \in \{0, \tilde{m}\}$ and $r^\star \in \{0, \tilde{r}\}$.
- CB_i chooses among his available career options, and either stays at the central bank or heads to the financial sector or government. If CB_i stays at the central bank, he sets period $2i$ monetary policy according to $\chi^\star = \chi_i$, and $\pi_{2i}^\star$ and $y_{2i}^\star$ result. Otherwise, the government appoints a new central banker, and the game begins again.

Player/Period	0	1	2	3	4	...
CB_a	Fin (0a)	CB (1a)	Fin (2a)			
CB_b		Fin (0b)	CB (1b)	Fin (2b)		
CB_c			Gov (0c)	CB (1c)	Gov (2c)	
⋮				⋮	⋮	⋱

Figure 2.6. *Example career tracks of successive central bankers.* Cell entries show the location of each player in each period (either the financial sector, Fin; the government, Gov; or the central bank, CB). In parentheses are shown the career-period number and agent letter; hence at time 1, player b is in period 1 of his career and serving as central banker while player a is finishing up his career in the financial sector. See also the schematic representation in Figure 1.2.

Implicit Contracts Equilibrium

Observers of politics often assume that organizations can consummate policy-for-career-rewards bargains. A game theorist, however, might wonder how these deals stick. Why don't organizations leave agents hanging after receiving the policy they want? Repeated play offers one way out of this conundrum. Whether this is the right explanation – and whether career deals actually stick – remain empirical questions.

In the one-shot version of the game previously described, would-be shadow principals face a time inconsistency problem. Even when Pareto superior outcomes are possible through job-for-policy bargains, once the second period is reached the offerer has no incentive to pay, so central bankers would refuse to make deals in the first place. However, a form of the folk theorem applies to repeated games played by long- and short-run players (Fudenberg, Kreps, and Maskin, 1990). Provided the long-run run players (F and G) play last in the stage game, as they do here, reputational concerns can enforce cooperation (assuming short-run players are aware of the past behavior of long-run players). Because shadow principals who want to deal with today's central banker also want to deal with tomorrow's central bankers, there exist in equilibrium worthwhile jobs-for-policy bargains so long as there are gains to trade between central bankers and shadow principals.

To characterize the equilibria allowed by the folk theorem, we must identify Pareto improving job-for-policy trades – job offers which are both *feasible* (the offerer would be willing to trade the job for policy) and *acceptable* (the best option facing the central banker). For example, the financial sector only offers jobs that cost less than the policy that would have been implemented otherwise; a central banker only accepts jobs that provide more utility than either independent policy making or any counteroffer from the government. Given the actors' preferences, there may be no such offers (in which case the central banker implements π_i), only one offer (which the central banker accepts), or two equally good offers (a knife-edge case of little interest).

A formal characterization of equilibrium in this game follows. For a graphical explanation of comparative statics leading to testable hypotheses, see the main text.

Define the difference in player k's utility across policies χ_1 and χ_2 as $\Delta_k(\chi_1, \chi_2) = \mathrm{E}(W_k(\chi_1) - W_k(\chi_2))$. W_k denotes the policy terms of k's utility function subject to job-for-policy trades; for central bankers, this amounts to $W_i(\chi_i) = (1 + \delta_i)\left[-(1 - \chi_i)(y - \hat{y}_i)^2 - \chi_i \pi^2\right]$, because the price CB_i pays for an outside offer in period $2i$ is not one but two periods of policy discretion. Yet for F (and analogously G), $W_{\mathrm{F}}(\chi_{\mathrm{F}}) = -(1 - \chi_{\mathrm{F}})(y - \hat{y}_{\mathrm{F}})^2 - \chi_{\mathrm{F}} \pi^2$, because the bargain only buys the present period's policy; another bargain with CB_{i+1} is needed to secure next period's policy. Define the reversion policy from F's view, which obtains when F makes no offer, as $\chi_{\mathrm{F}}^{\mathrm{R}} = \mathrm{E}(\chi^{\star} | \tilde{w} = 0)$. Using these definitions, we characterize the equilibrium behavior of F; the equilibrium offer of $\tilde{r}$ by G is defined analogously.

The folk theorem for games with short- and long-run players suggests F offers $\tilde{m} \in [\underline{m}, \overline{m}]$. The upper bound is the most F can credibly offer. The lower bound, $\underline{m}$, reflects that to win the auction, F must offer more (in CB_i's view) than either G or independent action. In stylized form, we have

$$\overline{m} = \frac{\text{F's added utility}}{\text{from policy control}}, \tag{2.22}$$

$$\underline{m} = \max\left(\begin{matrix}\text{CB}_i\text{'s added utility from} \\ \text{independent policy}\end{matrix}, \begin{matrix}\text{CB}_i\text{'s added utility from} \\ \text{best alternative bargain}\end{matrix}\right). \tag{2.23}$$

Specifically, CB_i knows that regardless of how much F promises (in Period $1i$) to offer in period $2i$, the most F is willing to pay once $2i$ is reached is the one-period value of the difference in policies, in units of m, or

$$\overline{m} = \frac{\Delta_{\mathrm{F}}(\chi_{\mathrm{F}}, \chi_{\mathrm{F}}^{\mathrm{R}})}{\theta_{\mathrm{F}}}. \tag{2.24}$$

To see this, it suffices to note that if F always reached and fulfilled bargains to pay $\overline{m}$, it would break even versus the no-bargain solution in every period, and a bargain of $\epsilon > 0$ less in each period would ensure that F gains from trade in every period. Given $\delta_F < 1$, F would be willing to promise $\overline{m}/\delta_F$ but not willing to pay it, hence $\overline{m}$ is the best deal the central banker will accept.

The lower bound is more complicated, because winning bargains must beat all alternatives facing CB_i:

$$\underline{m} = \max\left[\frac{(1+\delta_i)\Delta_i(\chi_i, \chi_F)}{\delta_i\theta_i}, \right. \\ \left. \max\left(0, \frac{\tau_i\Delta_G(\chi_G, \chi_F)}{\tau_G\theta_i}\right) + \frac{\Delta_i(\chi_G, \chi_F)}{\delta_i\theta_i}\right]. \qquad (2.25)$$

The first term is simply the utility CB_i loses from setting F's preferred policy; clearly any acceptable bargain must fully compensate this loss. Winning bargains must also be better than G's best offer. The net change in CB_i's utility given G's best offer is captured in the second term in equation 2.25, which consists of the value to CB_i of $\overline{r}$ and the government's preferred policy, respectively.

Successful bargains between F and CB_i depend on the existence of gains to trade; that is, $\overline{m} > \underline{m}$. But unlike most games between short- and long-run players, bargains can succeed even when the principal cares little for the future. This is because payment of $\tilde{m}$ for today's policy is deferred to the next period. If it is not paid, the next period's central banker (whether the current agent or a replacement) will not accept an offer from F. Because the costs and benefits of defection are deferred to the next period, any $\delta_F \in (0, 1]$ suffices so long as there are gains to trade in the next period as well.

Because CB_i always maximizes his return over one play of the stage game, he always employs a pure strategy of accepting the best offer made and setting policy accordingly. F and G, however, may choose to play either pure or mixed strategies. When both principals play pure strategies, they offer some $\tilde{m} \in [\underline{m}, \overline{m}]$ and $\tilde{r} \in [\underline{r}, \overline{r}]$. CB_i always accepts the best offer and implements policy accordingly. In period $2i$, the winning bidder, if any, makes good on its promise, and CB_i accepts. If there was no winning bidder, then CB_i remains as central banker and implements his own ideal policy implied by χ_i.

The arrangement of the game allows F or G to play mixed strategies, but they will not do so in any way that affects policy or career transitions. Suppose, given $\overline{m} > \underline{m}$, F offers to pay $\tilde{m}$ in Period $2i$ such that $m \in [\overline{m}, \underline{m}]$ with probability q, and $m = 0$ with probability $1 - q$. This will be the winning offer so long as F respects the constraint that $E(\tilde{m}) = qm \geq \underline{m}$. If the central banker expects any less from F, then he will rationally punish F by refusing F's bargain, but so long as CB_i expects at least $\underline{m}$, he will implement F's desired policy. Therefore, any mixed strategy with $qm < \underline{m}$ is strictly dominated by the pure strategy of paying $m = \underline{m}$ every round, because the latter assures F of unbroken policy influence, which is worth at least $\underline{m}$ per period. But failing to pay $m \geq \underline{m}$ in any particular round of the game leaves CB_i in place for a second period, in which he implements χ_i regardless. As we have shown F would rather pay at least $\underline{m}$ than reach this outcome, then we can conclude that under a mixed strategy, no realization of m falls below this threshold. (If we relax the assumption that central bankers receive job offers before choosing to leave the central bank in period $2i$, mixed strategies that occasionally pay nothing become viable, but the policy implications of the model remain the same.) In sum, mixed and pure strategy equilibria with the same $E(m)$ and $E(r)$ may differ with respect to job offer quality and perhaps the likelihood of CB_i receiving a job at all, but not with respect to any policies actually implemented. ■

3

CENTRAL BANKER CAREERS AND INFLATION IN INDUSTRIAL DEMOCRACIES

> Will it be sufficient to mark, with precision, the boundaries
> of these departments in the constitution of the government,
> and trust to these parchment barriers
> against the encroaching spirit of power?
>
> JAMES MADISON, *Federalist 48*

THE THEORY of career-based monetary policy suggests testable implications for central banker preferences, policy decisions and outcomes, and the hiring and firing of central bankers. In this chapter, I focus on the simplest empirical implication: monetary policy should be more anti-inflationary in the hands of financial sector types than government bureaucrats. Starting with inflation makes sense: inflation control is the ostensible object of monetary policy, and inflation is the outcome most widely measured over a broad array of countries and periods. I find that central bankers' careers not only influence the inflation rate, but that this effect can be split, using contextual clues, into a likely combination of career incentives and socialized preferences.

Measuring Career Effects

In developing measures of central bankers' careers, the first choice is whether to focus on what central bankers did before joining the central bank's board, or what they did after. There are theoretical, empirical, and practical reasons to concentrate on measures based on *past* career experience. Prior experience provides the context in which career socialization takes place and should therefore be a good measure to test the socialization hypothesis. But prior careers are important for incentives as well, because experience provides the specialized knowledge and social networks that are the foundation of job-for-policy exchanges. Choosing to work in a sector also reveals preferred career rewards, and I show in the following that earlier work in a sector also strongly predicts post-central bank career patterns. Though future careers are central to the career incentives story, from a given central banker's perspective they are uncertain. A central banker may aim toward a future career that fails to materialize for any number of reasons, including poor health, poor performance, or an unexpected better job offer elsewhere. To the extent a central banker's past reveals his expectations and preferences at the time he entered the central bank, pre-central bank careers are the most accurate measure of career effects.

There are also practical reasons to develop measures using prior experience. The alternative – using the future to explain the past – is not only causally discomfiting, but also precludes prediction using observable variables. Moreover, the quality of future jobs is hard to assess from extant records. It is often difficult to find information on post-bank activities, especially in the private sector, whereas complete pre-central bank career data are almost always available. Finally, we are interested in developing good measures of overall central bank conservatism, which may result not only from career concerns, but also from socialized policy preferences shaped by career backgrounds alone. Where available, future career data are useful; in particular, such data can help distinguish incentive and socialization effects, as I show in Section 2. But the primary indicator of career effects is *past* experience.

To measure the career background of a particular central banker at a particular time, I partition his past jobs into seven mutually exclusive and exhaustive categories (Table 3.1).[1] Most studies of political actors' background use binary variables to capture experience, but this practice has two key failings: it groups together specialists who have devoted their careers to one area with those who have spent perhaps no more than a year in one place, and it overlooks changes in careers over time.[2] In contrast, I focus on the composition of each person's career over time. For each job category, I calculate an *experience score*, which is

1 To improve the international comparability of the categories, I include only privately owned and operated financial firms in the Financial category. State-run banks face different incentives, and almost all central bankers who took a turn at such banks were career bureaucrats, not financiers. Thus, I include management of government-controlled banks in the Government category.

2 Stovel, Savage, and Bearman (1996), who explore detailed career histories of employers at Lloyd's of London, is an exception.

Table 3.1. *A typology of central banker job types.*

Job Category	Description
Financial	Private banking jobs
Government	Bureaucrats outside the central bank and finance ministry
Finance Ministry	Bureaucrats in the finance ministry
Central Bank	Staffers at the central bank, excluding policy makers
Economics	Academic economists
Business	The private sector, excluding banks
Other	International organization officials and staff, non-economist academics, labor union organizers, journalists, etc.

Each job held by a central banker throughout his career falls into exactly one category.

the fraction of the central banker's career spent in that job category up to the date of his most recent appointment to a monetary policy making post. To define experience scores, let j index central banks, let $i \in \{1, \ldots, I_j\}$ index central bankers, let t index time periods (months, quarters, or years), and let d count days from a universal reference date. Let Career_{ij} mark the start of i's career, in days, let Appoint_{ijt} be the day of i's most recent appointment to central bank j, and let Jobs_{ijd} indicate the number of jobs i held on day d. Then, define the financial experience of the ith central banker in the jth central bank in period t as

$$\text{FinExp}_{ijt} = \sum_{d=\text{Career}_{ij}}^{\text{Appoint}_{ijt}} \frac{\text{FinJob}_{ijd}}{\text{Jobs}_{ijd}} \Bigg/ \left(\text{Appoint}_{ijt} - \text{Career}_{ij}\right). \qquad (3.1)$$

Similar definitions obtain for GovExp_{ijt}, FMExp_{ijt}, CBExp_{ijt}, EcoExp_{ijt}, BusExp_{ijt}, and OthExp_{ijt}. Together with FinExp_{ijt}, the seven experience scores sum to one. Taken as a whole, the set of experience scores are an example of compositional data (Aitchison, 2003*b*) and require special care when used in regression models as either covariates or dependent variables.

To produce a set of experience scores for an entire central bank over period t we need an aggregation mechanism. Work on the Federal Reserve (Chappell, Havrilesky, and McGregor, 1993; Chappell, McGregor, and Vermilyea,

2004*a*,*b*) suggests that while the Fed Chair is not all-powerful, his agenda-setting power gives him extra influence in policy making. Still, Chappell, McGregor, and Vermilyea (2004*a*) find that the most important voice on the FOMC is the median voter's.[3] Unfortunately, it is difficult to extend this work across countries without recorded votes, which are usually unavailable or uninformative. Instead, I aim for a broad sweep across countries to establish the importance of career variables. I simply average the career experiences of all central bankers who enjoy *de jure* rights to set or vote on monetary policy, "tenure-weighted" by the proportion of the period they served.[4] In constructing a quarterly experience score, for example, a member who served the entire quarter would be weighted fully, but a central banker who departed a month into the quarter would receive only one-third as much weight. Where it is possible to combine central banker characteristics in a single index, I summarize the institution's characteristics by its tenure-weighted median member, relying on a loose application of the median voter theorem for leverage over the preference aggregation problem. Otherwise, when multiple variables are needed to summarize central bankers' preferences, I use the tenure-weighted *mean* of each score.

To define institution-wide experience scores formally, first let Duration_t indicate the length of period t in days, and let Office_{ijt} count the number of days that member i was in a monetary policy post at central bank j during period t. Then, define the financial experience of central bank j in period t as the weighted

3 In an interesting confirmation of the importance of legally defined voting rights, Chappell, McGregor, and Vermilyea (2004*a*,*b*) also study the bank presidents of the FOMC. These presidents rotate through a limited number of voting positions and attend FOMC meetings even when they are temporarily lacking voting rights. But it is the vote that matters: Chappell, McGregor, and Vermilyea find that non-voting bank presidents views carry no weight in policy decisions.

4 To determine which officials have voting authority on monetary policy questions, I turned to legal documents from the various central banks, along with data collected in Siklos (2002), Eijffinger and Geraats (2004), and Goodman (1992). Two special cases are worth mentioning. The first is the American FOMC, which has four rotating members representing the regional Federal Reserve Banks. I determined which regional bank presidents were voting members at any given time from the *Federal Reserve Bulletin*. The second case is Canada, which reserves *de jure* monetary authority for the central bank governor only but informally grants some power to a "Governing Council" within the bank. The results reported in the text follow from the *de jure* definition and include the Canadian Governor only.

average of individuals' scores with weights given by the fraction of the period each banker served

$$\text{FinExp}_{jt} = \sum_{i=1}^{I_j} \text{FinExp}_{ijt} \frac{\text{Office}_{ijt}}{\text{Duration}_t} \Bigg/ \sum_{i=1}^{I_j} \frac{\text{Office}_{ijt}}{\text{Duration}_t}. \qquad (3.2)$$

GovExp_{jt}, FMExp_{jt}, CBExp_{jt}, EcoExp_{jt}, and BusExp_{jt} are defined analogously. As in the case of an individual's experience scores, the experience scores of a given bank in a given period always sum to one.

Central Bankers' Careers: Data

In this chapter, I study an original dataset documenting central bankers' careers and educational backgrounds. The data consist of complete or near-complete career histories of nearly six hundred monetary policy decision-makers from twenty developed countries over the period 1950 to 2000.[5] Depending on the country, these may include governors, deputy governors, directors, policy board members, or their equivalents. For each policy maker, the database includes all jobs worked, by type; starting and ending dates for each job; all positions at central bank, with dates of service; educational history; birth, graduation, retirement, and death dates; and gender. (Monetary policy is remarkably male dominated; fully 95 percent of the central bankers in the sample were men.) Data were collected by the author from central banks' archives, biographical dictionaries, web resources, and business periodicals (see the Data Appendix for sources). Career histories were tabulated into individual- and central-bank-level experience scores for various period lengths (monthly, quarterly, annually) and differing collections of central banking officials (all officials, just governors, and so on).

A large majority (about 83 percent) of all work done by central bankers was in government (including the finance ministry and the central bank itself), private finance, or economics (Figure 3.1). This is a remarkable degree of convergence, given data on careers from university onwards for hundreds of individuals scat-

5 The countries are Australia, Austria, Belgium, Canada, Denmark, Finland, France, Germany, Ireland, Italy, Japan, the Netherlands, New Zealand, Norway, Portugal, Spain, Sweden, Switzerland, the United Kingdom, and the United States. I identified a total of 721 monetary policy officials and was able to assemble reasonably complete career histories for 598 of these, at least through their time at the central bank. See Table 3.3 in the Data Appendix to this chapter for further details. A complementary database for developing countries is examined in Chapter 5.

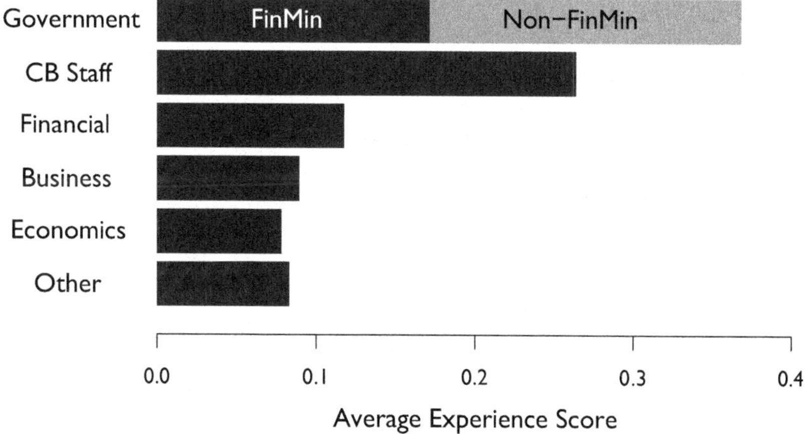

Figure 3.1. *Average prior career experience of twenty central banks, 1950 to 2000.* Career experience is the fraction of a central banker's prior career spent in a job type, averaged across a bank's monetary policy makers. Over the last half century, the past experiences of central bankers in twenty industrial democracies can be described almost entirely as falling within the state bureaucracy, central bank staff, private banking sector, and economics profession.

tered across twenty countries. Former bureaucrats (of all kinds) are the most common type of central banker, but less than half of past bureaucratic experience is in finance ministries; the rest is spread over a variety of ministries often lacking any substantive connection to monetary or economic policy. Private banking backgrounds are rarer than conventionally assumed, comprising only twelve percent of central bankers' backgrounds, making it the third-most common background, after bureaucrats and central bank staffers.

The average mixture of career types varies across nations (Figure 3.2; see Box 3.1 on "Star Plots"). Sweden, Belgium, and Finland rely heavily on bureaucrats and politicians to staff their banks; in Sweden, parliamentary backgrounds are common. New Zealand and Denmark depend more on financiers. The monetary policy authorities of France and Ireland are overwhelmingly veterans of the Finance Ministry, whereas those of the United Kingdom, Canada, and Italy tend to be career central bank staffers. The United States, Japan, Austria, and the Netherlands have more balanced boards.

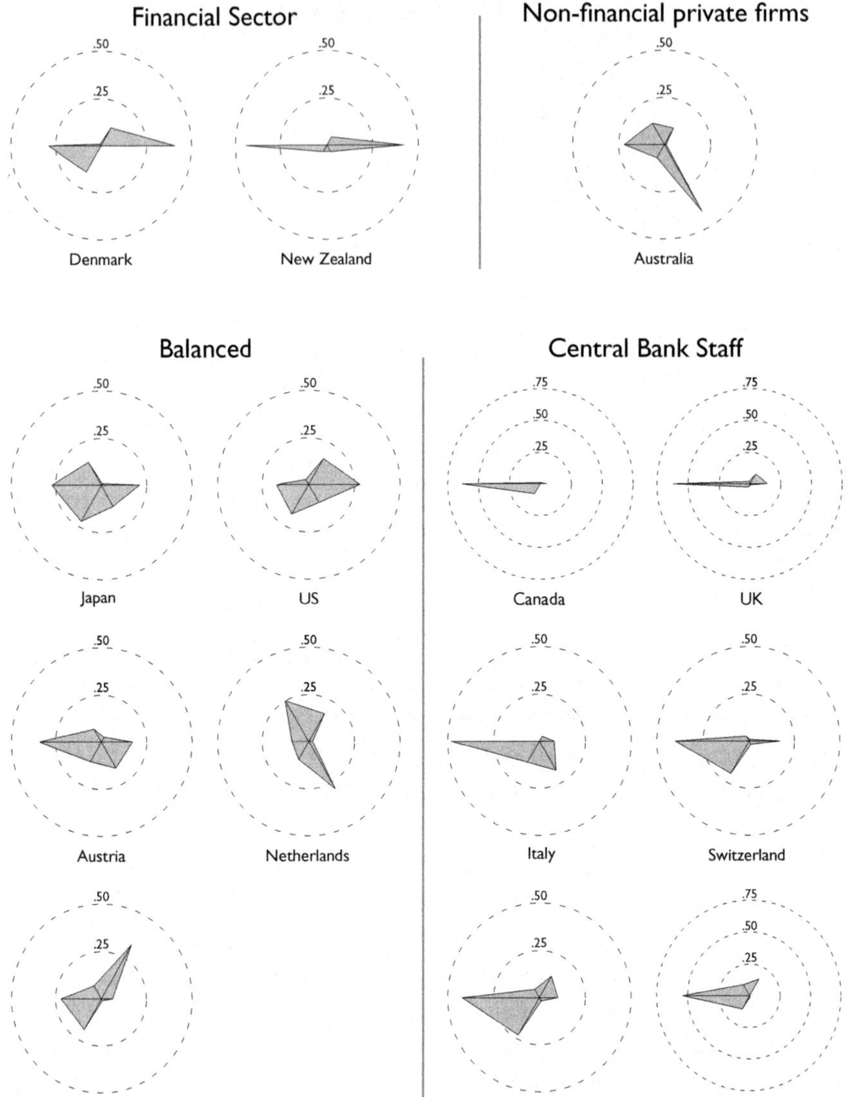
Financial Sector
Non-financial private firms
.50
.25
Denmark
New Zealand
Australia
Balanced
Central Bank Staff
.75
Japan
US
Canada
UK
Austria
Netherlands
Italy
Switzerland
Portugal
Germany
Spain

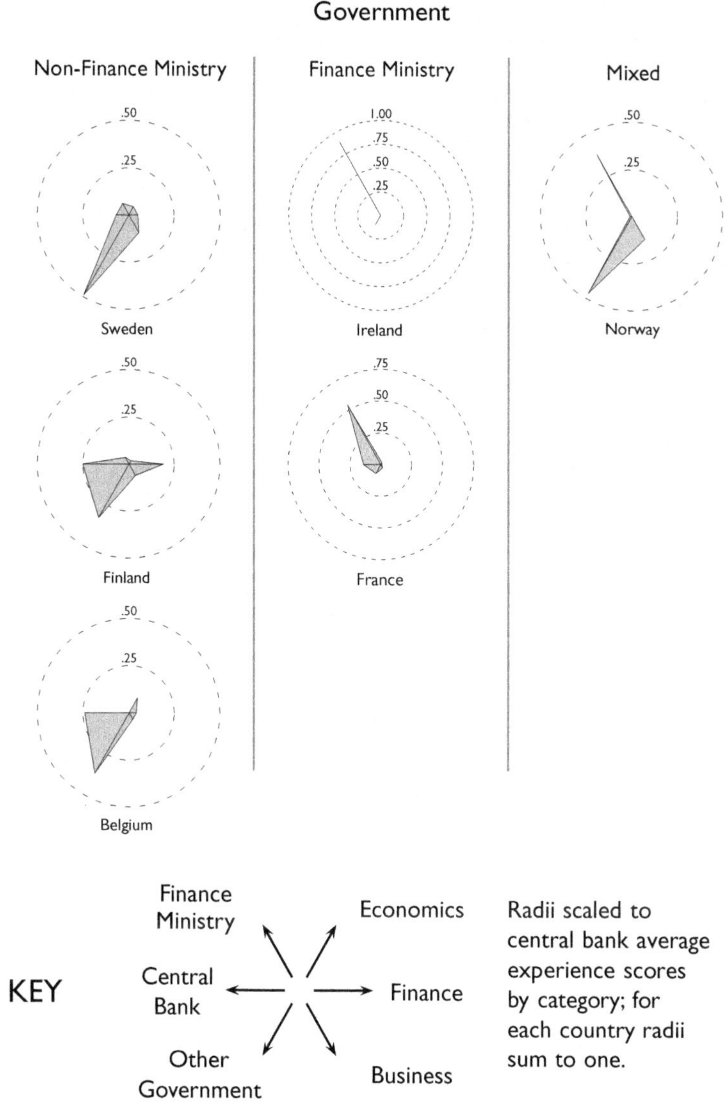

KEY

Finance Ministry, Economics, Central Bank, Finance, Other Government, Business

Radii scaled to central bank average experience scores by category; for each country radii sum to one.

Figure 3.2. *Cross-country variation in central banker types.* Countries are grouped by dominant central banker background over the period 1950 to 2000.

Box 3.1. Star Plots

Star plots such as Figure 3.2 attempt to solve the most challenging information visualization problem, the simultaneous display of many dimensions of data. In these figures, we create a separate plot for each country, averaging its data on six career experience variables over time. Each plot has not two but six axes, all of which radiate in a circle from the center of the plot. The values of six variables are plotted, one for each axis, and the values connected to create a star-like shape. Each case in the dataset thus gets a differently shaped star based on its unique combination of values on the six experience scores. Observations with similar patterns across many variables trace out similar polygons, so star plots can help us find similar clusters in the data – countries whose central bankers are similar on many career dimensions – just by matching up shapes.

Looking at individual characteristics, rather than at central bank board averages, supports the career typology as well. At first appointment to a monetary policy position, the average central banker was 47.8 years old, could expect to stay at the central bank for 6.1 years, and had spent 80 percent of his past career in just one of the sectors listed in Figure 3.1. Nine of ten central bankers spent at least half their pre-appointment careers in one sector, while a third spent all of their careers in just one type of job. Just 29 percent of new central bankers had ever worked in a private bank, whereas 23 percent had worked in the finance ministry, 47 percent elsewhere in government, and 23 percent in a private business. About two in five had worked previously as central bank staff; one in five as an academic economist. Almost half (47 percent) had *never* had a job outside either the financial sector or government (including the finance ministry and central bank) – which suggests most new central bankers would expect their next job, obtained perhaps at age 54, to be in one of these places as well.

Returning to aggregate central bank data, Figure 3.3 traces the evolving mixture of backgrounds within central banks over time. The most outstanding feature is the waning and waxing of financial sector experience. Starting at an average of 17 percent of the cumulative experience of the central bankers of 1950, financial experience steadily dropped until it made up only seven percent of the backgrounds of 1970s central bankers. Then, in the first half of the 1980s, financial backgrounds shot up to their former highs, and have remained around seventeen percent ever since. The second notable trend is the steady growth in economics backgrounds, totally absent in 1950, but comprising fifteen percent

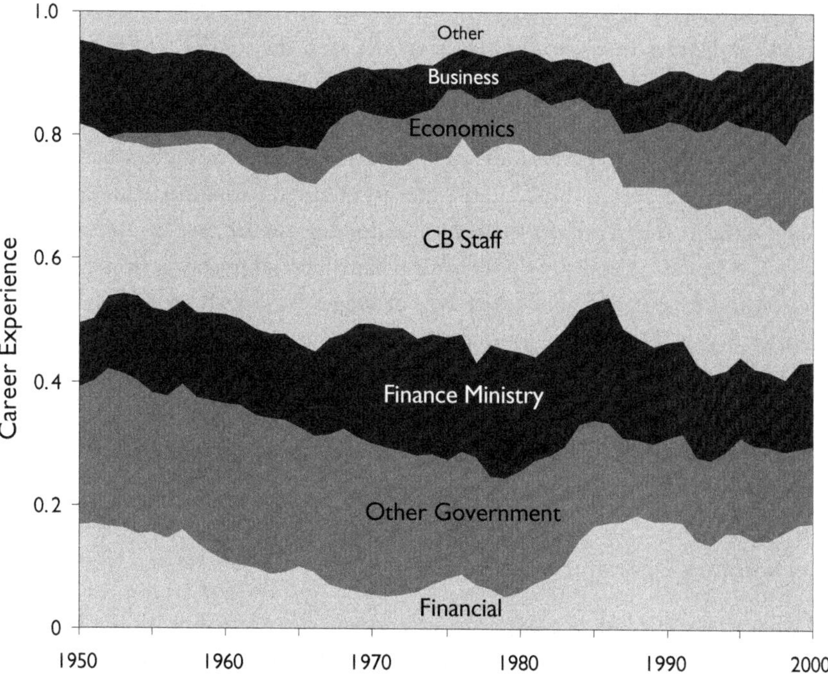

Figure 3.3. *Evolution of career experience in twenty central banks, 1950 to 2000.* Average career composition of central bank policy makers, by month.

of the past experience of central bankers in 2000. The gains of financiers and economists have come primarily at the expense of bureaucrats, especially those without finance ministry or central banking backgrounds. Overall, the public sector experience of central bankers comprised a majority of total experience in 1950 (65 percent of all past careers), grew to overwhelming dominance by 1979 (73 percent), then rapidly receded after 1980. In 2000, private sector experience – in finance, economics, and business – made up 41 percent of backgrounds, twice its 1979 low.

Besides career data, the central banker dataset includes information on central bankers' educational histories. Because of the technical nature of monetary policy, there is particular interest in central bankers' economics training. The data, summarized in Table 3.2, reveal unexpected educational pluralism. First, economics training beyond the undergraduate level is surprisingly uncommon among monetary policy makers. In the average country, only 30 percent held advanced degrees in economics (masters degrees, doctorates, or their equivalents). Second, cross-country variation in economics training is vast. Economics training is practically *de rigueur* for monetary policy makers in some countries, such as Norway, the Netherlands, and Switzerland. In the middle, a bare majority of central bankers in the United States and United Kingdom held economics credentials. At the other extreme, economics degrees are rare or unheard of in Japan and Ireland. Finally, OECD central bankers tend to stay at home to study economics: except in Canada, the lure of major American economics departments is weak. Moreover, domestically-trained central bankers tend to come from a broad array of schools, not just an elite few (with only a few unsurprising exceptions, like France). In short, economists neither dominate central banks, nor do a few select departments or countries dominate the economics training of central bankers.

The Revolving Door at the Central Bank

The hypothesized link between past careers and career socialization is straightforward: exposure to conservative ideas during a career engenders conservative preferences. But the association between career backgrounds and career incentives may be less clear to skeptics, who might reasonably ask why it matters what a central banker did before entering the central bank, especially if the central banker can always choose a new shadow principal while on the monetary policy board, then take up a new career in the financial sector or government afterwards. On this view, the central bank is not a revolving door sending people back to their old careers, but instead a waiting room through which ambitious financiers and bureaucrats may circulate easily among all three sectors: government, central bank, and high finance.

Chapter 2 suggested the revolving door is the more apt metaphor. First, past careers reveal central bankers' demands for career rewards. Former bankers likely entered banking in the first place for its financial rewards, just as bureaucrats joined the civil service for its security, power, and perquisites. To the extent central bankers' career goals remain constant, they should part ways again on leaving the central bank. Second, previous careers impart specific skills and create social ties that make rehiring into that sector more affordable to the shadow principal. If these suppositions are correct, post-central bank appointments will flow from pre-central bank careers, with financial sector veterans likely to return to private banks, and career bureaucrats likely to return to gov-

Table 3.2. *Central bankers' economics education, by country, 1950 to 2000.*

All figures are lower bounds Country	% of CBers with adv econ degree	% of these with own country degree	No. of sources of highest econ degree	Most common schools granting highest advanced economic degree (number of degree-holders)
Norway	100%	100%	1	Oslo (2)
Netherlands	80	100	3	Groningen (2)
Switzerland	75	83	5	GIIS-Geneva (2)
Denmark	63	100	1	*not available*
Belgium	56	80	3	Cath. Univ. of Louvain (2)
United Kingdom	52	73	6	LSE (3), Oxford (3), Camb. (2)
United States	52	97	19	Mich. (5), Chicago (4), Harv. (3)
Italy	47	86	3	MIT (2)
Canada	44	0	5	LSE (4)
Germany	42	100	18	Berlin (3), Freiburg (3)
New Zealand	36	80	5	various Antipodean (1)
Spain	31	80	6	Madrid (6)
France	23	100	1	Sciences Po (6)
Australia	21	44	8	Australia Nat. Univ. (2)
Portugal	20	67	5	ISCEF (4), Columbia (2)
Sweden	15	90	5	Stockh. Sch. Ec. (3), Stockh. (2)
Finland	14	100	1	*not available*
Austria	12	100	3	Vienna (2)
Japan	6	33	3	Tokyo (1), MIT (1), UCLA (1)
Ireland	0	—	1	*not available*
All countries	30	83	80	LSE (10), MIT (7)

Some policy boards include many central bankers with either a masters or doctorate in economics; others have few. In most countries, central bankers earned their highest degree domestically. Except in small countries and France, no school has a monopoly on central banker graduates. On average, there were about two central banker graduates per school.

ernment. Pre-central bank experience scores constitute valid measures of career incentives.

We can test whether the central bank is a waiting room or a revolving door with a pair of probit regressions modeling post-central bank jobs as a function of pre-central bank careers. First, I construct two binary dependent variables, FinJob_i and GovJob_i, which indicate whether a central banker obtained a job of corresponding type after leaving the central bank. (Note that GovJob_i includes all government jobs, including posts in the finance ministry and central bank, unlike our usual experience score categories. The rationale for contrasting these types in the first place rests on the hypothesis that they differentially predict future careers in banking or government as a whole. As *destinations*, there is no longer any reason to distinguish them.) I regress both of these indicators on the same six explanatory variables: pre-central bank levels of FinExp_i, GovExp_i, FMExp_i, CBExp_i, and EcoExp_i, along with the age of the central banker at the end of his service to the central bank (see Table 3.6 in the Data Appendix for estimated parameters).

We interpret these models through estimated first differences showing how the probability of a post-bank career changes as the corresponding pre-bank experience score shifts from 0 to 1. Calculating first differences in the response variable is always good practice, but especially useful here because of a subtle issue in the interpretation of compositional explanatory variables in regression models. By definition, a central bank(er)'s experience scores must sum to one. Therefore, any hypothetical that alters one component score is incomplete if it does not specify which other scores are adjusted to maintain this accounting identity. When multiple components enter a model separately, it is inappropriate to treat any one coefficient as a complete summary of the effect of a component score, because there could be countervailing or reinforcing effects working through other parameters. (I discuss this problem in greater depth in the Methods Appendix.)

In this particular example, there is a simple solution. In contrast to monetary policy boards, individual central bankers tend to have most or all of their experience concentrated in a single career category, so I calculate the probability of future jobs in either finance or government under the assumption that the central banker's prior career was entirely in a single category and hold all other categories at zero.

The analysis suffers from substantial missing data. We have fairly complete data on prior careers, but future jobs are often hard to document, and we cannot usually distinguish missing data on the dependent variable from an absence of post-bank jobs of that type. There is no easy imputation fix for this problem, and it surely introduces bias into the results; at a minimum, fitted probabilities of future jobs are likely too low on average (because many of the zeros are probably ones, but not *vice versa*).[6] Moreover, missing data afflicts the different outcome variables to varying degrees. Government jobs taken after central bank service are more likely to be recorded in the public record and are more likely to be noted in central bank archives. It is harder to discern whether central bankers took on private banking roles after leaving the central bank. These jobs are seldom tracked by the central bank and are often overlooked by biographical dictionaries, which usually emphasize public service. Internet searches turned up numerous cases where former central bankers joined private banks, raising the suspicion that post-central bank financial jobs in the pre-internet era are undercounted. For these reasons, there is also little hope of imputing more complete data.[7]

With these caveats, we turn to the results, summarized in Figure 3.4. Former private bankers (the first row of result in Figure 3.4) enter government at lower rates than other central bankers, and reenter the financial sector at higher rates. Non-specialist bureaucrats (the last row of results) reenter government at higher than normal rates, but are less likely than average to switch to private banking after the central bank. In these two cases, there is a clear revolving door – and a potential link between past career types and future career interests.

Now consider the more ambiguous cases of expert bureaucrats. I argue in the preceding that central bank and finance ministry staff may more easily join private banks than other bureaucrats, given their training and likely social connections with that sector. The right plot in Figure 3.4 shows this is the case. But note there is also a difference between the two types: past central bank experience makes future government jobs *more* likely, whereas finance ministry experience makes them *less* likely.[8] By calculating the difference in these con-

6 Constructing an appropriate imputation model is complicated by the difficulty of establishing *any* of the zeros on the dependent variable with complete confidence – there could always be an undocumented or overlooked job. (An exception is when central bankers die in office, but these cases are surely not representative of other zeros and are consequently of limited use in reducing bias through imputation.)

7 In the jargon of missing data imputation, future jobs likely involve "non-ignorable missingness," a pattern of missingness that cannot be successfully modeled using the observed data alone (Little and Rubin, 1987).

8 Although our findings on financial and government experience make intuitive sense and seem likely to hold out of this sample, the career patterns of central bank and finance ministry staff are likely to vary on a case by case basis, as we find in Chapter 4.

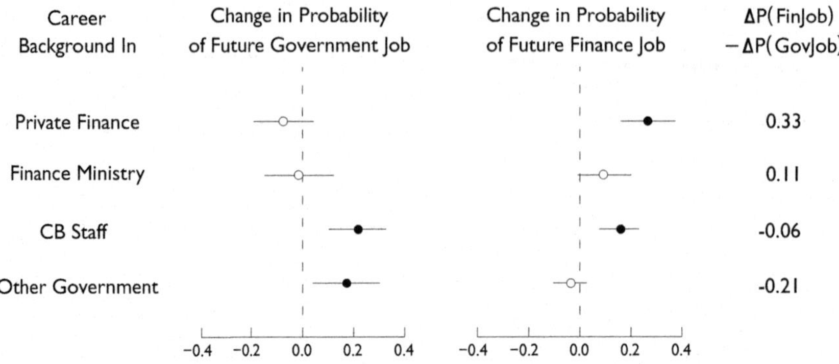

Figure 3.4. *The central bank's revolving door.* The two plots show first differences from probit regressions of post-CB careers on pre-CB experience scores; horizontal bars mark 90 percent confidence intervals. Central bankers' post-central bank careers in private finance (left plot) or in government (right plot) are correlated with their prior career experience (listed at left). The column at far right shows the change in probability of having a finance job rather than a government job.

ditional probabilities

$$P(\text{Future Fin Job}|\text{Past Career}) - P(\text{Future Gov Job}|\text{Past Career}), \qquad (3.3)$$

we can order career types based on their likelihood to lead to financial, rather than government, future appointments as Fin > FM > CB > Gov. We expect the same order to describe the effects of these career types on economic outcomes.

Career Effects and the Level of Inflation

The first step in exploring the connection between central banker characteristics and monetary policy outcomes is the linkage between central bankers and inflation in the post-Bretton Woods era.[9] To do this, I employ least squares time series cross-section regression with standard errors corrected for panel heteroskedasticity (Beck and Katz, 1995). Linear regression is appropriate because

9 That is, the data analyzed in this section and the next cover our twenty countries over 1973 to 2000, excluding ECB members after 1997 and Spain and Portugal before democracy (before 1979 and 1977, respectively).

the dependent variable, logged quarterly inflation, is approximately Normally distributed (a few cases of deflation are omitted). I include country fixed effects to mitigate omitted variable bias, and I include lags of the dependent variable to account for temporal dependence. The model is of the form

$$y_{it} = \sum_{q=1}^{Q} \phi_q y_{i,t-q} + \alpha_i + \mathbf{x}_{it}\beta + \epsilon_{it}, \tag{3.4}$$

where $\mathbf{x}_{it}$ is a vector of covariates, β is a vector of associated coefficients, α_i is a country fixed effect, and ϵ_{it} is a Normally distributed disturbance.

Model 1 regresses logged inflation on several career components – financial experience, finance ministry experience, economics experience, and government experience – while controlling for CBI using an average of three well-known indices.[10] I also control for imports as a share of GDP, which according to several theories should reduce the attraction of loosening the money supply (Campillo and Miron, 1997).[11] Tables 3.4, 3.5, and 3.7 in the Data Appendix provide estimated parameters, goodness of fit statistics, and data summaries.[12]

Results are presented in terms of counterfactuals calculated from the estimated model (Figure 3.5). I focus on counterfactuals because they more transparently handle the problem of compositional explanatory variables, which is described in detail in the Methods Appendix. In short, we cannot read a single component's coefficient as a "first difference" without implicitly assuming the increase in that category is made up by reductions in the omitted categories only – an assumption that can lead to misleading or even impossible inferences. The solution is to reduce *all* other categories proportionally and calculate expected values or first differences of the outcome variable. Such "ratio-preserving" counterfactuals deal neutrally with offsetting shifts in experience

10 These are the Cukierman, Webb, and Neyapti (1992) index, with updated data from Maxfield (1997), the Grilli, Masciandaro, and Tabellini (1991) index, and the Bade and Parkin (1982) index.

11 For example, Romer (1993) argues that openness lowers the benefits of raising output through monetary policy while raising the inflationary cost. Lane (1997) supposes the benefits of surprise inflation act through raising the output of rigidly priced non-tradables; hence the more open the economy, the less the benefit of money surprises.

12 Substantial serial correlation can endanger the consistency of time-series cross section regressions that include lags of the dependent variable. Lagrange multiplier tests for serial correlation reject the null hypothesis of autocorrelation when two lags of the dependent variable are included in the model

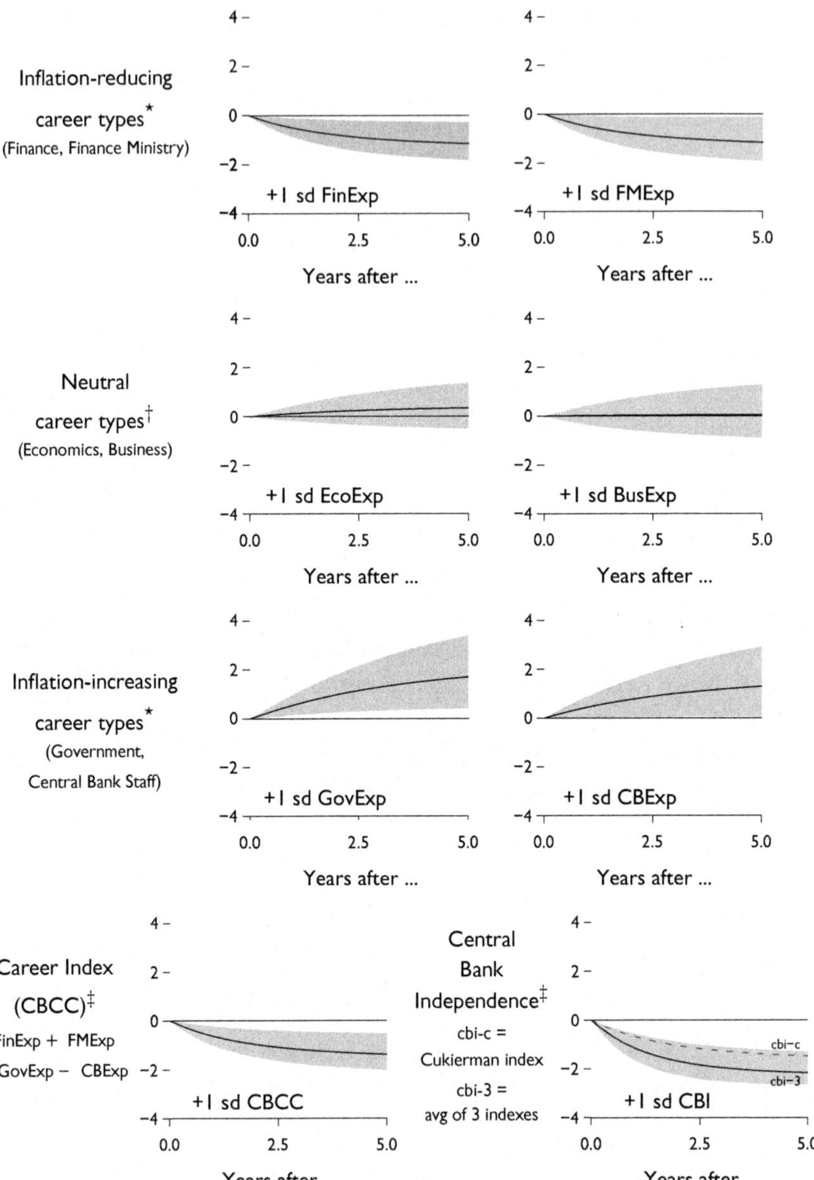

Change in inflation, over time, from changing career composition of the central bank
Inflation-reducing career types*
(Finance, Finance Ministry)
+1 sd FinExp
+1 sd FMExp
Neutral career types†
(Economics, Business)
+1 sd EcoExp
+1 sd BusExp
Inflation-increasing career types*
(Government, Central Bank Staff)
+1 sd GovExp
+1 sd CBExp
Career Index (CBCC)‡
FinExp + FMExp - GovExp − CBExp
+1 sd CBCC
Central Bank Independence‡
cbi-c = Cukierman index
cbi-3 = avg of 3 indexes
cbi-c
cbi-3
+1 sd CBI
Years after ...
4
2
0
−2
−4
0.0
2.5
5.0

Figure 3.5. *Effects of individuals and institutions on inflation, OECD sample.* Change in inflation following a permanent one standard deviation increase in a career type, the career conservatism index (CBCC), or central bank independence (CBI). Each solid line is a separate counterfactual. When one experience score is increased, all other scores are reduced proportionately from their means to maintain a sum of one. Initial lags are set at mean observed inflation. All plots show expected values as solid lines and mark 90 percent confidence intervals in gray. These intervals reflect the cumulative estimation uncertainty produced by iterating the model through twenty periods. *Counterfactuals from Model 1. †Counterfactuals from Model 1, with EcoExp and BusExp added. ‡Counterfactuals from Model 3.

scores, while meeting the logical requirement that all experience scores sum to one.

Figure 3.5 shows counterfactuals calculated from Model 1 using this method. According to the model, increasing the average financial experience of monetary agents by one standard deviation corresponds with a 1.1 point reduction in inflation over a five year period. That is, if the central bank board changed from having 17 percent of its collective experience in finance to having 30 percent, inflation would drop by a little over a point after five years with the new board in office.[13] In contrast, increasing government experience by one standard deviation presages a 1.7 point increase in inflation. Both findings are significant, substantial, and match our expectations under either the incentive or socialization hypotheses. Turning to our two more ambiguous cases, we find finance ministry experience is associated with significantly lower inflation (1.1 points), whereas central bank experience is associated with significantly higher inflation (1.4 points). The effects of the career types are ordered as hypothesized based on career transitions (from least to most inflationary, they run Fin $<$ FM $<$ CB $<$ Gov), supporting the career incentive view. The more a central banker expects a post-central bank career in finance relative to government, the lower the expected inflation rate under that central banker.

There are two other career categories of potential interest: experience in economics (EcoExp) and in the real economy (BusExp). We do not expect

13 The change in central banker characteristics constitutes a multi-period shock, persisting and accumulating in effect until the board changes again. Understanding its cumulative effect requires an iterated counterfactual. Chapter 7 looks at another kind of multi-period shock, changes in the party of government, using the same counterfactual techniques and provides further details on their construction.

these variables to have systematic effects on inflation. As noted previously, economists on central bank boards have diverse educational backgrounds, suggesting their policy positions are similarly varied. Economics experience is thus unlikely to tell us much on average. Likewise, although firms in the real economy may prefer lower interest rates, businesses in industrial democracies seldom if ever lobby over so indivisible a public good as monetary policy (Gowa, 1988). Therefore, we do not expect businessmen and women to be subject to pressure from their old firms for monetary policy favors. Unsurprisingly, when we respecify Model 1 to include these two categories along with the initial four, we find little change from the initial estimates and no effects of economics or business experience on inflation. Thus, economics and business fall into the neutral range in Figure 3.5, supporting the initial decision to exclude them from the model (that is, to treat these categories as indistinguishable from all other omitted career types). The explanatory power of EcoExp is no greater if we distinguish economists appointed by the left from those appointed by the right; if anything, economists appointed by the right are associated with higher inflation in this sample.

The results on individual career experience scores suggest we can produce a single number summary of central bank conservatism by simply summing experience in "conservative" job types and subtracting experience in "liberal" types. Define the Central Banker Career Conservatism (CBCC) index as

$$\text{CBCC}_{ijt} = \text{FinExp}_{ijt} - \text{GovExp}_{ijt} + \text{FMExp}_{jt} - \text{CBExp}_{ijt}. \qquad (3.5)$$

The index ranges from $\text{CBCC} = -1$ (all "liberal" career experience) to $\text{CBCC} = 1$ (all "conservative" career experience). Because this is a single dimension proxying the policy positions of central bank boards, taking the tenure-weighted median for each country-period makes more sense than taking the mean, at least according to the median voter theorem. Over the 1973 to 2000 period, this variable, CBCC^{med}, averaged -0.17 (s.d. = 0.53). It varied substantially over time within countries, and even more so across countries: about two-thirds of the variance in CBCC can be attributed to differences across countries, and about one-third to variation within them.[14] Overall, the median member of the average central bank first shot upward on the CBCC index, from -0.35

14 Examining monthly CBCC^{med} data over 1973 to 2000, in the average country, the standard deviation over time was 0.35, whereas for the average time period, the standard deviation across countries was 0.53. Including further time periods (for example, going back to 1950) raises the proportion of variance explained within countries.

in 1973 to a high of −0.01 in 1988, then drifted back to −0.16 in 1993, before rising again to −0.05 in 2000.

Model 2 regresses logged inflation on CBCC, controlling for CBI. I obtain similar results using either mean or median CBCC, and either the combined CBI index or just CWN's time-varying version. The plot in the center of the second row shows that a one standard deviation increase in the CBCC of the median central banker precedes a 1.4 point decline in inflation over five years.[15] This result is highly significant, virtually identical to the effect of a one standard deviation increase in CWN's CBI index (1.5 points), and somewhat smaller than the effect of the combined index (2.2 points) – CBCC is *as important* as CBI in explaining inflation. Because we expect central banker preferences to matter more when central bankers have greater autonomy, Model 3 adds an interaction between these two variables. Though correctly signed, this interaction is far from significant. I return to this puzzle in Chapter 6, where I show it results in part from an unclear concept of central bank independence.

CBCC will serve as a provisional measure of conservatism, especially because it explains inflation about as well as CBI. CBCC also has the distinct advantage of varying over time and is easy to recalculate as the leadership of a central bank changes. And because CBI and CBCC are uncorrelated (in this sample, $r = -0.02$ between CBI-3 and CBCC, and $r = 0.01$ between CBI-c and CBCC), the strong showing of CBCC casts doubt on the assumption that CBI alone is an adequate proxy for monetary policy non-accommodation. Preferences matter, and we ought not neglect them in favor of models relying only on institutional variables.

Robustness of Career Effects on Inflation

Empirical results are most convincing when they meet our prior expectations, are resistant to outliers, and robust to plausible respecifications. The key findings presented here perform well on all three criteria, as the ropeladder plots in Figure 3.6 concisely summarize (see Box 3.2 for an explanation of these graphics). First, the findings accord with the theory articulated in Chapter 2. The first row of the figure reiterates the main finding: after five years, inflation falls

15 The choice of equal weights for each component in CBCC is made for simplicity, but some plausible alternatives produce substantively similar results. For example, if we give only half weight to the two more ambiguous categories – FMExp and CBExp – the effect of one standard deviation higher CBCC is −1.1 points of inflation, with a 90 percent confidence interval of −0.3 to 1.8.

Box 3.2. Ropeladder Plots

Quantitative models often present one or two central findings based on dozens of simplifying assumptions. Assumptions are unavoidable in any model, but *robust* results – findings that emerge from the data under the full range of reasonable assumptions – are best. Analysts often start with a baseline model incorporating the most plausible assumptions, then check the robustness of baseline findings by reestimating the model while relaxing one assumption at a time. Summarizing how robust the baseline model is – and where it breaks down – presents an overlooked opportunity for statistical graphics.

I introduce a graphical display of model robustness called the *ropeladder plot* (Figure 3.6). The entries in a ropeladder plot are estimates of some quantity of interest as predicted by the model for a hypothetical scenario; typically, this scenario is either a one unit or one standard deviation increase in the covariate of interest, with all other covariates held at their means. (The quantity of interest could be an expected value, a first difference, a difference-in-differences, or a relative risk.) This quantity is shown as either a filled or open circle; filled circles indicate statistically significant results. The confidence interval associated with the estimate is shown as a thin horizontal line. In some ropeladder plots, arrowheads indicate cases where this is interval extends beyond the plotted range.

A single ropeladder plot efficiently compares the estimated effect of a covariate (such as FinExp) under a series of models making different assumptions. A gray box shows the full range of estimates under these assumptions. Three conditions are desired: for the box to be narrow, for the estimated effects to line up vertically, and for the confidence intervals to be of similar width. When all three conditions hold, the resulting picture looks like a stable ropeladder, safe to climb to a conclusion of robustness. When the ropeladder appears to blow in the wind, results vary according to modeling assumptions and trusting the baseline model is hazardous.

Because ropeladder plots are compact, it is easy to show several ropeladders testing the robustness of different findings all in the same display. Figure 3.6, for example, includes five ropeladder plots.

Ropeladder plots like those in this book can be made using the `tile` package for R, available at `chrisadolph.com`.

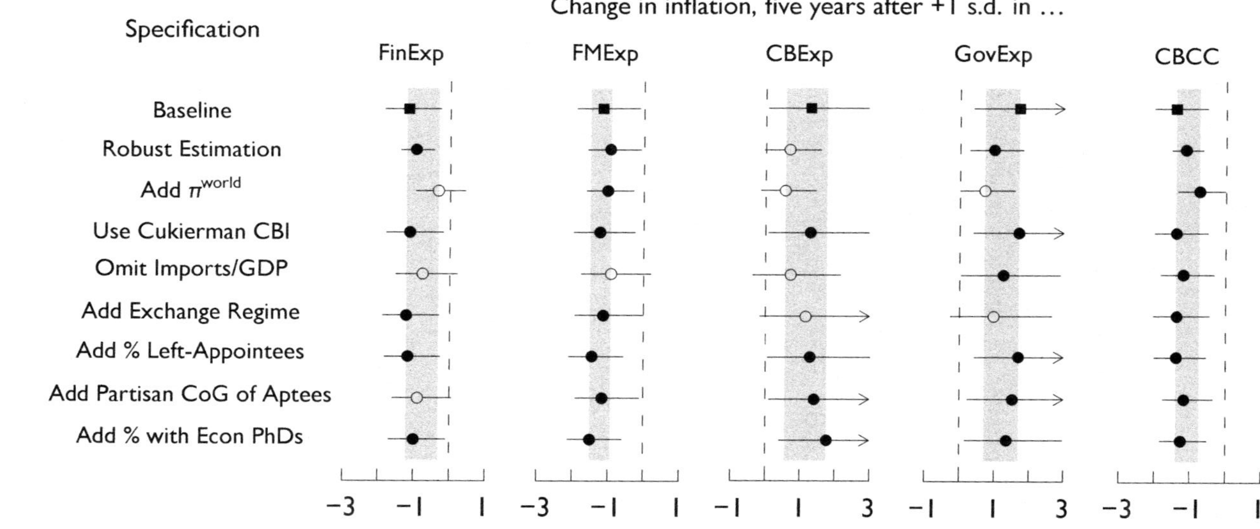

Figure 3.6. *The career-inflation link under alternative specifications.* Each plot shows the five-year first difference in inflation resulting from a one standard deviation increase in a career variable (FinExp, GovExp, etc.), given the specification noted at left. See the text for a description of the baseline model and alternatives. Circles and squares indicate point estimates of the first difference and horizontal lines show 90 percent confidence intervals. The results marked with a square are the same as those used in Figure 3.5. The shaded areas highlight the range of point estimates across all alternatives. Effects of controls not shown (of those considered, only π^{world} had a significant effect on inflation).

if FinExp, FMExp, or CBCC are raised, and it rises following appointment of central bankers with higher GovExp or CBExp. Second, these key relationships do not depend on a few influential observations. Because least squares is vulnerable to outliers, I re-estimate equation 3.4 using robust regression techniques and again find similar results.[16]

Third, the relationship between CBCC and inflation persists when we alter the right-hand side variables in various ways.[17] For example, starting with the baseline specifications (Models 1 and 2), we could include a control for the average level of inflation across the G7 countries to allay concerns that the relations among CBCC, CBI, and inflation are a spurious result of trends in these variables.[18] As the third row of Figure 3.6 shows, our explanatory variables remain potent even when this source of variation is removed. Likewise, we could change our measure of CBI to include just the Cukierman index, or omit the imports variable, and obtain similar results (rows 4 and 5). Another concern is that fixed exchange rate regimes, such as the Exchange Rate Mechanism (ERM), might preclude autonomous monetary policy and hence nullify career effects. In a sixth specification, I include a variable indicating membership in the ERM, and interact it with each career variable. I find the non-ERM cases show strong career effects (row 6). None of the ERM interactions was significantly different from zero, suggesting the ERM did not noticeably interfere with domestic sources of monetary policy.[19]

16 To test the resistance of the model to outliers, I re-estimated Model 2 using an *M*-estimator (specifically, one based on Huber's influence function). Using this less efficient but more robust technique, I obtain an effect parameter of −0.043 (s.e. = 0.013) for CBCC and −0.177 (s.e. = 0.062) for CBI. Both results are significant and accord with the LS results. Robust estimation of Model 1 also supports the LS findings. (For an accessible introduction to robust regression relevant to comparative political economy, see Western, 1995.)

17 The notion of specification robustness used here is similar to Levine and Renelt (1992), who investigate the robustness of cross-country growth regressions to the inclusion of various sets of extra regressors, while always keeping in the specification the variables of theoretical interest.

18 For countries in the G7, we instead control for the average inflation in the other six. In general, we weight the G7 (or G6) average by the real size of each country's economy.

19 There is an argument to be made that between capital controls and frequent recalibrations, the ERM did little to constrain domestic monetary policy autonomy (Downs, n.d.). This is consistent with Obstfeld and Rogoff's (1995) observation that post-Bretton Woods, very few countries (and within the ERM, only Austria, Luxembourg, and the Netherlands) maintained even ±2 percent fixed exchange rate bands over five consecutive years.

Chapter 2 suggests there may be partisan tendencies in central banker appointments: left-wing parties may favor the more liberal government-career central bankers, whereas right-wing parties may favor the more conservative financial types. I defer direct tests of partisan appointment to Chapter 8, but for now, let us suppose a partisan pattern in appointment exists. Do career backgrounds link government partisanship and central banker behavior – in which case, career effects would persist even controlling for the party of appointment, or is it just the partisanship of each appointee that matters – in which case, partisan controls would wipe out the effect of careers. I run two further robustness checks, including first the percentage of central bankers appointed by "left-wing" parties (as categorized by Alesina, Roubini, and Cohen [1997] and the author), and then controlling for the partisan center of gravity of the median central banker (Cusack and Engelhardt, 2002). In both cases, career effects persist strongly. In neither case did partisanship of appointment significantly affect inflation, controlling for career background. If there is a partisan cycle in central banker appointments, it must therefore work in large part through selection of central bankers by career type.

In a final specification check, I control for the fraction of central bankers holding advanced degrees in economics. Economics training may provide technical expertise enabling central banks to implement more efficient policies and hence produce lower inflation regardless of central banker preferences. If this expertise matters, however, it is not enough to simply complete an degree program: the presence of economically trained members had no effect on inflation (see Model 4, Table 3.7), whereas all career effects persisted unchanged (row 9, Figure 3.6).

Across an array of model specifications, the effects of career types on inflation are remarkably uniform and almost always statistically significant, providing strong confirmation of the career effects hypothesis. A similar pattern of robustness emerges if we keep the baseline model in place and instead vary the construction of the key explanatory variables. Most central banks have multiple, legally established monetary policy makers who must make collective decisions. Modeling the aggregation of policy makers' preferences is a key challenge. Taking the (tenure-weighted) means of all *de jure* policy makers seems like a good first approximation, although the median member is a better bet when a single dimension (like CBCC) can be established. But as Figure 3.7 shows, it makes little difference if we take means or medians of the career components or CBCC. In constructing the CBCC index, we have still more options. Rather than weighting FinExp, GovExp, FMExp, and CBExp equally, as in the main

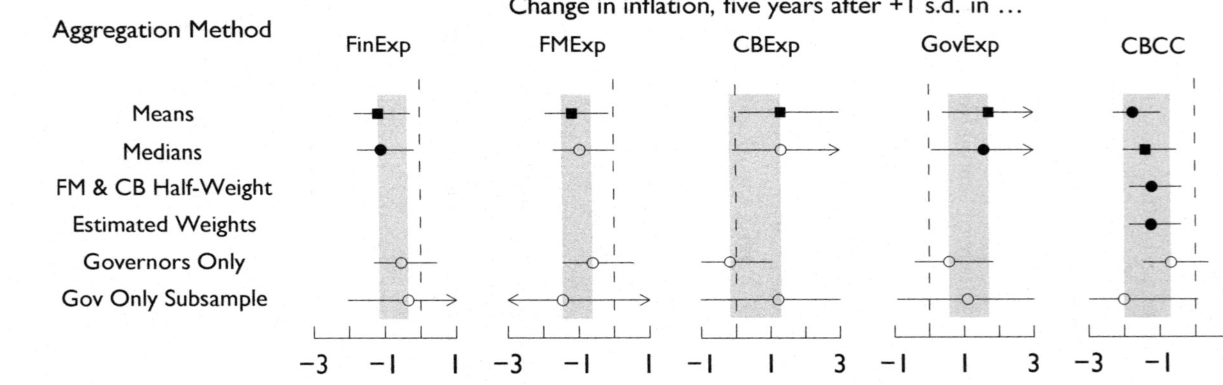

Figure 3.7. *The career-inflation link under alternative aggregation rules.* Each plot shows the five-year first difference in inflation resulting from a one standard deviation increase in a career variable (FinExp, GovExp, etc.), given the central-bank–level aggregation rule noted at left. See the text for a description of the baseline model and alternatives. Circles and squares indicate point estimates of the first difference and horizontal lines show 90 percent confidence intervals. The results marked with a square are the same as those used in Figure 3.5. The shaded areas highlight the range of point estimates across all alternatives. Effects of controls not shown (of those considered, only π^{world} had a significant effect on inflation).

text, we could give only half-weight to the more ambiguous categories (FM-Exp and CBExp), or we could use the point estimates of the coefficients on each category as weights. The middle rows of Figure 3.7 show that these alternative make little difference.

A final approach follows the common practice of ignoring all central bankers but the governor of the bank. The procedure eliminates the problem of aggregation by pretending it does not exist. Theoretically, the governors-only makes little sense; it is incompatible even with the strict legalist interpretation of CBI, because CBI usually grants autonomy not to a single leader but to a policy board. Rerunning the model using data on only governors produces correct signs for four of five variables, but none of the results are significant, and the fit of this model is inferior to any other model considered here. A final refinement restricts the sample of countries to those where the governor has sole legal authority. This discards three-quarters of the data, but produces correct signs on all five variables and an "almost significant" effect of CBCC. I conclude that those officials who are legally deemed to matter are the right ones to study, and restricting attention to governors is unjustified.

Career Effects on Monetary Policy: Native and Induced Preferences

Central bankers' past careers correlate with inflation outcomes, but is this the result of socialized policy preferences, career concerns, or both? To gain leverage over this question, I test whether factors that should increase the strength of career incentives also augment the effect of past experience on inflation. I consider three such conditions:

Condition 1: Future career rewards happen. As the expected reward for granting shadow principals their preferred policies, post-central bank jobs in finance and government may reflect either successful policy signaling or completed career-for-policy-bargains leading to lower or higher inflation, respectively. If we suppose, consistent with the model of monetary policy under career effects, that career incentives augment socialized preferences, then we should see stronger effects of career variables on central bankers whose future jobs are known to have materialized.

Condition 2: Shadow principals can monitor monetary policy votes. The models of career signals and bargains in Chapter 2 assume shadow principals can observe the policy decisions of particular central bankers, at least after the fact. We expect stronger career effects in countries where central banks eventually publish their voting records or where a single official makes policy. Secret voting procedures should hamper the career rewards mechanism.

Condition 3: Central bankers have many years left before retirement. Age may have two countervailing effects on career experience. Because younger central bankers have more "career" left to worry about, they should face stronger career incentives than central bankers nearing retirement. Central bankers at the end of their careers face far weaker career incentives. However, a 65-year-old central banker with, say, the same FinExp score as a 40-year-old has spent more years in the financial sector, which augurs for stronger socialization effects among older central bankers. The net effect of age for a given set of experience scores is thus a balance of declining incentives and deepening socialization.

The simplest of these tests to implement regards public voting. Let PV_{jt} be 1 for countries that (eventually) publish monetary policy voting records or have a single monetary decision maker, and 0 otherwise. A simple multiplicative interactive term between public votes and career conservatism should augment the effect of careers if public votes help shadow principals detect signals or apply career incentives, but have no effect if career effects work only through socialized preferences.

The other two tests require somewhat more complicated measures because they involve individual level "microinteractions," rather than the more customary institution-level interactions.[20] To capture the effect of youth on career effects, we need to multiply a measure of youth with individual level characteristics, then aggregate up to the central bank level using the weighted median

$$\mathrm{CBCCYY65}_{jt}^{\mathrm{med}} = \mathrm{median}(\mathrm{CBCC}_{ijt} \times \mathrm{YY65}_{ijt}, w_{ijt}). \qquad (3.6)$$

20 A common way to investigate the contingent nature of relationships among variables is to employ interaction terms. If we suspect that the relationship between X and Y depends also on the level of Z, we typically specify a model such as $Y = f(X, Z, X \times Z)$. The same technique can be used here to investigate the contingencies that arise from having a particular level of, say, FinExp, given a certain degree of CBI, or from any other interaction taking place at the institutional level. However, where the contingency arises at the level of individual central bankers, we must take the interaction into account *before* aggregating across the central bank. Therefore, to consider the effect of each banker's age on the contribution of their financial experience to policy, we construct $\mathrm{FinExpAge}_{jt} = a(\mathrm{FinExp}_{ijt} \times \mathrm{Age}_{ijt}, w_{ijt})$, where a is an aggregation function (either a weighted mean or a weighted median) and w are weights. For most $a(\cdot)$ and w_{ijt}, $\mathrm{FinExpAge}_{jt} \neq \mathrm{FinExp}_{jt} \times \mathrm{Age}_{jt}$.

In this case, our measure of youth is "years younger than 65,"

$$\text{YY65}_{ijt} = \max(0, 65 - \text{Age}_{ijt}). \tag{3.7}$$

If career incentives overshadow native preferences, this variable should carry a negative coefficient, augmenting the effect of career conservatism. But if socialization weighs more heavily, the coefficient should be positive, because an older central banker with the same CBCC score as a younger official has had more time to be socialized. Finally, to see whether career effects are stronger when central bankers are known to have returned to financial or government jobs later, we multiply the binary future job variables described previously by the relevant past experience. Because of the ambiguity of finance ministry and central bank experience, I include it in both categories:

$$\begin{aligned} \text{CBCCFJ}_{jt}^{\text{med}} = \text{median}[&\text{FinJob}_{ij,t+} \times (\text{FinExp}_{ijt} + \text{FMExp}_{ijt} + \text{CBExp}_{ijt}) \\ &+\text{GovJob}_{ij,t+} \times (\text{GovExp}_{ijt} + \text{FMExp}_{ijt} + \text{CBExp}_{ijt}), w_{ijt}]. \end{aligned} \tag{3.8}$$

As with the other variables, a negative coefficient is evidence of career incentives at work.

I included each of these terms separately in the inflation model and report the estimated parameters in the Data Appendix to this chapter (Table 3.8). The signs of the interaction terms are appropriate and the precision of the estimates reasonably good for future jobs and public votes, but because interactive coefficients are difficult to interpret, I focus on two kinds of counterfactual calculated from the estimated model. One shows the difference in inflation resulting from a standard deviation increase in CBCC under conditions that should either discourage or encourage career incentives. The second isolates the "extra effect," or difference-in-differences, due to career incentives alone. In each case, I show 90 percent confidence intervals.

Given the same one standard deviation increase in median CBCC, inflation falls more when the median central banker took a job later in finance than when he did not (1.9 points versus 1.4; left panel of Figure 3.8).[21] Even without observed job rewards, the reduction in inflation is significant, suggesting that socialization plays a role regardless of incentive effects. But a look at the

21 To calculate the appropriate hypothetical level of $\text{CBCCFJ}_{j,t-2}^{\text{med}}$, I assume the median central banker spent his career in only two sectors, government and private finance. If CBCC $= 0.35$ (one standard deviation above the mean), this implies a hypothetical FinExp $= (\text{CBCC}+1)/2 = 0.675$, which in this case is also the value of $\text{CBCCFJ}_{j,t-2}^{\text{med}}$.

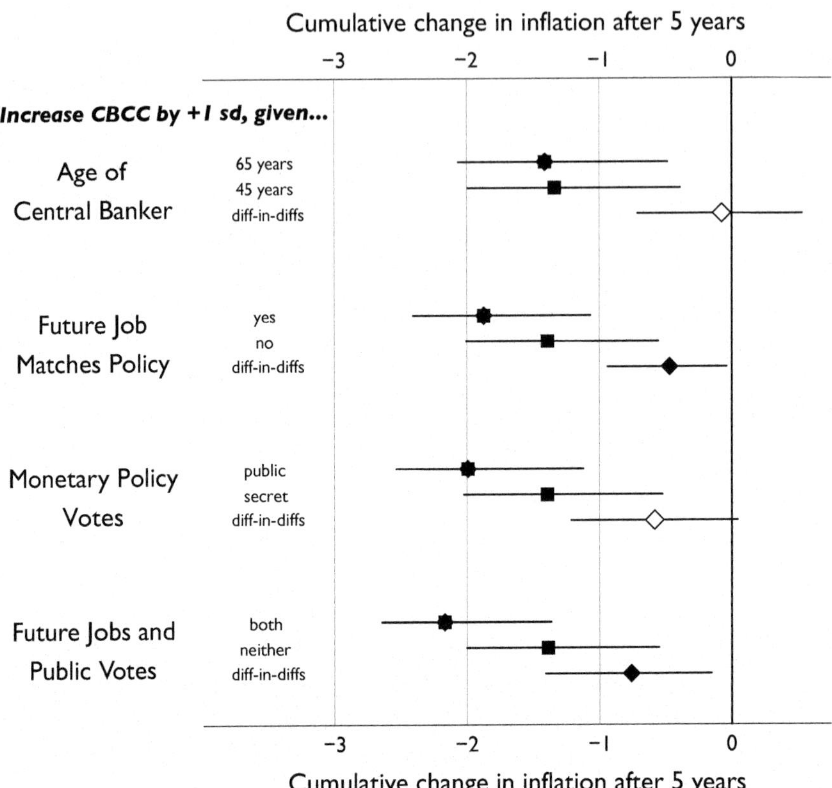

Figure 3.8. *First differences and difference-in-differences from interactive career effects models of inflation.* Each trio of results shows the cumulative change in inflation five years after a one standard deviation increase in central banker career conservatism *given* the condition listed at the left, which should enhance (top row; stars) or suppress (middle row; squares) career incentives. The bottom row of each trio (diamonds) shows the difference-in-differences from adding career incentives. Filled symbols indicate differences (or diffs-in-diffs) that are significantly different from zero at the 90% level, and horizontal lines mark 90% confidence intervals. All results taken from models in Table 3.8.

difference-in-differences shows that the added impact of future jobs is also significantly different from zero, supporting the presence of career incentive effects.

Public votes had a similar effect: CBCC lowered inflation rates whether votes were secret or not, but lowered them substantially more when votes were eventually revealed (2.0 points versus 1.4). However, the extra impact of public votes is not quite significant. Youth, on the other hand, appears to have no effect: central bankers young and old provided the same reduction in inflation for a given increase in CBCC.[22] The estimated difference-in-differences shows this null result is imprecisely estimated, so we cannot say with certainty that it is actually zero. But it is consistent with socialization and incentives sharing roughly equal responsibility for career effects.

Finally, I estimate a model with both vote and future job interactions included. (Adding the age interaction as well produces similar parameter estimates but larger standard errors.) Using this model, I find the effect of CBCC is 56 percent larger when votes are public and the median banker takes a financial job than otherwise. The extra effect of the combined interactions is also significantly different from zero. While I do not consider later jobs or revealed votes to be perfect proxies of career incentives, it seems clear that the two main career mechanisms of socialization and job rewards operate on the same order of magnitude. Central bankers' career backgrounds appear to affect both native and induced preferences over monetary policy.

The Evolving Role of Career Effects on Monetary Policy

The evidence so far points to a cross-national pattern of career-based monetary policy and inflation. But have these career-induced patterns of monetary policy been consistent over time? There is clear evidence that the ideas of policy makers change (as in the rise and fall of monetarism) and that institutions mediating monetary policy come and go (the collapse of the Bretton Woods regime). Might career effects be a similarly transient phenomenon? Or have we found something essential and seemingly inevitable about the nature of monetary policy delegation?

So far, I have restricted analysis of inflation performance to the period between the end of Bretton Woods and the rise of the euro. In this period, causal

22 I experimented with various transformations of age (squares, exponentials, logs, and binary divisions into young and old), but always obtained substantively similar results.

mechanisms in monetary policy were arguably constant. Industrialized countries allowed their currencies to float against each other, with the brief exception of the Exchange Rate Mechanism. Yet career patterns in inflation performance in central banks under the ERM were no different from other, explicitly floating central banks, perhaps owing to the partial flexibility ERM offered its members, especially those with capital controls. Did Bretton Woods-era central banks enjoy similar flexibility? And if so, did central bankers in the Bretton Woods era behave as the career theory predicts they would?

Time-Varying Accounts of Career Effects on Inflation

Because our career data range over 1950 to 2000 and usably complete data on inflation are available from 1957, we can investigate the effects of regime change – and more broadly, the question of how career effects on monetary policy have changed over time – by re-estimating the inflation performance model using subperiods within this half century. The simplest approach is to assume a structural break at 1973 and estimate the following baseline equation for each period:

$$\ln \pi_{it} = \phi_1 \ln \pi_{i,t-1} + \phi_2 \ln \pi_{i,t-2} + \beta_1 \text{CBCC}^{\text{med}}_{i,t-2} + \beta_2 \text{CBI-3}_{i,t-2} + \alpha_i + \epsilon_{it} \tag{3.9}$$

This model regresses quarterly inflation on indices of central banker careers and central bank independence, along with fixed effects and two lags of the dependent variable. This is exactly the model investigated previously, except trade openness (imports divided by GDP) has been dropped from the model because this variable is missing (at least at quarter intervals) for many countries in the pre-1973 period. This omission makes little difference in practice. Unfortunately, although CBCC and CBI are available back to 1950, quarterly inflation data are not, and the regressions in this section must take the third quarter of 1957 as their starting point. As before, the model is estimated by least squares with panel correction applied to standard errors (Beck and Katz, 1995), and results are reported in tables of estimated coefficients (see the Data Appendix, Table 3.9) and as first differences.

The first column of Table 3.9 shows a regression on data from the entire period (1957–2000). It finds strong and highly significant effects of both career conservatism and independence, essentially indistinguishable from the effects for the post-Bretton Woods period. Splitting the data into pre- and post-1973 samples, the next two columns show that, if anything, career effects were slightly stronger under Bretton Woods, although we cannot reject the hypothesis of equal effects of careers in each period. On the other hand, independence had no significant effect in the earlier period, a puzzle I return to in the following.

We need to look deeper into the data. Rather than assuming a structural break at a single, known moment, I systematically analyze a series of subperiods using the "moving-windows" method. This approach rolls a window across the last fifty years, re-estimating the model using the years currently in the window and tracking shifts in the estimated parameters as the window moves forward in time. This technique allows us to see gradual change and also lets the data reveal where structural breaks might lie, rather than imposing these breaks *a priori*.[23] To be sure, there is a trade off between maximizing the precision of the estimates and narrowing the width of the moving window. Twenty years appears to be the smallest practical window; smaller windows tended to produce unusably noisy estimates.

The moving windows results are shown in Figure 3.9; in discussing this plot, I refer to points on the horizontal axes as slices with a starting year and ending year. Looking at the right half of the first plot, we see that every twenty year slice from 1966–1985 to 1981–2000 shows significant and fairly constant inflation reduction under conservative median central bankers. The slices from 1958–1977 to 1965–1984 find no effect, while the earliest slices, containing the years 1957 to 1976, reveal career effects as large and significant as the late twentieth century. A reasonable interpretation is that in settled fixed or flexible ex-

23 The moving windows methodology involves five steps. Starting from the beginning of the sample period (here, 1957Q1):

1. Select the next *j* periods of data for all countries. (We use $j = 60$ quarters, or 15 years.)
2. Estimate the model on the selected data. (In our example, this is equation 3.9, which we estimate by least squares with panel-corrected standard errors.)
3. Calculate the quantities of interest and their confidence intervals. (Here, the quantities of interest are first differences of inflation with respect to one standard deviation increases in either $\text{CBCC}^{\text{med}}_{i,t-2}$ or $\text{CBI-3}_{i,t-2}$.)
4. Repeat steps 1 to 3 until the end of the sample is reached (here, 2000Q4).
5. Plot the collected results against time.

With 44 years of quarterly data, a twenty year moving window means we have 94 slices of data to analyze. For each slice, we plot the change in inflation that would result from a one standard deviation increase in either CBCC or CBI, based on the regression on that slice. Throughout, we use the full sample means and standard deviations in this calculation. The mean levels of CBI-3 and CBCC were 0.182 and −0.251, and their standard deviations were 0.182 and 0.516, respectively.

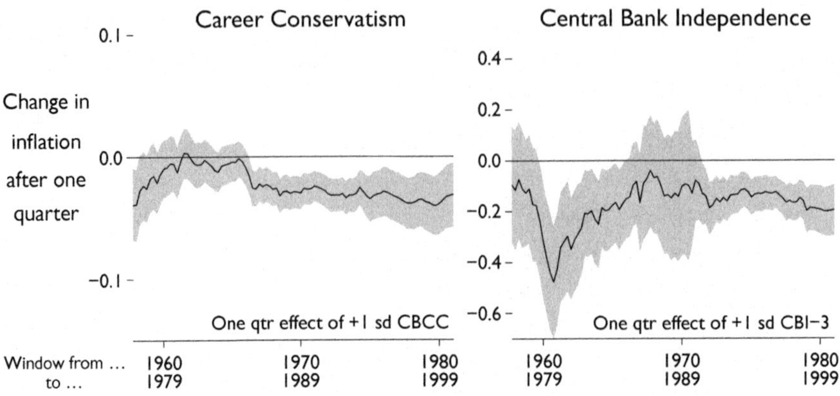

Figure 3.9. *Inflation moving windows.* Plot shows the effect of central banker careers (left panel) or central bank independence (right) on inflation in the first quarter after a one standard deviation increase in that variable from its mean (shaded areas are 90 percent confidence intervals around this estimate). The estimated effects and confidence intervals result from re-estimating the model in equation 3.9 over a series of windows that slice off a range of data within a 20 year subperiod. The horizontal axis labels each window. The graphs thus show the evolution of the effects of CBCC and CBI on inflation over time.

change rate regimes, so long as national central banks enjoy national monetary policy autonomy, central bankers' career patterns are reliable guides to their behavior and hence to monetary policy outcomes. But in unsettled periods between regimes, the factors explaining normal monetary policy behavior times may be much less reliable.

Turning to the effect of CBI, we find a more complicated picture. The most recent windows (in this case, the 1972 to 1991 slice onward) show steady, strong inflation suppression under independent central banks. Earlier windows show a mixed picture – mostly no effect of CBI, but a large negative effect in windows centered on the first years of the 1970s.[24]

24 The Bundesbank of the 1960s and 1970s was so legendarily anti-inflationary – to the point of intentionally creating recessions in Germany during times of plenty elsewhere in Europe (for example, during 1964 to 1966; see Hall, 1986; Kreile, 1978) – that one worries Germany's monetary regime confounds the CBI findings. However, the moving windows results are unchanged when we omit Germany altogether.

Conclusions

Despite being largely ignored by political economists, central bankers' career concerns guide their behavior in office. The financial sector and bureaucratic experience of central bankers affect inflation as much as central bank independence, the most commonly used measure differentiating monetary regimes. Some of the effects of central bankers' careers are likely a result of socialization and selection within the financial sector and government, but several pieces of evidence suggest that career ambitions play a significant role.

To the extent career effects rely on career incentives created by the government and private banks, legally-mandated central bank independence builds only a parchment barrier between government and central bank. It is true that laws may help central bankers act without the constant threat of government vetoes. But as long as monetary agents aspire to further wealth or office, paper autonomy alone cannot guarantee the insulation of monetary policy from outside interests. Whether one advocates or opposes insulation, it is clear that the monetary policy interests and ideas of central bankers and governments should no longer be shoved under the central bank independence carpet.

Methods Appendix to Chapter 3

This appendix explains how conventional intepretation of linear regression coefficients can led to massive substantive misinterpretation – including sign reversals – when several covariates in the model are compositional, or parts of a greater whole. The value of these regression coefficients depends, perhaps surprisingly, on the arbitrary construction of a reference category; they do not – and mathematically cannot – cleanly capture how a change in a single compositional covariate affects the response. As a solution, I provide appropropriate methods and software for interpreting models with compositional covariates that rely on the concept of ratio-preserving counterfactuals.

Compositional Covariates in Regression Models

Consider a regression model of the form

$$y_i = b_0 + \sum x_{ki} b_{ki} + \epsilon_i, \tag{3.10}$$

where k indexes M different covariates x_k. In this appendix, I suppress error terms and subscripts for individual observations for simplicity, so we can rewrite the model as

$$y = b_0 + \sum x_k b_k. \tag{3.11}$$

In most cases, an estimate of the parameter b_1 can be interpreted as the marginal effect of x_1 on the response or a nonlinear transformation of the response. One exception occurs when there is a perfect linear relationship among the covariates, in which case no unique $\widehat{b_k}$'s exist. This is the well-known problem of perfect collinearity. Perfect collinearity is simply an extreme case of a more general challenge for the interpretation of regression coefficients: logical dependencies among the covariates.

Regression on compositional covariates presents a particular kind of logical dependency. We say that data are *compositional* when these constraints hold (Aitchison, 2003*b*)

$$\sum_{k=1}^{M} x_k = 1, \tag{3.12}$$

$$0 \leq x_k \leq 1. \tag{3.13}$$

Examples of compositional data include shares of a budget devoted to different programs, the ethnic breakdown of a population (if ethnicities are mutually exclusive), and the allocation of time within a meeting. Put another way, compositional data include any set of measures of the share of some population belonging to each category of an exhaustive and mutually exclusive typology. Compositional data are ubiquitous in political science and the social sciences generally, but they are often modeled incorrectly, whether they appear on the left-hand or right-hand side of a regression equation.

Suppose we model a response variable y using a set of M compositional explanatory variables satisfying conditions 3.12 and 3.13. We might begin with a model including all M components

$$y = b_0 + \sum_{k=1}^{M} x_k b_k, \tag{3.14}$$

but this model is unidentified due to the linear dependence of the composition. That is, because

$$x_M = 1 - \sum_{k=1}^{M-1} x_k, \tag{3.15}$$

we cannot include x_M along with the other x_k's. Substituting equation 3.15 into equation 3.14 shows that a model on x_k, for $k = 1, \ldots, M-1$, contains the effects of all M components of x:

$$y = b_0 + b_M + \sum_{k=1}^{M-1} x_k(b_k - b_M). \tag{3.16}$$

From equation 3.16, the problems inherent in interpreting compositional explanatory variables begin to emerge. The partial derivative of y with respect to x_k is not b_k, as we would expect in most linear models, but $b_k - b_M$. By construction, (3.16) reflects the fact that when we increase x_1 by, say, 0.2, and leave all x_k, $k = 2, \ldots, M-1$, unchanged, x_M must decrease by 0.2. Therefore, the resulting change in y is not $0.2b_1$ but $0.2b_1 - 0.2b_M$. The effects of increasing x_1 and decreasing x_M have been mixed together; we can no more separate them than we can estimate the unidentified equation 3.14 above.

The difficulty in stating the effect of a change in x_1 on y runs deeper still, because we can never change $x_j, j \in \{1, \ldots, M\}$ without simultaneously altering some other component, $x_{\sim j}$. When we contemplate a differential Δx_j, equation 3.12 requires us to account for all the changes in the remainder of the composition, such that $\Delta x_j = -\sum \Delta x_{\sim j}$. In equation 3.16, we implicitly assumed this slack was accounted for by a complementary change in x_M, but there are arbitrarily many ways to divide x_j among the remaining categories, and each produces a different effect on y.

Without loss of generality, assume $j = 1$. We can represent the change in $\Delta x_{\sim j}$ as $x_k - w_k \Delta x_1$, where the set of weights w_k adjust for the change in x_1 to maintain the compositional constraint. So long as $\sum w_k = 1$, the compositional constraint is satisfied. This procedure is known as a perturbation of the composition (Aitchison, 2003*b*). We can now restate the model as

$$y = b_0 + b_M + (x_1 + \Delta x_1)(b_1 - b_M) + \sum_{k=2}^{M-1} (x_k - w_k \Delta x_1)(b_k - b_M). \tag{3.17}$$

Differentiating, we find the "true" marginal effect of x_1 to be

$$\frac{\partial y}{\partial x_1} = b_1 - b_M - \sum_{k=2}^{M-1} w_k (b_k - b_M). \tag{3.18}$$

When we estimate equation 3.17, we obtain the estimated parameters given by

$$\widehat{y} = \beta_0 + x_1 \beta_1 + \sum_{k=2}^{M-1} x_k \beta_k. \tag{3.19}$$

Clearly, it is inappropriate to treat β_1 as the marginal effect of x_1. Instead, β_1 is an estimate of $b_1 - b_M$, which is not equal to $\partial y / \partial x_1$, except in the special case where x_M takes up all the slack, and $w_k = 0 \; \forall k, \; k = 2, \ldots, M - 1$. These are strong assumptions. In many cases, it is logically impossible for x_M to take up the slack and stay within the $[0, 1]$ bounds as logic requires. Even within the set of logically possible reallocations, different assumptions about w_k could change either the magnitude or even the sign of the estimated effect of x_1.

To see this, consider the following example using a four-part composition:

$$y = 0 + 10x_1 - 50x_2 + 100x_3.$$

We are interested in the effect of increasing x_1 by, say, 0.1. If we treat the coefficient of x_1 as the marginal effect (thus assuming the omitted component x_4 declines by 0.1 in turn), we obtain $\Delta y = 1$. But if we instead assume x_2 declines by 0.1 to maintain the composition, we find a much larger effect of changing

x_1: $\Delta y = 6$. Finally, if we assume x_3 declines by 0.1, we observe a sign-reversal: $\Delta y = -9$. All three answers are correct given the assumed allocations of the full composition.

Fortunately, there is a better way to summarize the marginal effects of compositional covariates. Given estimates β_k and an assumed set of weights w_k, we can represent the true marginal effect of any change in the overall composition by the first difference in y. Because of the compositional properties of $x_1, \ldots, x_M$, we can never state the marginal effect of any particular x_j without reference to the corresponding hypothetical values of $x_{\sim j}$. But we can set up counterfactuals that show the effect of increasing x_j when the reductions in $x_{\sim j}$ are assigned in a "neutral" fashion. To accomplish this, we need to choose the weights w_k with care.

Formulating Counterfactuals for Compositional Covariates

Given a hypothetical new value for the jth component, x_j^{hyp}, our task is to assign the remaining $x_{\sim j}^{\text{hyp}}$ in a way that satisfies the two requirements of compositional data – that all components sum to one and that each component lies in the interval $[0, 1]$. Moreover, we seek a "neutral" reassignment, to avoid unnecessarily conflating the effect of a change in x_j with the effect of a particular $x_{\sim j}$. An appealing choice is to reassign the slack in a manner that preserves the ratios among all components $\sim j$. Consider the following example:

	x_1	x_2	x_3
Initial composition	0.10	0.30	0.60
New composition, after increasing x_1 by 0.15	0.25	0.25	0.50

In addition to increasing x_1 by 0.15, we have reduced x_2 and x_3 by a total of 0.15 but have allocated this reduction so that the ratio of x_2 to x_3 remains 0.5. I call this reassignment the *ratio-preserving counterfactual* (RPCF). Any other perturbation would conflate the change in x_1 with the relative effect of x_2 compared to x_3.

Ratio-preserving counterfactuals are appealing because they focus attention as much as possible on the change in x_j itself. The procedure for calculating RPCFs is simple. First, choose some $x_j^{\text{hyp}} = x_j + \Delta x_j$, taking care to select Δx_j such that x_j^{hyp} remains within the $[0, 1]$ bounds. Next, reduce each other component $x_{\sim j}$ according to

$$x_{\sim j}^{\text{hyp}} = x_{\sim j} - \frac{x_{\sim j}}{1 - x_j} \Delta x_j. \tag{3.20}$$

Counterfactuals set up according to equation 3.20 have all three desired properties: they ensure each component of the composition is not less than zero and not greater than one; they meet the overall unit constraint on the composition; and they (uniquely) preserve the ratios among all components of the composition, save the component of counterfactual interest.

The recommendations made herein require no change in estimation strategy, only in how regression estimates are interpreted.[25] When regression models include compositional covariates, researchers should avoid interpreting parameter estimates directly – as even the signs of these coefficients can be misleading – and instead calculate the difference in the response variable given a counterfactual change in the compositional vector. Such first differences can be easily calculated by hand or with the aid of free packages like `simcf` or `Zelig` (for `R`) or `Clarify` (for Stata). The key is to properly set up the hypothetical values of the covariates, so that a logically consistent, ratio preserving counterfactual is calculated. The `R` package `simcf` can help: given new hypothetical values of one or more components of a composition, its `rpcf()` function returns the appropriate counterfactual levels of the remaining components.[26]

25 "Do I need to include 'all but one' of the components of $x_1, \ldots, x_M$ in the equation, or can I leave out more than one?" The division of a whole into components is usually arbitrary; in most examples, the omitted category or categories could have been sliced into still more subcategories or lumped together into a single catch-all group. Taking a "model's eye view," whatever components you exclude from the regression are lumped together in a single category and assumed to have homogenous effects on y. Whether this assumption is tenable is up to the applied researcher.

26 The `simcf` package is available from `chrisadolph.com` under Software.

Data Appendix to Chapter 3

Sources of Data

Central bankers' experience data were coded by the author and tabulated into experience scores and other quantities using Escore, available at chrisadolph.com. The twenty central banks studied in this chapter provided invaluable assistance in gathering information on past and present central bankers, though naturally none of these institutions is responisble for the contents of this book. In many cases, the central bank's records were incomplete, but even a simple list of historical central bankers was an indispensable starting point. I turned to a variety of print and web resources to fill in the details of central bankers' careers; print sources are listed in the references. Back issues of country-based biographical dictionaries proved invaluable and will likely provide the backbone of any similar study of state official's careers.

Central bank independence data were taken from Cukierman, Webb, and Neyapti (1992), whose dataset ranges over 1950 to 1989. These data were supplemented using Maxfield's (1997) coding of the same countries through 1994. Additional CBI indices were taken from Grilli, Masciandaro, and Tabellini (1991) and Bade and Parkin (1982).

Inflation, GDP, imports, and exchange rate data were obtained from the IMF *International Financial Statistics*.

The left and right leanings of governments were coded based on the scheme of Alesina, Roubini, and Cohen (1997), extended and supplemented with exact election dates by the author using the Europa World Yearbook (various years).

Table 3.3. *Contents of the Central Banker Database: Developed country sample.*

		Governors	*Deputy Governors*	*Policy Board*	*Directors*
Australia	1950–2001	•	•	•	
Austria	1950–2001	•	•	•	
Belgium	1950–2001	•	•		•
Canada	1950–2001	•			
Denmark	1950–2001	•	•		
Finland	1950–2001	•	•		•
France	1950–2001	•	•	○	
Germany	1953–2001	•	•	•	
Ireland	1969–2001	•			
Italy	1950–2001	•			
Japan	1950–2001	•	•	•	
Netherlands	1950–2001	•			○
New Zealand	1950–2001	•			
Norway	1950–2001	•	•	○	
Portugal	1975–2001	•	•	•	
Spain	1950–2001	•	•	•	
Sweden	1950–2001	•	•	•	
Switzerland	1950–2001	•	•	•	
United Kingdom	1950–2001	•	•	•	
United States	1950–2001	•	•	•	

Monetary policy makers: • (nearly) all included ○ (mostly) missing

Sources: I relied on Fry, Julius, Mahadeva, Roger, and Sterne (2000), Siklos (2002), and country sources to determine which officials enjoyed *de jure* monetary policy making authority.

Descriptive Statistics

Table 3.4. *Summary statistics for data used in Table 3.7 regressions.*

	Mean	Std. Dev.	Min	Max
FinExp	0.131	0.172	0.000	1.000
GovExp	0.166	0.161	0.000	0.729
FMExp	0.133	0.195	0.000	1.000
CBExp	0.279	0.254	0.000	1.000
$CBCC^{med}$	-0.200	0.493	-1.000	1.000
CBI-c	0.436	0.186	0.141	0.852
CBI-3	0.383	0.157	0.090	0.690
ln(Inflation)	1.417	0.940	-3.664	3.466
Inflation	5.976	5.130	0.026	32.012
Imports/GDP	0.290	0.133	0.064	0.756

Data cover all twenty countries over 1973 to 1997 and non-ECB members from 1973 to 2000. Cases of deflation are omitted.

Table 3.5. *Correlations across career types and institutions*

	FinExp	GovExp	FMExp	CBExp	EcoExp	BusExp
GovExp	-0.14					
FMExp	-0.33	-0.08				
CBExp	-0.18	-0.34	-0.39			
EcoExp	0.04	-0.14	-0.20	-0.23		
BusExp	-0.10	-0.10	-0.08	-0.31	-0.02	
CBI-3	0.17	-0.08	-0.15	0.10	-0.01	-0.13

Table 3.6. *Post-central bank appointments as a function of pre-central bank careers.*

	$\text{FinJob}_{i,t+}$	$\text{GovJob}_{i,t+}$
$\text{FinExp}_{i,t-}$	0.98	-0.27
	(0.25)	(0.21)
$\text{GovExp}_{i,t-}$	-0.39	0.43
	(0.31)	(0.20)
$\text{FMExp}_{i,t-}$	0.41	-0.07
	(0.29)	(0.23)
$\text{CBExp}_{i,t-}$	0.67	0.56
	(0.21)	(0.16)
$\text{EcoExp}_{i,t-}$	-0.12	0.04
	(0.32)	(0.21)
$\text{Age}_{i,t}$	-0.02	-0.03
	(0.01)	(0.00)
Constant	-0.19	0.82
	(0.34)	(0.29)
log-likelihood	-0.42	-0.64
Correctly predicted	83%	62%
N	928	928

Data drawn from twenty countries over the period 1950 to 2000. The unit of analysis is each appointment (indexed *i*) to the monetary policy authority. Appointments end at time *t*; hence, *t*- refers to pre-appointment experience and *t*+ to jobs obtained after the appointment ends. Entries are probit parameters and standard errors. See the text and Figure 3.4 for interpretation.

Table 3.7. *Log inflation regressed on central banker characteristics, twenty countries, 1973 to 2000, quarterly.*

Variable	Expected Sign	DV: ln(Inflation) 1	2	3	4
$\text{FinExp}_{j,t-2}$	$-$	-0.14			-0.09
		(0.08)			(0.07)
$\text{FMExp}_{j,t-2}$	$-/+$	-0.08			-0.13
		(0.06)			(0.06)
$\text{CBExp}_{j,t-2}$	$+/-$	0.12			0.12
		(0.05)			(0.05)
$\text{GovExp}_{j,t-2}$	$+$	0.23			0.19
		(0.08)			(0.08)
$\text{CBI}_{j,t-2}$	$-$	-0.91	-0.92	-0.90	-0.94
		(0.30)	(0.29)	(0.29)	(0.30)
$\text{CBCC}^{\text{med}}_{j,t-2}$	$-$		-0.09	-0.03	
			(0.03)	(0.07)	
$\text{CBI}_{j,t-2} \times \text{CBCC}^{\text{med}}_{j,t-2}$	$-$			-0.12	
				(0.15)	
$(\text{Imports/GDP})_{j,t-2}$	$-$	-0.02	0.02	0.05	-0.25
		(0.26)	(0.25)	(0.26)	(0.26)
$\%\text{EcDegree}_{j,t-2}$	$-$				0.04
					(0.06)
$\ln \pi_{j,t-1}$		0.97	0.97	0.97	0.96
		(0.04)	(0.04)	(0.04)	(0.04)
$\ln \pi_{j,t-2}$		-0.03	-0.03	-0.03	-0.01
		(0.04)	(0.04)	(0.04)	(0.04)
Fixed effects		x	x	x	x
N		1696	1696	1696	1645
s.e.r.		0.304	0.305	0.305	0.306
$\bar{R}^2$		0.887	0.887	0.888	0.886
LM test (critical = 3.84)		2.60	2.64	2.57	3.84

Least squares estimates with panel-corrected standard errors in parentheses. ECB members excluded after 1997. LM test refers to a Lagrange Multiplier test for serial correlation.

Table 3.8. *Log inflation regressed on central banker characteristics, twenty countries, 1973 to 2000, quarterly: Interactive models.*

		DV: ln(Inflation)			
Variable	E(sign)	5	6	7	8
$\text{CBCC}^{\text{med}}_{j,t-2}$	–	-0.087	-0.068	-0.082	-0.073
		(0.028)	(0.031)	(0.034)	(0.032)
$\text{CBCCFJ}^{\text{med}}_{j,t-2}$	–	-0.039			-0.030
		(0.022)			(0.022)
$\text{CBCC}^{\text{med}}_{j,t-2}$	–		-0.096		-0.080
$\times\text{PV}_{j,t-2}$			(0.062)		(0.064)
$\text{CBCCYY65}^{\text{med}}_{j,t-2}$	?			-0.0004	
				(0.0024)	
$\text{CBI}_{j,t-2}$	–	-0.980	-0.932	-0.913	-0.981
		(0.294)	(0.292)	(0.294)	(0.293)
Imports/	–	0.047	0.023	-0.002	0.052
$\text{GDP}_{j,t-2}$		(0.257)	(0.253)	(0.254)	(0.257)
$\ln\pi_{j,t-1}$		0.967	0.970	0.970	0.967
		(0.038)	(0.038)	(0.038)	(0.038)
$\ln\pi_{j,t-2}$		-0.027	-0.030	-0.029	-0.028
		(0.038)	(0.038)	(0.038)	(0.038)
Fixed effects		x	x	x	x
N		1683	1696	1688	1683
s.e.r.		0.306	0.305	0.305	0.306
$\bar{R}^2$		0.886	0.889	0.885	0.886
LM test (critical = 3.84)		2.388	2.476	2.840	2.369

Least squares estimates with panel-corrected standard errors in parentheses. ECB members excluded after 1997. LM test refers to a Lagrange Multiplier test for serial correlation.

Table 3.9. *Inflation regressions by period, twenty industrialized countries*

	Period					
Variables	*1957.3 –2000.4*	*1957.3 –1972.4*	*1973.1 –2000.4*	*1957.3 –1970.2*	*1970.2 –1975.2*	*1975.3 –2000.4*
$CBCC^{med}_{j,t-2}$	-0.067	-0.117	-0.059	-0.122	0.024	-0.057
	(0.018)	(0.058)	(0.020)	(0.069)	(0.031)	(0.022)
$CBI\text{-}3_{j,t-2}$	-0.866	0.633	-0.858	0.770	-2.157	-0.915
	(0.234)	(0.873)	(0.243)	(0.905)	(0.734)	(0.257)
$\ln \pi_{j,t-1}$	0.957	0.857	0.994	0.828	1.195	0.970
	(0.025)	(0.047)	(0.035)	(0.051)	(0.090)	(0.037)
$\ln \pi_{j,t-2}$	-0.043	-0.080	-0.045	-0.090	-0.278	-0.035
	(0.025)	(0.045)	(0.035)	(0.049)	(0.087)	(0.037)
Fixed Effects	x	x	x	x	x	x
N	3035	1000	2035	822	336	1855
s.e.r.	0.337	0.410	0.288	0.442	0.139	0.297
$\bar{R}^2$	0.844	0.668	0.897	0.615	0.901	0.889
F-Test		3.942		4.062		1.934
		p =0.000		p =0.000		p =0.004

All regressions are estimated by least squares with panel-corrected standard errors. Entries are estimated regression parameters, with standard errors in parentheses. F-test refers to a test for structural breaks across the corresponding columns, also known as a Chow test.

4

CAREERS AND THE MONETARY POLICY PROCESS

Three Mechanism Tests

> A man's thinking goes on within his consciousness in a seclusion in comparison with which any physical seclusion is an exhibition to public view.
>
> LUDWIG WITTGENSTEIN

CHAPTER 2 ARGUED THAT central bankers' monetary policy choices, and through them interest rates and inflation, are influenced by their past careers. Both career socialization and incentives to advance one's career encourage central bankers to tilt monetary policy decisions toward the sectoral-level preferences of their previous careers, whether those careers were in private finance (hawks) or the public bureaucracy (doves). Chapter 3 tested this argument, uncovering an empirical link between central bankers' career paths and inflation outcomes. But these macro-level tests leave out several steps. If career effects exist, they must work through the policy process. If we can show career effects flow through individual central bankers' policy preferences to their votes in committee, and through committee votes to interest rate policies and economic outcomes, our faith in the mechanisms linking careers and inflation outcomes will be much stronger.

This chapter uses data from the United States, as well as a broader panel of industrialized countries, to trace career effects through the monetary policy process. I conduct three separate tests of career effects on monetary policy (Figure 4.1). The first test looks at the relationship between the median central banker's career conservatism and nominal interest rates, using the same panel of advanced democracies studied in the last chapter. The second test takes a step

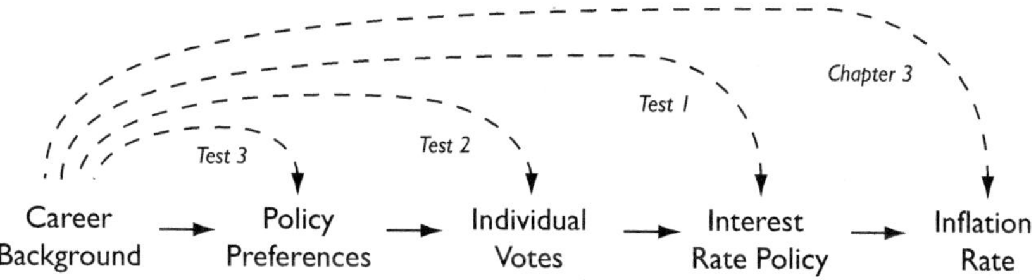

Figure 4.1. *Testing the effect of central bankers' career backgrounds on monetary policy in stages.*

further back, linking dissenting votes on the United States Federal Open Market Committee (FOMC) to individual members' career characteristics. Finally, I look at the revealed interest rate ideal points of FOMC members and show how these too can be traced back to career types.

The Policy Mechanism: Short-Run Real Interest Rates

The expected relationship between careers and interest rates follows directly from the theory of Chapter 2. When there is an inflation shock, central bankers with backgrounds in private finance should react more conservatively: to rein in prices, they should raise real interest rates more vigorously than central bankers with government backgrounds. Conversely, following a negative shock to output, former bureaucrats should more eagerly lower rates to stabilize the economy.

Reaction Function Models of Monetary Policy

To embed these insights in a model of interest rate policy, we must first make some assumptions. We suppose that central bankers make monetary policy decisions as if they were obeying a reaction function, a simple equation relating their preferred interest rate to a set of variables that the central banker observes. These variables could consist of either current economic indicators or expectations of future economic conditions. The intuition behind the model is simple: central bankers should lower interest rates when they expect the economy to underperform and raise them when they expect it to overheat.

Some notation helps fix ideas. Let r_t stand for the nominal interest rate in period t, r_{LR} the long-run nominal interest rate, π_t^{e} expected next-period inflation, and $\tilde{y}_t$ the gap between observed and expected economic output. In a seminal paper, Taylor (1993) suggested that central bankers should set interest rates according to the rule

$$r_t = r_{\mathrm{LR}} + \gamma_y \tilde{y}_t + \gamma_\pi \pi_t^{\mathrm{e}}, \tag{4.1}$$

where γ_y and γ_π are parameters reflecting the responsiveness of monetary policy to exogenous shocks. Much of the Taylor Rule literature in monetary economics is prescriptive, investigating whether central bankers *should* consciously employ one or another rule, set of variables, or vector of parameters (Ball, 1999; Levin, Wieland, and Williams, 1999; McCallum and Nelson, 1999; Orphanides, 1999; Rotemberg and Woodford, 1999; Rudebusch and Svensson, 1999; Svensson, 2003; Taylor, 1999*b*; Woodford, 2003).[1] Other studies use the Taylor Rule as a framework for empirical research (Clarida, Galí, and Gertler, 1998, 1999, 2000; Hetzel, 2000; Judd and Rudebusch, 1998; Siklos, 2002; Taylor, 1993, 1999*a*). The empirical Taylor approach assumes that the Taylor Rule (or some equally tractable reaction function) captures the essence of monetary decision making well enough to be used as the functional form for a regression model on historical data. The estimated parameters from such regressions are then taken to describe the preferences of the central bank and can be assessed as either hawkish or dovish. In terms of equation 4.1, high values of γ_π imply greater sensitivity to inflation shocks and a stronger desire to keep prices stable. High values of γ_y, on the other hand, suggest more sensitivity to output shocks and a greater desire to keep output stable. We therefore take high γ_π as a shorthand for hawkish policy and high γ_y as a shorthand for dovishness. Note the emphasis on stabilization: the parameters γ_π and γ_y reflect differential responses to shocks, not different preferences regarding the optimal interest rate in a stable economy, which are absorbed into the intercept, r_{LR}.

This chapter is an example of the empirical use of the Taylor Rule. I take for granted that central bank decisions more or less follow equation 4.1. One of the virtues of this approach is the simplicity of the model, which renders

1 Taylor (1993) recommended that the Fed set interest rates using $r_t = r_{\mathrm{LR}} + 0.5\tilde{y}_t + 1.5\pi_t^{\mathrm{e}}$. Later authors disagree on the optimal parameter values, while generally agreeing that γ_π should always be greater than one to ensure inflation stabilization (this is sometimes called the Taylor principle; see Taylor, 1999*a*; Woodford, 2003). Based on regressions on historical data, Taylor (1999*a*), Clarida, Galí, and Gertler (2000), and others criticize the pre-Volcker Fed for setting interest rates according to $\gamma_\pi < 1$ and praise the Volcker–Greenspan Fed for adopting $\gamma_\pi > 1$.

it more robust than more intricate models of the policy process.[2] The task for this section is to ask whether the variables investigated in the last chapter help explain the empirically observed values of γ_π and γ_y.

Before operationalizing the Taylor Rule as an empirical model of central banker behavior, I highlight three controversies in the reaction function literature that bear on our modeling choices: whether central bankers are forward or backward-looking observers of the economy, whether they adjust to shocks quickly or gradually, and whether central bankers reliance on contemporaneous, unrevised economic data limits the prescriptive or empirical application of monetary rules.

Are central bankers *adapting* to observed economic outcomes, or are they *anticipating* future developments? Although early work on reaction functions assumed central bankers react adaptively to current economic indicators, later work found that forward-looking rules focused on expected economic performance produce slightly better economic outcomes (Batini and Haldane, 1999; Clarida, Galí, and Gertler, 1998, 1999, 2000). The differences are not large, and either a backward- or forward-looking rule fits the available data fairly well (see Taylor, 1999*b*). I assume central bankers are rational and forward looking; that is, they make decisions based on expected inflation and the output gap, rather than current levels of inflation or output.

Do Taylor Rule estimates depend on whether we use revised data or real time data? Orphanides (1999, 2001) criticizes the Taylor Rule literature's reliance on final (that is, revised) time series data. He shows that estimates of the optimal and historical FOMC reaction function hinge on whether real-time or revised

2 The strategy of this section is not to ask whether the Taylor Rule (in contrast to some other specification) best captures how policy makers respond to shocks. Like other models, the Taylor rule greatly simplifies a complex cognitive and social process and cannot capture the full details of central bankers' decision making. It is instead a *useful* model of policy making with some cross-national validity; a baseline from which to investigate how different central bankers behave. Several studies find the Taylor Rule closely fits historical interest rate data in the United States and Europe (Clarida, Galí, and Gertler, 2000; Judd and Rudebusch, 1998; Taylor, 1999*a*), and simple monetary rules typically outperform (in a prescriptive sense) more complex rules in simulations across varied economic outcomes (Levin, Wieland, and Williams, 1999; Rudebusch and Svensson, 1999; Taylor, 1999*c*,*b*). If simple rules like equation 4.1 are normatively more robust than more complex alternatives, it is reasonable to expect a similar degree of empirical robustness compared to more complex functional forms.

inflation and output data are used. According to real time data, 1970s policy makers seem less naïve and the parameters of their implicit reaction functions less inflationary. In particular, Spencer (2004) argues that faulty real-time output gap assessments led the Fed astray in the 1970s. It is clearly hazardous to rely on data that may have been revised after the fact, but comparable and comprehensive real-time data is unavailable in the cross-section time series context. Instead, we must be satisfied with, and appropriately skeptical of, final time series data. Later, when we turn to individual voting and preference expression, we restrict our attention to a single country, the United States, and use only real-time data.

Are central bankers interest rate smoothers? Of the controversies in the Taylor Rule literature, the most salient to an analysis of how personal characteristics of central bankers affect policy choices is whether central bankers try to spread out adjustments over time. In empirical studies of monetary behavior, this question is typically interpreted as asking whether the lagged interest rate enters the policy rule. Although it is usually the case that lagged dependent variables included in a Taylor Rule regression turn out to be large, positive, and significant, the proper interpretation of these findings is far from clear. On one hand, several authors argue the lag terms are *prima facie* evidence of smoothing (Castelnuovo, 2003; Clarida, Galí, and Gertler, 2000; Levin, Wieland, and Williams, 1999; English, Nelson, and Sack, 2003). But there are many alternative explanations. Lagged dependent variable specifications could be picking up (a) serially correlated shocks (Rudebusch, 2001, 2002), (b) persistent exogenous influences on central bank decision making (Carey, 2001), (c) reactions to uncertainty about the size of the output gap (Smets, 2002), or (d) the spurious effect of using revised data to estimate Taylor Rules, rather than the real time data to which the policy makers had access (Lansing, 2002). Possibilities (a) and (b) suggest including a lagged dependent variable in our models may hide the persistent effect of career backgrounds on central bankers' preferences.

It is worth keeping these three controversies – adaptive versus rational expectations, revised versus real time data, and the ambiguous interpretation of lagged dependent variables – in mind throughout this section on interest rate policy and the next, in which we consider individual central banker's monetary policy votes and preference declarations.

Adding Career Effects to Reaction Functions: Hypotheses and Specification

In a time series cross-section context, the Taylor Rule lends itself to the econometric specification

$$r_{it} = \Gamma_{\mathrm{LR}} + \Gamma_y \tilde{y}_{it} + \Gamma_\pi \pi^{e}_{it} + \epsilon_{it}, \tag{4.2}$$

where the Γ's are parameters reflecting central bank behavior, and ϵ_{it} is a random disturbance (Taylor, 1993). We can estimate this equation directly (the usual practice), or we can add more structure to the preference parameters. That is, we can suppose the Γ's are linear functions of the median central banker's career characteristics (CBCC) and the degree of institutional autonomy enjoyed by the central bank (CBI). We represent these relationships according to the following set of equations:

$$\Gamma_{\mathrm{LR}} = \gamma_{\mathrm{LR}} + \gamma_{\mathrm{LR,C}}\mathrm{CBCC}_{it} + \gamma_{\mathrm{LR,I}}\mathrm{CBI}_{it}, \tag{4.3a}$$

$$\Gamma_\pi = \gamma_\pi + \gamma_{\pi,\mathrm{C}}\mathrm{CBCC}_{it} + \gamma_{\pi,\mathrm{I}}\mathrm{CBI}_{it}, \tag{4.3b}$$

$$\Gamma_y = \gamma_y + \gamma_{y,\mathrm{C}}\mathrm{CBCC}_{it} + \gamma_{y,\mathrm{I}}\mathrm{CBI}_{it}. \tag{4.3c}$$

Equation 4.3a says that the long-run nominal interest rate is a function of both career conservatism and central bank independence. Because both CBCC and CBI suppress inflation, we expect that in the long run, nominal interest rates should be lower when central bankers are conservative or independent. Thus, we expect to see $\gamma_{\mathrm{LR,C}} < 0$ and $\gamma_{\mathrm{LR,I}} < 0$. These parameters might also reflect different preferences among central bankers regarding the long-run interest rate, but at the country-level we expect these differences to be swamped by the effects of CBCC and CBI on long run inflation and (therefore) long nominal interest rates.

Equations 4.3b and 4.3c allow conservatism and independence to influence the sensitivity of the central bank to short-run fluctuations in either expected inflation or the output gap. Because monetary conservatives tend to believe the only responsibility of the central bank is to guarantee price stability, rather than output stability, we expect conservatism to heighten responsiveness to inflation but to lower responsiveness to output gaps. Therefore, we expect to find $\gamma_{\pi,\mathrm{C}} > 0$ and $\gamma_{y,\mathrm{C}} < 0$.

Turning to the effect of central bank independence on responsiveness to shocks, we again highlight the difference between preferences and institutions. Controlling for preferences, the principal effect of CBI is to make the central bank's policies more credible. More credible central banks should be able to achieve desired responses in inflation with smaller interventions than less credible central banks. This allows a highly independent central bank to be more responsive to output gaps – and less responsive to inflation shocks – than a dependent central bank.[3] Therefore, we expect $\gamma_{\pi,1} < 0$ and $\gamma_{y,1} > 0$, the reverse of our expectations about conservative reactions to shocks.

There are many variations on monetary rules available in the literature and corresponding bells and whistles that could be added to this model. For example, suppose increases in inflation and declines in output are more worrisome than declines in inflation or increases in output. In this case, we would want to allow asymmetric sensitivity to increases or decreases in expected inflation and the output gap (Surico, 2003). However, entertaining this and other hypotheses about the form of the reaction function lies beyond our scope. The goal is not to search through all the possibilities for the best possible approach to interest rate decision making, but instead to show the utility of career proxies for conservatism, and the intuitive relationship between these proxies and interest rates, in a basic model allowing differential responses to shocks.

Data and Methods

The data analyzed cover twenty industrialized democracies in the post-Bretton Wood era (1973 to present, quarterly; see note 5 in Chapter 3 for a list of countries). Most relevant economic variables come from Siklos (2002), who offers panel estimates of the Taylor Rule. For each of twenty countries (the same twenty industrialized countries studied in Chapter 3), Siklos provides a set of roughly comparable short-run interest rates, along with inflation forecasts and output gap estimates.[4] I complement these economic data with measures of central bank conservatism, using the median central banker's score, $CBCC^{med}$, measured quarterly, and autonomy, using an index of central bank indepen-

3 As Siklos puts it, an independent central bank can afford to "focus on long-term stability and not to react to every wiggle in inflation" (Siklos, 2002, 169). Smets (2002) shows that when the central bank's credibility has established an anchor for inflation, inflation becomes relatively less persistent than the gap in output, and the optimal response to output gaps grows larger.

4 Siklos (2002) calculates forecast inflation using moving windows regressions on lagged values of the policy instrument (the interest rate), inflation, the output gap, and exogenous factors such as world interest rates, equity and commodity prices, and real exchange rates.

dence, CBI-3, which combines the three most popular scorings of the concept into a single 0 to 1 scale.

I analyze these data using an interactive specification that substitutes equations 4.3a, 4.3b, and 4.3c into equation 4.2. I estimate the resulting linear model by least squares, with heteroskedasticity and autocorrelation consistent standard errors. With so many interaction terms, one might expect this to be a difficult model to estimate with any precision. However, as noted in Chapter 3, CBI and CBCC are (perhaps surprisingly) orthogonal, which maximizes the potential for estimating their distinctive effects. The key methodological question turns out to be how to model dynamics and in particular, whether to include a lag of the dependent variable.

Past studies of interest rate reaction functions find that a lagged dependent variable is always significant. Besides the popular interest rate smoothing explanation, I noted four other explanations of this finding. Of these four, the most worrisome for the present study is the danger of conflating persistent exogenous influences on monetary policy (such as individual central bankers' personalities and preferences) with the lagged term, a possibility that leads Carey (2001) to recommend dropping the lag altogether. This concern is consistent with Achen's (2000) warning that when both observed and omitted exogenous variables are serially correlated, the effects of lagged dependent variables are biased upwards toward one (regardless of whether this effect is truly zero, or instead positive), and the effects of other serially correlated explanatory variables are biased downward to zero:

> Intuitively speaking, the problem is that when a lagged dependent variable is entered into a regression equation with serial correlation, it acts as a proxy, picking up some of the effect of unmeasured variables. However, the autoregressive term does not conduct itself like a decent, well-behaved proxy. Instead, it is a kleptomaniac, picking up the effect, not only of the excluded variables, but also of the *included* variables if they are sufficiently trended. As a result, the impact of the included substantive variables is reduced, sometimes to insignificance (Achen, 2000, 9, emphasis original).

Achen's argument leads to a simple (perhaps simplistic) conjecture about the role of lagged dependent variables in political economy. In models of the influence of politics on the economy, policy choices impart force to an economic outcome already carrying its own momentum. (This is obvious for any real variable like employment, investment, or productivity but applies as well to inflation, which generates private expectations of continued inflation.) In these cases, a lagged specification is a reasonable default choice on theoretical grounds, although we should bear in mind Achen's warning. But lagged dependent variables may be especially misleading when the dependent variable is a policy choice than can be (and in some sense *is*) made *de novo* each period. In such cases, we should start without a lagged dependent variable, control for institutional constraints that may lead to policy inertia, and correct standard errors for serial correlation. The intuition behind this distinction is simply this: when unconstrained by veto players or institutions, political actors can make policy turn on a dime; the economy they can bring about but slowly.[5]

Accordingly, although in other chapters I use lagged specifications to study economic outcomes such as inflation and unemployment, in this chapter I emphasize lagless models of policy choices. Omitting the lag induces massive autocorrelation in the errors of the model, so I follow the advice of Achen (2000) and the example of Carey (2001) and calculate heteroskedastic and autocorrelation consistent standard errors (Newey and West, 1987). This approach balances the countervailing risks of bias due to "kleptomaniacal" lags on the one hand, and incorrect standard errors due to serial correlation of the errors on the other.

Results: Career Effects in Interest Rate Policy

We start with a simple specification estimating the parameters of the forward-looking Taylor Rule directly, without accounting for the diverse career backgrounds of central bankers or the varied independence of central banks (see Table 4.2, Model 1, in the Data Appendix for details). For our twenty country panel, we find that a one point increase in expected inflation leads to an 0.57 point increase in nominal interest rates two quarters later. Although positive, the effect is clearly smaller than the one-for-one rate suggested as a floor by Taylor (1993). Moreover, central banks were even less responsive to output shocks, reducing rates only 0.1 points in response to a one point output gap.

In Model 2, we broaden the specification to include measures of conservatism and independence, but only allows the long-run interest rate to vary based on

5 This is not to say that policy choices are in practice simply unconstrained, only that policies can, conditional on politics, be moved arbitrarily, whereas most economic outcomes cannot. Clearly, some policies are "stickier" than others because of institutional arrangements that make them difficult to change; consider, for example, the mostly automatic nature of social entitlement spending. The best approach is to model institutional constraints on the use of policy instruments explicitly; otherwise, reaction function estimates may be misleading, especially in a comparative context (Alt and Woolley, 1982).

these factors and not short-run responses to shocks. The results suggest slightly higher long-run interest rates under conservative boards and much lower rates under independent ones.

A more interesting picture develops when we allow both long-run interest rates *and* short-run sensitivity to shocks to depend on central bank preferences and institutions, as we do in Model 3. The signs of the estimated model suggests close agreement with the hypotheses given in the preceding. Because of the numerous interaction terms, I focus on a graphical presentation of these results. As the first row of plots in Figure 4.2 shows, the long-run nominal interest rate depends on conservatism (measured on the horizontal axis) and independence (which is low in the first plot and high in the second). All else equal, more independent banks have much lower nominal rates (2.5 points lower) than their less autonomous cousins, in accordance with the better inflation performance produced by independent central banks. Conservatism is also associated with lower rates, but the difference is smaller and not statistically significant: a shift from minimal to maximal career conservatism lowers long-run rates by just 0.8 points.

Why does independence have a much larger effect on long-term rates than conservatism, when they have similar effects on inflation? If the central bank is more conservative than the government – as is usually the case for industrialized democracies – the credibility granted by independence unambiguously allows lower inflation and interest rates. Conservative preferences also lower inflation, but their effect on interest rates may be dulled (though not completely erased) by the central banker's preference for tighter monetary policy. Hawks can achieve lower interest rates than doves, but are more reluctant to accept them, opting instead to fight inflation a bit harder.

Conservatism plays a key role in short-term responses to inflation shocks, as the middle row of plots shows. If expected inflation rises by one point, interest rates rise under any combination of institutions and preferences. But the hike is 0.25 points steeper under maximum conservatism compared to the minimum. A typical interest rate adjustment is usually 0.25 or 0.50 points, so this difference is not only statistically significant, but substantively important as well.

Unlike conservatism, independence is associated with milder responses to inflation. A highly independent central bank raises interest rates a statistically significant 0.11 points less than a weak central bank. This result makes sense if independent central banks can signal tightness more credibly than less independent ones: they get more bang for their basis points and can afford to soften the real consequences of price level stabilization. Notably, this helps explain

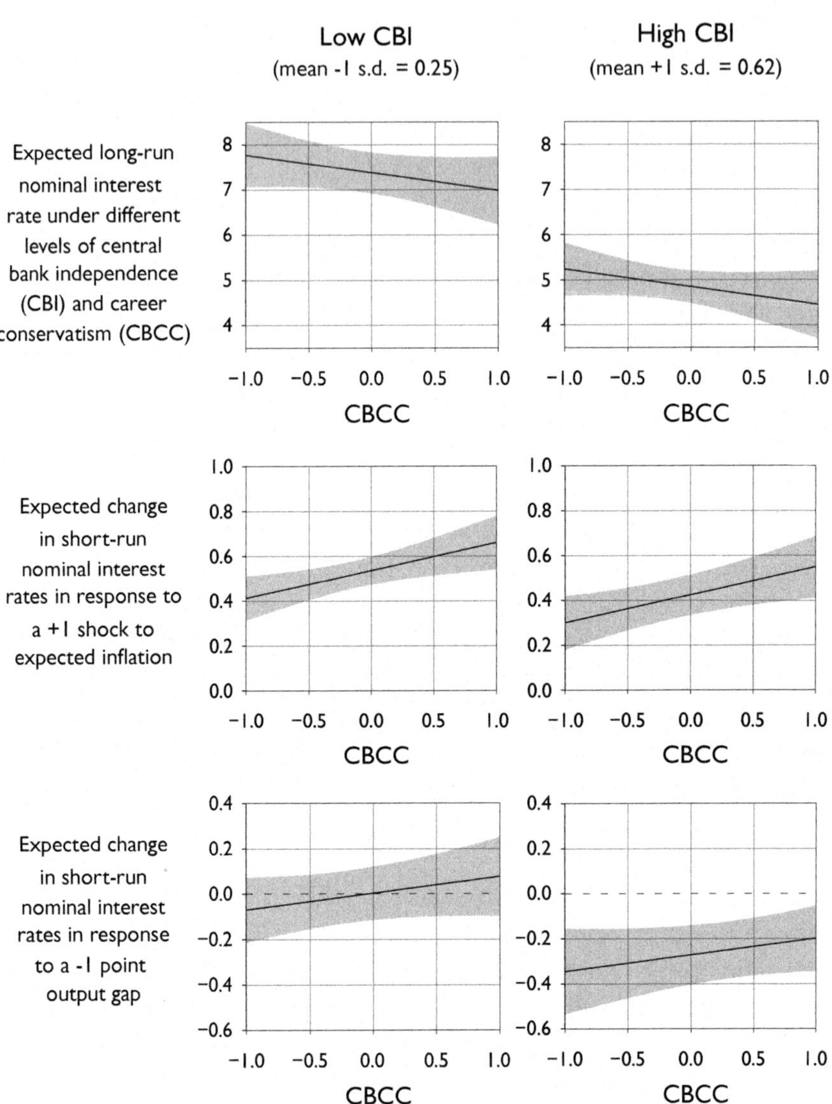

Low CBI
(mean -1 s.d. = 0.25)
High CBI
(mean +1 s.d. = 0.62)
Expected long-run nominal interest rate under different levels of central bank independence (CBI) and career conservatism (CBCC)
Expected change in short-run nominal interest rates in response to a +1 shock to expected inflation
Expected change in short-run nominal interest rates in response to a -1 point output gap
CBCC

Figure 4.2. *Estimated monetary policy responses to institutions, preferences, and economic shocks.* Solid lines mark the expected interest rate associated with a given career background score (CBCC, shown on the horizontal axis). The left column of plots assumes low central bank independence and the right high CBI. The top row of plots shows the expected level of interest rates for each CBI/CBCC combination, absent any change in expected inflation or the output gap. The middle row of plots shows how much interests change in response to an anticipated inflation shock, and the bottom row shows the change in interest rates in response to a one point growth in the estimated output gap. All results are calculated from Model 3. Gray areas indicate 90 percent confidence intervals.

the old puzzle that CBI lowers inflation without increasing output volatility (Grilli, Masciandaro, and Tabellini, 1991).

The bottom row of plots show similar responses to short-run developments in the gap between actual and potential output. Most (but not all) central banks lower nominal interest rates when the economy underperforms. Career conservatives, however, seem more wary of sharply lowering rates. In reaction to a one point output gap, maximally conservative central bankers lower interest rates 0.15 points less than minimally conservative ones, although the difference is not statistically significant. Once again, independent central banks can afford to be more dovish and lower rates 0.27 points more than their less credible peers, a difference that *is* statistically significant.

In sum, a central bank with legal independence can respond gently but firmly to expected inflation, and can react to output gaps decisively. A conservative central bank prefers vigorous responses to inflation and tepid reactions to output gaps. Because conservatism and independence need not go together, a variety of outcomes are possible.

Finally, we note the above results are not robust to including a lag of the interest rate, as in Model 4. Comparing Models 3 and 4, we find the lagged dependent variable suppresses the effects of all our explanatory variables. They remain for the most part correctly signed, but few are significant at conventional levels. The lag term is doing most of the explaining in this specification. The conventional interpretation from the monetary reaction function literature would be to conclude central banks are intentionally smoothing out interest rate changes. But whether there is smoothing or not, the lag term is stealing explanatory power from the serial correlated measures of conservatism and independence. I suspect interest rate movements reflect both intentional smoothing and the (serially correlated) effects of career conservatism and institutions, but these effects are difficult to disentangle.

Career Incentives and Individual Behavior: Dissenting Votes in the Federal Open Market Committee

Chapter 2 offered a micro-theory of central bankers' motivations and behavior; Chapter 3 tested this theory with macro-data on policy instruments and economic outcomes. This leaves a gap between our understanding of how individual central bankers behave and how committees of central bankers reach decisions. Were we to leave this gap unfilled, Chapter 3 would still constitute strong indirect evidence of this book's central claim that central bankers' careers influence the economy. But testing the links in the causal chain binding central bankers' micro-behavior to macro-consequences is an important further confirmation: career backgrounds should also explain *individual* central bankers' monetary policy preferences and behavior. We turn now to this micro-level test.

Although in most countries, a committee of central bankers vote on monetary policy decisions, these votes go unpublished in all but a handful of cases (Fry et al., 2000; Siklos, 2002). Secrecy greatly limits our ability to test the propositions of this study at the micro-level. The country with the longest and most accessible public record of monetary policy votes is the United States, where the Federal Open Market Committee meets ten times a year and publishes dissenting votes after a lag of one meeting (Chappell, McGregor, and Vermilyea, 2004*a*).

A first glance, the FOMC voting record seems the perfect arena for testing the career effects approach to monetary policy, which holds that the career backgrounds of central bankers influence their monetary policy preferences. In countries like the United States, where there is a written record of monetary policy votes, it would seem clear that the pattern of assents and dissents to interest rate proposals should reflect differences in individual preferences – and, if they matter, differences in career types. Indeed, prior works on career incentives in monetary policy focused on patterns of FOMC dissent (Belden, 1989; Canterbery, 1967; Gildea, 1990; Havrilesky and Schweitzer, 1990; Havrilesky and Gildea, 1991*a*,*b*, 1992).

In practice, however, FOMC votes are not as informative as one might hope. The chairman canvasses the FOMC in the days leading up to a meeting to determine the range of acceptable policies. Because chairmen are loath to end

Table 4.1. *Three samples of FOMC members' behavior.*

	Count of...			Period Average...		
Period	Meetings	Assents	Dissents	Fed Funds	Infl	Unem
All data ('60–'96)	319	3077	262	6.7	4.7	6.1
Burns ('70–'78)	99	1153	55	6.5	6.5	6.3
Greenspan ('87–'96)	75	771	63	5.9	3.7	6.1

Author's calculations using data from Chappell, McGregor, and Vermilyea (2004*a*), the Federal Reserve, the IMF International Financial Statistics, and the OECD Statistical Compendium.

up on the losing side, they are constrained to make only those proposals that can muster a majority. In fact, chairmen never lose these votes; if one did, many would expect him to resign (Chappell, McGregor, and Vermilyea, 2004*a*; Meyer, 2004). Nevertheless, the invariable agreement of the chair and median voter is consistent with a great deal of latent influence by committee members, as by most accounts, the chair actively seeks to satisfy the majority (Chappell, McGregor, and Vermilyea, 2004*a*). Moreover, the central bank as a whole benefits from the appearance of unanimity and the confidence it inspires on the part of market observers (Woolley, 1984; Greider, 1987; Krause, 1994; Chappell, McGregor, and Vermilyea, 2004*a*). These collective benefits dissuade members from dissenting over minor differences of opinion. The result is that dissents are rare, occurring only when dissenting members strongly disapprove of the majority policy and wish to send a costly message to the chairman.[6] From 1960 to 1996, members of the FOMC formally assented to the chair's agenda 92 percent of the time (Table 4.1). Either monetary policy was uncontroversial, or votes carry incomplete information about the controversy, coming after it is settled and a winning position is evident.

Fortunately, richer data on FOMC member preferences exist. Before voting, the FOMC holds a discussion in which each member of the committee voices an opinion on the proper course of action. Usually, these presentations include an explicit statement of the member's preferred Fed Funds rate or enough information to deduce it. Chappell, McGregor, and Vermilyea (2004*a*) collect these

6 Put another way, the chair can set an agenda no closer to his ideal point than is allowed by take-it-or-leave-it bargaining (Romer and Rosenthal, 1978; Ferejohn and Shipan, 1990), with the median member willing to depart from his ideal point to some degree to avoid the appearance of a divided board.

revealed interest rate preferences for all voting FOMC members at each meeting between 1970 and 1978 (under Arthur Burns' chairmanship) and between 1987 and 1996 (under Alan Greenspan) and argue these revealed interest rate targets contain far more information than dissenting votes.

In the remainder of this chapter, I analyze both measures of individual preference: dissenting votes, of which we have more observations, and revealed interest rate targets, which carry more information.

Modeling Dissenting Votes

Given a proposed Fed Funds target, a member of the FOMC has three choices. In order of increasing monetary conservatism, he can either dissent in favor of an easier policy, assent, or dissent in favor of a tighter policy. An ordered probit model provides an appropriate representation of the probability of each vote choice. That is, we assume there is some normally distributed latent variable corresponding to central bankers' preferred interest rates. The estimated model allows us to calculate the probability of dissents for ease, votes for the proposal, and dissents for tightness, and condition these probabilities on the state of the economy and the characteristics of central bankers themselves.[7] Except for central banker career data, all variables are drawn from Chappell, McGregor, and Vermilyea (2004*a*).

Expected inflation and unemployment. As in the preceeding Taylor Rule models, I assume that central bankers make monetary choices based on expected inflation and real economic performance. For the FOMC, we are fortunate to have real-time forecast of inflation and unemployment – the very Green Book forecasts on which FOMC members relied when making their decisions. Even though these forecasts have a large effect on the interest rate chosen by the Fed, they should have a much smaller effect on dissents, precisely because the Chair's pro-

7 Of course, there are other variables we could consider. For instance, Meyer (2004, 53, note 27) suggests that because FOMC members vote in alphabetical order (excepting the chair and vice-chair), there may be a correlation between the alphabetical order of FOMC member names and their propensity to dissent. The reasoning is that members who disagree with the proposed policy may desire at least a modicum of dissent, but prefer to avoid all-out revolt (say, three or more dissents) against the chairman once a proposal has been made. If an early voter or two dissents, later voters who would otherwise dissent may instead defer to the chairman. However, a logistic regression of dissents on the voting order of members fails to support this hypothesis, and I consider it no further.

posed interest rate already adjusts to meet the changing forecasts. To the extent there is a status quo bias in the Chair's proposals, there may be more dissents in favor of aggressively fighting anticipated increases in either inflation or unemployment. But if the Chair accurately gauges the sentiment of the committee, expected inflation and unemployment should have little effect on the probability of dissent.

Partisanship and elections. I control for the party appointing each member and expect Republican appointees to be inflation hawks (dissenters for tightness), given right-wing constituencies' greater inflation sensitivity (Powell and Whitten, 1993; Hibbs, 1987). Indeed, a large literature has found a correlation between monetary policy tightness, on one hand, and the partisanship of the president (Alesina and Sachs, 1988; Havrilesky, 1987) or the partisanship of Congressional oversight committees (Grier, 1991, 1996), on the other. There is also evidence of a correlation between FOMC votes for tightness and Republican appointees (Havrilesky and Gildea, 1992; Tootell, 1996).

But election pressures may override the usual partisan policy preferences. Following Chappell, McGregor, and Vermilyea (2004*a*), I also include a variable flagging members appointed by parties with a president up for reelection that year. According to political business cycle theory, sitting presidents put pressure on the Fed to deliver low interest rates prior to an election (Niskanen, 1971; Nordhaus, 1975; Kettl, 1986; Grier, 1987, 1989; Clark and Hallerberg, 2000). In the year before elections, we expect the president's partisan allies in the FOMC to respond with more votes in favor of easing and to be less likely than at other times to push for tightness, regardless of whether their party is ordinarily associated with easy money.

Career backgrounds, conservatism, and reliable partisanship. The key explanatory variables are the career backgrounds of central bankers. However, because we are now restricting our attention to a single country, rather than the twenty country panel, we do not use the CBCC index as our measure of career effects, but instead include each career component separately to allow for the idiosyncrasies of the American case. We retain the strong expectation of finding conservative financiers and less conservative generalist (that is, non-central bank and non-finance ministry) bureaucrats: we expect experience in finance (FinExp) to lead central bankers to dissent more for tightness and less for ease, and we expect experience in government (GovExp) to have the opposite effect. More specialized experience in the Treasury (FMExp) or as staff in the

Federal Reserve (CBExp) should have intermediate effects, both because such appointees are more likely to have their own opinions, and thus may be more willing to resist government pressure for ease, and because specialized bureaucrats may be more appealing job candidates for top positions in the financial sector, especially if they have more social contacts in the banking sector.

These career hypotheses match the ones we made in Chapter 3. We now add a new hypothesis, drawn from past studies of the Fed, finding economist appointees to be "reliable partisans" (Havrilesky and Gildea, 1992). Although we did not find any such pattern internationally, the large number of economists on the FOMC makes it easier to detect partisan differences in their preferences. We include in our specification academic economics experience (EcoExp) interacted with the party of appointment. We expect Republican-appointed economists to be hawks and economists appointed by Democrats to be doves.

Unlike the Taylor Rule regressions, we do not include interactions of experience scores and expected economic performance. Because the median member on the board tends to respond to shocks, dissents against the median voter's position are unlikely to be much influenced by them. In any case, with six experience score terms an interactive specification would be unwieldy, difficult to estimate precisely, and too demanding of the information contained in a trichotomous outcome. As in the Taylor Rule regressions, we do not include lags of the dependent variable. This omission is minor, given the rarity of dissent and our desire to model explicitly any autocorrelation in dissents resulting from personal characteristics.

Results: Dissenting Votes

Because of the difficulty of directly assessing probit parameters for compositional covariates, we focus our discussion on a graphical display of the expected probabilities of dissent under different hypothetical values of the explanatory variables (Figure 4.3).[8] Each row of this plot represents a different counter-

8 The estimated parameters of the ordered probit of dissents are shown in Table 4.3 in the Data Appendix. There are two reasons to be cautious in directly interpreting these estimates. The first is the usual opacity of probit coefficients. The second is the peculiar properties of compositional covariates. Recall that a set of compositional variables like experience scores must logically always sum to one. Any counterfactual we construct must fulfill this constraint. For example, if we assume a central banker had 100 percent of his experience in the financial sector, his experience in every other sector must be held at zero. Therefore, if we wish to compare the probability of dissent by a central banker with the average career background to one who has only worked in fi-

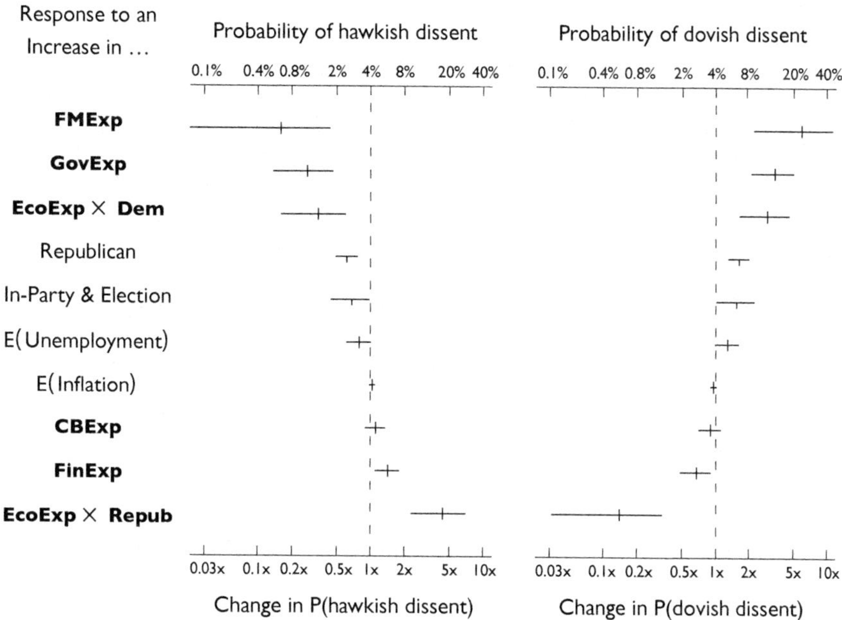

Figure 4.3. *Probability of casting a dissenting vote on the FOMC.* The plots show the estimated effect of increasing the variable listed at left on the probability of dissenting votes favoring tightening (left plot) or easing of interest rates (right plot). The counterfactual increase in the covariate of interest is +1 unit, except for experience scores, which are instead raised to their maximum of one. For each row, all covariates besides the variable listed are set at their means where logically possible. The top scale shows the estimated probability of a dissenting vote, while the bottom scale shows the relative risk of dissent compared to the the baseline level. Horizontal bars mark 90 percent confidence intervals. Career variables are printed in bold.

factual drawn from the estimated model. We discuss the construction of each counterfactual in turn, but the general idea is to construct only logically possible scenarios. When the variable in question is a career component, we take advantage of the fact that most individuals have uninterrupted prior careers in a single sector and focus on scenarios where one experience score is set to one and all others to zero.

Figure 4.3 uses several tricks to make the ordered probit model's implications easier to understand. First, the dashed vertical lines show as reference the rate at which the average member, with average characteristics, dissented in favor of easier policy (the left panel) or tighter policy (the right panel). Second, because the probability of dissent can vary over a wide range, the plots are logarithmically scaled. Finally, we can simultaneously read off the probabilities of dissent (the bottom axis) and the relative risk of dissent (the top axis) compared to the mean scenario.[9]

The strongest predictors of dissenting votes are the career experience variables, which follow our expectations with a single exception. A central banker who spent his entire career in the financial sector dissents for tightness 5.8 percent of the time (43 percent more often than the average central banker), and

nance, the change in dissent probability flows not only through the FinExp coefficient, but also through every other parameter attached to a compositional covariate, because each of those covariates fall to zero. See the Methods Appendix to Chapter 3 for a full treatment of compositional covariates.

9 For continuous covariates, like central banker characteristics and economic conditions, a straightforward way to interrogate our model is to compare the predicted probability of each kind of dissent under a counterfactual value of a covariate of interest (say, the mean plus one standard deviation) to the predicted probability of each kind of dissent under the mean level of that covariate, with all other covariates held at their means in both scenarios. For these cases, results are plotted against the top axis (expected probabilities) and the bottom axis (relative risks). But our political variables are binary, and the most appealing comparison is between their presence and *absence*, not their mean value in the data. Figure 4.3 shows the change in probability of dissent given a change from Democratic to Republican appointees and the change in probability of dissent comparing central bankers who are not subject to a looming election to those who are. This causes a slight complication for presentation: whereas the baseline probability of dissent for each continuous covariate is the same, the baseline probabilty of dissent for each binary covariate differs. To make the covariates' effects easier to compare, the two binary scenarios are plotted against only on the bottom axis (relative risks), not the top axis (expected probabilities). As a guide to readers, for each scenario plotted in Figure 4.3, the vertical mark indicating the point estimate points toward whichever axis or axes can be read for that scenario.

dissents for ease 2.7 percent of the time (33 percent less often than the baseline). A former generalist bureaucrat dissents for tightness only 1.1 percent of the time (73 percent less often than the baseline) and in favor of ease 13.8 percent of the time (340 percent more often than the baseline). All these results are statistically significant. In contrast, a former Fed staffer's behavior lies in the middle and cannot be distinguished from the average central banker. Ex-Treasury officials are the anomalous case: contrary to expectations, they are more likely to dissent for ease and less likely to dissent for tightness than other bureaucrats. However, this result is imprecisely estimated and its confidence interval mostly overlaps with generalist bureaucrats.

As anticipated, economists are reliable partisans. Economists appointed by Democratic presidents are about as dovish as generalist bureaucrats. Economists appointed by Republicans are the most hawkish type of all, dissenting for tightness 17.8 percent of the time (439 percent more often than the mean) and for easing 0.6 percent of the time (86 percent less often than the average central banker). Again, these results are statistically as well as substantively significant.

Compared to career experience, the remaining covariates all have smaller (but still statistically significant) effects on dissent behavior. Expected economic conditions have the weakest effect – a one point increase in inflation makes dissent in favor of tighter policy just four percent more likely; a one point increase in unemployment makes dissent for ease 30 percent more likely. These weak relationships show that the committee's decision mostly tracks changing economic conditions, but is slightly biased towards the status quo.

Turning finally to our political variables, we find appointees of the president's party to be more dovish during election years: all else equal, they dissent for tighter policy 2.5 percent of the time (32 percent less often than their peers) and for easier policy 3.8 percent of the time (56 percent more often than their peers). These findings are significant and consistent with the predictions of opportunistic political business cycles.[10]

10 One might suppose that finding the president's party is more likely to *dissent* for ease and less likely to *dissent* for tightness suggests efforts at pre-electoral manipulation failed, because these central bankers are "dissenting," but that would be reading too much into the model. Although we have framed our interpretation in terms of "dissents," the estimates are equally consistent with two different scenarios: a majority that defies efforts at electorally-motivated easing, thereby provoking dissents in favor of ease by in-party governors; *or* a majority, including the in-party governors, which successfully cuts rates to benefit the incumbent party, thereby provoking dissents for tightness from the out-party members. The model is agnostic as to which collective outcome results.

With the exception of the reliable economists and controlling for career types, Republican partisanship has a mild and surprisingly dovish effect in our sample. There are several possible explanations for this finding: 1) the thinness of information in the dissenting vote data may be misleading us; 2) perhaps partisan effects are largely absent from the FOMC, or 3) partisan effects may work through the career types selected by the parties, with economists the only exception, as their published writings and academic reputations make it easier to identify hawks and doves. For other types, careers are probably the best signal a government has. Indeed, Republican appointees are more likely to be bankers and less likely to be bureaucrats than Democratic appointees.

Based on these results, I suspect the answer is a combination of (1) and (3). Presently, we check whether the revealed preferences of FOMC members reflect partisan leanings. In Chapter 8, we explore the connection between partisan appointment and career backgrounds in the comparative context.

Modeling Revealed Interest Rate Targets

Dissenting votes are rare protests made at the end of policy deliberations. The policy discussion itself is a richer source of information about FOMC member preferences. At every meeting, each member presents his views – and in most cases, an explicit interest rate ideal point – in a formal policy "go-round." Through March 1976, these discussions were published after a lag of five years as the *Memoranda of Discussion*. After that date, the Fed ceased formal publication of its discussions, but continued to tape-record, transcribe, and release them after five years. Thanks to the painstaking data collection of Chappell, McGregor, and Vermilyea (2004*a*), we can analyze the stated preferences of FOMC members regarding the Fed Funds rate. This allows us to tackle the micro-level connection between career backgrounds and policy preferences in a richer and cleaner context.

The dependent variable is the revealed interest rate target, measured each meeting for each voting member. Chappell, McGregor, and Vermilyea code these data for two eras in which data were available and the Fed Funds rate was the unquestioned primary policy instrument: the Burns years (1970–1978) and the available Greenspan years (1987–1996). The authors found explicit statements of policy preference for 80 percent of the 1782 Burns-era member–votes, and 92 percent of the 1292 Greenspan-era member–votes.[11] In the remaining

11 Explicit policy statements include personal statements of preferred quantitative targets, endorsements of staff scenario targets, or endorsements of fellow members' statements.

cases, they recorded the direction the member was leaning and imputed a specific target.[12]

The covariates of the model are exactly those used in the dissenting vote regressions: real-time Green Book inflation and unemployment forecasts, party of appointment, the "in-party during an election year" indicator, and career experience scores for financial, government, Treasury, Federal Reserve, and economics backgrounds, with economics experience further broken down by party of appointment to reflect reliable partisanship. Our expectations are unchanged, though we now expect to see large effects of expected inflation and expected unemployment on the desired interest rate, just as in the Taylor Rule regressions considered earlier.[13] Estimation by least squares is once more appropriate. As with other policy response variables, we omit lags of the response variable and rely on heteroskedastic and autocorrelation consistent standard errors to cope with serial correlation of the errors.

Results: Revealed Interest Rate Targets

The estimated parameters for the Fed Funds ideal point regressions are listed in Table 4.3. The model appears to fit the data well, and most parameters are highly significant by conventional tests. A graphical summary (Figure 4.4) allows easy comparison with the dissenting votes results.

Inflation and unemployment forecasts have strong and predictable effects on members' target interest rates. A one point expected rise in inflation is associated with a tightly estimated 0.74 point increase in interest rate goals. Notably, this is lower than the 1-for-1 minimum recommended by the Taylor principle. In contrast, FOMC members' preferences were more responsive to the real economy: a one point increase in expected unemployment was associated with a 1.45 decline in interest rate preferences.

Elections and partisanship have smaller but still significant effects. Controlling for careers and the reliable partisanship of economists, non-economist Republican appointees favored higher Fed Funds rates (+0.20 points). This makes more sense than the findings on dissenting votes, where Republicans

12 Because the Chappell, McGregor, and Vermilyea (2004*a*) imputation model includes fixed effects for members, the imputed values should contain information regarding the effect of careers on preferences even though career variables are not included in Chappell, McGregor, and Vermilyea's model.

13 Ideally, we would include similar interactions between inflation, output, and career conservatism, but these cannot be precisely estimated for our data, especially given the many career variables included in the model and the limited number of observations.

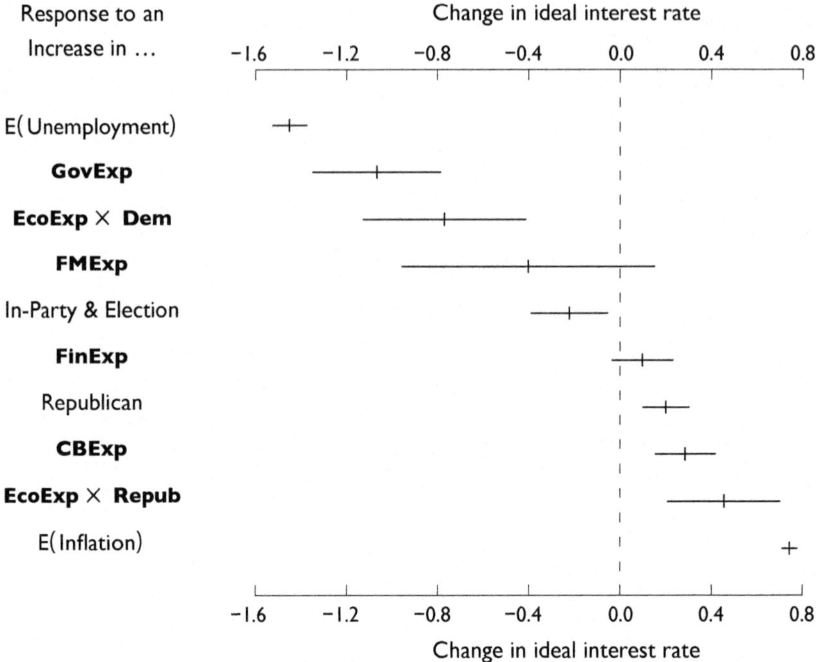

Figure 4.4. *Determinants of interest rate preferences.* The plot shows the effect of increasing the variable listed at left on the central banker's ideal interest rate target. The counterfactual increase in the covariate of interest is +1 unit, except for experience scores, which are raised to their maximum of one. For each row, all covariates besides the variable listed are set at their meanns where logically possible. Horizontal bars mark 90 percent confidence intervals. Career variables are printed in bold.

were paradoxically more dovish than Democrats. On the other hand, regardless of partisan ideology, in the year before an election appointees of the president's party wanted interest rates to be lower (−0.22 points). These findings suggest both partisan and opportunistic political cycles operate through the channel of central bank appointment.

The effects of careers were sizable and for the most part in line with our expectations. Non-specialist bureaucrats favored much easier money (−1.07 points), as did economists appointed by Democrats. Republican economists were reliable hawks (+0.46 points). Central bank staff were hawkish as well (+0.29 points), at odds with our cross-country regressions (Chapter 3) and the dissenting vote regressions. Former private bankers were slightly hawkish (+0.10 points), but this result is not significant (the 90 percent confidence interval runs from −0.04 to 0.23). As in the dissenting vote regressions, former Treasury staff have poorly estimated preferences, mostly leaning dovish, but with a very wide confidence interval.

In sum, the evidence suggests that members of the FOMC form their policy preferences based first on economic considerations, followed by their career backgrounds. Partisan and electoral considerations play a part, but are less important.

Conclusions

This chapter traced career effects through expressed preferences to votes, policy choices, and policy outcomes, and in every case reached the same conclusion: differences among central bankers, measurable through their career backgrounds, matter for monetary policy. This microfoundation supports the claim that career-types of central bankers influence inflation and economic performance generally. Accordingly, monetary policy scholars should consider career-based indexes of central bank conservatism to complement widely used measures of central bank independence.

Recent Federal Reserve decisions continue to follow the pattern laid down here: at a time when many influential economists question whether the Fed might pursue further unconventional zero-bound policies to dig the United States out of unrelenting recession, three members of the FOMC dissented against keeping interest rates low in August 2011, the largest number of dissents in almost two decades.[14] Public debate continues over the need for greater macroeconomic stimulus, yet inside the Fed, these dissenting voices instead feared future inflation – even with core inflation contained below two percent and near its postwar low. The disconnect between the risk of contraction

14 On the August dissents, see David Leonhardt, "Dissecting the Mind of the Fed," *New York Times*, August 28, 2011, SR8, and Benyamin Appelbaum, "Conflict and Confusion over Economy at the Fed," *New York Times*, October 13, 2011, B4. For a forceful example of economic criticism of the Bernanke Fed's reluctance to pursue aggressive stimulus at the zero-bound, see Paul Krugman, "Earth to Ben Bernanke: Chairman Bernanke should listen to Professor Bernanke," *New York Times Magazine*, April 24, 2012, MM18. For a critical but slightly more sanguine view, see Mark Thoma, "Has Bernanke Learned an Important Lesson?" *CBS Money Watch*, February 29, 2012, www.cbsnews.com/8301-505123_162-57387707/has-bernanke-learned-an-important-lesson.

in the macroeonomy and the anti-inflation rallying cry of internal Fed critics is baffling – until one notes that all three dissents can be explained by career backgrounds. One dissenting hawk, Dallas Fed President Richard W. Fisher, is a financial sector veteran; the two others, Narayana Kocherlakota of the Minneapolis Fed and Charles I. Plosser of Philadelphia, are conservative economists trained at the University of Chicago.

At a broader level, the evidence collected here recommends more exchange, synthesis, and cooperation between students of the Federal Reserve and comparative scholars of monetary policy. In particular, we can use the same framework to study the behavior of FOMC members and central bankers across the industrialized world. The Taylor rule shows itself to be a useful tool for empirical work, though some results are anomolous; for example, the surprisingly dovish reaction of the average central banker to rising expected inflation is inconsistent with the Taylor principle, yet over this period inflation performance improved.

Finally, this chapter demonstrates that we can study the micro-logic of delegation in a step-by-step fashion, tracing the mechanism by which agents' preferences become policy. The data to do this are not always available or complete. Here we have made do with data of varying quality available for different countries and time periods but nonetheless generally supporting a single logic transforming career backgrounds of agents into policy outcomes. Similar sets of tests might explore the mechanisms of delegation in other policy arenas, to better tease out the interaction of principals, agents, and institutions, a topic I return to in the concluding chapter.

Data Appendix to Chapter 4

Table 4.2. *Nominal interest rate regressions, twenty industrialized countries, 1973 to 1998.*

Covariate	Parameter	E(sign)	DV: Nominal Interest Rate (r_{it}) 1	2	3	4
$\pi^{e}_{i,t-2}$	γ_{π}	+	0.572	0.474	0.613	0.094
			(0.030)	(0.031)	(0.073)	(0.034)
$\tilde{y}_{i,t-2}$	γ_{y}	+	0.089	0.101	-0.193	0.025
			(0.040)	(0.038)	(0.155)	(0.06)
$\text{CBCC}^{\text{med}}_{i,t-2}$	$\gamma_{\text{LR,C}}$	−		0.376	-0.395	-0.147
				(0.225)	(0.345)	(0.115)
$\text{CBI}_{i,t-2}$	$\gamma_{\text{LR,I}}$	−		-8.064	-6.997	-0.826
				(0.574)	(0.891)	(0.338)
$\pi^{e} \times \text{CBCC}^{\text{med}}_{i,t-2}$	$\gamma_{\pi,\text{C}}$	+			0.124	0.025
					(0.054)	(0.019)
$\pi^{e} \times \text{CBI}_{i,t-2}$	$\gamma_{\pi,\text{I}}$	−			-0.307	-0.072
					(0.181)	(0.074)
$\tilde{y} \times \text{CBCC}^{\text{med}}_{i,t-2}$	$\gamma_{y,\text{C}}$	−			-0.073	-0.018
					(0.065)	(0.025)
$\tilde{y} \times \text{CBI}_{i,t-2}$	$\gamma_{y,\text{I}}$	+			0.759	-0.001
					(0.360)	(0.135)
$r_{i,t-1}$	ϕ_1	+				0.865
						(0.022)
Intercept	γ_{LR}		5.477	9.683	9.132	1.131
			(0.183)	(0.377)	(0.467)	(0.234)
N			1927	1927	1927	1925
s.e.r.			3.674	3.385	3.365	1.681
R^2			0.345	0.444	0.451	0.863

All regressions are estimated by least squares with heteroskedastic and autocorrelation consistent standard errors. Entries are estimated regression parameters, with standard errors in parentheses.

Table 4.3. *Regression models of FOMC member behavior: Dissenting votes and revealed interest rate targets.*

Covariates	FOMC Votes (1 = ease, 2 = accept 3 = tighten)	Revealed Fed Funds Target
FinExp	-0.021	0.105
	(0.146)	(0.194)
GovExp	-0.753	-1.059
	(0.188)	(0.254)
FMExp	-1.039	-0.393
	(0.324)	(0.399)
CBExp	-0.142	0.292
	(0.141)	(0.202)
EcoExp × Repub	0.934	0.299
	(0.281)	(0.224)
EcoExp × Dem	-0.826	-0.622
	(0.202)	(0.287)
E(Inflation)	0.019	0.743
	(0.015)	(0.02)
E(Unemployment)	-0.035	-1.449
	(0.022)	(0.045)
In-Party, election year	-0.182	-0.223
	(0.103)	(0.102)
Republican	-0.485	0.305
	(0.102)	(0.126)
Constant	2.49	11.776
	(0.148)	(0.303)
Cutpoint	3.745	
	(0.067)	
Method	ordered probit	linear regression
N	2957	1402
ln likelihood	-871.7	
% predicted	93.0	
R^2		0.72
s.e.r.		1.10

Entries are estimated regression parameters, with standard errors in parentheses. Standard errors for the revealed interest rate target regression are heteroskedastic and autocorrelation consistent. Votes data cover 1960 to 1996; revealed interest rate data cover 1970 to 1978 and 1987 to 1996.

5

CAREERS AND INFLATION IN DEVELOPING COUNTRIES

> The IMF reports to the ministers of finance and the governors of the central banks, and one of the important items on its agenda is to make these central banks more independent – and less democratically accountable... it always puts far more weight on inflation than on jobs. The problem with having the rules of the game dictated by the IMF – and thus by the financial community – is not just a question of values (though that is important) but also a question of ideology. The financial community's view of the world predominates – even when there is little evidence in its support.
>
> Joseph Stiglitz, *former chief economist of the World Bank**

In developed countries, central bankers' past careers shape their preferences over monetary policy. This happens directly, through socialization, and indirectly, by giving central bankers incentives to select the monetary policy preferred by likely future employers. Put another way, central bankers can use monetary policy to grease a revolving door connecting the central bank and private finance and the state. These career effects lead former financiers to be monetary policy hawks and make doves of former bureaucrats.

In this chapter, I turn to the developing world. Past scholarship on developing country central banks finds little traction for concepts such as central bank independence that seem important to monetary policy making elsewhere. Some conclude that developing economies have weak institutions and give up hope of deciphering the implications of developing countries' laws.

Perhaps we have misunderstood the motivations of developing world central bankers from the start. I explore the career socialization and career ambitions of central bankers in less developed countries. Can we identify central banker types

* Joseph Stiglitz, "Globalism's Discontents," *American Prospect*, Winter 2002.

with different policy beliefs and career incentives – such as the conservative financier and the dovish bureaucrat – around the globe? If so, can we finally understand the role of developing country central banking institutions?

Central Banking in Developing Countries

Before laying out career-effects hypotheses for developing country central banks, I review some of the features that make central banking in the developing world different from the countries examined so far. Some types of central bankers, including *financiers*, *businesspeople*, and *economists*, may play somewhat different roles in developing country central banks. Moreover, these institutions are often *less developed*, *more politicized*, and according to most empirical work, *less effective* than their industrialized economy counterparts.

The role of finance. Governments' thirst for credit shapes central banking in developing countries in several ways. Providing loans to the state remains a key function of many central banks in the developing world (Maxfield, 1994). Domestic sources of capital are often inadequate, leaving governments at the mercy of international capital markets (Mosley, 2003). Maxfield (1997) argues that developing country governments may elevate central bank independence to signal their creditworthiness to the international banking community. We can extend this argument to the appointment of central bankers: choosing private bankers or other agents trusted by international financiers should also help governments win the trust of international financial firms. In this signaling process, domestic private banks may play their familiar anti-inflation role, with some exceptions. A banking sector weighed down by bad debt might welcome inflation to clear their balance sheets. And in a country experiencing hyperinflation, banks make costly adaptations that reduce or even nullify their opposition to inflation.[1] When considering the role of financial sector representatives at developing country central banks, it is crucial to keep these exceptions in mind.

1 Posen (1998) argues that under hyperinflationary conditions financial institutions make technological investments to deal with price volatility, making a return to stable inflation less urgent for these firms or even costly. Likewise, Mas (1995) argues that in developing countries, as inflation rises, banks' resistance to inflation declines due to widespread indexation of inflation, shortening of loan maturities (which reduces pressure on banks balance sheets), and currency substitution. In Russia from 1991 to 1994, commercial banks adapted well to inflationary conditions and resisted efforts to restore stable prices, an urgent priority of the government (though not, ironically, of the independent Central Bank of Russia; see Johnson 2000).

Greater potential for pro-growth pressure from business. The role of business lobbying in first world central banking gets little attention because there is little scope for interest group politics in an area with indivisible policies, decentralized pressure groups, and uncaptured externalities from any successful bargain. Instead, businesses concentrate their lobbying efforts on trade policy, regulation, and subsidies (Gowa, 1988; Olson, 1965). But this Olsonian logic flips around in many developing countries, where capital is scarcer and concentrated in fewer hands (Amsden and Hikino, 1994). Often a single domestic conglomerate, spanning multiple sectors of the economy, stands to gain enough from loose monetary policy to put pressure on the government (Haggard, Maxfield, and Schneider, 1997).[2] But this pressure may not take the form of lobbying. As Evans (1995) notes, in many developing countries, employer organizations tend to be relatively unimportant players, and large firms prefer to use informal social networks and revolving doors between industry and government to influence policy.

Higher status for economics Ph.D.'s, especially in Latin America. In the 1980s and 1990s, U.S.-trained economists played a key role in liberalizing many developing economies, especially Latin American countries emerging from years of authoritarianism, protectionism, and statism (Valdés, 1995; Domínguez, 1997; Centeno and Silva, 1998; Dezalay and Garth, 2002). Neoliberal economists from Chicago, Harvard, and other elite schools served as presidents and economics ministers in Mexico, Argentina, and Chile, cutting budgets, lowering trade barriers, and fighting inflation. In fact, there were more holders of economics Ph.D.'s from elite U.S. universities running Latin American central banks than could be found on the Federal Open Market Committee itself. But the rise of technopols was not uniform: American educated Ph.D.'s found it easier to rise to the top in some countries, yet were nowhere to be found in others.[3] All this raises a question central banker biographical data is ideally suited to answer: Is appointing a central banker with a Ph.D. in economics from an American university the ticket to price stability?

2 For indirect evidence, see Clark (1993), who finds that CBI in developing countries is inversely correlated with labor and industry strength.

3 Schneider (1998) reviews a variety of possible pathways of technocratic success, including elite networking and pluralist competition, and argues that in part politicians appoint technocrats to signal credibility to international investors, a clear echo of Maxfield's argument.

More politicized central banks. Developing country central banks are stepping stones to political power. Countries in transition from communism in particular had porous boundaries between the central bank and government.[4] An incomplete list of developing country central bankers turned president or prime minister around the turn of the century includes Siim Kallas (Estonian prime minister, 2002 to 2003), Mugur Isarescu (Romanian prime minister, 1999 to 2000), Mekere Morauta (Papua New Guinean prime minister, 1999 to 2002), Einars Repse (Latvian prime minister, 2002 to 2004), Josef Tosovsky (Czech prime minister, 1997 to 1998), Guntis Ulmanis (Latvian president, 1993 to 1999), and Victor Yushchenko (Ukrainian prime minister, 1999 to 2001). Many other central bankers went on to be economics and finance ministers; most had entered the central bank with established political careers and party ties.[5]

4 The liberalization of Latin America pales in comparison to the transformation of the postcommunist states of Eastern Europe and Central Asia. The successor states faced the triple challenge of building new central banking institutions out of old command-economy monobanks, while liberalizing their economies and struggling to create new, often democratic, political orders. Unlike Latin American societies, post-Soviet countries lacked officials with expertise and experience in private banking, economics, or central banking. Instead, these central banks were dominated by former government officials and monobank managers. Nevertheless, these unlikely central bankers enthusiastically embraced the concept of central bank independence as a shield against critics and rivals (Johnson, 2002).

5 A few developing country central bankers also become involved in the darker side of politics. Khudayberdy Orazov, a former Turkmen central bank governor, fell out with his former boss, president-for-life Saparmurat Niyazov, and joined the opposition. Orazov paid a heavy price for standing up for "sound policy": Niyazov accused Orazov of embezzlement and attempted assassination. Convicted in absentia by a show trial, Orazov went into exile in Russia. He insisted the assassination attempt was staged, because he would know better than to try to gun down Niyazov's motorcade:

> Everyone in Turkmenistan knows that Niyazov's cars are invulnerable. When I was central bank chairman, we bought two cars – a Mercedes and a jeep – in Stuttgart specially for the president. They were already armoured, but they were sent to the Czech Republic for additional armour to be fitted. An additional 200,000 dollars was paid for each car. Even a grenade launcher could not pierce those cars now.

Orazov's successor was more pliant – some central bankers have more on their minds than getting prices right. (See "It wasn't me," *Central Bank Newsmakers*, London: Central Banking Publications, December 16, 2002; Agence France Presse, "Turkmenistan's Niyazov blames exiled opponents for assassination bid," November 26, 2002; "Turkmen central bank under a tyrant's rule," *Central Bank Newsmakers*, October 21, 2002; and Amnesty International, Urgent Action EUR 46/005/2003, January 2002.)

Legal Central Bank Independence in Developing Countries

The final difference between developing and developed world is familiar to any scholar of central banking: according to Cukierman, Webb, and Neyapti (1992), Campillo and Miron (1997), and others, legal CBI does not predict inflation performance in developing countries.[6] Cukierman, Webb, and Neyapti (1992) suppose that laws in developing countries tend to be poorly enforced, and separation of powers seldom respected, so that legal guarantees of central bank autonomy are not worth the paper they are printed on. Likewise, Acemoglu, Querubín, Johnson, and Robinson (2008) argue that central bank independence only reduces inflation in developing countries if other institutional constraints on governments are sufficiently strong to prevent them from undermining statutory independence. But is high inflation always an indication that are developing countries' institutions are "weak"? Perhaps we have misunderstood the aims of developing country central bankers. What if central bank independence has been put to purposes unanticipated by its developed world advocates?

Recent history in Peru and Russia shows that central bank independence can backfire when strong institutions combine with anti-conservative preferences. Peru's central bank gained greater autonomy from the government under a 1993 reform that included guaranteed terms for its seven directors.[7] Ten years later, four left-wing members of this board – holdovers from a less conservative government – used their protected positions to harass the central bank's more conservative governor, Richard Webb, firing his closest economic advisor, general manager, and other staff. A frustrated Webb resigned amid ironic calls from conservative members of the legislature for *less* central bank independence, as under existing law the four so-called "heterodox" central bankers could remain in place.[8] The government chose instead to name the finance minister, Javier

6 The literature, of course, is larger than this handful of studies, though most other papers consider a subset of the developing world. See Bodea and Popova (2004), who find CBI reduces inflation in former Communist countries that have become democratic.

7 Gould and Rosenbaum (1998) describe Peru's 1993 reforms. One ranking of central bank independence across fourteen Latin American countries considered Peru the second-most autonomous central bank (Jácome, 2001).

8 Several sources, including Webb, corroborate the infighting at the Peruvian central bank, which culminated in Webb's resignation on July 10, 2003. See Lucy Conger, "The ugly battle at Peru's central bank," *Institutional Investor*, August 2003; "'Upside-down world' in Peru," *Central Bank Newsmakers*, London: Central Banking Publications, July 28, 2003; and "Toledo's own goals," *The Economist*, May 17, 2003.

Silva Ruete, the new governor, assuaging international investors' concerns.[9] Nevertheless, the doves on the central bank board had shown they could make life unpleasant for an inflation hawk, precisely because they are independent of the (presently conservative) government.

Peru's misadventures with CBI pale compared to Russia's experience in the 1990s. Åslund (1995) pins the blame for Russian hyperinflation not on the machinations of the elected government – the usual villain in the CBI story – but on completely *independent* central bankers who even refused to accept the quantity theory of money and printed currency with abandon. Legal independence shielded the dangerously incompetent and corrupt head of the Central Bank of Russia, Victor Gerashchenko, from effective government oversight (Johnson, 1999).[10] As Johnson (2000) relates, at first the newly privatized Russian banks simply did not care about inflation because Gerashchenko gave the most important banks something better – large negative-interest loans, which they used to buy up state industries and become the pivot of the new Russian economy. They were kingmakers, too, funneling their gains back into politics to bankroll President Boris Yeltsin and other candidates.

Gerashchenko's role in this corrupt circle helped the man Jeffrey Sachs called the "world's worst central banker" cling to office far longer than his performance merited. Even Gerashchenko could not survive as head of the central bank after he allowed the ruble to fall 40 percent in a single day in 1994. Like many Russian politicians, he entered a revolving door between the state and the banking sector, resurfacing as chairman of a major Moscow bank (Johnson, 2000).[11] Despite his horrendous record, Gerashchenko returned to head the central bank in 1998. He didn't have another chance to engineer hyperinflation, though: a decline in the central bank's independence saw to that.

9 See "Peru Central Bank's President Richard Webb Resigns," Bloomberg, July 11, 2003; "Analysts' view on the Peruvian Economy," September 2003, ProInversión, www.proinversion.gob.pe, and Global Insight, "Monthly Outlook: Peru," December 2003, www.globalinsight.com.

10 Some contemporaneous western observers assumed the cause of Russian hyperinflation must be a shortsighted government overriding a prudent central bank. In fact, the central bank was so independent it introduced a new currency without so much as informing the finance ministry or parliament, and so anti-conservative as to print money pell-mell (Johnson, 2000).

11 Of course, Gerashchenko was already financially secure – he had earned higher salaries in office than his American counterpart, Alan Greenspan, and had embezzled untold sums, even diverting IMF money to an offshore account (Black, Kraakman, and Tarassova, 2000).

One way to read the experiences of Peru and Russia is that formal independence may not always lower inflation because agents need not use independence to that end. Independence and conservatism are *not* the same thing. In 1993, the Central Bank of Russia was independent, but as Russian finance minister Boris Fedorov put it, "[t]he problem with the Central Bank is that there are practically no central bankers over there" (quoted in Johnson, 2000, 64). The CBI prescription offered by so many western advisors relied not just on the right legal institutions, but on having the right sort of people, with the right interests and incentives, running the central bank – a *coincidence* of preference and autonomy (Johnson, 2002). But instead of recognizing the multiple uses of any real independence, the CBI literature has labored to explain the absence of a simple CBI–inflation link by questioning the effectiveness of *formal* independence in developing countries.

Central Banker Turnover: Behavioral Independence or Political Outcome?

With legal CBI seemingly irrelevant to developing country inflation performance, scholars constructed measures of "behavioral" independence, the most important being the rate of turnover of central bank governors. A number of studies find higher turnover rates of central bank governors to be correlated with higher inflation (Cukierman, Webb, and Neyapti, 1992; Cukierman, Kalaitzidakis, Summers, and Webb, 1993; de Haan and Kooi, 2000; Sturm and de Haan, 2001). Cukierman (1992) suggests the correlation between turnover and inflation is evidence that central bank governors are either dismissed for not giving in to government demands or resist these demands successfully and stay in office. If so, turnover would constitute a behavioral indicator of central bank independence.

Work in this literature assumes that governments are always less conservative than their central bankers, and that a central banker who manages to hang on has won the battle over monetary policy. Neither assumption necessarily holds. A governor may last because his preferences (hawkish *or* dovish) match those of the government, and he be fired because they do not. Tenure, an outcome of politics, captures more than just central banker independence or conservatism, and it certainly cannot distinguish various combinations of these two key characteristics.

Nor is this the only problem with the turnover proxy. In general, we should cautiously interpret the relationship between an official's performance and his tenure, because they are surely subject to reciprocal causation. Governors who perform well are likely to be invited to stay; those who disappoint – or fail to salvage crises – risk dismissal.[12] In this case, inflation is the cause of turnover, not the other way around.[13] This is especially likely under hawkish governments. That is, a correlation between central banker tenure and low inflation could occur precisely because of the dominance of central bank appointment by a conservative government, not because of greater "behavioral" independence. The correlation could also hold under liberal governments, which may fire central bankers who make less of economic conditions – in terms of both inflation and unemployment – than a more competent alternative agent would. (We return to the issue of central banker tenure in Chapter 9.)

Cukierman and others are aware of the difficulties in using turnover metrics to represent independence, but believe the variable retains some merit. Cukierman argues that "above some critical turnover rate CBI is lower the higher the turnover rate of CB governors" because "for sufficiently high turnover rates the tenure of the CB governor is shorter than that of the executive branch" (Cukierman, 1992, 385). In other words, above some level of turnover *k*, turnover is primarily result of central bankers resisting government demands and being sacked for it. Cukierman (1992) also performs Granger causality tests that purport to show turnover precedes inflation, not the reverse.[14] When I

12 A large literature in political economy considers whether electorates (or political principals generally) can sort out the competence of elected or appointed agents in the presence of random shocks to performance; see Rogoff and Sibert (1988), Rogoff (1990), Persson and Tabellini (2000, Ch. 4), and Drazen (2001, Ch. 7). So long as a principal thinks agent competence varies, *ceteris paribus* he will be tempted to take a new draw from the pool of prospective agents if he suspects the current agent is subpar. This logic surely applies to a central bank that is independent in the sense of Lohmann (1992). Suppose the government can only dismiss the central bank governor at substantial cost, and will only do so given a big economic shock, which, for the sake of argument, could include an unexpectedly incompetent central banker. Whether dismissal occurs because the agent is truly incompetent (that is, the cause of high inflation) or an unlucky bystander (there was a negative economic shock which the principal was unable to distinguish from agent incompetence), there obtains a correlation between turnover and inflation that has nothing to do with independence *per se*.

13 Cukierman and Webb (1995) and Cukierman et al. (1993) partially recognize this problem, noting that negative shocks may lead to changes in government which may in turn cause turnover in central banks, but their effort to isolate "non-political" turnover does not fully address the simultaneity problem raised here because it identifies only turnover after elections as politically induced.

14 Granger causality tests, of course, are not necessarily proofs of actual causality. Kevin Hoover (2001) describes the Granger causality test as a probabilistic version of *post hoc*

turn to empirical models of inflation, I consider the turnover hypothesis, but given the murky interpretation of this variable, it is just as well if the effect of our variables of interest are unchanged whether we control for turnover rates or not.

Career Effects in Developing Countries

Studies of developing country monetary institutions have reached a frustrating impasse. The institutions that "should" matter don't appear to make any difference. But the real barrier to understanding central bank institutions is the assumption that they are always used to the same ends by identically conservative central bankers. In borrowing this faulty assumption from the developed world, studies of developing country central banks have been stymied from the start.

We need to consider central banker preferences regardless of how the CBI debate turns out. If legal central bank constraints matter in developing countries, we should study the preferences of central bankers to understand how that autonomy is used (a point emphasized by Mas, 1995). If developing country institutions prove irrelevant, all the more reason to focus on the types of political actors actually making policy. As with industrial democracies, I argue we can understand central banker preferences by examining their career paths leading to the central bank.

The stereotype of the worried central banker perpetually spying inflation just around the corner does contain a grain of truth, but isn't the whole story. Central bankers may be more conservative on average than elected governments, but there is still variation among them – not every central banker is Paul Volcker. In this chapter, I show that central bankers in developing countries are as diverse as their first world colleagues, and that a reluctance to recognize and measure central banker diversity lies behind the failure to find reliable explanations for central bank behavior in these states. Once again, I use career variables – supplemented at times with educational histories – to explain this variation. Hopefully, readers do not doubt central bankers vary, but instead worry that they vary even more than occupational measures can convey.[15] Rather than

ergo propter hoc and points out the test mistakenly classifies as directly causally related any two variables with a common third cause.

15 The anecdotes related so far suggest that where institutions are underdeveloped or riven with corruption, the incentives and choices facing central bankers are more complex than the standard model suggests. Country studies of the politics of monetary policy

tackle all the motivations that may face central bankers, I will show the utility of career-based measures as a foundation for further work, although my formulation of career effects is surely not the last word.

As in rich democracies, I expect central bankers' career backgrounds to reveal two things: first, how *socialization* in a particular sector influences central bankers' *a priori* perceptions of appropriate monetary policy goals and strategies and second, how career paths create *incentives* to set policy according to a shadow principal's wishes in exchange for career advancement. We consider four types: the financier, the bureaucrat, the businessman, and the economist.

Private bankers. It is a fair first guess that most private bankers in developing countries are socialized to prefer low inflation and to see the task of central banking as resisting pressure to inflate. Meanwhile, former bankers' career incentives to produce low inflation may be quite strong; they may seek the favor of the international financial community and perhaps an important post in a multinational bank. But the assumption that developing country financial sectors have uniformly conservative monetary policy preferences is harder to sustain. National banking systems operating under hyperinflation often adapt to rapidly changing prices and may even come to prefer them; hence I focus on countries with "normal" inflation rates. A higher percentage of developing country banks are publicly-owned institutions, tasked to provide credit to the state rather than maximize profits. Therefore, I expect central bankers with *private*, but not public, financial experience to be associated with lower inflation.

---

can broaden our understanding of the pressures facing central bankers. See for instance Shih (2009), who examines the Chinese case. Shih argues a factional tug-of-war within the Chinese Communist Party creates an inflationary cycle. This is a different kind of career incentives theory, showing how unusual economic and political institutions can create different career effects. In China, members of factions with either provincial or central government bases have different preferences over money creation. To advance their faction – and their career within it – provincial bureaucrats seek decentralized monetary creation to increase the flow of capital to their province's enterprises. But decentralized printing of money quickly leads, through a prisoners' dilemma, to high inflation. This gives central government factions an excuse to recentralize money creation and simultaneously tighten their grip on macro-economic policy. But as soon as recentralization occurs, provincial factions begin pushing for more money creating power, and the cycle restarts. In an open economy, the pain of rapid inflation would be enough to convince political actors to solve this problem once and for all; the ruble zone collapsed in the early 1990s under similar pressures. But capital controls allow China's inflationary cycle to persist without capital flight.

Government bureaucrats. Career bureaucrats appointed to the monetary policy board are likely to want to continue their political careers, and getting the next appointment depends on pleasing the government and ensuring its survival. Satisfying the government usually means supporting easy money to stimulate the economy, in opposition to the preferences of more conservative financial sector types. To the extent a civil servant has little economic policy experience, once on the central bank he is more likely to be reliant on political patrons' instructions – and thus more dovish than financiers. But bureaucrats with the expertise to choose their own policies – finance ministry or central bank staff promoted to the board – may be a middling category, not as liberal as other bureaucrats, but not as conservative as financial sector appointees. This is even more likely if these staff enjoy some prospect of a financial sector job after their central bank rotation – a reward made possible by their greater expertise and opportunities to forge relationships with private financial actors.

Representatives of the real economy. Firms in the real sector of the economy are likely to be the most consistently dovish actors on inflation, but in the industrialized world, the large number of firms and high cost of lobbying make business pressure on monetary policy weak. In developed countries, business representatives on central bank boards – few as they are – are unlikely to see any career rewards for making dovish policy choices. But in smaller economies with bigger conglomerates, it would not be surprising to find firms willing to cultivate or reward central bank members who vote for easy credit; such firms could do no better than to put their own employees on the policy board. Therefore, I expect business experience to be correlated with higher inflation in developing countries (Evans, 1995; Haggard, Maxfield, and Schneider, 1997).

Economists. In industrialized countries, we found that economists were too diverse to make useful general predictions about their monetary policy behavior. The same holds for developing countries, whose central banker economists range from graduates of Soviet universities – where even the word "price" was politically incorrect – to neo-liberal Chicago Ph.D.'s. A more useful way to look at economics experience may be to consider the country where the Ph.D. was granted. I entertain the simple hypothesis is that holders of U.S. economics Ph.D.'s are more conservative on monetary policy.

Data

This chapter combines original data on developing country central bankers with existing measures of political institutions and economic performance. Our first empirical task is to discover what developing country central bankers' careers and educational histories look like.

Central Banker Career Data

To construct experience scores for developing country bankers, I again sought out career histories from the central banks themselves, internet resources, and biographical dictionaries. Unfortunately, complete biographical data for developing world officials is difficult to collect. Thus, while I gathered data on central bankers with monetary policy authority from 110 countries (see Table 5.5 at the end of the chapter), of these, only 31 had time series long enough for meaningful time series cross-section analysis. I call these countries, scattered all over the world, the "long series" sample.[16]

As with central bankers of developed countries, I classify the jobs held over a central banker's career into six mutually exclusive and exhaustive categories: Financial (private banking jobs), Government (bureaucrats outside the central bank and finance ministry), Finance Ministry (bureaucrats in the finance ministry), Central Bank (staffers at the central bank), Economics (academic economists), Business, and Other (international organization officials and staff, other academics, labor union organizers, journalists, and so on).[17] To create aggregate measures of career experience for an entire central bank board, I again simply average (with weights for the portion of the period served) the career experiences of all central bankers who, by virtue of their positions, appear to have significant influence on monetary policy.[18] Where it is possible to com-

16 The countries in the long series sample are Argentina, Barbados, Bulgaria, Chile, Croatia, Cyprus, Czech Republic, Estonia, Israel, Jamaica, Jordan, Kazakhstan, Kuwait, Latvia, Lesotho, Lithuania, Maldives, Mexico, Netherlands Antilles, Philippines, Poland, Romania, Russia, Samoa, Slovenia, South Africa, Thailand, Tonga, Trinidad and Tobago, Uganda, and Venezuela.

17 As with the industrial democracy cases, I made substantial efforts to include only privately owned and operated financial firms in the Financial category. As before, state-run banks face different incentives, and most individuals in the dataset who took a turn at such banks were career bureaucrats, not bankers. Once again, I include management of government-controlled banks in the Government category.

18 I relied on Fry et al. (2000), Siklos (2002), and country sources to determine which officials enjoyed *de jure* monetary policy making authority.

bine central banker characteristics into a single index, I summarize the institution's characteristics by its tenure-weighted median member. Otherwise, when multiple variables are needed to summarize central banker's preferences, I use tenure-weighted means.

Looking at the average experience scores of central bankers across time and space gives a good first impression of the data. Recall that experience scores measure experience over the career, so that when we say "the average financial sector career experience of all central bankers was 0.11," we mean that 11 percent of the average central bankers' career was in finance, not that only eleven percent of central bankers ever worked in a private bank. (The "ever worked" figure is higher to the extent careers are heterogenous.) Figure 5.1 presents the global average of experience scores across countries and time for six different groupings of central banks, constituting our broadest summary of central bankers origins.

Studying the first three plots, it appears the types of central bankers appointed in the developing world are similar to those in the industrial countries.[19] In the full 107 country developing country dataset, about 40 percent of central bankers' career experience prior to appointment was in state bureaucracies, a somewhat higher proportion than seen in the developed world, but in either context the most common category by far. In developing countries, fewer bureaucrats – indeed, only half as many – punched their tickets in the finance ministry, but in the remaining categories of central bank staff, economics, and business, developing country central bankers have résumés remarkably similar to their industrial colleagues. As before, private financiers are a distinct minority, with only 11 percent of career experience. The percentage of central bankers who ever worked in finance is also a minority (29 percent).

As in developed countries, the prior career tracks of developing country central bankers frame the possibility of a revolving door. Most (61 percent) gained all their prior experience in a single sector. The average developing country central banker was 47.8 years old on appointment (the same age as in the developed world) and could expect to serve an average of 4.96 years at the central bank (slightly less than the average developed country central banker). Considering this, it seems likely that many would seek to keep ties to the old sector strong, as the most likely next career destination.

19 As in the industrialized world, central bankers in developing countries are overwhelmingly male: in our sample, men account for 93 percent of officials with monetary policy authority.

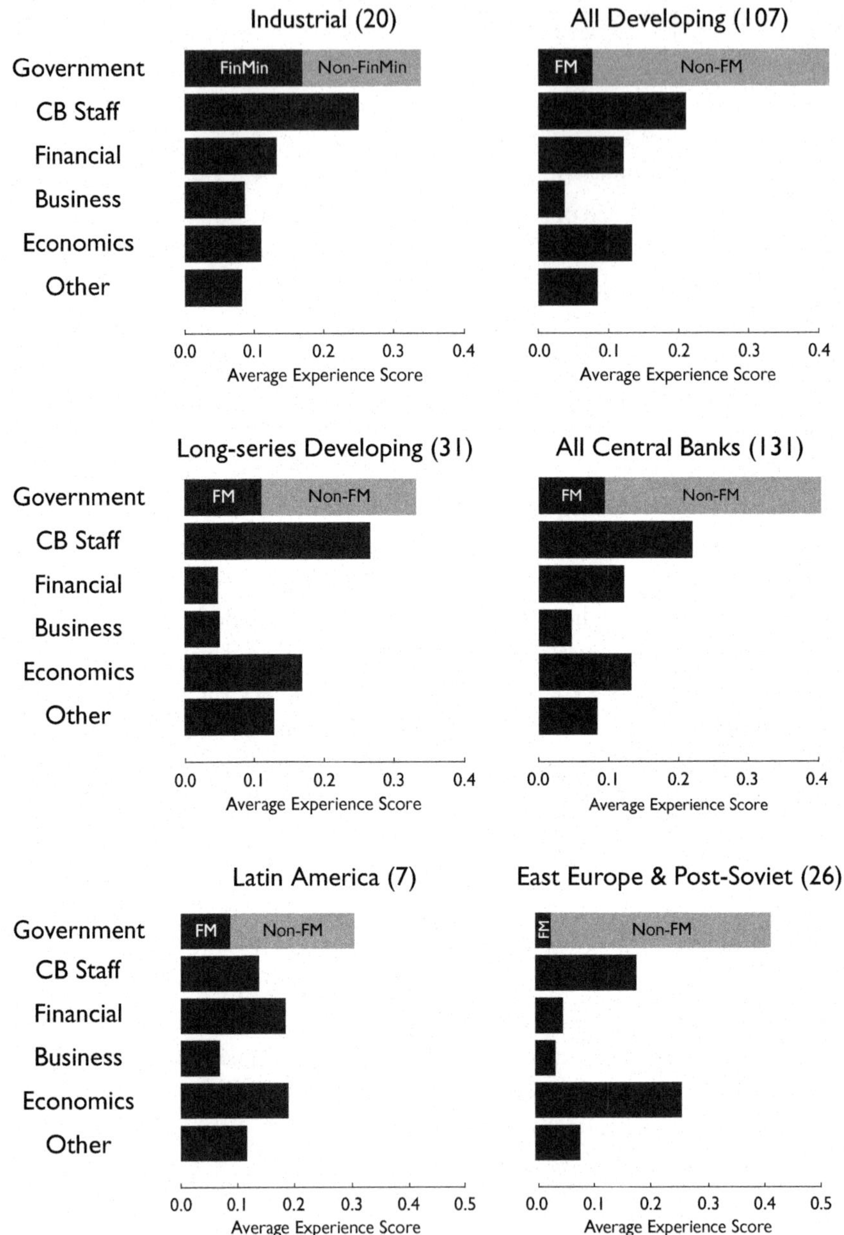

Industrial (20)
All Developing (107)
Long-series Developing (31)
All Central Banks (131)
Latin America (7)
East Europe & Post-Soviet (26)
Government
CB Staff
Financial
Business
Economics
Other
FinMin
Non-FinMin
FM
Non-FM
0.0
0.1
0.2
0.3
0.4
0.5
Average Experience Score

Figure 5.1. *Average composition of central banker backgrounds, 1973 to 2003.* Career experience is the fraction of a central banker's prior career spent in a job type, averaged across a central bank's monetary policy makers. These plots show how the average career experience varies across samples of central banks. In large part, the career makeup of central bankers is similar around the world and largely consists of backgrounds in the bureaucracy, central bank, private banking sector, economics, and business. The number of countries in each sample is indicated in parentheses.

Some regional differences are worth noting. Compared to the world average, Latin American central bankers have more experience in finance and economics and less bureaucratic exposure. The transition countries of Eastern Europe and the former Soviet republics, on the other hand, have far fewer financiers and many more (Soviet-trained) economists.[20] Still, the differences across regions are well accommodated by the career typology: in no case is the "other" category noticeably larger than ten percent.

Central Banker Education Data

I collected data on the education of central bankers throughout the developing world with a focus on economics training, which I measure as possession of an advanced degree (a masters, a doctorate, or their equivalents). These data are summarized in Figure 5.2 and Table 5.1. Overall, a similar fraction of OECD and developing country central bankers have Ph.D.'s (about 20 percent) and M.A.'s (an additional 20 percent). The origins of these degrees differ somewhat: 83 percent of central bankers in developed countries obtained their degrees from own-country universities, compared to 70 percent of developing country central bankers and only half of "long series" central bankers. In particular, Latin American central bankers overwhelming held North American economics degrees and received them from a handful of elite schools, especially Chicago, Columbia, and Harvard. At the other extreme are central bankers in transition countries, who included few Western-trained economists.

20 I treat pre-transition service in the massive state monobanks as non-finance ministry government work, and I code post-transition work in the central bank as central bank staff experience. There is little reason to suspect communist monobank experience compares to central bank or finance ministry work in a capitalist economy.

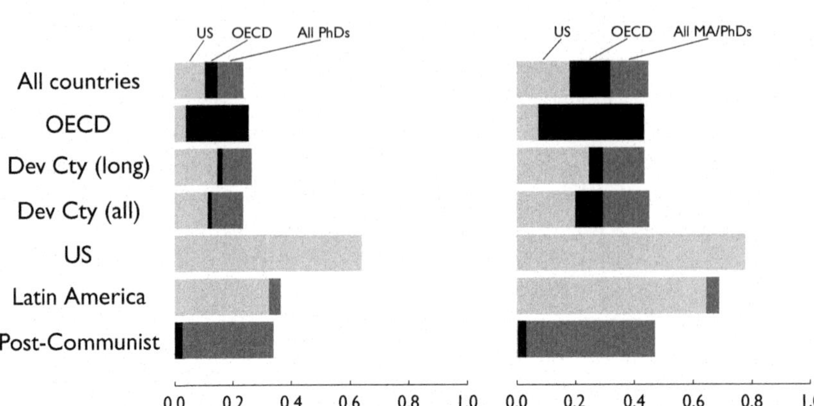

Figure 5.2. *Economics Ph.D.s among central bankers, 1973 to 2003.* Bars stack cumulatively from left to right: the lightly shaded first bar indicates U.S. degrees, the darkly shaded second bar indicates all other OECD degrees, and the medium-shaded final bar indicates all non-OECD degrees. Central bankers holding the same degree from several origins (for example, multiple masters in economics from the United States and some other OECD country) are included in the left-most eligible category only (in this example, the United States). Honorary degrees are not included.

Other Variables

Central bank independence. The central bank independence index with by far the best coverage among developing countries is the Cukierman, Webb, and Neyapti (1992) index, which CWN coded through 1989. Maxfield (1997) updates the index through 1994 for all of CWN's countries, and Cukierman, Miller, and Neyapti (2001) update it through 2000 for the former Soviet bloc countries.[21] In this chapter, I refer to this index simply as CBI.

Central banker turnover. Most studies that consider the effect of central bank governor turnover on inflation regress decade-average inflation on decade-average

21 Where Cukierman, Miller, and Neyapti's coding disagrees with Maxfield's, I use the former. Lacking updates for central bank reforms outside the transition economies over 1995 to 2000, I assume that previous institutions remained in place, which is correct for a large fraction but surely not all of the observations. Post-2000 observations are treated as missing.

Table 5.1. *Central bankers' economics education, by country group, 1973 to 2003.*

All figures are lower bounds Country	% of CBers with adv econ degree	% of these with own country degree	No. of sources of highest econ degree	Most common schools granting highest advanced economic degree (number of degree-holders)
Industrial countries	30%	83%	80	LSE (10), MIT (7)
All developing	45	70	96	Columbia (8), LSE (7)
Long-series develop	48	49	48	Columbia (8), LSE (6)
Latin America	46	40	14	Chicago (5), Buen. Aires (3)
East Eur/Post-Sov	49	83	37	Prague Sch. Ec. (6), Sofia (5)
All central banks	37	62	158	LSE (18), Columbia (13)

Advanced degrees include M.A.'s, Ph.D.'s, and their equivalents.

turnover, which leaves the direction of causality in doubt, especially because the turnover in question could temporally follow the inflation. To mitigate this problem, I control for the average annual changes in governor over the preceding five (or ten) years, which I denote TO^k. For example, if we observe $\text{TO}^5 = 0.4$ in 1988, the central bank in question had $5 \times 0.4 = 2$ changes in governor over the years 1983 to 1987. Central bank turnover data is constructed from the central bank biographical dataset and supplemented with data from Sturm and de Haan (2001).

Economic variables. I obtained most quarterly economic data – imports, consumer prices indexes used to calculate inflation, and gross domestic product – from the IMF's International Financial Statistics. I obtained annual data on gross government debt from the World Bank's World Development Indicators. Using these data, I construct quarterly inflation rates for each country, denoted π; quarterly averages of inflation for the G7 countries, which I call π^{world}; a measure of economic openness, Imports/GDP; and a measure of government indebtedness, Debt/GDP.

Political Instability. Violent political instability is likely to increase inflation by reducing the ability and incentives of politicians to commit to low inflation (Campillo and Miron, 1997). I construct a measure of instability based on the number of assassinations, *coups d'etat*, general strikes, anti-government demonstrations, purges, and civil wars observed in each country in a given year. The data are drawn from Arthur Banks' Cross-National Dataset (Banks, 2004). Because the desired covariate is the latent instability in the country, I calculate the first principal component of these counts, and name this variable Chaos.

Methods

Estimation

Throughout the rest of this chapter, I analyze the relationship between inflation and central banker careers using time series cross-section regressions. I estimate these models by least squares and apply a correction for country-level heteroskedasticity to the variance-covariance matrix of parameters (Beck and Katz, 1995). The model follows the form of the time series cross-section models of Chapter 3. This modeling strategy places a few constraints on the data. First, the covariates of interest must be time-varying (because of the fixed effects) and second, the time series involved must have some overlap (to allow us to calculate panel-corrected standard errors). Because the variables of greatest interest – the careers of individual central bankers – naturally vary as central bankers are replaced, the first constraint is not too onerous. However, we are limited to series long enough to contain multiple central bank boards; otherwise, we cannot separate the effects of the people in power from the effects of the institutions they work within. This restricts us to 31 "long series" available in the developing country portion of the central banker database. Moreover, fewer countries may be available for particular regressions, depending on the controls added. I run multiple specification adding different controls in turn and show that in general the effects of key variables of interest remain unchanged.

To reduce causal heterogeneity, I exclude quarters in which hyperinflation occurs (defined, arbitrarily, as inflation above 50 percent). The conditions that set off hyperinflation are not necessarily the same as those that cause variation at more ordinary levels; likewise, the behavior of central bankers under hyperinflation may be very different. If we include hyperinflation cases, even with inflation logged, the hyper-inflation/ordinary-inflation divide dominates the analysis, masking the effects of careers on "normal" inflation policy and making comparisons with the developed world impossible. The decision to exclude hyperinflation cases is consistent with past work finding the effect of CBI depends on the range of inflation in the sample (Temple, 1998). See the Data Appendix for discussion and a sensitivity analysis.

As in Chapter 3, the inclusion of compositional data in the regression model complicates interpretation of the regression coefficients. Because the career components must always sum to one, a change in any one experience score necessarily changes the others. As a result, the effects of a particular career type work through not one but *all* of the career parameters, so we cannot interpret the coefficients as marginal effects – not even the signs of these parameters can be taken at face value. In practice, it is easiest to see career effects by calculating the expected value of inflation under different hypothetical career combinations, in which we increase one component while lowering all others proportionally (see the Methods Appendix to Chapter 3).

Inflation Results

Although the empirical link between CBI and inflation is widely celebrated, it is not particularly robust. It fails to extend beyond the industrialized world and even within that context is sensitive to minor changes in specification (Cukierman, Webb, and Neyapti, 1992; Campillo and Miron, 1997). In this chapter, I show that career-based measures of central bank behavior are more robust and portable. To help the reader digest results from numerous samples and model specifications, I present all findings using comparable quantities of interest: the effect of a one standard deviation change in the career backgrounds of central bankers on the change in inflation, measured over time. Although the results differ from those obtained in Chapter 3 for the developed world in several expected ways, they share many points of agreement and show once again the utility of the career effects approach for exploring the interaction of agents and institutions. In the end, by looking to agent preferences, we may even help rehabilitate the study of developing world central bank institutions.

Career Conservatism and Inflation: A First Cut

I start by regressing the natural log of quarterly inflation on the average experience scores of the central bank board for the entire 31 country long sample. I control for country fixed effects, political instability, the average level of inflation in the world's largest economies, and two lags of the dependent variable. The controls have reasonable effects: political instability and world inflation positively correlate with domestic inflation (see Table 5.2, Model 1 in the Data Appendix). The ordering of the career effects on inflation is essentially as expected: financial experience depresses inflation the most, and business experience the least, with the other types arrayed in between. However, *all* of the estimated coefficients are negative. Do all of these types actually reduce inflation? Or is the compositional constraint misleading us?

Treating coefficients of compositional variables as marginal effects is dangerous because it ignores the compositional constraint. A +0.1 increase in one compositional covariate mandates a collective −0.1 decrease in some combination of the remaining components, some of which may also be regressors. I show in the Methods Appendix to Chapter 3 that the best way to express the effects of compositional covariates is to calculate ratio-preserving counterfactuals (RCPFs), which raise one component while reducing all other components in proportion to their *ex ante* levels.

In this case, RPCFs show the coefficients are indeed misleading (Figure 5.3). Whereas a one standard deviation increase in either financial or finance ministry experience suppresses inflation by about one point, a similar increase in business types on the monetary policy board actually raises inflation by the same amount. Both results are statistically significant. On the other hand, appointing other bureaucrats, central bank staff, or economists leaves inflation unchanged, placing these types between the finance and business extremes.

Compared to other variables in the literature, career experience scores turn out to be decidedly robust. Controlling for CBI – which, as others have found, has no significant *direct* effect on inflation – careers have essentially the same effects (Table 5.2, Model 2). Indeed, careers maintain their potency when we control for both legal CBI and observed central bank governor turnover over the previous five years (Table 5.2, Model 4). (We return to the relationship between turnover and inflation in Chapter 9, focusing on the developed world sample.) Finally, we check whether the educational background of central bankers matters. Controlling for career experience, it made no difference what percentage of central bankers had Ph.D.'s in economics from an American university (Table 5.3, Model 6), nor did it matter how many central bankers had Ph.D.'s from OECD countries, Ph.D.'s of any origin, or even any advanced degree in economics. For the full long series developing country sample, central bankers' economics training is simply too diverse to tell us anything systematic about their monetary policy views.

To gain a better perspective on the relative effects of career experience in developing country central banks, it helps to recall their effects in industrial democracies. We can compare the impact on inflation of a one standard deviation increases in each career type using estimates from Chapter 3 and the present chapter's Model 2. The left panel of Figure 5.4 places these first differences side by side. Before interpreting this comparison, however, recall the compositional constraint that governs these career scores: all central bankers must be of *some* type, so the effects of each type can only be judged relative to each other. We can compare the relative order of career effects across samples, but we cannot put them on an absolute underlying scale. For example, even if all OECD central bankers favored price stability and all developing country central bankers favored rising inflation, there must be relative doves and relative hawks in each case. Put another way, a central banker who looks relatively dovish among the OECD cohort may find himself in the middle of the developing country scale. Without a frame of reference, the question of whether he is "truly" a dove is ill-posed.

With the subtleties of compositional covariates in mind, we find the order of career effects is basically similar in the developed and developing countries, with one anticipated exception. Businessmen, who were neutral in advanced industrial democracies, lie at the inflationary end of the spectrum in developing countries, where business pressure on monetary policy is more likely. The contrasting behavior of business representatives has a side effect: non-finance ministry bureaucrats, strongly inflationary in the developed world, now lie in the middle range of developing country types between the two poles of financial and business types. Of course, this doesn't necessarily imply that developing country bureaucrats are more hawkish than OECD bureaucrats (they likely aren't); only that they fall in a different relative position within the scale of career types, compared to the more inflationary stance of business veterans.

Once again, it is useful to create an index summarizing the effect of careers on inflation. In the developed world, the index CBCC = FinExp + FMExp − GovExp − CBExp served to measure overall career conservatism. For developing countries, where financial and business experience have equal and opposite effects, a more appropriate index of Central Banker Conservatism in Developing Countries (CBCD) is given by

$$\text{CBCD} = \text{FinExp} + \text{FMExp} - \text{BusExp}. \tag{5.1}$$

As the right panel of Figure 5.4 shows, CBCD is a broadened version of CBCC, expanded to include the inflationary effect of business in the smaller, more concentrated economies of the developing world.

Including the median level of CBCD in a regression with CBI, we find that a one standard deviation increase in CBCD lowers inflation by about one point after two years. Controlling for CBCD, legal CBI has no significant effect (Table 5.3, Model 5; and the bottom row of Figure 5.3). I return to these two indexes at the close of this chapter to explore their potential interactive effects.

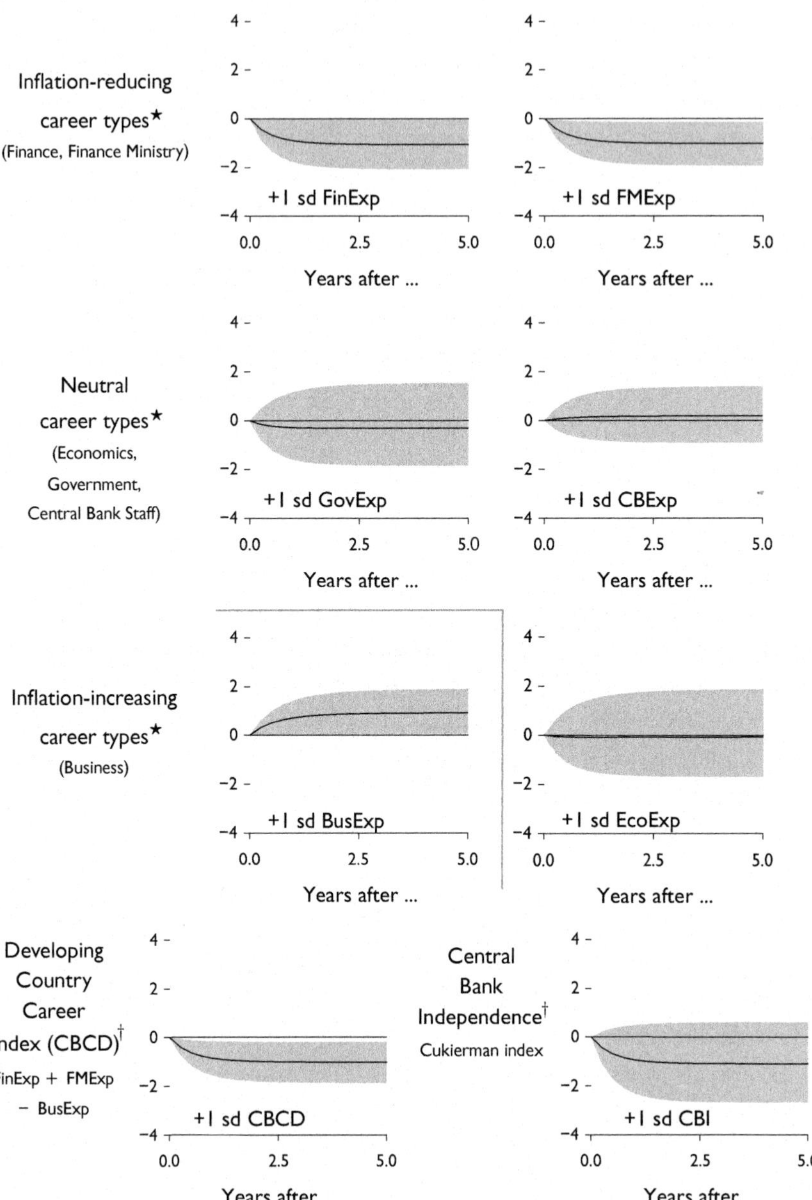

Change in inflation, over time, from changing career composition of the central bank
Inflation-reducing career types★ (Finance, Finance Ministry)
+1 sd FinExp
+1 sd FMExp
Neutral career types★ (Economics, Government, Central Bank Staff)
+1 sd GovExp
+1 sd CBExp
Inflation-increasing career types★ (Business)
+1 sd BusExp
+1 sd EcoExp
Developing Country Career Index (CBCD)†
FinExp + FMExp − BusExp
+1 sd CBCD
Central Bank Independence†
Cukierman index
+1 sd CBI
Years after ...
4
2
0
-2
-4
0.0
2.5
5.0

Figure 5.3. *Additive effects of individuals and institutions on inflation, developing country sample (facing page).* Change in inflation following a permanent one standard deviation increase in a career type, the career characteristics index for developing countries (CBCD), or central bank independence (CBI). Each solid line is a separate counterfactual; the first six plots summarize Model 2, while the final two summarize Model 5. In the first six plots, when one experience score is increased, all other experience scores are reduced proportionately from their means to maintain a sum of one. Initial lags are set at the mean observed inflation rate. All plots show expected values as solid lines and mark 90 percent confidence intervals in gray. These intervals reflect the cumulative estimation uncertainty produced by iterating the model through twenty periods. *Counterfactuals from Model 2. †Counterfactuals from Model 5.

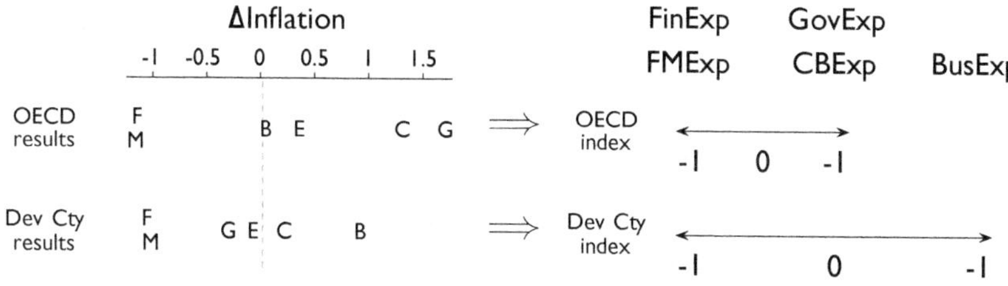

Figure 5.4. *Comparing career effects and career indexes for the industrial and developed worlds.* For the OECD and developing country samples, the left panel shows the estimated change in inflation two years after a one standard deviation increase in the central bank board average career experience in each of six career types. F stands for financial experience, M for finance ministry, B for business, E for economics, C for central bank staff, and G for other government. The right panel translates these findings into appropriate career indexes summarizing the career conservatism of central banks in a single number.

Robustness checks and regional differences

I check the robustness of the findings in three ways, examining alternative *estimators*, *specifications*, and *samples*. To make it as easy as possible to assess the robustness of the results under alternative models, I construct a series of ropeladder plots showing the two-year first difference and its 90 percent confidence interval for a one standard deviation increase in each explanatory variable of interest (Figure 5.5, and see Box 3.2 for a discussion of ropeladder plots). These plots show clearly in a single page what we could otherwise only vaguely discern across several pages of regression tables. Simply put, if we look up and down these plots and see an unswaying ladder, we can conclude the results are robust. In particular, we want to know the range in which the various estimates lie (shaded as a gray box); the narrower this region, the better.

Alternative estimators. To complement the least squares estimates, I consider two alternative estimation techniques: the Cochrane-Orcutt transformation and robust estimation.

Cochrane-Orcutt corrects for the mild but statistically significant degree of serial correlation in the errors of the least squares models revealed by Lagrange multiplier tests. Serial correlation can threaten the consistency of estimates in a time series cross-section regression that includes lags of the dependent variable, but in practice its effects are often negligible (Beck, 2001; Keele and Kelly, 2006). Fortunately, the present analysis appears to be a benign case: the Cochrane-Orcutt transformation eliminates serial correlation and still yields similar results to the untransformed models (compare the first and second rows in Figure 5.5 or Models 2 and 3 in Table 5.2). The only difference is that business experience is no longer significant though its magnitude remains the same. The overall index remains clearly significant and associated with lower inflation.

The second approach is robust estimation (using an M-estimator) to reduce the effect of any outliers in the data.[22] Once again, our initial results are largely confirmed. The effect of financial experience appears muted in this regression, but the effect of the overall index remains steady and highly significant.

Alternative specifications. Returning to the original estimator (least squares with panel-corrected standard errors), I now consider a variety of alternative controls. Because these controls are available for different sets of countries, we enter

22 Robust estimation can reduce bias in the presence of outliers but carries efficiency costs. The robust estimator employed here uses a Huber influence function to downweight observations with large residuals.

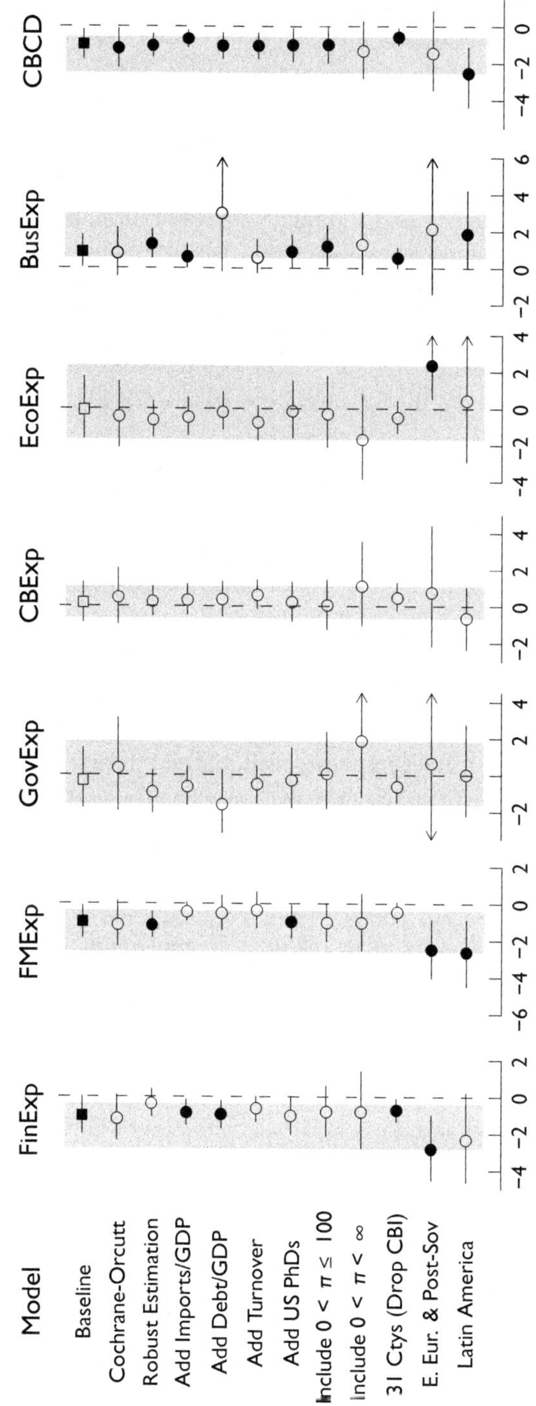

Figure 5.5. *The career-inflation link in developing countries under alternative estimators, specifications, and samples.* Each plot shows the two-year first difference in inflation resulting from a one standard deviation increase in a career variable (FinExp, GovExp, and so on), using the estimator, specification, or sample noted at left. See the text for a description of the baseline model and alternatives. Circles and squares indicate point estimates of the first difference, and horizontal lines 90 percent confidence intervals. The results marked with a square are the same as those used in Figure 5.3. The shaded areas highlight the range of point estimates across all alternatives. Arrows indicate confidence intervals that extend outside the plotted range.

them *seriatim* into the model to reduce the loss of observations through listwise deletion. These controls are trade openness (measured as Imports/GDP) and gross government debt (also measured as a fraction of GDP), both of which should increase the benefits of inflation to the government (Romer, 1993; Lane, 1997; Campillo and Miron, 1997; Temple, 2002); central banker turnover (annual rate over the previous five years); and the fraction of central bankers with Ph.D.'s in economics from an American university. Turnover is correlated with higher inflation (though the arrow of causation is unclear), as is higher government debt (an extra 10 percentage points of debt is associated with 0.76 points more inflation, with a confidence interval of 0.25 to 1.30, when all other variables are held at the means). On the other hand, neither economically trained central bankers nor trade openness seem to matter.

Controlling for these variables does not, for the most part, mute our initial findings of career effects. Regardless of specification, the career conservatism index remains significantly associated with lower inflation. A few components are more sensitive; for example, the effect of business experience is much less precisely estimated when debt is controlled. But when one considers that the set of countries in each robustness check differs somewhat, the career effects seem rather stable across these different models.

Alternative sampling schemes. Career hypotheses should fail during hyperinflation, both because the goals of shadow principals may change, and because we do not expect career types to explain the occurrence of this pathological outcome. It is no surprise that including hyperinflation cases is the one robustness check that definitely "breaks" the career theory. Nevertheless, the results remain similar when we include cases up to 100 percent annual inflation. Only if we include all cases, even those with inflation in the 10,000 percent range, do our results become non-significant (though they are still properly signed; see the Data Appendix for more details).

I also investigated the effects of careers and education in two subsamples: Latin American central banks and the transition economies of Eastern Europe and the former Soviet Union.[23] Results for both regions were largely consistent

23 The Latin American countries included in this sample are Argentina, Brazil, Chile, Mexico, and Venezuela. The transition economies included are Albania, Armenia, Azerbaijan, Bulgaria, Croatia, Czech Republic, Estonia, Georgia, Hungary, Kazakhstan, Kyrgyz Republic, Latvia, Lithuania, Moldova, Poland, Romania, Russia, Slovakia, Slovenia, and Ukraine. Countries are included solely on the basis of data availability.

with the full sample, raising our confidence that we have identified career effects that are largely consistent from country to country.

There are three exceptional findings worth highlighting. First, businesspeople on the central bank exerted more inflationary pressure in Latin America than elsewhere, consistent with the hypothesis that business pressure for loose money is more effective when domestic industry is concentrated in fewer hands. Second, Soviet-bloc-trained economists in transition central banks were associated with substantially higher inflation; elsewhere in the world, economics experience is neutral on average.

Finally, while holding an economics Ph.D.'s made little difference in the OECD or developing country full samples, U.S. Ph.D.'s (but not Ph.D.'s from other regions) did correlate with lower inflation in Latin America. When the percentage of board members holding Ph.D.'s from American economics departments increased from its mean (31 percent) to one standard deviation above the mean (77 percent), inflation fell by 2.4 points over two years, although the confidence interval of the difference includes zero [90% CI: −4.9, 0.2]. This is about the same effect as a one standard deviation increase in career conservatism in the Latin American sample. In no other sample did economic degrees correlate with inflation performance. Taken together, these findings suggest that in most of the world, the economics training central bankers bring to monetary policy is too diverse to tell us much about how they will behave, but that in Latin America, where many central bankers have very similar economics training, the stereotype of the neo-liberal economist–central-banker may capture some of the truth.

Career Effects on Inflation in Institutional Context

Peru and Russia illustrate a central claim of this book: granting bureaucratic agents legal independence leads to different policy outcomes depending on agents' preferences. Overlooking this obvious point, past research on central banks has generally assumed that an independent central bank must, *ipso facto*, be a conservative one. Researchers studying developing country central banks have been puzzled to find no correlation between the legal independence of those institutions from governments and inflation. But there is no puzzle. Instead, there are several different kinds of central bankers in the developing world who, given independence, naturally pursue different policy goals.

To test the proposition that independence and preferences interactively shape inflation outcomes, I add an interactive term, CBCD × CBI, to the model

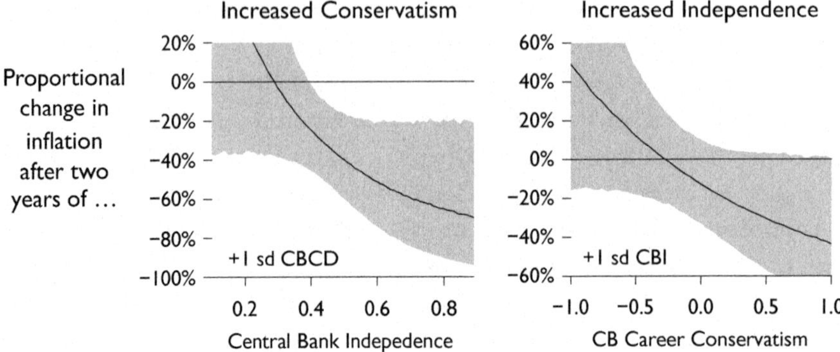

Figure 5.6. *Inflation as a function of careers and independence: Interactive results.* The left plot shows the percent reduction in inflation after a one standard deviation increase in central bankers' career conservatism, across the observed range of CBI. The right plot shows the percent reduction in inflation after a one standard deviation increase in independence, over the range of conservatism. Gray shading indicates the 90 percent confidence interval. Both plots are calculated from the estimated Model 7 in Table 5.3.

(see Model 7, Table 5.3, in the Data Appendix). This model allows the effect of changes in either central bank independence or the central banker career conservatism index to be mutually contingent. The estimated coefficients fit exactly with our theoretical expectations: independence does not appear to matter, except through the conduit of agent preferences.

We can most easily understand the interactive effects of conservatism and independence by calculating expected inflation under various combinations of each. I focus on proportional changes in inflation to simplify comparisons across different starting conditions.[24] The left plot in Figure 5.6 shows the change in inflation (on the vertical axis) two years after an increase in conservatism, given different levels of legal independence (covering the range observed in the data; shown on the horizontal axis). Conservatism has different effects in different institutional contexts. When the central bank has little legal independence from

24 In our time series cross-section model, the starting conditions (the status quo *ex ante*) affect the size of the first difference in two ways. First, the starting conditions enter the right-hand side of the model through the lag terms. Second, the dependent variable is logged, so on a linear scale, a unit change in a covariate has a bigger impact on inflation when inflation starts out at a high level. Looking at proportional changes in the dependent variable helps take into account both features of the model.

the government, switching from one kind of central banker to another makes no difference for inflation. But when the central bank has substantial legal independence, the type of central banker matters a great deal. At the highest observed levels of CBI, a one standard deviation increase in central banker conservatism is enough to cut the inflation rate by two-thirds.

Now we consider what happens when we increase independence, holding fixed the career conservatism of the central bank board. The right panel of Figure 5.6 shows inflation falls by as much as 40 percent of its existing level when independence rises, but only if the central bank board is conservative. Likewise, when a more liberal board is granted more autonomy, inflation may rise by a similar amount. Though large, neither effect is quite statistically significant. However, under stronger assumptions about the nature of this interaction, we do see a statistically significant difference between the inflation performance of independent liberals and independent conservatives (Model 8, Table 5.3).[25]

Past work explored central banks' legal independence while ignoring the preferences of officials entrusted with that independence. The evidence here suggests that monetary policy agents' autonomy and interests are inextricably linked. Preferences and institutions interact, limiting our ability to study each in isolation.

Conclusions

A major argument of this book is that central bankers' behavior can be understood by looking at the effect of career paths on policy preferences. In Chapters 3 and 4, I show the career effects approach could explain each step of the monetary policy making process in industrialized countries. Although the central banks of the developing world often resist systematic study, in this chapter I found that we can place a common career-based foundation under studies of central banks around the world. Moreover, this foundation is a flexible one, as the economic and political structure of particular countries may alter our intuition about how career effects work in context.

25 Note that the uninteracted terms CBCD and CBI are indistinguishable from zero. If we are willing to assume these parameters really *are* zero, we can respecify the model to obtain a more precise estimate of the interaction of CBI and CBCD. That is, assuming the effect of the career index is nil when CBI is zero, and the effect of CBI is nil when the career index is zero, we obtain an interaction between the two that is significant at the 95 percent level

Finally, I find that the legal independence of developing country central banks may matter after all, but because independence can be put to conservative or liberal uses, we can only understand its role by accounting for the interaction of career conservatism and independence. But intuitive estimates of this interaction in the developing world remind us of the puzzling anomaly in Chapter 4, that no such interaction appeared in the industrialized world. In the next chapter, I return to this puzzle, taking a closer look at what we mean by central bank independence.

Data Appendix to Chapter 5

Hyperinflation sensitivity analysis

Figure 5.7 shows the distribution of logged inflation in less developed countries (specifically, the observations included in the long-series regressions). Unlike the developed countries, there are many quarters of hyperinflation in the data, causing a bulge of inflation cases over 50 percent per year. This mars the Normality of the distribution – there are instances of inflation as high as 18,000 percent. The distribution appears to mix two data generating processes, one for countries in the normal range of inflation and another for countries caught in hyperinflation. There is no reason to think the causal mechanisms relating politics and inflation performance are the same in each process. How hyperinflation starts, how far it goes, and how it ends in one country are all different questions from why inflation varies between five in fifteen percent in another. In particular, career concerns that may tell the difference between a hawkish or dovish policy within the normal range of inflation performance and expectations do not clearly translate to hyperinflationary contexts. In the extreme, banks may adapt to hyperinflation and governments may rue it, reversing the usual order of inflation preferences.

Including hyperinflation in the sample analyzed risks introducing causal heterogeneity, producing estimates that inappropriately pool over different contexts. Because hyperinflation cases have high leverage, the risk of obtaining es-

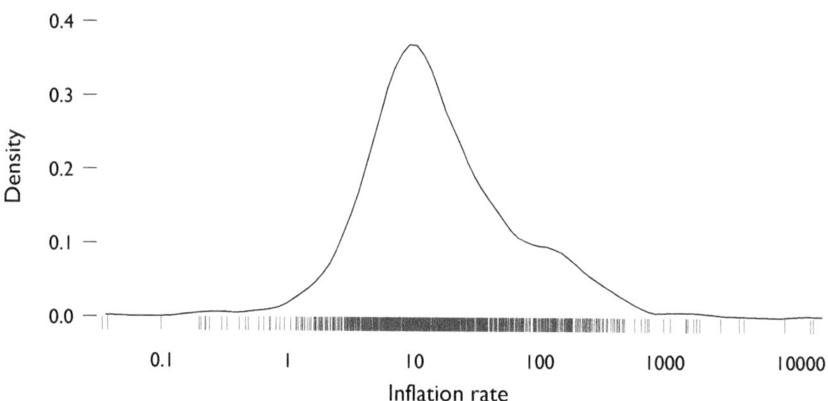

Figure 5.7. *The distribution of inflation in developing countries.* A smoothed histogram of the natural log of inflation in the 31 "long series" less developed countries, 1973 to 2003. Deflationary observations omitted.

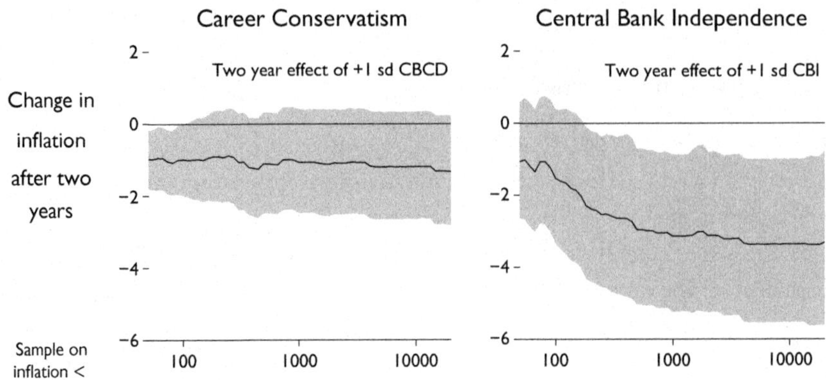

Figure 5.8. *Hyperinflation sensitivity analysis.* Estimated effect and 90 percent confidence interval for a one standard deviation increase in the career conservatism index (left panel) or central bank independence (right panel) in a series of rolling regressions. The regression samples include cases of inflation between 0 and the level indicated on the horizontal axis. The first sample considered (at extreme left of each plot) includes inflation rates between 0 and 50, as in the main text.

sentially meaningless estimates is acute. This is an instance where we can legitimately select on the dependent variable. Selection on the dependent variable is usually best avoided, as it can introduce bias (usually, but not always, shrinking slope estimates towards zero; see King, Keohane, and Verba [1994] and Geddes [1990]), but careful selection can occasionally improve inference by partitioning causally distinct processes (Collier and Mahoney, 1996). In this situation, selecting cases under, say, 50 percent inflation focuses attention on the causal process in question – what causes inflation to vary under normal conditions – rather than submerging this variation in the separate question of what causes hyperinflation.

As an added precaution, I explore the effects of including hyperinflation cases in Model 5, borrowing a moving windows technique from Temple (1998). I set an inflation threshold k such that observations with inflation higher than k are excluded from the analysis. Then, I run the analysis for a range of k's between 50 and positive infinity and report estimates of the key quantities of interest. This sensitivity analysis shows how the estimated effects of career conservatism and central bank independence shift as higher inflation observations enter the sample.

Figure 5.8 shows the results of the sensitivity analysis. The far left of each plot shows the effect of CBCD and CBI on inflation using the $0 < \pi < 50$ dataset used in the main text. For the career index, expanding the dataset to include higher inflation cases does not noticeably change the point estimate – conservative career types are still associated with lower inflation – but when cases higher than 100 percent annual inflation enter the sample, the confidence interval around this estimate widens substantially and includes zero. This fits with the intuition that CBCD matters in the "normal range" of inflation but does not help explain hyperinflation. In contrast, the effect of CBI becomes stronger and significantly negative as higher inflation cases enter the dataset. This is the opposite of what Temple found, although he was working with a larger sample, different controls, and no fixed effects.

Table 5.2. *Log inflation regressed on central banker characteristics, developing country long series sample, 1973 to 2000, quarterly.*

Data: developing countries (Long Series)			Dep. Var.: ln(Inflation)	
Covariate	1	2	3	4
$\text{FinExp}_{j,t-2}$	-0.328	-0.328	-0.438	-0.273
	(0.111)	(0.133)	(0.232)	(0.139)
$\text{GovExp}_{j,t-2}$	-0.210	-0.187	-0.174	-0.136
	(0.076)	(0.099)	(0.205)	(0.099)
$\text{FMExp}_{j,t-2}$	-0.241	-0.383	-0.537	-0.382
	(0.072)	(0.131)	(0.283)	(0.141)
$\text{CBExp}_{j,t-2}$	-0.135	-0.168	-0.185	-0.111
	(0.059)	(0.072)	(0.164)	(0.078)
$\text{EcoExp}_{j,t-2}$	-0.221	-0.186	-0.256	-0.198
	(0.069)	(0.080)	(0.165)	(0.081)
$\text{BusExp}_{j,t-2}$	-0.053	-0.035	-0.047	-0.020
	(0.081)	(0.091)	(0.171)	(0.092)
$\text{CBI}_{j,t-2}$		-0.200	-0.179	0.076
		(0.220)	(0.324)	(0.307)
$\text{TO}^{05}_{j,t-2}$				0.239
				(0.132)
$\text{Chaos}_{j,t-2}$	1.382	1.265	1.623	1.523
	(0.675)	(0.713)	(1.276)	(0.784)
$\ln \pi^{\text{world}}_{jt}$	0.099	0.104	0.124	0.113
	(0.021)	(0.027)	(0.040)	(0.030)
$\ln \pi_{j,t-1}$	0.744	0.823	0.458	0.785
	(0.043)	(0.068)	(0.066)	(0.073)
$\ln \pi_{j,t-2}$	0.057	-0.015	0.308	-0.005
	(0.039)	(0.063)	(0.044)	(0.067)
Method	LS/PCSE	LS/PCSE	Cochrane–Orcutt	LS/PCSE
Fixed effects	x	x	x	x
N	1639	987	933	882
Countries	31	22	22	21
s.e.r.	0.449	0.444	0.436	0.447
$\bar{R}^2$	0.79	0.783	0.603	0.779
LM test	21.929	10.415	$\rho = 0.325$	4.172
(crit = 3.841)			(0.064)	

Parameter estimates with standard errors in parentheses.
Cases of inflation below 0% or above 50% per year are excluded.
LM test refers to a Lagrange Multiplier test for serial correlation.

Table 5.3. *Log inflation regressed on central banker characteristics, developing country long series sample, 1973 to 2000, quarterly (continued).*

Data: developing countries (Long Series)			Dep. Var.: ln(Inflation)	
Covariate	5	6	7	8
$\text{CBCD}^{\text{med}}_{j,t-2}$	-0.105	-0.110	0.205	
	(0.052)	(0.059)	(0.208)	
$\text{CBI}_{j,t-2}$	-0.254	-0.255	-0.217	
	(0.228)	(0.227)	(0.218)	
$\text{USPhD}_{j,t-2}$		0.011		
		(0.051)		
$\text{CBI}_{j,t-2}$			-0.742	-0.297
$\times\text{CBCD}^{\text{med}}_{j,t-2}$			(0.485)	(0.125)
$\text{Chaos}_{j,t-2}$	1.111	1.104	1.151	1.062
	(0.696)	(0.702)	(0.697)	(0.688)
$\ln \pi^{\text{world}}_{jt}$	0.101	0.101	0.104	0.110
	(0.025)	(0.025)	(0.026)	(0.025)
$\ln \pi_{j,t-1}$	0.828	0.828	0.826	0.829
	(0.068)	(0.068)	(0.068)	(0.068)
$\ln \pi_{j,t-2}$	-0.012	-0.012	-0.012	-0.012
	(0.063)	(0.063)	(0.063)	(0.063)
Method	LS/PCSE	LS/PCSE	LS/PCSE	LS/PCSE
Fixed effects	x	x	x	x
N	987	987	987	987
Countries	22	22	22	22
s.e.r.	0.444	0.444	0.444	0.444
$\bar{R}^2$	0.783	0.783	0.783	0.784
LM test	10.787	10.816	10.651	10.406
(crit = 3.841)				

Parameter estimates with standard errors in parentheses.
Cases of inflation below 0% or above 50% per year are excluded.
LM test refers to a Lagrange Multiplier test for serial correlation.

Table 5.4. *Log inflation regressed on central banker characteristics, Latin American and Eastern Europe/Post-Soviet samples, 1973 to 2000, quarterly.*

Data: Regional Samples			Dep Var.: ln(Inflation)		
Covariate	9	10	11	12	13
$\text{FinExp}_{j,t-2}$	-0.616			-0.235	
	(0.330)			(0.317)	
$\text{GovExp}_{j,t-2}$	-0.275			-0.086	
	(0.180)			(0.067)	
$\text{FMExp}_{j,t-2}$	-0.712			-0.710	
	(0.302)			(0.315)	
$\text{CBExp}_{j,t-2}$	-0.300			-0.273	
	(0.149)			(0.085)	
$\text{EcoExp}_{j,t-2}$	-0.244			-0.216	
	(0.136)			(0.057)	
$\text{BusExp}_{j,t-2}$	-0.086			-0.479	
	(0.142)			(0.319)	
$\text{CBCD}^{\text{med}}_{j,t-2}$		-0.188	-0.131		-0.463
		(0.070)	(0.067)		(0.279)
$\text{CBI}_{j,t-2}$	-0.038	0.223		-0.055	0.058
	(0.286)	(0.314)		(0.171)	(0.163)
$\text{USPhD}_{j,t-2}$			-0.096		
			(0.059)		
$\text{Chaos}_{j,t-2}$	1.993	1.789	1.831	0.145	0.063
	(1.33)	(1.376)	(1.214)	(2.553)	(2.391)
$\ln \pi^{\text{world}}_{jt}$	0.057	0.074	0.036	0.097	0.076
	(0.04)	(0.036)	(0.033)	(0.079)	(0.078)
$\ln \pi_{j,t-1}$	0.833	0.853	0.939	0.979	1.019
	(0.144)	(0.141)	(0.127)	(0.088)	(0.088)
$\ln \pi_{j,t-2}$	0.009	0.004	-0.069	-0.144	-0.153
	(0.131)	(0.130)	(0.119)	(0.079)	(0.080)
Region		Latin America		East Eur & post-Sov	
Fixed effects	x	x	x		
N	249	249	288	429	429
Countries	4	4	5	19	19
s.e.r.	0.332	0.331	0.317	0.445	0.449
$\bar{R}^2$	0.874	0.875	0.883	0.803	0.800
LM (crit=3.841)	2.482	2.204	3.775	7.655	7.075

All models estimated by least squares with panel-corrected standard errors.
Parameter estimates with standard errors in parentheses.
Cases of inflation below 0% or above 50% per year are excluded.
LM test refers to a Lagrange Multiplier test for serial correlation.

Table 5.5. *Contents of the Central Banker Database: Global sample.*

		Governors	*Deputy Governors*	*Policy Board*	*Directors*
Albania	1997–2001	●	○	○	
Algeria	1992–2002	●			
Argentina	1950–2003	●			
Armenia	1998–2001	●	○		○
Aruba	2000–2001	●			
Azerbaijan	1994–2001	●			
Bahamas	1997–2001	●	○		○
Bahrain	2001–2001	●			
Barbados	1972–2001	●		○	
Belarus	1998–2001	●			
Bermuda	1993–2001	●			
Bosnia	1997–2003	●	●		
Botswana	1999–2001	●	○		○
Brazil	1999–2003	●			
Bulgaria	1991–2003	●	●	●	
Burma	1997–2003	●			
Burundi	1992–2001	●			
Cambodia	1998–2001	●			
Cameroon	1995–2001	●			
Cape Verde Islands	1999–2001	●			
Cayman Islands	1997–2001	●			
Chile	1989–2003	●			
China	1995–2002	●	●	○	
Comoros	1996–2001	●			
Congo	1997–2001	●			
Croatia	1992–2001	●	●		
Cyprus	1982–2003	●			○
Czech Republic	1990–2003	●	●	●	
East Caribbean	1989–2003	●			
Egypt	1993–2001	●	○		○
Eritrea	1995–2001	●			
Estonia	1990–2003	●		○	
Fiji	1988–2001	●	○		○
Georgia	1998–2001	●	●		○
Ghana	1997–2001	●	○	○	○
Greece	1994–2002	●	●	●	
Hong Kong	1993–2001	●	○		●
Hungary	1993–2001	●	●	●	

Monetary policy makers: ● (nearly) all included ○ (mostly) missing

		Governors	Deputy Governors	Policy Board	Directors
Iceland	1991–2002	●	●	●	
India	1994–2003	●	●		○
Indonesia	1998–2003	●	●		
Iran	1994–2003	●	●		
Iraq	1994–2003	●			
Israel	1976–2003	●	○	○	○
Jamaica	1960–2001	●			
Jordan	1963–2003	●	○	○	
Kazakhstan	1991–2003	●	○	○	○
Kenya	1993–2003	●	○		○
Kuwait	1986–2001	●	○	○	
Kyrgyz Republic	1994–2001	●	○		○
Laos	1998–1999	●			
Latvia	1990–2003	●	●	●	
Lebanon	1993–2001	●	○		
Lesotho	1980–2001	●	●	●	
Liberia	1999–2003	●			
Libya	1996–1999	●			
Lithuania	1990–2003	●	●	●	
Luxembourg	1998–2003	●			
Macao	1996–2003	●			
Macedonia (FYR)	1997–2003	●	○	○	
Malawi	2000–2003	●			
Malaysia	1994–2003	●	●		○
Maldives	1981–2003	●			
Malta	1997–2003	●	○		○
Mauritania	1993–1997	●			
Mauritius	1996–2003	●			○
Mexico	1952–2003	●	○		
Moldova	1991–2003	●	●		○
Mongolia	2000–2003	●			○
Namibia	1997–2003	●	○	○	
Nepal	1995–2003	●			
Neth. Antilles	1991–2003	●			
Nigeria	1999–2003	●			
Oman	1991–2003	●			
Pakistan	1993–2003	●	●		
Panama	1999–2003	●			
Peru	2003–2003	●	○		○
Philippines	1950–2003	●			

Monetary policy makers: ● (nearly) all included ○ (mostly) missing

		Governors	Deputy Governors	Policy Board	Directors
Poland	1991–2003	•		•	
Qatar	1990–2003	•			
Romania	1990–2003	•	○	○	
Russia	1991–2003	•	○	○	
Samoa	1989–2003	•			
Sierra Leone	1993–2003	•	○		○
Singapore	1998–2003	•	•	•	
Slovakia	1993–2003	•	•		
Slovenia	1991–2003	•	•	○	
Solomon Islands	1993–2001	•			
South Africa	1989–2001	•	•	•	
South Korea	1998–2003	•	•	•	
Sri Lanka	1995–2001	•			○
Swaziland	1997–2001	•			
Taiwan	1960–2001	•			○
Thailand	1950–2001	•	○		○
Tonga	1991–2001	•		○	
Trinidad & Tobago	1984–2002	•			
Tunisia	2001–2003	•			
Turkey	1994–2003	•	•		
Turkmenistan	1993–2002	•			○
Uganda	1986–2001	•			
Ukraine	1993–2002	•			
United Arab Emir.	1991–2003	•			
Uzbekistan	1991–2003	•			
Vanuatu	1993–1998	•			
Venezuela	1950–2003	•			
Vietnam	1999–2003	•			
West Africa	1990–2003	•	○		
Yemen	1997–2003	•			
Yugoslavia	2000–2003	•			
Zambia	1995–2002	•	○		○
Zimbabwe	1993–2003	•			

Monetary policy makers: • (nearly) all included ○ (mostly) missing
Sources: I relied on Fry et al. (2000), Siklos (2002), and country sources to determine which officials enjoyed *de jure* monetary policy making authority.

6

HOW CENTRAL BANKERS USE THEIR INDEPENDENCE

Bernard WOOLLEY, *Principal Private Secretary to the Minister for Administrative Affairs*: That's how the civil service works in practice – each department is controlled by the people it's supposed to be controlling.... Every department acts for the powerful sectional interest with whom they have a permanent relationship.

Jim HACKER, *Minister of the Department of Administrative Affairs*: So the whole system is designed to stop the cabinet from carrying out its policies?

WOOLLEY: Well, somebody's got to.

HACKER: But shouldn't the civil service be committed to helping the government carry out its wishes?

WOOLLEY: So it is, as long as the government's wishes are practical.

HACKER: Meaning?

WOOLLEY: As long as the civil service agrees with them.

"The Bed of Nails," *Yes Minister*

The career theory of central banker motivations lets us revisit old questions and gain new insights. An important example is the debate among Iversen (1999), Hall and Franzese (1998), and Cukierman and Lippi (1999), who explore the interactive effects of central banks and labor unions on economic performance. This intriguing literature emerged from the insight that if unions have any wage-setting power, then central bankers have the ability to shape the real economy using monetary policy, even over the long run. Yet to date, this work lacks any way to measure a concept at its theoretical core: the conservatism of the central bank. In this chapter, I combine measures of central bank *autonomy* and *conservatism* into a new measure of overall central bank *nonaccommodation*. We can use this improved measure of nonaccommodation to gain a richer understanding of the role central banks and unions jointly play in shaping economic performance, and in particular, inflation and unemployment.

I find that inflation is lower after conservative central bankers take the helm of an autonomous central bank, but if the central bank lacks independence, the career-induced preferences of the central banker matter little. As a source of central bank nonaccommodation, central banker conservatism has significant unemployment costs in decentralized economies (those with firm-level wage negotiation) and highly centralized labor markets (with peak association agreements), but not in economies with a moderate degree of centralization (such as sector-level bargaining).

The broader goal of this chapter and the next one is to add a realistic dose of politics into institutional modeling in order to better discern how institutions filter policy makers' preferences to produce economic outcomes. Because the long tradition of scholarship on monetary policy institutions often minimizes the role of political actors, especially within central banks, these institutions are ripe for an investigation centered on the interaction of agents and institutions.

The Institutional Interactions Approach to Monetary Policy

Political economists recognize the importance of institutional context in determining the effects of monetary policy, but the details of this interaction remain theoretically and empirically uncertain. At a minimum, scholarship in this area agrees that central banks and labor markets matter.[1] Thus, it is helps to review the literatures on central banks and labor markets taken separately before turning to the question of how these institutions interact.

For the most part, students of central bank independence assert the price-level is determined by monetary policy alone. They suppose individual wage setters will fully anticipate the monetary authority's actions, so monetary policy is neutral with respect to unemployment and output. Because anticipated money supply growth yields higher inflation and no real gain, governments

1 Later studies added exchange rate regimes to the argument (see Franzese [2003] as well as the contributions to the Autumn 2002 special issue of *International Organization* on the relationship between CBI and exchange rate regimes), but I do not address that innovation here.

should prefer to set their ideal inflation rate by a rule. But this policy is plagued with time inconsistency (Kydland and Prescott, 1977). To whatever extent economic actors believe the promised rule, governments are tempted to create unexpected money growth, and the rule fails to attain optimum outcomes. Therefore, governments preferring both low inflation and high output are better off credibly delegating authority to a more conservative agent who is independent from the government (Barro and Gordon, 1983; Rogoff, 1985). Some have argued that independent central banks empirically combine price stability with the same expected level of real output as looser monetary arrangements (Grilli, Masciandaro, and Tabellini, 1991; Alesina and Summers, 1993). The central bank independence literature offers a simple explanation of comparative inflation performance, leaving the question of what causes unemployment open.

A key comparative perspective on unemployment performance comes from the study of corporatism. In an important paper, Calmfors and Driffill (1988) suggest the relationship between labor union concertation and unemployment is hump-shaped, owing to two countervailing forces. The market power of unions to demand higher wages grows with the centralization of wage bargaining, because the elasticity of demand for goods produced by a bargaining unit falls as the unit grows to encompass entire industries. But at the same time, more encompassing bargaining systems foster union restraint by internalizing the inflationary effects of wage demands (Olson, 1982). Working against each other, these forces render industry-level bargaining the worst of all worlds, because sectoral concentration creates market power without containing temptations to raise nominal wages. According to Calmfors and Driffill, moving in either direction from moderately centralized bargaining should improve economic performance. In one direction, the market restrains decentralized unions' wage demands, yielding better outcomes. In the other, nationally coordinated labor markets may be the best case of all, because unions representing most workers (and thus most consumers) self-restrain to avoid poor aggregate outcomes. Therefore, according to the Calmfors–Driffill model, the relationship between unemployment and labor concertation is hump-shaped.

Later work (Iversen, 1999; Hall and Franzese, 1998; Cukierman and Lippi, 1999) argues the Calmfors–Driffill effect depends on central bank nonaccommodation (CBNA), defined as the combination of conservatism and independence. As long as labor market agents are not simply price takers, unions and central banks are in strategic interaction. That is, central banks must consider the behavior of wage-setting unions and employers when setting monetary policy, while unions must anticipate the reaction of the central bank to wages. In theory, any positive degree of wage bargaining centralization can impart real effect to monetary policy, because the threat of nonaccommodation by an independent central bank may lead a union to rethink its wage demands. Beyond this basic point, there is little agreement on the details of this strategic interaction. Three approaches deserve particular note. Iversen (1998*a*,*b*, 1999) models the strategic interaction by incorporating Calmfors and Driffill's insights into a two-stage game between wage-setting unions and inflation-setting central banks. Cukierman and Lippi (1999) undertake a similar project, but reach different conclusions. Finally, Hall and Franzese (1998) substitute labor market coordination for centralization to yield a third set of hypotheses. The theoretical predictions of these models are summarized in Figure 6.1.

In Iversen's model, wage setters weigh real wage demands against fears of unemployment and wage inequality while anticipating the central bank's reaction (which, in turn, balances inflation and aggregate unemployment). Following the Calmfors–Driffill model, unions' ability to set real wages and the inflationary consequences of those wages both rise with wage bargaining centralization. Thus, if the central bank accommodates wage demands, the relationship between unemployment and centralization is hump-shaped, but with a non-accommodating central bank the hump is suppressed or even inverted (Figure 7.1, top panel). For centralization near zero, unemployment is unchanged, because money remains neutral where unions are price takers. In moderately centralized labor markets, CBNA lowers unemployment, because the central bank's credible threat discourages wage demands. Yet for highly centralized economies, unions' efforts to maintain wage equality may mitigate the effectiveness of restrictive monetary policy, leading to higher unemployment under CBNA.[2]

Cukierman and Lippi's approach is broadly similar, but in contrast to Iversen, they suppose unions are organized by craft and care only about their own real wages and within-union unemployment, not within-union wage equality or economy-wide unemployment. They also assume labor is perfectly substitutable across industries but not across unions. Cukierman and Lippi's model predicts that the Calmfors–Driffill hump in unemployment occurs in some

2 According to Iversen, encompassing unions face pressure from the median wage earner to maintain wage equality but find it difficult to impose wage compression on their most productive workers, who often receive raises outside the bargaining agreement. To erode this "wage drift," unions demand higher nominal wages across the board, trading inflation for wage equality. Unless the central bank accommodates these demands, unemployment rises as well.

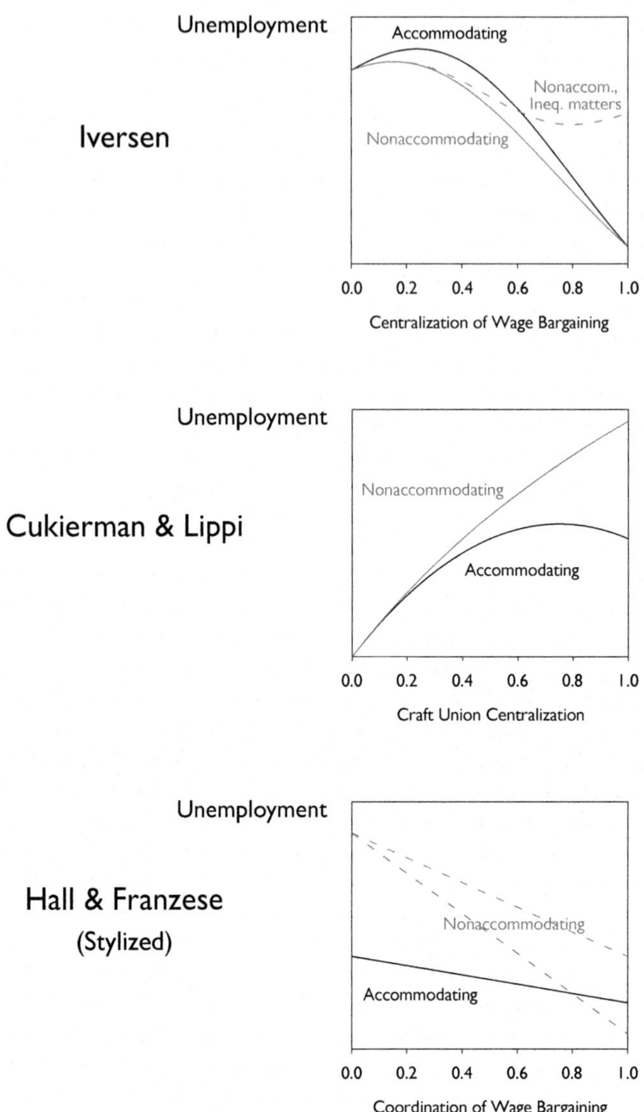

Figure 6.1. *Predictions of interactive models of unemployment.* Note the conceptually different horizontal axes. Vertical axis scaling is incommensurate and hence omitted, but in the Iversen and Cukierman and Lippi models, unemployment performance varies over a substantively large range in terms of the formal model specification and parameter values. The Hall and Franzese graphic is my interpretation of their model.

form, regardless of CBNA, as long as unions are sufficiently inflation averse. But if unions have any market power, restrictive monetary authorities impose an unemployment cost: the more nonaccommodating the central bank, the faster the rise of the Calmfors–Driffill curve, and the more rightward its peak (see Figure 6.1, middle panel). For Cukierman and Lippi, CBNA almost always creates a tradeoff between unemployment and inflation.

Taking a different approach, Hall and Franzese argue that union coordination better captures variation in the strategic interaction of central banks and unions than centralization of wage bargaining.[3] In their view, effective coordination offers the same benefit as centralization by forcing the lead union to consider the inflationary consequences of its demands for the whole economy. Therefore, even seemingly decentralized labor movements may reliably *coordinate* on the leading union's contract. A conservative, independent central bank can nudge a coordinated labor market toward better economic outcomes by credibly threatening to punish inflationary wage demands, but without labor market coordination, high CBNA may actually raise unemployment (see Figure 6.1, bottom panel). Franzese (2001, 2002) argues that in this case, wage bargainers tend to be too small to be credibly threatened with monetary nonaccommodation, because monetary policy is indivisibly applied to the whole economy, which may include hundreds or thousands of unions. Nevertheless, even decentralized unions are often large enough to exert some market power, so their wage demands can create "incipient inflation pressures." As centralization drops, central banks rely more on preemptive action to slow the economy (undermining unions' bargaining position and checking inflation) and less on threats (which can be simultaneously credible and largely unexecuted only when unions are large). The result is negative real consequences of nonaccommodation in low centralization economies.

That much is theory. Most empirical results suggest nonaccommodation – usually proxied by CBI alone – produces the best (or least bad) unemployment performance in moderately centralized or coordinated economies, but empirical models disagree about other cases. Using a fine-grained, time-varying measure of *centralization*, Iversen finds that CBI substantially raises unemployment where labor markets are most centralized; other authors, using simpler, time-invariant codings of *coordination*, find slightly lower unemployment in this case. Though Iversen observes no effect of CBI in decentralized economies, Hall and Franzese and Cukierman and Lippi find higher unemployment where CBI is

3 Some systems may be highly coordinated but not centralized (such Germany), although not the reverse (Soskice, 1990).

combined with uncoordinated economy labor markets. Finally, the small number of observed cases of high centralization means even small differences in measurement can produce substantively different results.

Any conclusions we draw from these results face two challenges. First, scholars disagree on the appropriate labor market measure. In this chapter, I use centralization, especially because time-varying data are available. Second, and more problematically, past work has lacked a measure of central bank conservatism and thus had no way to adequately capture nonaccommodation. Despite a theoretical emphasis on conservatism, all extant studies use measures of independence alone, implicitly assuming that all central banks would act in the same way if unconstrained by governments. If some central bankers dislike inflation more than others, these studies empirically miss the theoretical point.

Career Effects on Monetary Policy in Institutional Context

Breaking from past studies in the institutional interaction literature, I employ an explicit measure of central bank career conservatism. In broad terms, central bankers who hail from the financial sector tend to be conservative, favoring tight money and low inflation, whereas former bureaucrats tend to be more liberal and accepting of inflation. Chapter 3 shows that private finance and finance ministry careers are associated with lower inflation, while other government bureaucrats and central bank staff are associated with higher inflation, even controlling for central bank independence (which is, in any case, uncorrelated with these career types). The observed ordering of career effects matches with the post-central bank careers of central bankers: conservative types (private finance and finance ministry) are more likely to end up in the private banks, whereas the less conservative bureaucrats are more likely to return to government.

As in Chapter 3, I summarize the career conservatism of a particular central banker i in country j at time t using the Central Banker Career Conservatism (CBCC) index

$$\text{CBCC}_{ijt} = \text{FinExp}_{ijt} + \text{FMExp}_{ijt} - \text{CBExp}_{ijt} - \text{GovExp}_{ijt}, \qquad (6.1)$$

where FinExp, FMExp, CBExp, and GovExp denote the percentage of central banker i's career spent in private finance, the finance ministry, the central bank staff, and the rest of the government, respectively. I aggregate CBCC_{ijt} across a single central bank using the tenure-weighted median of *de jure* policy makers over period *t*, which this chapter refers to simply as CBCC.

Many studies of the effects (real or nominal) of central bank nonaccommodation implicitly assume that central banks are uniformly conservative, conditional on CBI. An incomplete list of empirical papers conflating independence and conservatism includes Cukierman, Webb, and Neyapti (1992), Cukierman and Lippi (1999), Cukierman, Miller, and Neyapti (2001), Grilli, Masciandaro, and Tabellini (1991), Hall and Franzese (1998), Franzese (1999, 2003), Temple (1998), and Banaian and Luksetich (2001); an exhaustive search would likely find dozens more. This assumption is unjustified and ultimately untenable.

To be sure, some authors attempt to estimate or proxy for central banker preferences. Cukierman and others have argued that directives to produce price stability written into central bank charters constitute a sort of conservatism, but these dictates hardly describe actual central bankers' preference or even effectively bind their behavior. Posen (1995) argues the financial sector is more likely to overwhelm the independence of the central bank under certain conditions, which include federalism, a fractionalized party system, universal banking, and central bank responsibility for banking regulation. Yet Posen's approach likewise revolves around variation in central bank institutions, not central banker preferences. His argument is that if the institutional setting is ripe for a powerful financial sector, private banks can dominate the central bank, regardless of the central bankers' own preferences. Iversen (1999) uses a measure of relative currency appreciation as a proxy for conservatism (or "behavioral" CBI), but this measure is indirect – an outcome of monetary policy rather than a source of it. Indeed, the only direct measure of central banker preferences is Chang (1998, 2003), who uses the published votes of members of the Federal Reserve to estimate central banker ideal points. Still, this method cannot be employed for countries that keep central bankers' votes secret votes, and it can be fooled by the *kabuki* consensus votes central banks sometimes use to mask internal disagreement (Chappell, McGregor, and Vermilyea, 2004*a*).[4] Given the limitations of other approaches, the best cross-country, time-varying measure of central bankers preferences we possess is the career-based index, CBCC.

The interactive relationship between CBCC and CBI in producing inflation remains a puzzle. Agent preferences should matter more when the agent has greater autonomy. Likewise, the effect of autonomy should depend on agent

4 See also Morris (2004), who worries that Chang's rankings are often contrary to members' widely perceived reputations as hawks or doves.

preferences. Yet in Chapter 3, we failed to find a significant interaction between these two variables. We now resolve this puzzle by refining our concept of central bank independence. This refinement also helps explain how monetary policy affects the real economy through the strategic interaction of central bankers and wage bargainers.

To complement our measures of central bank preferences, we need a measure of the ability of central bankers to set monetary policy without the interference of the government. Although this idea lies at the heart of the concept of the independent central bank – at least as construed by Lohmann (1992), Banaian, Burdekin, and Willett (1995), Franzese (1999), and others – it is not necessarily the only element of the most commonly used measures of central bank independence. For example, Cukierman, Webb, and Neyapti (1992) include characteristics such as whether the central bank plays a role in budgeting (which might distract the central bank or complicate the weighing of policy objectives), whether the central bank may lend to the public sector (on the same justification), and whether the charter pledges the central bank to pursue price stability only (a presumed measure of central banker conservatism, despite being neither a characteristic of central bankers nor enforceable in practice; see McCallum [1995]). Including these concepts in what is ostensibly a measure of autonomy is a puzzling strategy: While it is possible that these institutions may have *something* to do with inflation performance – although Berger, de Haan, and Eijffinger (2001) suggest price stability directives do not – they are not actually components of the *independence* of central bankers from the government.[5]

In more precise terms, CBI can be divided into two sets of institutions: *Monetary Policy Autonomy* (MPA) institutions that define the central banker's role in monetary policy decision-making vis-à-vis the government; and other, potentially *Inflation Mitigating Institutions* (IMI) that have no direct connection to legal central bank independence.[6] The key point is that the effect of MPA depends on central bankers' preferences, whereas the effect of IMI likely does not.

5 Narrowing the focus of our CBI measure carries other benefits. For such a widely used measure, the Cukierman score and its fellow CBI indexes have received relatively little scrutiny for intercoder reliability, subjectivity, missing data, and other problems inherent in reducing complex and often vaguely written statutes into comparable numerical ratings. Mangano (1998) points out the vast interpretative spread between common indexes. Armstrong and Morris (2003) note the pernicious effects of missing component data throughout the Cukierman index. Numerous authors bemoan the failure of the field produce updated CBI scores.

6 That is, $\text{CBI} = a(\text{MPA}, \text{IMI})$, where $a(\cdot)$ is some form of weighted average.

MPA augments the inflation-suppressing effect of having conservative central bankers, but given sufficiently liberal central bankers, high MPA actually *increases* inflation. In contrast, if IMI has any effect on inflation, it is probably always suppressive.[7] From this vantage point, models that include CBI × CBCC interactions are misspecified efforts to capture the effects of institutions on preferences, which could be better modelled using the interaction of CBCC and MPA.

I define MPA as an average of six variables, all drawn from Cukierman, Webb, and Neyapti (1992), with updates by the author for the 1990s.[8] The six components are:

1. The Governor's term of office.
2. How much say the government has in the Governor's appointment.
3. How easily the Governor may be dismissed.
4. Whether the Governor may hold other political office simultaneously.
5. Whether the central bank formulates monetary policy.
6. Whether the central bank has the final say on monetary policy.

These variables either capture the relative decision-making power of government and central bank (3, 5, and 6) or affect the career autonomy of central bankers (1, 2, 3, and 4). To create MPA, I simply average these six variables. This produces a variable with a similar distribution to CBI (see the Data Appendix for descriptive statistics), but a more focused institutional interpretation.

To measure labor market institutions, I rely on Iversen's scoring of the degree of centralization of wage bargaining (Iversen, 1999). Finally, I draw economic data from the IMF's International Financial Statistics (inflation, GDP, and imports) and the OECD's Economic Compendium (unemployment and export market growth). Generally, the data cover up to twenty countries over the post-Bretton Woods period (1973 to 2000), by quarter.

7 In symbols, $\pi = f(\text{MPA} \times \text{CBCC} + \text{IMI})$, with $\partial\pi/\partial\text{IMI} < 0$ and $\partial\pi/\partial\text{MPA} \propto$ CBCC.

8 The updated countries are New Zealand (based on the 1990 reforms), France (1993), Italy (1993), Spain (1994), Portugal (1996), and the United Kingdom (1998). The European Central Bank is excluded from the model and left uncoded. I selected and coded the six components of the MPA prior to any analysis of component effects and did not contemplate any other versions of the index.

Methods

As is standard in the political economy literature, I estimate time series cross-section regressions using least squares with panel-corrected standard errors. The model includes lags of the dependent variable to account for the dynamics of inflation and unemployment and fixed effects to cope with omitted country characteristics. To clarify the interactive and dynamic implications of the model, I intepret it using counterfactuals that show how the inflation or unemployment effects of changing one covariate depend on the levels of other covariates. Although the model is estimated on quarterly data, institutional changes tend to be sticky, so for the most part I show the cumulative change in inflation or unemployment and 90 percent confidence interval of that change, summed up over the five years following a permanent shift in a covariate.

Inflation Analysis

The dependent variable is the natural log of inflation (a few negative values are omitted) ensuring the dependent variable is approximately Normally distributed. I also control for imports as a share of GDP, following the intuition of Romer (1993) and Lane (1997).[9] Tables 6.4 and 6.5 in the Data Appendix summarize the analyzed variables. The specification is straightforward, in part because the central bank is clearly the most important institution in determining inflation. If we expected conservatism and independence to have only independent effects, we would include the usual additive terms on the right-hand-side of the regression:

$$\text{additive effects} \qquad \beta_1 \text{CBCC} + \beta_2 \text{CBI},$$

and expect to find $\hat{\beta}_1 < 0$ and $\hat{\beta}_2 < 0$. But because conservatism and independence are mutually reinforcing, we must also include a multiplicative interaction term, leading to a more flexible specification:

$$\text{multiplicative effects} \qquad \beta_1 \text{CBCC} + \beta_2 \text{CBI} + \beta_3 \text{CBCC} \times \text{CBI}.$$

For the interactive model, we expect to find $\hat{\beta}_1 \leq 0$, $\hat{\beta}_2 \leq 0$, and $\hat{\beta}_3 < 0$.

The first two columns of Table 6.2 recapitulate results from Chapter 3. In the first of these two models, CBCC and CBI have similar but separate effects on inflation. Under the additive model, a one standard deviation reduction in CBCC lowers inflation by 1.3 points over five years, with a 90 percent confi-

9 See Chapter 3, note 11.

dence interval of [−0.8,−1.9]. Compare this to the effect of CBI: a 2.7 point decline, with a confidence interval of [−1.8,−3.5]. The second model adds an interaction between CBI and CBCC. We expect that just as CBI and CBCC each reduce inflation, so should their conjunction lower inflation; hence the interaction of these two variables should be negative.[10] Though correctly signed, this interaction is not remotely significant.

It makes sense that both CBCC and CBI are related to lower inflation, but it is puzzling to find their interaction insignificant. Several things might explain this result. First, career conservatism may operate regardless of formal independence. Even when the government has some power to legally overide the bank, threatening a veto could damage the central bank's credibility. To avoid paying this political price, governments can simply appoint ambitious bureaucrats as central bankers, then quietly hold their careers hostage in exchange for monetary accommodation. This works in both directions: if the government wants conservative monetary policy, appointing a private banker may be easier than changing the laws governing the central bank to increase its independence.

Measurement error is a simpler (but not mutually exclusive) explanation of the non-significant interaction. We have assumed CBI is a proxy for autonomy, when it actually includes many ostensibly inflation mitigating institutions that have little directly to do with central bankers' freedom to set policy. If we isolate the appropriate parts of CBI, the interaction of preferences and institutions may emerge more cleanly.

To test the measurement error explanation, I substitute the narrowly defined MPA measure for the conceptually diverse CBI. Model 3 shows that when CBCC and MPA enter the model independently, the effect of CBCC remains essentially the same as in a model with CBI, while MPA has a similarly strong effect on inflation: a one standard deviation increase in MPA lowers inflation by 1.8 points over five years [−1.1, −2.5]. Model 4 adds an interaction term

10 Note that this specification does not assume $\partial\pi/\partial\text{CBI} = \text{CBCC}$, only that $\partial\pi/\partial\text{CBI} \propto \text{CBCC}$. To see this, suppose

$$\pi = f(\alpha\text{CBI} + \gamma(\text{CBCC} + k) \times \text{CBI}),$$

so that $-k$ is the point at which CBCC is neutral. Reparameterization using $\alpha' = \alpha + \gamma k$ reveals a simple interaction specification:

$$\pi = f(\alpha'\text{CBI} + \gamma\text{CBCC} \times \text{CBI}).$$

Thus, so long as we include an uninteracted CBI term, we can estimate the interactive effect of conservatism and autonomy without assuming $k = 0$.

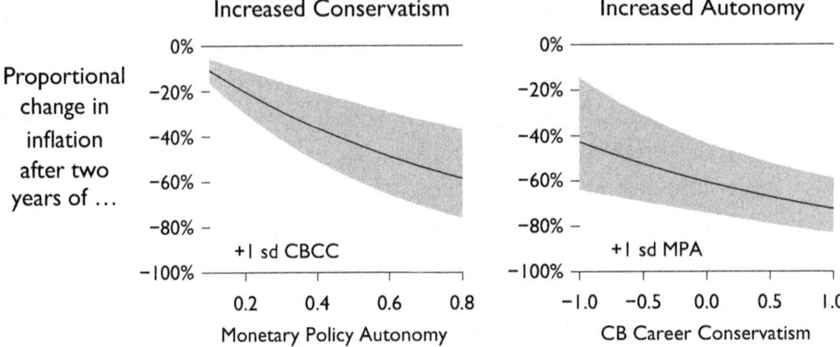

Figure 6.2. *Inflation as a function of careers and autonomy.* The left plot shows the percent reduction in inflation after a one standard deviation increase in central bankers' career conservatism, calculated across the observed range of institutional autonomy. The right plot shows the percent reduction in inflation after a one standard deviation increase in autonomy, calculated across the range of conservatism. Gray shading indicates the 90 percent confidence interval. Both plots are calculated from Model 5 in Table 6.2.

to this specification. It is correctly signed, but still insignificant. The additive effect of CBCC is now essentially zero, just what we would theoretically expect if the transformation of preferences into policy depends on institutional opportunity. If we re-estimate the model without this additive CBCC term – in effect *assuming* that CBCC has no effect except in conjunction with MPA – then we obtain a more precise but substantively unchanged estimate of the interaction term.

To explore the interaction between autonomy and conservatism, we can hold one fixed (say, conservatism), then vary the other (autonomy), and calculate the gap in inflation that results after a certain period of time. We repeat this procedure for other levels of conservatism and plot out the effect of increased autonomy under the observed range of central banker preferences. Then we swap variables and repeat the procedure to see the effect of increased conservatism over the observed range of autonomy.

The mechanics of these calculations are fairly simple (King, Tomz, and Wittenberg, 2000), although a few details should be noted. First, in calculating counterfactuals from a model with a lagged dependent variable, we must make some assumption about the *ex ante* level of that variable. Here, I assume that inflation starts at the sample mean. Then I iterate over two scenarios. In the first, either conservatism or autonomy changes permanently at time zero. In the second, there is no change in the explanatory variables. The quantity of interest is therefore the difference between these two scenarios after a given time has passed (say 20 quarters, or five years). A second detail involves how this difference is calculated. Because the model is linear in the natural log of inflation, and not inflation itself, it is simpler to speak of the proportional reduction in inflation under the "changed" scenario compared to the "unchanged" scenario.

Applying this approach to Model 5 shows that conservatism and autonomy reinforce each other. Under the unconditional model 3, conservatism reduces inflation by 41 percent [90% CI: −23 to −56] after five years. But this turns out to be an average across countries with different central bank institutions. The left panel of Figure 6.2 shows that the effect of conservatism (CBCC) at the lowest observed levels of autonomy (MPA) is a mere eleven percent reduction in inflation [90% CI: 6 to 16]. At the sample average level of autonomy, career conservatism reduces inflation by 42 percent [90% CI: 24 to 57], and the effect tops out at 58 percent [90% CI: 37 to 76] in the most autonomous banks. The effect of career conservatism, then, appears almost wholly dependent on the institutional autonomy of the bank.

But that does not make conservatism irrelevant, for the effect of institutional autonomy depends closely on the preferences of the central bankers it empowers. A one standard deviation increase in MPA reduces inflation by 72 percent [90% CI: 59 to 83] if the median central banker is a pure financial-type, but only 43 percent [90% CI: 14 to 64] if the median central banker is a government-type.[11] MPA thus has some inflation-reducing effect regardless of the career background of central bankers. This may reflect the credibility benefits of high MPA or a tendency of governments to follow the Rogoff prescription to appoint central bankers more conservative than themselves; more generally, MPA might pick up residual conservatism uncaptured by career effects.

Unemployment Analysis

For the unemployment regressions, I calculate the response variable, UDIFF, as the difference between the unemployment in country *j* and the contemporaneous GDP-weighted average of unemployment in the G7 countries (excluding country *j*). This follows Alesina, Roubini, and Cohen (1997), and helps remove

11 For comparison, Model 3, which does not condition the effect of MPA on CBCC, finds an across-the-board 58 percentage reduction in inflation from a one standard deviation increase in MPA [90% CI: −39 to −72].

exogenous world shocks from consideration. Tables 6.6 and 6.7 in the Data Appendix summarize the analyzed variables.

The unemployment specification is considerably more complex than the inflation model. Several different empirical specifications appear in the literature; I follow Iversen (1999) and estimate a polynomial interaction model. The goal is to allow either a linear or hump-shaped relationship between centralization and unemployment, and to allow that line or hump to be inverted as central bank nonaccommodation varies. Suppose the right-hand side of the unemployment model includes the following terms:

hump or line $$\beta_1\text{CWB} + \beta_2\text{CWB}^2 + \beta_3\text{CBNA},$$

where CWB is a labor centralization measure and CBNA is some measure of central bank nonaccommodation (we consider several such measures). If we find $\hat{\beta}_1 > 0$ and $\hat{\beta}_2 < 0$, a Calmfors–Driffil hump appears. Other combinations of signs allow a U-shape or a straight line to emerge.

To capture effects of centralization that depend on the degree of monetary accommodation, we need an even more flexible specification. Now suppose that we multiply the first two terms by $k - \text{CBNA}$, where k is a constant:

$$\left(\beta_1\text{CWB} + \beta_2\text{CWB}^2\right)(k - \text{CBNA}) + \beta_3\text{CBNA}.$$

This specification still allows for a hump-shaped relationship between centralization and unemployment, but that hump may be flattened out or even inverted as CBNA increases. We can transform this nonlinear specification into a linear one by first rearranging

$$\begin{aligned}&\beta_1 k\text{CWB} + \beta_2 k\text{CWB}^2\\ &\quad -\beta_3\text{CWB} \times \text{CBNA} - \beta_4\text{CWB}^2 \times \text{CBNA} + \beta_3\text{CBNA}\end{aligned}$$

and then reparameterizing using $\alpha_1 = \beta_1 k$, $\alpha_2 = \beta_2 k$, $\alpha_3 = \beta_3$, $\alpha_4 = -\beta_1$, and $\alpha_5 = -\beta_2$:

conditional hump or line $$\begin{aligned}&\alpha_1\text{CWB} + \alpha_2\text{CWB}^2\\ &\quad +\alpha_3\text{CBNA} + \alpha_4\text{CWB} \times \text{CBNA} - \alpha_5\text{CWB}^2 \times \text{CBNA}.\end{aligned}$$

This specification offers a great deal of flexibility. It allows the effect of CBNA to differ in sign across the low, medium, and high centralization cases; and the relationship between centralization and unemployment to be a hump, U, or straight line. It can also be estimated easily using least squares, but it is a fairly complicated specification and easiest to interpret graphically.

Table 6.1. *Modeling central bank nonaccommodation and unemployment: Non-nested goodness of fit tests.*

J-test p-values
low values → reject column in favor of row

	CBI	CBCC	CBI× CBCC	MPA× CBCC
CBI	—	0.084	0.067	0.106
CBCC	**0.005**	—	0.463	0.585
CBI × CBCC	**0.003**	0.113	—	0.689
MPA × CBCC	**0.002**	0.120	**0.034**	—

Cox-Pesaran-Deaton test p-values
low values → reject column in favor of row

	CBI	CBCC	CBI× CBCC	MPA× CBCC
CBI	—	0.155	0.067	0.162
CBCC	**0.000**	—	0.493	0.407
CBI × CBCC	**0.000**	0.108	—	0.283
MPA × CBCC	**0.000**	0.078	**0.015**	—

Entries are *p*-values from non-nested goodness of fit tests pitting models using the row variable to proxy central bank nonaccommodation against models using the column variable (that is, the column variable is used in the null hypothesis). *p*-values less than 0.05 are shown in bold. The tests support models that include career conservatism (CBCC) against those relying on institutions only (CBI).

For the remainder of the chapter, I consistently use the same measure of labor market concentration – Iversen's centralization of wage bargaining – but I vary the measure of central bank nonaccommodation. The first measure of CBNA I consider is the conventional favorite, the three-index average of CBI. Table 6.3, column 1 reports these results, which comport (at least in sign) with Iversen's expectations. The results, however, are not significant.[12]

While a purely institutional measure fails to capture central bank nonaccommodation, measures incorporating career-induced preferences perform much better. As the remaining three columns of Table 6.3 show, whether we use

12 Iversen (1999) obtains significant results using a combination of CBI and currency appreciation as a behavioral measure of central bank nonaccommodation.

career conservatism alone, or interact it with a measure of institutional independence (either CBI or MPA), we obtain significant and correctly signed results. Tests of non-nested model fit (Davidson and MacKinnon, 1981; Pesaran and Deaton, 1978) suggest any of the three models that include conservatism (CBCC, CBCC × CBI, or CBCC × MPA) beats the model using CBI by itself. We cannot conclusively reject any of the models that include conservatism, but non-nested tests offer some evidence that CBCC × MPA is the best choice (see Table 6.1).

To understand these empirical models, I plot in Figure 6.3 several quantities calculated from the estimated parameters. In the first column of plots, I show the level of unemployment an economy would converge to in the long-run if CBNA were kept at a low level (1.5 standard deviations below the mean). The second column shows long-run unemployment under nonaccommodation. Comparing the plots in these two columns confirm the centralization of wage bargaining strongly influences long-run unemployment. The third column shows the cumulative difference in unemployment after five years of nonaccommodation compared to five years of accommodation, in either case under a fixed wage bargaining system and starting from the same initial unemployment rate. Looking across the wage bargaining axis in the third column is the easiest way to see where non-accommodation is relatively helpful or harmful.

The second row of Figure 6.3 shows results from a model that takes career conservatism as its measure of nonaccommodation. When the median central banker has a non-conservative career path (such as a generalist bureaucrat), unemployment rates follow a Calmfors–Driffill hump: good performance when wage bargaining happens at the firm or peak level, and poor performance when bargains are struck across sectors of the economy. When the median central banker has a conservative career background (private finance or the finance ministry), unemployment performance is quite different, and is worse the greater the centralization of wage bargaining. Taken together, these two plots of long-run performance correspond reasonably well with Cukierman and Lippi's predictions.

Another way to look at these results is through a first difference. Consider the counterfactual in which two identical economies choose different central bankers: one with a conservative career and the other with a liberal career. Suppose both economies have decentralized labor markets, like the United States or United Kingdom. The model predicts that five years later, the country with the conservative central bank will have 2.3 percent higher unemployment [90% CI:

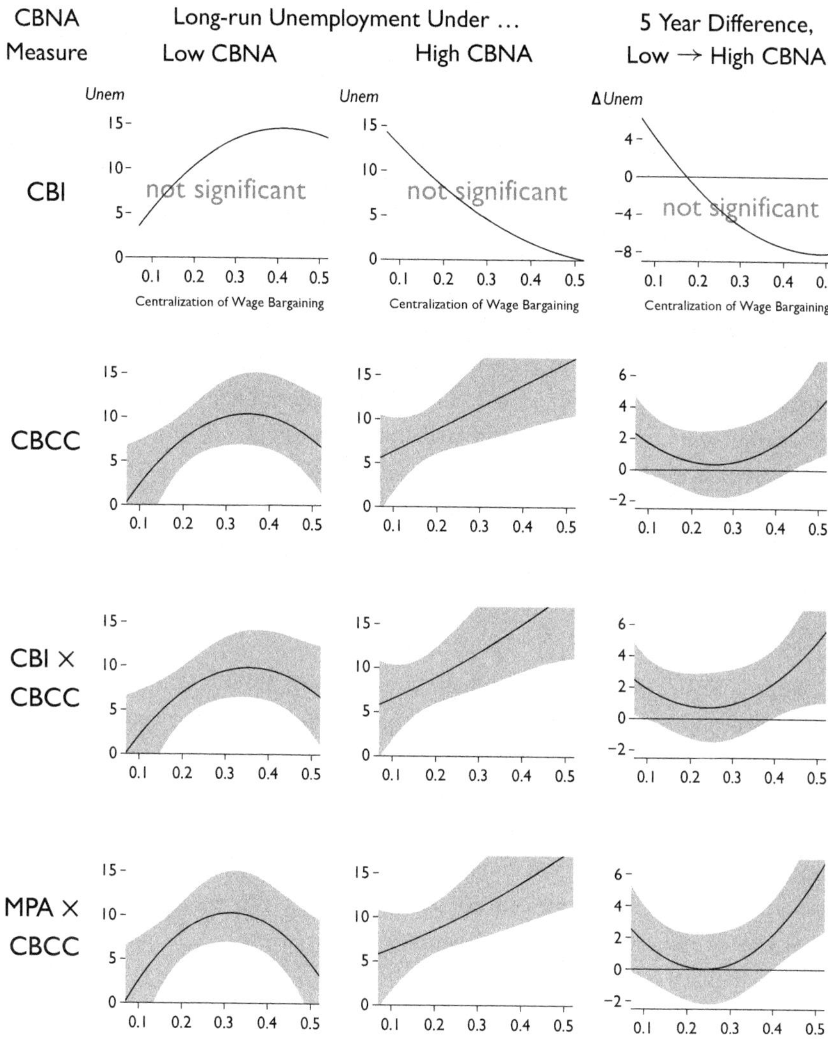

Figure 6.3. *Unemployment as a function of central bank nonaccommodation and wage bargaining centralization.* Long-run expected values and five year first differences calculated from the estimated models in Table 6.3. Gray areas indicate 90 percent confidence intervals. High CBNA is 1.5 standard deviations above the mean; low CBNA is 1.5 standard deviations below.

−0.02 to 4.7]. If the economies are instead highly centralized, as in Scandinavia, the unemployment penalty for conservatism may be even greater. In choosing central bankers, these economies face sharp inflation–unemployment tradeoffs. But for countries with moderate centralization, like Germany, there is no significant difference in unemployment when a conservative sets monetary policy and thus no tradeoff between inflation and real economic performance.

In analyzing inflation performance, we find that both career conservatism and legal independence matter. For unemployment, we find that if we combine central bank preferences and institutions into one measure, whether it is CBCC × CBI or CBCC × MPA, we obtain consistent results similar to those emerging from the CBCC-only regressions. Taken together, these results suggest there is an inflation–unemployment tradeoff in decentralized and highly centralized economies, but not in moderately centralized ones. Economists sometimes refer the possibility of real long-run effects of monetary policy, which involve real returns to merely nominal adjustments, as a "free lunch." The findings here suggest that there may a free lunch available through accommodative monetary policy, but not on every central bank's menu.

Conclusion

Monetary institutions and monetary agents have different macroeconomic consequences in different types of economies. Decentralized economies are the setting for a traditional tradeoff between inflation and unemployment, in which either more conservative agents or more autonomy, but especially their combination, lowers inflation at a real cost in unemployment. The inflation–unemployment tradeoff is even stronger in highly centralized labor markets. Yet in moderately centralized economies, the unemployment consequences of conservatism and autonomy appear to be nil, leaving only the inflation-reducing benefits.

The three-way debate among Iversen, Hall–Franzese, and Cukierman–Lippi remains a draw. The results in this chapter look remarkably like Cukierman and Lippi's predictions, except that Cukierman and Lippi expected no real effects of money in decentralized economies. In those cases, Hall and Franzese find support. From another view, the empirical model backs Iversen's hypotheses, finding a real cost of nonaccommodation in highly centralized markets and showing nonaccommodation to be least painful in moderately centralized cases.

These findings suggest different political conflicts over monetary policy in different contexts. Moderately centralized countries, like Germany in the Bundesbank era, may find consensus on conservative, autonomous central banks because for such economies, nonaccommdation imposes no real costs on the economy as a whole. But in decentralized economies, citizens, interest groups, and political parties with different tastes for inflation and unemployment may disagree on the choice of monetary institutions and agents. It is no accident that the extension of German-style central banking to the Eurozone has produced increasingly contentious debates over monetary policy and the conservative, Bundesbank-inspired approach of the European Central Bank. These debates reflect a profound mismatch between the monetary institutions and agents that worked well in the moderately centralized Germany economy, and the monetary institutions and agents best suited for a diverse and decentralized Europe.

Data Appendix to Chapter 6

Table 6.2. *Log inflation regressed on central banker characteristics, central bank institutions, and interactions across twenty countries, 1973 to 2000, quarterly.*

		DV: ln(Inflation)				
Covariate	E(Sign)	1	2	3	4	5
$\text{CBCC}^{\text{med}}_{j,t-2}$	–	-0.09	-0.03	-0.08	0.01	
		(0.03)	(0.07)	(0.03)	(0.08)	
$\text{CBI}_{j,t-2}$	–	-0.92	-0.90			
		(0.29)	(0.29)			
$\text{MPA}_{j,t-2}$	–			-0.44	-0.47	-0.47
				(0.13)	(0.13)	(0.13)
$\text{CBI}_{j,t-2} \times \text{CBCC}^{\text{med}}_{j,t-2}$	–		-0.12			
			(0.15)			
$\text{MPA}_{j,t-2} \times \text{CBCC}^{\text{med}}_{j,t-2}$	–				-0.19	-0.18
					(0.17)	(0.05)
$\text{Imports/GDP}_{j,t-2}$	–	0.02	0.05	-0.08	-0.05	-0.06
		(0.25)	(0.26)	(0.25)	(0.25)	(0.25)
$\ln \pi_{j,t-1}$		0.97	0.97	0.97	0.97	0.97
		(0.04)	(0.04)	(0.04)	(0.04)	(0.04)
$\ln \pi_{j,t-2}$		-0.03	-0.03	-0.03	-0.03	-0.03
		(0.04)	(0.04)	(0.04)	(0.04)	(0.04)
Fixed effects		x	x	x	x	x
N		1696	1696	1696	1696	1696
s.e.r.		0.305	0.305	0.305	0.305	0.305
$\bar{R}^2$		0.887	0.888	0.887	0.887	0.887
LM (crit = 3.84)		2.64	2.57	3.78	3.29	3.26

Least squares estimates with panel-corrected standard errors in parentheses. ECB members are excluded after 1997. LM refers to a Lagrange multiplier test for serial correlation.

Table 6.3. *Unemployment difference regressed on central banker characteristics, institutions, and interactions across fifteen countries, 1975 to 1998, quarterly.*

DV: UDIFF		CBNA defined as ...			
				CBI ×	MPA ×
Covariate	E(Sign)	CBI	CBCC	CBCC	CBCC
CWB_{jt}	+	3.06	0.69	1.43	0.73
		(3.00)	(0.60)	(0.66)	(0.57)
CWB^2_{jt}	−	-3.25	-0.47	-1.95	-0.55
		(3.63)	(0.80)	(0.97)	(0.74)
$CBNA_{jt}$	+/0	0.86	0.13	0.52	0.28
		(0.71)	(0.07)	(0.30)	(0.15)
$CWB_{jt} \times CBNA_{jt}$	−	-6.07	-0.92	-3.62	-2.29
		(8.82)	(0.63)	(2.79)	(1.30)
$CWB^2_{jt} \times CBNA_{jt}$	+	6.19	1.82	7.57	4.75
		(10.58)	(1.09)	(5.28)	(2.36)
$Exmar_{jt}$	−	-0.01	-0.01	-0.01	-0.01
		(0.00)	(0.00)	(0.00)	(0.00)
$UDIFF_{j,t-1}$		1.34	1.33	1.33	1.33
		(0.04)	(0.04)	(0.04)	(0.04)
$UDIFF_{j,t-2}$		-0.36	-0.35	-0.36	-0.35
		(0.04)	(0.04)	(0.04)	(0.04)
Fixed effects		x	x	x	x
N		1316	1316	1316	1316
s.e.r.		0.358	0.357	0.357	0.357
$\bar{R}^2$		0.993	0.993	0.993	0.993

Least squares estimates with panel-corrected standard errors in parentheses. ECB members are excluded after 1997.

Table 6.4. *Descriptive statistics for data underlying unemployment regressions.*

	Mean	St. dev.	Min	Max
UDIFF	1.27	4.18	-8.28	12.69
C	0.29	0.16	0.07	0.65
CBI	0.46	0.19	0.25	0.85
CBCC	-0.35	0.49	-1.00	0.93
MPA	0.47	0.17	0.20	0.75
Exmar	5.44	4.66	-13.52	24.59

Fifteen industrial democracies, 1975 to 1998.

Table 6.5. *Bivariate correlations of data underlying unemployment regressions.*

	UDIFF	C	CBI	CBCC	MPA
C	-0.381				
CBI	-0.087	-0.222			
CBCC	-0.089	0.060	0.001		
MPA	-0.251	-0.178	0.551	-0.118	
Exmar	0.045	-0.130	0.090	-0.009	0.090

Fifteen industrial democracies, 1975 to 1998.

Table 6.6. *Descriptive statistics for data underlying inflation regressions.*

	Mean	St. dev.	Min	Max
ln(Inflation)	1.44	0.91	-3.66	3.47
CBCC	-0.28	0.50	-1.00	1.00
MPA	0.48	0.16	0.10	0.77
CBI	0.44	0.19	0.14	0.85
Imports/GDP	0.29	0.13	0.06	0.76

Twenty industrial democracies, 1973 to 2000.

Table 6.7. *Bivariate correlations of data underlying inflation regressions.*

	ln(Inflation)	CBCC	MPA	CBI
CBCC	-0.130			
MPA	-0.138	-0.144		
CBI	-0.317	-0.109	0.586	
Imports/GDP	-0.104	-0.015	-0.163	-0.037

Twenty industrial democracies, 1973 to 2000.

7

PARTISAN GOVERNMENTS, LABOR UNIONS, AND MONETARY POLICY

All short sentences in economics are wrong.

Alfred Marshall*

Political economists' explanations of 1980s economic performance often focused on labor market arrangements or elections and partisan governments. Starting in the 1990s, political economists turned to central bank institutions. Literatures based around each of these explanations developed in isolation, grew in popularity, then faded, for the most part, into the background. More recently, comparative political economists revisited these ideas in the context of richer, interactive models of economic performance. These new models focused on the interplay of labor markets and central banks. Yet there has been little effort to update earlier interactive models of parties and unions, and no tests for three-way interactions among parties, unions, and monetary authorities. This chapter fills these gaps to better understand how political actors and institutions affect the real economy. As in Chapter 6, I test these interactive models using direct measures of central bank conservatism, so that our results do not rest on weak proxies or dubious assumptions.

The focus of this chapter is the unemployment rate, which results from the interaction of wage bargaining centralization and monetary accommodation. Introducing partisan governments to the framework, I develop a model of unemployment in which partisan governments and unions reach bargains exchanging wage restraint for social policy, with both sides anticipating the cen-

* Marshall's comment earned the reply, "Including that one" (Stigler, 1987).

tral bank may respond to excessive wage demands with restrictive monetary policy. According to the theory developed here, union–government bargains will be most effective to the extent that (1) labor markets are moderately centralized, (2) central banks are inflation hawks, and (3) governments are willing to spend significant sums to reduce unemployment.

Testing the model on fifteen industrial democracies over twenty-four years yields two main findings. First, monetary and labor market institutions interactively determine unemployment. For countries with accommodating central banks, the Calmfors–Driffill curve still holds: Unemployment is highest in moderately centralized labor markets and lower elsewhere. But nonaccommodating central banks – those that are both independent and *conservative* – change this pattern. Nonaccommodating central banks essentially flip the Calmfors-Driffill curve (Iversen, 1999): They produce unemployment outcomes no worse than accommodating central banks in moderately centralized labor markets but raise unemployment everywhere else. Against neoclassical economic theory, the theory and findings of this chapter confirm the existence of meaningful economic tradeoffs in decentralized labor markets, such as the United States and the Eurozone today.

Second, unemployment is subject to both temporary partisan cycles after elections and permanent partisan effects, both of which are consistent with rational expectations. As Lange and Garrett (1985) argue, labor market centralization mediates permanent partisan cycles. *Contra* Lange and Garrett, these cyles reach maximum impact in moderately centralized labor markets, where left-wing government lowers unemployment the most. Central bank independence does not affect temporary partisan cycles. Moreover, permanent partisan cycles are actually larger where the central bank is nonaccommodating.

The Conditional Political Economy of Economic Performance

Before considering interactive models of unemployment, I review three building blocks from which these syntheses developed: theories of corporatism, central bank independence, and partisan cycles. I proceed to pairwise interactions between these institutions, and finally a fully interactive model. As a guide to the different perspectives reviewed, Table 7.1 collects hypotheses regarding the impact of labor markets, partisan governments, and central bank independence on unemployment.

Unions

In the 1980s, labor market structure was a popular explanation for better economic performance in corporatist countries such as Sweden, Austria, and Norway (Cameron, 1984; Katzenstein, 1985). As noted in Chapter 6, Calmfors and Driffill (1988) suggest the relationship between labor union concertation and economic performance may be hump-shaped, owing to two countervailing forces. First, the market power of unions to demand higher wages grows with the centralization of wage bargaining, because the elasticity of demand for goods produced by a bargaining unit falls as the unit grows to encompass entire industries. But at the same time, more encompassing bargaining systems foster union restraint by internalizing the inflationary effects of wage demands (Olson, 1982). Working against each other, these forces render industry-level bargaining the worst of all worlds, because sectoral concentration creates market power without curing the temptation to raise nominal wages. According to Calmfors–Driffill, moving in either direction from moderately centralized bargaining should improve economic performance. In one direction, the market restrains decentralized unions' wage demands, yielding better outcomes. In the other, nationally coordinated labor markets may be the best approach of all, because unions that represent most workers self-restrain to avoid imposing collective negative economic consequences on themselves.

Central Banks

In contrast to the corporatism literature, which supposes labor market institutions affect inflation and unemployment, most scholarship on central banks asserts the price level is determined by monetary policy alone. In particular, the literature presumes individual wage setters anticipate the monetary authority's incentives to inflate, so monetary policy is neutral with respect to unemployment and output. Because anticipated money supply growth yields higher inflation and no real economic benefit, governments should prefer to set their ideal inflation rate by a rule. But this policy is plagued by time inconsistency (Kydland and Prescott, 1977). To whatever extent economic actors believe the promised rule, governments are tempted to create unexpected money growth. Yet so long as the market rationally anticipates cheating, inflation expectations and inflation itself will be higher than under a credible rule. Thus governments preferring both low inflation and high output are better off credibly delegating authority to a conservative, independent central banker (Barro and Gordon, 1983; Rogoff, 1985). As noted in Chapter 6, some economists argue that independent central banks (assumed by these authors to be generally conservative) empirically achieve price stability at no real cost (Grilli, Masciandaro, and Tabellini, 1991; Alesina and Summers, 1993), though in theory, central bank nonaccommodation should increase the instability of the real economy.

Partisan Governments

Whereas work on corporatism and central bank independence concerns the long term institutional sources of economic performance, the political business cycle literature deals with transitory and generally smaller variation in performance before and after elections. Economic theory's turn to rational expectations narrowly confined the role of partisanship in the economy, undercutting Hibbs' (1987) claim that partisan monetary policy had persistent effects on real economic variables. But according to Alesina (1987), elections provide a temporary exception. Firms and unions writing wage contracts before elections are unsure who will win, so contractual assumptions regarding future inflation rates are bound to be less accurate the more unexpected the election outcome. This creates a brief post-election window for parties to use monetary policy to real effect. According to Alesina, left-wing electoral victories are followed by economic booms and right victories by recessions, but by the time most pre-election contracts lapse (say, two years), partisan performance should be indistinguishable. Alesina, Roubini, and Cohen (1997) test this model in the United States and in fifteen OECD countries and find modest temporary partisan cycles. Alesina, Roubini, and Cohen also suppose partisan cycles are less intense where central banks are independent, on the presumption that legally independent central bankers' behavior is unaffected by a change in government. Surprisingly little supporting evidence exists. Indeed, some of the largest partisan cycles appear in Germany and the United States (Alesina and Roubini, 1990), countries with independent central banks. This led Drazen (2000) to question whether Alesina's partisan cycles derive from monetary policy at all, rather than fiscal policy.

Partisan Governments and Unions

In an early effort to examine the interactive effects of political economic institutions on performance, Lange and Garrett (1985) and Alvarez, Garrett, and Lange (1991) argued the effects of labor market institutions depend on the party in power. Only if the left is in power can encompassing unions be sure the benefits of restraint go to workers, rather than the owners of capital (Przeworski

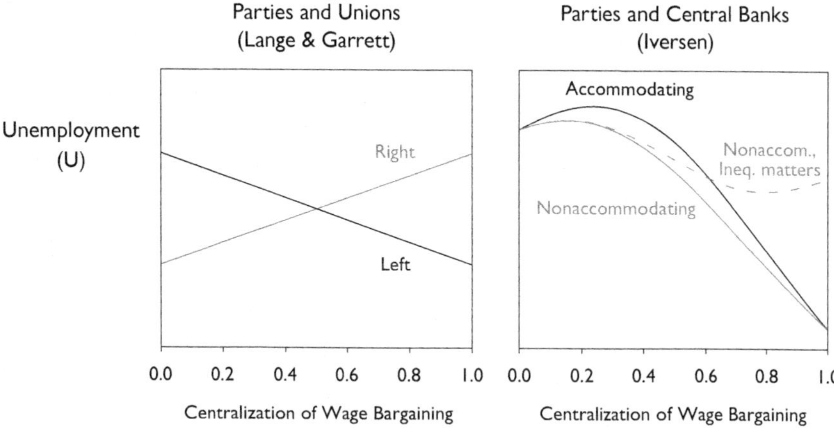

Figure 7.1. *Two interactive models of unemployment.* The left panel shows Lange and Garrett's expected relationship between parties, labor markets, and unemployment: left government complements a centralized labor market, and right government a decentralized economy. The right panel shows equilibrium employment in Iversen's model of union–central-bank interaction under three different scenarios: an accommodating central bank (dark line), a nonaccommodating central bank interacting with unions unconcerned with inequality (solid gray line), and a nonaccommodating central bank faced with unions that care about wage equality (dashed gray line).

and Wallerstein, 1982). Dependent on labor to win elections, the left pursues policies that ensure investment and employment remain high, fulfilling labor's long run goals. But when the right is in power, encompassing unions may be better off using their market power to win immediate wage gains – at the cost of higher unemployment and poorer long-term performance than under the left. On the other hand, where unions are weak and market conditions more closely approximate the neoclassical model, right governments may produce higher growth, lower unemployment, and lower inflation than the left by pursuing *laissez faire* policies. According to Lange and Garrett, the optimal combinations are weak unions and right government, or strong, encompassing unions and left government. At moderate levels of union centralization and strength, partisan changes should make little difference (Figure 7.1, left panel).

Unions and Central Banks

Political economists have recently focused on another institutional interaction. To the extent that labor market agents can set their own wages, central banks must consider the behavior of unions and employers when choosing a monetary policy. At the same time, because the threat of nonaccommodation by an independent central bank can lead a union to rethink its wage demands, any positive degree of wage bargaining centralization can give real effect to monetary policy. This idea lies behind the literature on union–central-bank interactions summarized in Chapter 6.

Within this literature, there is substantial agreement that at least in moderately centralized labor markets, nonaccommodating central banks lower unemployment (Iversen, 1999; Hall and Franzese, 1998; Cukierman and Lippi, 1999). But where wage bargaining centralization is high or low, monetary effects remain unclear. Iversen (1999) plausibly argues that pressure to maintain equality in centralized labor markets clashes with strict monetary regimes, but because these arrangements are rare his theory is hard to test. On the other hand, whereas standard rational expectations theory rejects the idea of lasting real monetary policy effects in decentralized labor markets, Franzese (2001, 2002) persuasively argues that hawkish central banks in mostly decentralized labor markets drive up unemployment to check inflation pressures from unions too small to be credibly threatened. Because of disagreement on the appropriate measure of centralized wage bargaining and a want of direct measures of central bank conservatism – compelling scholars to use outcome-based proxies or assume conservatism to be invariant – the debate remains unresolved.

Partisan Governments, Unions, and Central Banks

Lange and Garrett's argument led the field to consider interactive institutional theories of political economy. Their argument also supports the schema of complementarity, shared by many political economists, that considers ideologically consistent economic institutions – be they labor market structures, welfare state policies, or partisan governments – best for economic performance, as in the varieties of capitalism literature (Hall and Soskice, 2001). Nevertheless, we should examine critically the idea that left- and right-wing utopias constitute the best of all possible worlds. The insight that left-wing governments might suppress labor demands by promising more social policy is a powerful one, but Lange and Garrett's emphasis on highly centralized labor markets is misplaced. In such countries, left-wing governments need not offer social policy to restrain

Table 7.1. *Expected effects of parties, unions, and central banks on unemployment.*

	Theoretical Framework	Effect of Labor Market Institutions		Effect of Left Government given wage bargaining at				Effect of CBI given wage bargaining at		
				Firm	Industry	Peak		Firm	Industry	Peak
Building Blocks	Corporatism (*Calmfors–Driffill*)	Firm or peak bargaining best		—	—	—		—	—	—
	Partisan Cycles (*Alesina*)	—		Temporary decrease only				Moderates partisan cycle		
	CBI (*Barro–Gordon*)	—		—	—	—		No effect		
Synthetic Models	Lange–Garrett	Varies with Party		Perm. Increase	No Effect	Perm. Decrease		—	—	—
	Iversen	Varies with CBI		—	—	—		No Effect	Lower Unemp.	Higher Unemp.
	Hall–Franzese	Varies with CBI		—	—	—		Higher Unemp.	Lower Unemp.	Lower Unemp.
	Proposed Theory	Varies with Party & CBI	1	Weak perm. decrease	Big perm. decrease	Weak perm. decrease	1	Higher Unemp.	Lower Unemp.	Higher Unemp.
							2	Augments permanent partisan cycle		
			2	Temporary decrease from RPC						
							3	Suppresses temporary partisan cycle		

unions, because encompassing unions already internalize the inflationary cost of wage militancy. Instead, following a Calmfors–Driffill logic, the promise of social guarantees from the left should matter most where unions are sorely tempted by their market power – in *moderately* centralized labor markets. On the other hand, the precise benefit of right-wing government in decentralized economies is unclear in Lange and Garrett's work and may amount to the absence of discord, rather than any positive synergy. One might suppose that conservative parties take a hard-line on union wage demands, but if the market is sufficient to restrain atomized unions, there may be little left for the right to do. Instead, by combining Calmfors–Driffill and Lange–Garrett, we arrive at the conclusion that the left, as a credible provider of social policy bargains, can always lower unemployment but does so the most in moderately centralized labor markets, where unions' wage temptations are greatest. Finally, there is an extra dimension to party–central-bank interactions: because partisan governments choose central bankers' replacements when they leave office, parties can also directly shift the degree of central bank nonaccommodation, albeit at lag if the central bank is legally independent.

This chapter focuses on the conditions for successful social policy bargains and their effects on economic performance. Although I do not pursue the policy details of the mechanism here, a search for them could focus on "social pacts" among governments, unions, and employers (Pochet and Fajertag, 2000). These pacts often center on exchanges of wage restraint and labor market reform for social policy compensation, which may include increased education and training spending, more public sector employment, lower taxes and social contributions, or a greater role for unions in directing social policy (Hassel and Ebbinghaus, 2000). A key puzzle in this literature is the success of social pacts in the 1990s in countries, such as Ireland and Italy, that lacked highly centralized wage bargaining, traditionally the signal feature of corporatism (Rhodes, 2001). But a link between *moderately* centralized labor markets and social pacts is exactly what the theory presented here leads us to expect.

Formalizing the Argument: Wage Restraint for Sale

A formal version of the argument sharpens its implications considerably. To this end, I generalize Iversen's model of union–central-bank interaction to include a preliminary round of party–union bargaining over wages. Implicitly or explicitly, the government offers larger social policy benefits in exchange for lower wage demands by unions. The government could be seen as lobbying each union, offering "contributions" of social policy to influence the "policy" of union wage demands. Accordingly, I apply one of Grossman and Helpman's (2001) models of interest group bargaining to the unions' wage decision.

The details of this model can be found in the Theory Appendix to this chapter; here I focus only on the model's implications. The model holds that wage-policy bargains lower unemployment most in moderately centralized labor markets and have smaller effects given either centralization or decentralization. In particular, the model predicts that if unions do not care about policy, the government does not care about the economy, or the central bank and government are both "ultra-liberal" on inflation, then no bargain occurs and Iversen's equilibrium holds as a special case. But in all other cases, social policy bargains reduce unemployment by an amount that is increasing in centralization, the inflation-hawkishness of the central bank and government, and unions' desire for policy, but decreasing in the government's fiscal conservatism. Moreover, the effect of the central bank's inflation preferences is always stronger than the effect of government preferences.

Because the theoretical model involves many moving parts, I use visual displays of comparative statics to tease out testable hypotheses. Figure 7.2 maps expected unemployment at various levels of centralization given any combination of (high or low) monetary accommodation and (present or absent) social policy bargaining. In the first row of plots, solid lines show the equilibrium for Iversen's model of union-central bank interaction in which unions care about wages and unemployment only; dotted lines add social policy bargains for wage restraint. Setting aside differences between monetary regimes and focusing first on the reduction in unemployment under social policy bargains (highlighted in the second row of plots), the model confirms that bargains most effectively reduce unemployment at *moderate* levels of centralization. The effects of bargains are negligible at low levels of centralization because in this case, the connection between a given union's behavior and the average wage is weak. At high levels of centralization, peak associations self-restrain to avoid the inflationary consequences of high wage demands, minimizing – but not entirely eliminating – the scope of further gains from bargains with the government.

Comparing across monetary regimes, the examples in Figure 7.2 demonstrate that when the central bank is more nonaccommodating, social policy bargains reduce unemployment more and have maximum impact on unemployment at lower levels of centralization. A systematic survey across parameter values confirms these examples. Figure 7.3 uses image plots to display the average amount of unemployment reduction given each possible combination of

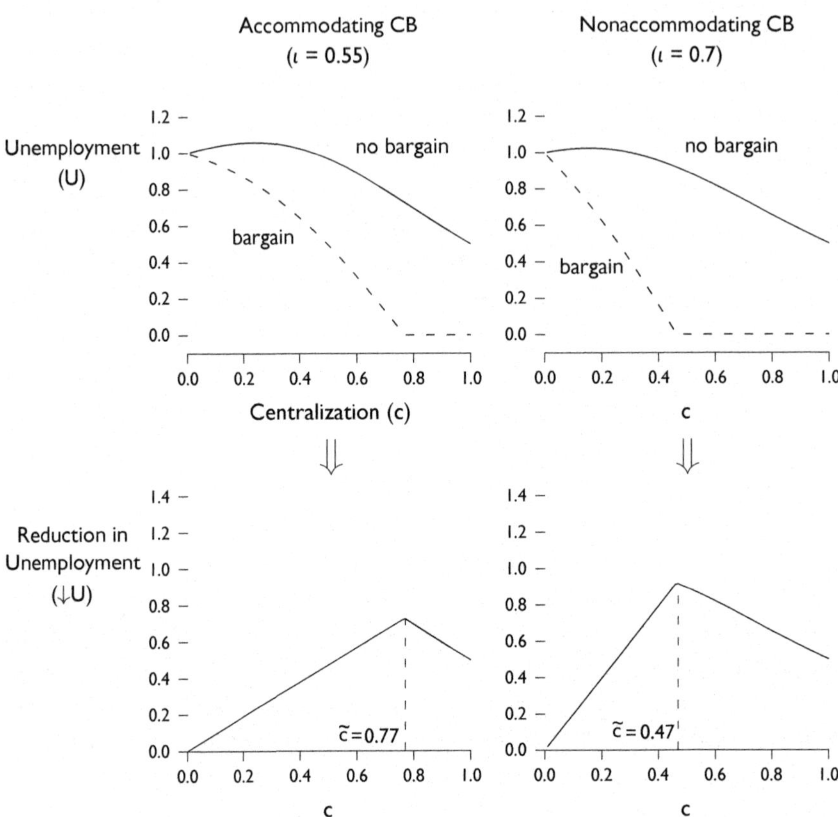

Figure 7.2. *Social policy bargains lower unemployment most given moderately centralized labor markets and hawkish monetary authorities.* In the top row, the unbargained cases (solid lines) are from Figure 7.1 and represent unemployment under Iversen's model (or, equivalently, the present model with $\zeta = 0$ or $\tau = 1$, and $a = 0.5$). The bargained cases (dashed lines) assume unions and governments care equally about inflation, unemployment, and social policy ($a = \lambda = 0.5$, $\zeta = \tau = 0.33$). The bottom row shows the difference between these scenarios, which is the reduction in unemployment under social policy bargains.

central bank inflation preferences (on the horizontal axis) and government inflation preferences (on the vertical axis), under two different scenarios for centralization (the left and right plots).[1] The left panel of this figure shows that regardless of government inflation preferences (λ), more restrictive central banks (those with higher ι) produce larger employment gains from social policy bargains (that is, the shading grows darker to the right of the plot). Although partisan governments' inflation preferences also affect unemployment, the benefit of partisan governments' economic conservatism turns out to be trivial, especially if the central bank is already strongly anti-inflation.

These results are intuitive implications of the model. When the central bank is nonaccommodating, unions and governments anticipate harsher consequences for failing to reach agreement, because wage militancy will be offset with higher unemployment. Acting alone, unions are at least partially compensated by their higher real wages. But because the government cares about unemployment and inflation, and not union wages *per se*, it offers a bargain substituting social policy for wages, averting unemployment and inflation to leave both sides better off.[2] The central bank's preferences are crucial, because the necessity and scope of the bargain is a function of the central bank's threat to hold the line on inflation. On the other hand, because both unemployment and inflation are lower when unions practice wage restraint, it matters little which economic indicator is paramount for the government.

So far, I have established two propositions: social policy bargains tend to be hump-shaped in centralization and increasing in central bank nonaccommodation. Now I show that social policy bargains are also likely to be partisan. Although the role of government inflation preferences is trivial, the impact of goverment fiscal conservatism is not. First, assume the central bank cares about inflation at least as much as unemployment. Then, if we compare the two plots in Figure 7.3, we see that when the government is more liberal on spending (the left plot), social-policy-for-wage-restraint bargains are far deeper and have peaks closer to the midrange of wage bargaining centralization. In contrast, a government that strongly resists spending on social policy produces only small

1 The total unemployment reduction is the area between the curves in Figure 7.2, $\int_0^1 U_a \, dc - \int_0^{\min(\tilde{c},1)} U_b \, dc$, where $\tilde{c}$ denotes the level of centralization at which social policy bargains reduce unemployment to zero. Because c ranges over $[0, 1]$, the total unemployment reduction is also the average unemployment reduction.

2 Even if the government's preference function included real wages, it would care not for union i's real wages but the average real wage in the economy, so like an encompassing union, the government would favor restraint.

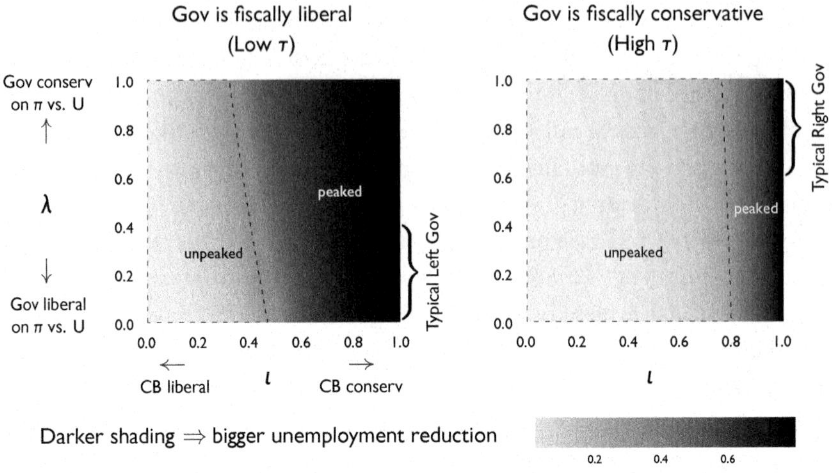

Figure 7.3. *Policy-for-wage-restraint bargains are strengthened by government willingness to spend and central bank nonaccommodation.* Shading indicates average unemployment reduction across all levels of centralization for the given scenario, though in general unemployment reducatons are largest in moderately centralized wage bargaining systems. Specifically, social bargains in the region marked "peaked" reach their unemployment reduction maxima in moderately centralized economies, and in the region marked "unpeaked" at $c = 1$. The left plot assumes a fiscally liberal government ($\tau = 0.25$); the right plot assumes a fiscally conservative government ($\tau = 0.75$). Both plots assume unions care equally about inflation, unemployment, and social policy ($\alpha = 0.5$, $\zeta = 0.33$).

unemployment reductions, unless the central bank is ultra-conservative. Thus for any sensible values of the model parameters, social policy bargains significantly reduce unemployment only when left-wing governments are in office. The result is a permanent, labor market contingent partisan cycle.[3]

The permanent partisan cycle interacts with central bank independence in opposite fashion to Alesina's temporary partisan cycles: labor market contingent cycles are augmented by higher CBI, whereas temporary cycles should

3 There is another reason to expect these cycles to be strongly associated with left government. Government promises of social policy compensation must be credible to spur unions to sign restrained labor contracts. Because the left relies on union members for electoral support, it has a strong incentive to keep its word, but the right, needing neither labor votes nor particularly eager to spend on social programs, may be less credible to unions. This makes right-wing policy-for-wage restraint bargains harder to achieve, or at least less extensive, and inflationary wage increases more likely under the right.

be reduced.[4] Empirical efforts to test for the institutional contours of partisan cycles must therefore take both types of cycles into account, to avoid mistaking one institutional interaction for the other. For example, if the labor market conditional partisan cycle is more important than the temporary rational partisan cycle, but we tested only for the latter and its interaction with CBI, we might find that temporary cycles were *stronger* in high CBI countries, rather than weaker. To avoid misleading results, I test for both cycles simultaneously.

Testing Competing Views of the Interactive Politics of Performance

I evaluate competing theories of the interactions of institutions and parties using data from fifteen industrial democracies collected over the years 1975 to 1998 (see the Data Appendix to this chapter for sources and coding). The countries and period included are those with available data, which is limited mainly by the labor market centralization variable. Fortunately, and in contrast to most measures used in the field, my measures of the characteristics of labor markets, central banks, and parties vary meaningfully over time as well as across countries. This key advantage lets us sort out interactive institutional effects while controlling for unmeasured country characteristics using fixed effects. The analysis proceeds as follows. As a first step, I present basic models testing Alesina's rational partisan cycle and Iversen's model of strategic interaction between unions and central banks. Then I explore a synthetic model including interactions among three institutions: partisan governments, unions, and central banks. Throughout, I employ graphical presentations of model estimates to make results tangible and comparable across models.

Data and Methods

The dependent variable is quarterly unemployment. As in Alesina, Roubini, and Cohen (1997), unemployment in country j and time t is measured as the difference between country j's unemployment and the G7 average for that period, excluding country j. To further mitigate autocorrelation, two lags of the dependent variable are included in all specifications. Another concern is heteroskedasticity across countries, a small amount of which appears in the residuals. Thus,

4 This is a counterexample to Franzese's (1999) claim that CBI reduces the magnitude of all other institutional determinants of nominal outcomes. In this case, credible nonaccommodation spurs more extensive wage restraint through government policy incentives precisely because the government does not control monetary policy.

following Beck and Katz (1995), the model is estimated by least squares with panel-corrected standard errors. Finally, country fixed effects help control for unmeasured, time-invariant country characteristics.

For complex interactive specifications such as the ones investigated in this chapter, tables of regression results leave most substantive questions unanswered (King, Tomz, and Wittenberg, 2000; Cam and Franzese, 2007). Moreover, it is hard to tell at a glance when interactive effects are significant because more than one standard error is involved. I employ the usual solution of calculating changes in the conditional expected value of unemployment in response to hypothetical shifts in a covariate, holding other controls constant. In this way, I can quantify the expected change in unemployment given a change in CBNA (or the party in government, or both) under any level of centralization of wage bargaining and establish a confidence interval around that expected change.

Another interpretive challenge is the time series nature of the model. Because the data are quarterly time series, regression coefficients convey per quarter effects. But the real quantity of interest is the cumulative effect of institutional change over longer periods of time, since political institutions tend to persist for years. Fortunately, we can use the estimated model to calculate first differences and their confidence intervals for any period we like. To calculate the effect of an institutional change in period 1 that persists through period T, I first calculate the period 1 expected value and its confidence interval; then use this point estimate and interval as the lag in calculating period 2, and so on until period T is reached. To obtain the first difference, I subtract the expected unemployment levels for period 0, the last time the old institutions were in place.

Thus, I need to make some assumptions about the *ex ante* values of the dependent variable prevailing before period 0. A reasonable approach is to set these initial lags to the level at which unemployment would have converged if the *ex ante* institutions had been in place indefinitely. Beside being useful for first difference calculations, the expected value of the convergent unemployment rate portrays the ultimate tendency of a particular institutional configuration.[5]

5 Because the model is a second-order difference equation with lag coefficients $\phi_1 + \phi_2 < 1$, the convergent level of unemployment under fixed values of the independent variables, $\mathbf{x}_c$, follows the usual formula, so that

$$\mathrm{E}(\mathrm{UDIFF}_t|\mathbf{x}_c, \beta) \rightarrow \frac{\mathbf{x}_c\beta}{1 - \phi_1 - \phi_2} \text{ as } t \rightarrow \infty;$$

Variables

Central Bank Non-Accommodation (CBNA): Chapter 6 investigated several measures combining central bank independence and central bank conservatism into a single index of central bank nonaccommodation (CBNA). Each of these variables combined the same proxy of central bank conservatism – the Central Banker Career Conservatism (CBCC) index developed in Chapter 3 – with a different measure of independence. The first combination used Cukierman, Webb, and Neyapti's (1992) measure of Central Bank Independence (CBI). However, that index includes some extraneous components, such as directives to maintain price stability, that do not bear immediately on the question of independence. The second measure of independence, Monetary Policy Autonomy (MPA), employed a focused subset of CBI components dealing directly with the central bank's separation from the elected government. In this chapter, I use the term CBNA to indicate the interaction of CBCC and MPA, which performed slightly better than other proxies of this concept in Chapter 6.

This approach differs from and improves upon Hall and Franzese (1998) and Cukierman and Lippi (1999), who assume CBI (measured either using the Cukierman index or an average of three popular indexes) sufficiently captures nonaccommodation, neglecting altogether variation in central bank conser-

---

as two of our institutions, CWB and CBNA, tend to remain relatively constant for years at a time, the convergent unemployment rate could be a good initial lag. But for parties that cycle in and out of office over the years, it is less than ideal. However, it does provide a useful baseline from which to consider alternative scenarios of partisan history. Readers interested in the effect of a change from left to right government when recent history includes both left and right governments might suppose that the unemployment rate in period 0 reflects some linear combination of the long-run tendencies of each party, conditional on the institutional setting:

$$\text{UDIFF}_0(\theta) = \theta \text{E}(\text{UDIFF}_\infty|\mathbf{x}_c, \text{Left}) + (1-\theta)\text{E}(\text{UDIFF}_\infty|\mathbf{x}_c, \text{Right}),$$

for $0 \leq \theta \leq 1$. If we assume *ex ante* unemployment had converged to the left government's long-run tendency, the calculated first difference for a right electoral victory reflects the case where $\theta = 1$ at time 0. Call these results $\text{E}(\Delta_t\text{UDIFF}_t|\mathbf{x}_c, \text{Right}, \text{UDIFF}_0(1))$. It follows that

$$\text{E}(\Delta_t\text{UDIFF}_t|\mathbf{x}_c, \text{Right}, \text{UDIFF}_0(\theta)) = \theta\text{E}(\Delta_t\text{UDIFF}_t|\mathbf{x}_c, \text{Right}, \text{UDIFF}_0(1)).$$

For example, if the initial level of unemployment lies halfway between the left and right tendencies at the start of a right-wing government, the appropriate first difference estimates are exactly half those shown in the text.

vatism. And though Iversen (1999) recognizes the need to incorporate a proxy of conservatism into his measure of CBNA, his approach is quite indirect, averaging three popular measures of CBI with a "behavioral" measure of restrictiveness, exchange rate stability. (Adolph [2004] presents an analysis similar to this chapter, but using Iversen's measure.[6]) One concern with using such a behavioral proxy is that by mixing economic outcomes with their determinants, we may induce endogeneity bias and overstate the effects of nonaccommodation. The regression models in this chapter use only the preexisting characteristics of institutions and agents to explain the unemployment rate and so avoid this problem.

Centralization of Wage Bargaining (CWB): Coded by Iversen, this variable captures the weight given to each level of bargaining and the percentage of workers covered at each level (the Data Appendix contains further details). CWB ranges from 0 to 1 in theory and is observed to vary between 0.01 and 0.43.

Challenging Party Electoral Victory within the last 6 quarters (CV6): As noted by Alesina, Roubini, and Cohen, challenger victories are likely to be a decent proxy for "surprising" elections. I follow their lead in coding a variable, $CV6_{jt}$, which takes on the value −1 for the six quarters following a left-wing challenger victory, 1 for the six quarters after a right-wing challenger win, and 0 otherwise. I expect this variable to have a positive effect on unemployment (that is, right-wing victory temporarily raises unemployment). Experimentation with various lag structures and lengths of partisan effects reveals that the second lag of this variable, $CV6_{j,t-2}$, best captures the temporary partisan cycle.

Partisanship of Current Administration (ADM): To test for permanent partisan effects, I use a simple coding of whether the government is right-wing (1) or left-wing (−1), which I updated from Alesina, Roubini, and Cohen. I have no expectations regarding ADM except in interaction with other variables.

Export Market Growth (Exmar): Following Iversen, I control for shocks impacting a country's export market using OECD data on the growth in each country's export markets.

6 The findings in Adolph (2004) differ from the present analysis mainly in respect to unemployment under nonaccommodating central banks. Under Iversen's measure, nonaccommodating banks appear to produce less unemployment, particularly in moderately centralized economies, but are still worse than accommodating central banks in decentralized labor markets.

Results

Empirical investigation of the interactive effects of partisan governments, unions, and central banks on unemployment takes place in two stages: first we test some basic building blocks, then move on to novel hypotheses. Table 7.3 in the Data Appendix presents raw regression results for comparison with previous research. For substantive clarity, I focus my discussion on graphical displays of these complex models.

First, I test Alesina's rational party theory, for which the most data are available (1960Q1 to 1998Q2). The model to be fitted is

$$\text{UDIFF}_{jt} = \phi_1 \text{UDIFF}_{j,t-1} + \phi_2 \text{UDIFF}_{j,t-2} + \beta \text{CV6}_{j,t-2} + \alpha_j + \epsilon_{jt}, \quad (7.1)$$

where α_j is a country fixed effect and ϵ_{jt} is a Normally distributed disturbance. The results (Table 7.3, column 1) echo Alesina, Roubini, and Cohen (1997): a change in government from left to right temporarily raises unemployment, and vice versa for right-to-left transitions. First differences show this effect is significant but small. Two and a half years after the election – the point of maximum accumulated impact – temporary partisan cycles shift unemployment only 0.52 points from the pre-election rate [90% CI: 0.28 to 0.75].

Next, I test Iversen's theory of union–central-bank interaction using his preferred specification, now applied to quarterly data (1975Q1 to 1998Q4) instead of four-year averages. Iversen's expectations are shown below each parameter.[7]

$$\begin{aligned} \text{UDIFF}_{jt} = {} & \phi_1 \text{UDIFF}_{j,t-1} + \phi_2 \text{UDIFF}_{j,t-2} \\ & + \underset{+}{\beta_1} \text{CWB}_{jt} + \underset{-}{\beta_2} \text{CWB}^2_{jt} + \underset{+}{\beta_3} \text{CBNA}_{jt} + \underset{-}{\beta_4} \text{CWB}_{jt} \times \text{CBNA}_{jt} \\ & + \underset{+}{\beta_5} \text{CWB}^2_{jt} \times \text{CBNA}_{jt} + \beta_6 \text{Exmar}_{jt} + \alpha_j + \epsilon_{jt} \end{aligned} \quad (7.2)$$

By including CWB and CWB^2, the model tests for the presence of a Calmfors–Driffill hump-shaped relationship between centralization and unemployment; by including interactions of these terms and CBNA, the model allows this curve to flip to a U in the presence of high nonaccommodation. Finally, by

7 To understand Iversen's specification, recall that it tests whether the Calmfors–Driffill hump is inverted for sufficiently high CBNA. A model testing just Calmfors-Diffill would include $\psi_1 \text{CWB} + \psi_2 \text{CWB}^2$, anticipating $\psi_1 > 0$ and $\psi_2 < 0$. But if instead we include $(\psi_1 \text{CWB} + \psi_2 \text{CWB}^2)(\kappa - \text{CBNA})$, $\kappa > 0$, then for CBNA $< \kappa$ the specification producea a hump, and for CBNA $> \kappa$ the hump is inverted into a U. Multiplying and reparameterizing yields the specification in the text.

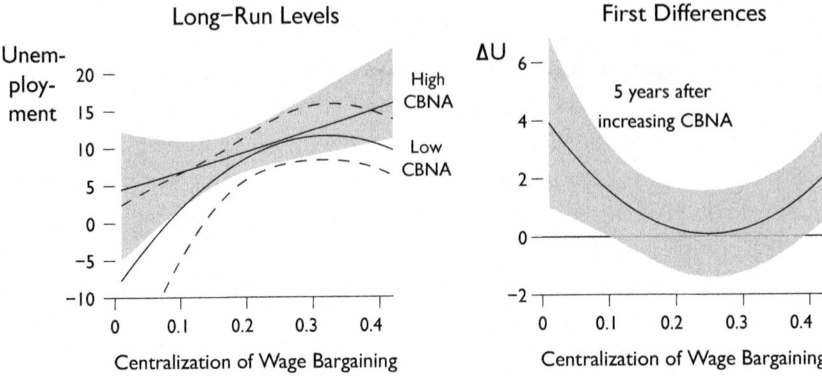

Figure 7.4. *Iversen's model of central banks and unions: Long- and medium-run results.* In the left panel, solid lines reflect the level of unemployment to which an economy would eventually converge given fixed institutions. The line marked "Low CBNA" assumes accommodating central banks (1.5 s.d. below the mean level), while the line marked "high CBNA" assumes nonaccommodating central banks (1.5 s.d. above the mean). The right panel shows the expected change in unemployment five years after an increase from low to high nonaccommodation. In all plots, shaded regions or dashed lines show 90 percent confidence intervals. All expectations and confidence intervals are based on Model 3, with partisanship and other controls held at their mean values.

including an uninteracted CBNA term, the model allows nonaccommodation to increase or decrease unemployment in decentralized economies.

As Table 7.3 shows, testing Iversen's theory on more finely grained economic data allows us to estimate his parameters more precisely. (These results recapitulate Model 2 from Chapter 6.) In terms of the signs of estimated parameters, all of Iversen's expectations are met and all but β_2 are significant, adding to our confidence that the Calmfors–Driffill relationship is inverted by monetary nonaccommodation. Once again, β_3 is positive and significant, supporting Hall and Franzese's view that nonaccommodation can raise unemployment in decentralized economies.

Expected values and first differences combine the various interaction terms to show how institutional effects accumulate over time. As in Chapter 6, one way to summarize these results is to calculate the level to which unemployment would converge given fixed CWB and CBNA. Figure 7.4 (left panel) shows this convergent unemployment rate over the observed range of labor market centralization, given either high CBNA (1.5 standard deviations above the mean observed level) or low CBNA (1.5 standard deviations below the mean), and holding other regressors at their means.[8] As in Chapter 6, monetary nonaccommodation carries no unemployment penalty in moderately centralized economies: there, the long-term unemployment rate is the same regardless of CBNA. For decentralized and highly centralized labor markets, nonaccommodation imposes significant unemployment costs.

Figure 7.4 (right panel) uses five-year first differences to show the expected change in unemployment after an increase in central bank nonaccommodation. Five years later, a decentralized economy can expect unemployment to rise 3.9 points, although the 90 percent confidence interval suggests this effect could be as low as 1.0 or as high as 6.9 points. At high levels of centralized wage bargaining, CBNA raises unemployment by two points, give or take 1.5 points. Moderately centralized labor markets experience no change in unemployment.

To test for labor-market contingent partisan cycles, I combine partisan, labor market, and central bank variables in a single specification. Model 3 adds three terms: ADM, ADM $\times$ CWB, and ADM $\times$ CWB^2. Because I expect left parties to lower unemployment more where centralization is moderate, ADM $\times$ CWB should be positive and ADM $\times$ CWB^2 negative. To avoid confounding temporary cycles with permanent, labor market contingent partisan effects, I also add Alesina's temporary cycle variable. The estimated model (reported in Table 7.3) meets our expectations regarding labor market contingent partisan cycles, which take place alongside the temporary partisan cycle. Iversen's variables remain robust to the inclusion of partisan variables and interactions – his parameters have grown in magnitude and remain as precise as ever – and CBNA still raises unemployment in decentralized labor markets.[9]

8 Because the outcome of interest is the unemployment level, while the dependent variable is the difference between the unemployment level and the G7 mean, I add the G7 mean (which was 6.72 percent, after adjusting for excluded cases) back in before plotting the results in Figures 7.4 and 7.5. To provide a more comprehensive test, the simulation results in these figures are actually drawn from Model 3, with partisanship held at its mean. Readers can refer back to the bottom row of plots in Figure 6.3 to review the results for this chapter's Model 2. The similarity of simulation results across these figures confirms that our first order results on union–central-bank interactions are insensitive to the inclusion or exclusion of party interactions.

9 As a check, I reestimated Model 3 excluding each country in turn. Across all of these robustness checks, the signs and approximate size of coefficients remained unchanged without exception. In the vast majority of cases, significant results from the full sample also remained significant in each subsample. However, in a few cases individual coefficients that were significantly different from zero in the full sample just missed

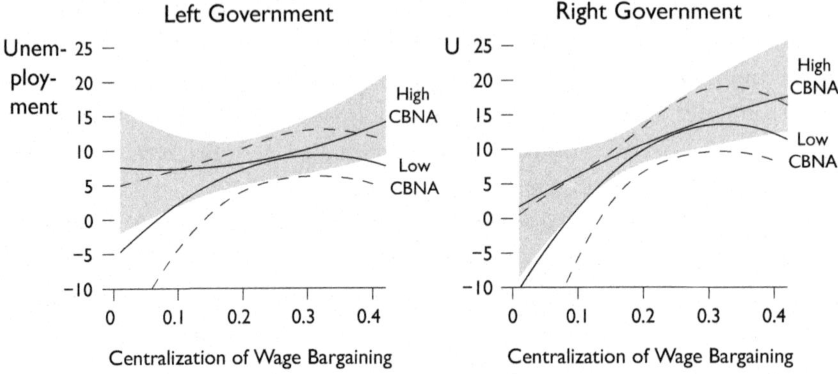

Figure 7.5. *Long-run results from the three-way model of central banks, unions, and partisan governments.* Solid lines reflect the level of unemployment to which an economy would converge given fixed institutions and government, with a left-wing government in power in the left plot, and a conservative government in the right plot. The line marked "Low CBNA" assumes an accommodating central bank (1.5 s.d. below the mean level), and the line marked "High CBNA" assumes an nonaccommodating central bank (1.5 s.d. above the mean). Shaded regions and dashed lines indicate 90 percent confidence intervals. Expectations and confidence intervals are calculated using Model 3, with other controls held at their mean values.

Graphics of expected values and first differences show the complex interactive effects of parties, unions, and central banks more clearly. Figure 7.5 shows the long-run tendencies of unemployment under continuous rule by either the left or the right, given either high or low CBNA and various levels of centralization. Partisan effects are greatest at moderate to moderately-high levels of

significance at conventional levels in analyses of datasets with one or another country removed. Coefficients of variables capturing the labor market contingent partisan cycle (ADM × CWB, ADM × CWB^2) proved especially robust, remaining significantly different from zero at the 95% level with only three borderline cases. The four terms crucial to Iversen's hypotheses (CWB, CWB^2, CWB × CBNA, and CWB^2 × CBNA) were somewhat more sensitive, but only because the terms CWB and CWB^2 are on the borderline of significance in the full model and slight changes in these estimates in subsamples shift them back and forth across conventional significance cutoffs. The additive impact of CBNA is sensitive to the exclusion of Austria – even then only barely missing significance at the 90 percent level. Alesina's measure of temporary cycles is always significant.

centralization, with unemployment lowered by the left and raised by the right. Comparison of the left and right panels echoes the predictions of this chapter's formal model of wage–policy bargaining, which held that a government able to credibly offer policy rewards for wage restraint lowers unemployment most where wage bargaining is moderately centralized. However, the wide range of long-run equilibrium unemployment rates across different labor market institutions shown in these graphics makes substantively large partisan effects appear smaller to the eye than they are. Moreover, the very long run is the wrong place to look for partisan cycles, which operate over the short and medium run following elections.

For these reasons, cumulative first differences over a period following a change in government – say, one year, three years, or five years – are a better way to show the combined effect of temporary and permanent partisan cycles. According to our hypotheses, unemployment should fall in all economies immediately after a left-wing victory. Over time, this effect should intensify in moderately centralized economies and vanish in labor markets closer to the extremes. Simulations through one and five years following partisan change reveal most, but not all, of these features, although assumptions about the government's influence over central banker appointment turn out to be crucial.

To explore labor market contingent partisan cycles in detail, Figure 7.6 displays two sets of simulations. In the first set (left panel), we assume a left-leaning government has replaced a right-leaning one. We allow the centralization of wage bargaining to take on any extant value, but assume central bank nonaccommodation is fixed at its mean, both before and after the change in government. In effect, we are holding the monetary regime fixed and examining the net nonmonetary consequences of partisan government. Three patterns emerge from this picture: first, the unemployment-reducing benefits of left government grow with increasing wage bargaining centralization, reaching a maximum at moderate to high levels of CWB, then tailing off; second, holding CBNA constant, left governments raise unemployment in decentralized labor markets, supporting – but only for the moment – the claims of Lange and Garrett; and third, partisan effects grow over time: permanent, not temporary, partisan cycles dominate.

Still, the left panel of Figure 7.6 tells an incomplete story. Governments influence monetary policy as well as fiscal and social policy, so to puzzle out the full effect of partisanship on unemployment, we must look ahead. In Chapter 9, I show that when control of government passes from right to left, central bankers appointed by the old right-wing government tend to leave office faster

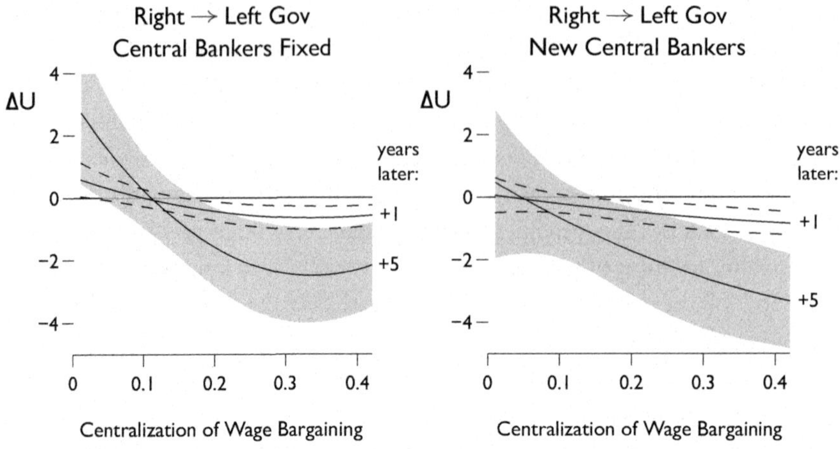

Figure 7.6. *Expected partisan effect on unemployment from the three-way interaction of central banks, unions, and partisan governments: Evidence from Model 3.* The left panel shows the cumulative change in unemployment either one year or five years after left-wing electoral victory over a long-standing right-wing government, given the indicated degree of centralized wage bargaining and assuming the level of central bank nonaccommodation remains unchanged at its mean. The right panel shows the same quantities but assumes the incoming left-wing government replaces a central bank board consisting of typical right government appointees with a board typical of left governments. Shaded regions and dashed lines indicate 90 percent confidence intervals. Predictions are calculated from Model 3, iterated through twenty periods with temporary partisan variables changing appropriately over time.

than they otherwise would. This happens despite legal guarantees of independence, in part because central bankers initially appointed by the current government's ideological opponents tend not to be reappointed when their terms end. New governments thereby have an opportunity to place their stamp on central bank policy boards. As Chapter 8 shows, partisan governments appoint central bankers whose careers suggest they have (native or induced) policy preferences that accord with the government's partisan goals.On average, left-wing governments prefer central bankers with Central Banker Career Conservatism scores 0.315 points lower than right-leaning governments' appointees.

The right panel of Figure 7.6 assumes the new left-leaning government has an opportunity to immediately reduce the median central banker's CBCC score by 0.315 points (in reality, this opportunity is idiosyncratically delayed by central banker terms of office). The resulting change in unemployment therefore comprises the total estimated monetary and nonmonetary effect of partisan government. We find no net impact of partisan government in decentralized labor markets and a gradual, permanent increase in the unemployment-reducing effect of left government as unionized bargaining grows more centralized. The total effect of partisanship does not tail off at high levels of CWB, but this is because under different wage bargaining systems, the components driving partisan cycles vary. In decentralized and highly centralized labor markets, the left's tendency to appoint more accommodating central bankers is critical, whereas in moderately centralized markets, left-leaning governments directly lower unemployment, even in combination with highly conservative central bankers. Labor market contingent permanent cycles still overwhelm temporary cycles, regardless of whether power changed hands recently or long ago. Finally, it bears repeating that our conclusions for decentralized labor markets depend crucially on the kinds of central bankers governments appoint: the results in Figure 7.4 suggest that any government willing to tolerate higher inflation could permanently reduce unemployment in mostly decentralized economies by choosing still more accommodating central bankers than they typically do.

This inflation–unemployment tradeoff does not appear in moderately centralized economies. Indeed, the theoretical model's final hypothesis is that left-wing government should be able to lower unemployment *more* in moderately-centralized labor markets when monetary nonaccommodation is high. As an aid to readers, the left panel of Figure 7.7 recalls how the reduction in unemployment from left-wing government should theoretically vary with CWB and CBNA. (These predictions are redrawn from the lower panels of Figure 7.2.) To fully test the theoretical model, I add two more interaction terms to the regression equation: ADM $\times$ CWB $\times$ CBNA, which should be positive, and ADM $\times$ CWB^2 $\times$ CBNA, which should be negative. These terms allow for an interaction between the central bank's stance and the permanent partisan cycle. The regression results appear in the last column of Table 7.2 and fit our expectations.[10]

10 In an alternative specification, I also add an interaction between temporary partisan cycles and central bank nonaccommodation. Because delegating monetary policy to a nonaccommodating central bank should lower uncertainty about future economic policy regardless of the party in government, this interaction should carry a negative coefficient and suppress the temporary partisan cycle. However, this is not the case. If we add this interaction term (and, if they are not already present, the CV6 and CBNA base terms) to the four models in Table 7.3, we find the interactive effect of temporary

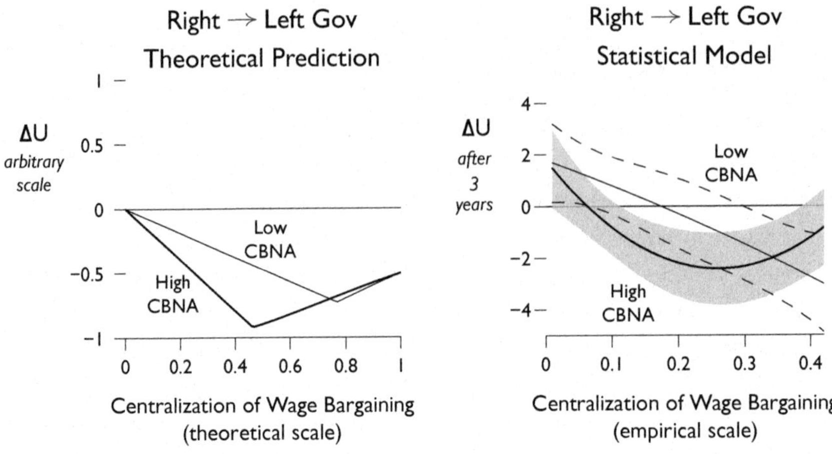

Figure 7.7. *Expected partisan effect on unemployment from the three-way interaction of central banks, unions, and partisan governments: Theory compared with evidence from Model 4.* The left panel recalls from Figure 7.2 the theoretically predicted change in unemployment after a change in the partisanship of government. The right panel summarizes the empirical model's findings regarding the change in unemployment following partisan transition (calculated from Model 4, iterated through twelve periods with temporary partisan variables changing appropriately over time). Solid lines show the change in unemployment three years after a left-wing government replaces a long-standing right-wing government, as conditioned by the monetary regime (either 1.5 s.d. below the mean level of CBNA or 1.5 s.d. above it) and the degree of wage bargaining centralization. Shaded regions and dashed lines indicate 90 percent confidence intervals.

But the real test is the visual comparison of the theoretical predictions with the unemployment first differences simulated from our analysis of the data (right panel of Figure 7.7). These first differences capture the cumulative unemployment effects of a change in the governing party after three years for either high or low CBNA. (In either case, CBNA is assumed to remain fixed

partisan cycles and central bank nonaccommodation is always *positive* and far from statistically significant. (The rest of the regression results, including the estimate of the effect of CV6, remain unchanged.) Nor does it help to interact CV6 with central bank independence alone, leaving out the effects of central banker conservatism (Adolph, 2004). Though the small size of temporary partisan cycles hinders empirical investigation of second-order institutional mediation, this is discouraging news for rational partisan theory, and adds evidence to Drazen's (2000) contention that temporary cycles are nonmonetary.

at that level across the pre- and post-election periods.) With the possible exception of highly centralized economies, where our confidence is lower, the match between prediction and result is remarkably close. Labor market contingent partisan cycles are stronger when central banks are nonaccommodating, and maintain their U-shaped relationship with centralization of the labor market. Indeed, when nonaccommodation increases, the peak of the partisan cycle moves to lower levels of centralization, as anticipated by the model. This result is consistent with the idea that left-leaning governments reach more efficient unemployment-reducing bargains with industry-level unions when unions fear central bank reprisals. To a remarkable degree, the partisanship of government, restrictiveness of the central bank, and centralization of wage bargaining interact as expected in shaping unemployment outcomes.

Conclusions

This chapter emphasized the possibility of bargains between labor unions and left-wing governments who trade policy concessions for wage restraint to lower unemployment. Leaving aside for the moment partisan governments' ability to shift monetary policy by appointing new central bankers, we find partisan governments' impact on unemployment matters most in moderately centralized labor markets, rather than the more extreme cases the literature has tended to emphasize. My argument echoes earlier findings that monetary nonaccommodation carries smaller unemployment costs under industry-level bargaining: theoretically and empirically, left parties and conservative central banks are strongly complementary – but *only* when labor markets are moderately centralized.

The evidence suggests political economic institutions have deeply interactive effects on economic performance. Further research should consider exactly how partisan governments, unions, and central banks interact, and how that interaction changes over time and with repeated bargaining. Clearly, the policy mechanisms governments use to encourage union restraint need to be isolated. Social pacts are one place to search, but extensions should also go beyond the bargaining framework to recognize the multiple avenues by which governments can affect monetary policy, labor market organization, and the interaction of these institutions in the wage determination process. After all, governments regulate unions and employers, appoint central bankers, and codify the degree of central bank independence. Thus, the literature developing around the proposition that labor markets and central banks interact should make explicit the role of the government itself.

One such extension contemplates the possibility that central banks threaten nonaccommodation of governments as well as labor market actors. Although central banks normally have statutory authority only over monetary policy, they can use that authority to gain leverage over fiscal policy as well, in a mirror image of the role governments play in this chapter. Some claim the Greenspan Fed made a bargain with the Clinton White House in which the president moderated fiscal policy in exchange for aggressive monetary stimulus. In June 2012, the European Central Bank appeared to make a similar threat, promising to hold back even the tepid amount of monetary stimulus needed to achieve ECB inflation targets unless Eurozone governments reached an accord to restrain fiscal stimulus.[11] From a political economy perspective, these episodes, even if isolated and publicly deniable, show the sort of bargaining logic used in this chapter can flow in multiple directions, so that power to make policy in one area gives leverage over others. In this view, instead of creating autonomous islands of monetary and fiscal authority, legal charters of central bank independence generate competition and mutual influence between rival economic powers within the state. A further unsettling implication is that legal independence allows central banks' power to exist outside the routine channels of democratic accountability, yet have significant influence over not just supposedly technical monetary issues, but the inarguably substantive questions of fiscal policy. This raises the stakes for democracies as we turn to the limited ways in which elected governments can hold central banks accountable for their policies.

11 Draghi repeatedly denied the ECB is holding interest rates hostage to E.U. fiscal agreements (Jana Randow, "Draghi Says a Few ECB Council Members Wanted to Cut Rate," *Bloomberg BusinessWeek*, June 6, 2012, businessweek.com/news/2012-06-06/draghi-says-a-few-ecb-council-members-wanted-to-cut-rate). But markets seem to have received the signal – backed up by an otherwise-puzzling refusal to lower rates in the midst of economic freefall. See Ezra Klein, "Mario Draghi: The banker holding Europe hostage," *Washington Post*, June 7, 2012, washingtonpost.com/blogs/ezra-klein/post/mario-draghi-the-banker-holding-europe-hostage-wonkbook/2012/06/07/gJQAnyxqKV_blog.html and Matthew Yglesias, "Toff Doctrine monetary policy from Alan Greenspan to Mario Draghi," *Slate*, June 6, 2012, slate.com/blogs/moneybox/2012/06/06/toff_doctrine_monetary_policy_from_alan_greenspan_to_mario_draghi.html.

Theory Appendix to Chapter 7

Sequence of Play and Economic Assumptions

In the first stage of the game, the government and a representative union i set the level of social policy, P, and union wage demands, w_i, according to the Nash bargaining solution. In the second stage, the central bank sets the price level, π, in response to the average wage, w, which results in the equilibrium level of unemployment, U.

A few economic assumptions are needed to establish the model (these mirror Iversen (1999), which should be consulted for further details). Assume the economy consists of n equally sized unions, so the centralization of the labor market can be represented by $c = 1/n$.[12] To understand the incentives facing unions in wage bargaining, we must consider the out-of-equilibrium effect of wages on unemployment. Iversen shows that the change in unemployment for any given union i is

$$\Delta U_i = w_i(c^2 - c + 1) + w_o c(1 - c) - \pi, \tag{7.3}$$

and the overall change in unemployment resulting from the wages of union i is

$$\Delta \overline{U} = cw_i + (1 - c)w_o - \pi, \tag{7.4}$$

where w_i is the wage demand of union i, and w_o the wage rate set by other unions (see derivations below). Because in equilibrium all unions set the same wage rate (that is, $w_i = w_o$), the equilibrium change in unemployment is $\Delta\overline{U} = w^\star - \pi$, which is also equal to zero – firms cannot raise the wage bill any faster than prices.

Derivation of Equations 7.3 and 7.4. Iversen decomposes the effects of wage-setting by union i into a relative price effect (π_i^r) and an aggregate price effect (π_i^a).

12 The assumption that the number of unions proxies their concentration can be empirically justified. Using data from Ebbinghaus and Visser (2000) for the year 1995, I find a correlation of 0.69 between the inverse of the number of unions and the Herfindahl index of union concentration in the dozen industrial democracies for which adequate data exist. Instead of all unions, however, the correlation between the number of and concentration of *bargaining units* – which in some countries may be sectoral confederations or peak associations rather than unions *per se* – is most relevant. Using Iversen's (1999) assessment of the primary bargaining level in each country, this correlation is 0.88.

According to Calmfors and Driffill, a union's ability to pass on wage increases through prices is proportional to its size, because larger unions imply poorer substitution among products from different bargaining areas. This is captured using the simple functional form $\pi_i^r = cw_i$. Analogously, the relative price effect for all other unions can be written $\pi_o^r = cw_o$. The aggregate price effect of union i's wage demand is also proportional to its size; therefore, $\pi_i^a = c^2 w_i$, while the aggregate effect of all other union's wage demands is $\pi_o^a = c(1-c)w_o$.

Assuming increases in real wages lower profits and raise unemployment, Iversen captures the change in unemployment within union i as the sum of the real increase in wages across the economy and the real increase in wages within union i, or

$$\Delta U_i = (\pi_i^a + \pi_o^a - \pi) + (w_i - \pi_i^r), \tag{7.5}$$

which simplifies to (7.3) in the text. Analogously, the increase in aggregate unemployment is the weighted average

$$\Delta U_i = (\pi_i^a + \pi_o^a - \pi) + c(w_i - \pi_i^r) + (1-c)(w_o - \pi_o^r), \tag{7.6}$$

which simplifies to equation 7.4 above (Iversen, 1999).

Players

As in Iversen's model, unions gain utility from real wages and low unemployment; however, they now receive utility from social policy as well. The preference function of the ith union is given by

$$V_{\mathrm{U_i}} = \zeta P + (1-\zeta)\left[\alpha(w_i - \pi) - (1-\alpha)U_i\overline{U}\right]. \tag{7.7}$$

The parameter ζ captures the weight given to social policy objectives, whereas α measures the relative importance of real wages and unemployment. Following Iversen, unions care about unemployment both within the union (U_i) and economy-wide ($\overline{U}$). To simplify exposition, I neglect the possibility that unions act to reduce wage inequality.

The monetary authority, on the other hand, cares only about economic outcomes. Its preference function is

$$V_{\mathrm{M}} = -\iota\pi^2 - (1-\iota)\overline{U}^2, \tag{7.8}$$

where ι captures the conservatism of the monetary authority in terms of its preference for inflation versus unemployment.

Finally, the government has three objectives: to minimize the cost of social policy while producing low inflation and low unemployment. Therefore, its preference function is

$$V_G = -\tau P - (1-\tau)\left[\lambda\pi - (1-\lambda)\overline{U}\right], \qquad (7.9)$$

where τ captures the budgetary conservatism of the government (the rate at which extra spending reduces its utility), and λ measures the economic conservatism of the government (its concern for inflation relative to unemployment).[13]

Equilibrium

I solve the game by "backwards induction." I find that unions and government anticipate the monetary authority will set the price level subject to the following maximization condition, expressed in terms of a given union's wage choice:[14]

$$\pi^{\star}(w_i) = (1-\iota)\left[\overline{U} + cw_i + (1-c)w_o\right]. \qquad (7.10)$$

The central bank accommodates wage increases through prices only to the extent that it is sensitive to unemployment resulting from nonaccommodation. If the central bank is hawkish on inflation (high ι), it holds a tighter line on inflation and allows unemployment to rise.

In the first stage, I assume the government and labor unions reach the Nash bargaining solution. That is, they agree on the wage and social policy that maximizes the geometric average of what each would gain under the agreement, relative to the status quo without the agreement and given the monetary authority's best move in the second stage. Thus, the government and unions choose (w_i, P) to maximize

$$\gamma \ln\left[V_{U_i}(w_i, P) - V_{U_i}(\hat{w}_i, 0)\right] + (1+\gamma)\ln\left[V_G(w_i, P) - V_G(\hat{w}_i, 0)\right], \qquad (7.11)$$

13 I assume government utility is linear in inflation and unemployment to simplify exposition, though these terms could be made quadratic (mirroring the central bank's preferences) without changing the thrust of the argument.

14 Once the second stage is reached, the central bank responds to the average wage, w, which in equilibrium is equal to w_i, as all unions are identical by assumption. Thus (7.10) simplifies to $\pi^{\star}(w) = (1-\iota)(\overline{U} + w)$.

where γ is a constant reflecting the bargaining power of union i relative to the government, and $\hat{w}_i$ denotes the wage that would prevail absent social policy payoffs.[15]

I show in the following that solving this maximization problem leads unions to demand wages strictly less than Iversen's equilibrium, in exchange for social policy gains. In turn, the equilibrium level of unemployment consists of the sum of two terms

$$\overline{U} = \frac{\alpha(1 - c + c\iota)}{(1-\alpha)(c^2 - 2c + 2\iota c + 1)} + \frac{\zeta}{1-\zeta}\frac{1-\tau}{\tau}\frac{\iota}{1-\iota}c(\lambda\iota - \lambda - \iota). \quad (7.12)$$

This is simply the equilibrium level under Iversen's model (the first term, which I denote U_a), reduced by social policy bargains (the second term, denoted U_b). Because no mechanism can lower unemployment below zero, I impose the additional restriction that $U^\star = \max(0, \overline{U})$.

Solution of the game. To solve the bargaining problem, it helps to isolate the non-social-policy components of the player's preferences. I rewrite union preferences as $V_{U_i} = \zeta W_{U_i}(w_i) + (1-\zeta)P$, where $W_{U_i} = \alpha(w_i - \pi) - (1-\alpha)U_i\overline{U}$. As in Iversen, W_{U_i} can be written as a function of the wage w_i by substituting the disequilibrium conditions $U_i + \Delta U_i$ for U_i and $\overline{U} + \Delta\overline{U}$ for $\overline{U}$. I rewrite government preferences in similar fashion as $V_G = W_G(w_i) - P$, again substituting $\overline{U} + \Delta\overline{U}$ for $\overline{U}$. We also need the derivatives of these preferences functions:

$$\frac{\partial W_{U_i}}{\partial w_i} = \alpha(1 - c + c\iota) - (1-\alpha)(c^2 - 2c + 2\iota c - 1)\iota(w + \overline{U}) \quad (7.13)$$

and

$$\frac{\partial W_G}{\partial w_i} = c(\lambda\iota - \lambda - \iota). \quad (7.14)$$

We can now rewrite the Nash bargaining problem facing unions and governments as

$$\max_{w_i, P} \gamma \ln\left\{\zeta P + (1-\zeta)\left[W_{U_i}(w_i) - W_{U_i}(\hat{w}_i)\right]\right\}$$
$$+ (1-\gamma)\ln\left\{-\tau P + (1-\tau)\left[W_G(w_i) - W_G(\hat{w}_i)\right]\right\}. \quad (7.15)$$

This yields first order conditions for w_i and P, respectively:

15 That is, $\hat{w}_i$ is the equilibrium of Iversen's model, *sans* inequality motives.

$$\frac{\gamma(1-\zeta)\partial W_{\mathrm{U_i}}/\partial w_i}{\zeta P+(1-\zeta)[W_{\mathrm{U_i}}(w_i)-W_{\mathrm{U_i}}(\hat{w}_i)]} + \frac{(1-\gamma)(1-\tau)\partial W_{\mathrm{G}}/\partial w_i}{-\tau P+(1-\tau)[W_{\mathrm{G}}(w_i)-W_{\mathrm{G}}(\hat{w}_i)]}=0, \qquad (7.16)$$

$$\frac{\gamma\zeta}{\zeta P+(1-\zeta)[W_{\mathrm{U_i}}(w_i)-W_{\mathrm{U_i}}(\hat{w}_i)]} - \frac{(1-\gamma)\tau}{-\tau P+(1-\tau)[W_{\mathrm{G}}(w_i)-W_{\mathrm{G}}(\hat{w}_i)]}=0. \qquad (7.17)$$

Equation 7.17 establishes the increase in social policy the government offers unions:

$$P=\gamma\frac{\tau}{1-\tau}\Big[W_{\mathrm{G}}(w_i)-W_{\mathrm{G}}(\hat{w}_i)\Big]+(1-\gamma)\frac{1-\zeta}{\zeta}\Big[W_{\mathrm{U_i}}(\hat{w}_i)-W_{\mathrm{U_i}}(w_i)\Big]. \qquad (7.18)$$

Equation 7.16 defines the equilibrium wage demand made by a representative union i:

$$\tau(1-\zeta)\frac{\partial W_{\mathrm{U_i}}}{\partial w_i}+(1-\tau)\zeta\frac{\partial W_{\mathrm{G}}}{\partial w_i}=0. \qquad (7.19)$$

Note that the bargaining power parameter, γ, has fallen out of the equation.

To find equilibrium unemployment, I first substitute for $\partial W_{\mathrm{U_i}}/\partial w_i$ and $\partial W_{\mathrm{G}}/\partial w_i$, and solve for the equilibrium wage $w^\star$ (noting, of course, that in equilibrium, $w_i=w_o=w^\star$):

$$w^\star=\frac{\alpha(1-c+c\iota)-(1-\alpha)\iota\overline{U}(c^2-2c+2\iota c+1)}{(1-\alpha)(c^2-2c+2\iota c+1)} + \frac{1-\tau}{\tau}\frac{\zeta}{1-\zeta}c(\lambda\iota-\lambda-\iota). \qquad (7.20)$$

This is simply the equilibrium wage under Iversen's model (first term), adjusted for social policy bargains (second term). Finally, recalling that in equilibrium $\Delta\overline{U}=w^\star-\pi=0$, I solve for $\overline{U}$ to obtain equation 7.12 in the main text. ■

Comparative Statics

If unions do not care about policy ($\zeta=0$), if the government does not care about the economy ($\tau=1$), or if the central bank and government are both "ultra-liberal" on inflation ($\iota = \lambda = 0$), then no bargain occurs and Iversen's equilibrium holds as a special case. But in all other cases, social policy bargains reduce unemployment by an amount that is increasing in centralization (c), the inflation-hawkishness of the central bank (ι) and government (λ), and unions' desire for policy (ζ), but declining in the government's fiscal conservatism (τ). Moreover, the effect of the central bank's inflation preferences is always stronger than that of government preferences.

Proof. To see that within the parameter space, social policy bargains either reduce unemployment or have no effect, note that $U_b < 0$ for all $\{\zeta, (1-\tau), c\} \in (0, 1]$ and $\lambda\iota - \lambda - \iota < 0$. The last condition holds if either of λ or ι is positive. Otherwise, $U_b = 0$.

Next, note that

$$\frac{\partial U_b}{\partial c} = \frac{\zeta}{1-\zeta}\frac{1-\tau}{\tau}\frac{\iota}{1-\iota}(\lambda\iota - \lambda - \iota), \tag{7.21}$$

which is negative given $\{\zeta, (1-\tau), \iota\} \in (0, 1]$. All else equal, the reduction in U gets larger as c increases, up to the zero unemployment constraint.

Further, note that

$$\frac{\partial U_b}{\partial \lambda} = -c\iota\frac{\zeta}{1-\zeta}\frac{1-\tau}{\tau}, \tag{7.22}$$

which is also negative for all $\{\zeta, (1-\tau), c, \iota\} \in (0, 1]$. Therefore, the government's distaste for inflation augments unemployment reduction, up to the zero unemployment constraint.

Turning to the central bank's preferences, observe that

$$\frac{\partial U_b}{\partial \iota} = c\frac{\zeta}{1-\zeta}\frac{1-\tau}{\tau}\left[\frac{\iota(\iota-2)}{(1-\iota)^2} - \lambda\right], \tag{7.23}$$

and because $\iota^2 < 2\iota$ for all $\iota \in (0, 1]$, we have $\partial U_b/\partial\iota < 0$ given $\{\iota, c, \zeta, (1-\tau)\} \in (0, 1]$. Thus, the central bank's inflation aversion also strengthens unemployment reduction, up to the zero unemployment constraint.

To show that central bank preferences on inflation have greater marginal effect than government preferences, $\partial U_b/\partial\iota > \partial U_b/\partial\lambda$ must hold. To prove this, it suffices to show $\lambda - \iota(\iota-2)/(1-\iota)^2 > \iota$. Because the left-hand side is greatest when $\lambda = 0$, we need only show $2 - \iota > (\iota - 1)^2$. This holds for all $\iota \in [0, 1]$. ■

Data Appendix to Chapter 7

Data and Sources

CBNA_{jt} represents the degree of central bank nonaccommodation of inflation in country *j* and time *t* and is the product of two time-varying measures, the median central banker's score on the Central Banker Career Conservatism (CBCC) index described in Chapter 3 and the central bank's score on the Monetary Policy Autonomy (MPA) index described in Chapter 6. CBCC reflects the percentage of each central banker's past career spent in private finance or the finance ministry, minus the percentage spent in the rest of the public bureaucracy or as central bank staff. MPA is based on the Cukierman, Webb, and Neyapti index of central bank independence (as updated by Maxfield [1997] and the author for the 1990s) but includes only six components chosen to focus on the legal separation of central bank policy decisions from government oversight. See Chapter 6 for further details.

CWB_{jt} measures the centralization of wage bargaining, and is taken from Iversen (1999). $\text{CWB}_{jt} = \left(\sum_{\forall k,\ell} w_{\ell jt} p_{k\ell jt}^2\right)^{\frac{1}{2}}$, where $w_{\ell jt}$ is the weight given to each level of bargaining ℓ (firm, industry, or peak level) in country *j* at time *t*, and $p_{k\ell jt}$ is the percentage of workers covered by union *k* at level ℓ. (The weights are chosen such that $\sum_{\forall \ell} w_{\ell jt} = 1$.) This variable is the main constraint on the available time periods, because Iversen coded it for 1973 to 1993, and the other variables typically exist through 1998. However, for the periods CWB is available, with a few notable exceptions, centralization mostly varies across countries rather than within them. A reasonable guess of the missing centralization scores for 1994 to 1998 is to assume that these figures did not change much from the 1993 levels. I ran the full analysis twice, first using 1993 values of centralization for later years (shown in the main text), and then deleting observations after 1993Q4 (not shown). The regression and simulation results were very similar, subtantively and statistically. In the interest of getting the most out of the available data, I show results for the larger dataset.

ADM_{jt} is a simple indicator of the partisan leaning of the administration, coded 1 when the right is in office and -1 when the left is in power. This variable is taken from Alesina, Roubini, and Cohen (1997) for 1960Q1 to 1993Q4. Data for 1994-1998 were coded by the author from the *Europa World Yearbook*.

CVN_{jt} stands for Challenger Victory and is coded 1 in the N quarters after the right wins as a challenger, as −1 in the N quarters after the left wins as a challenger, and 0 otherwise. The most effective variable for picking up temporary partisan cycles was $CVN_{j,t-2}$, indicating the six quarters after a challenger victory taken at two lags (or quarters 3 to 8). This variable is borrowed from Alesina, Roubini, and Cohen (1997) for 1960Q1 to 1993Q4 and updated by the author through 1998 using the *Europa World Yearbook*.

$Exmar_{jt}$ measures the growth rate of country *j*'s export markets at time *t*. It has been reported semi-annually since 1975 as part of the OECD Main Economic Indicators, available in the *OECD Statistical Compendium*.

$UDIFF_{jt}$ is the difference between the quarterly unemployment rate in country *j* at time *t* and the weighted average quarterly unemployment rate in the seven largest economies at time *t* (excluding country *j* as necessary). For every period, the seven largest economies were the United States, Japan, Germany, France, the United Kingdom, Italy, and Canada. These seven countries are weighted by their real quarterly GDP in dollars at time *t*. All GDP data are taken from the IMF International Financial Statistics. These data are essentially the same as those used in Alesina, Roubini, and Cohen (1997) but have been recollected and extended (where possible) through 1998 by the author. The quarterly unemployment rate is taken from the *OECD Main Economic Indicators*.

Table 7.2. *Summary statistics, 1975Q1 to 1998Q2*

Variable	Mean	Std. Deviation	Minimum	Maximum
$UDIFF_{jt}$	0.47	4.01	-7.80	11.71
CWB_{jt}	0.11	0.11	0.01	0.43
$CBNA_{jt}$	-0.18	0.27	-0.71	0.61
ADM_{jt}	0.04	0.96	-1.00	1.00
$CV6_{j,t-2}$	0.02	0.46	-1.00	1.00
$Exmar_{jt}$	5.43	4.67	-13.52	24.59

Table 7.3. *Institutional determinants of unemployment in fifteen industrial democracies, 1975 to 1998.*

		Model			
Covariate	E(sign)	1	2	3	4
CWB_{jt}	+		0.733	1.107	1.327
			(0.573)	(0.612)	(0.628)
CWB^2_{jt}	−		-0.546	-1.014	-1.254
			(0.740)	(0.789)	(0.798)
$CBNA_{jt}$	+		0.278	0.358	0.338
			(0.153)	(0.160)	(0.160)
$CWB_{jt} \times CBNA_{jt}$	−		-2.294	-2.808	-2.747
			(1.296)	(1.345)	(1.364)
$CWB^2_{jt} \times CBNA_{jt}$	+		4.755	5.622	5.519
			(2.358)	(2.434)	(2.454)
$CV6_{j,t-2}$	+	0.065		0.053	-0.043
		(0.018)		(0.024)	(0.024)
ADM_{jt}	0			-0.078	-0.075
				(0.035)	(0.035)
$ADM_{jt} \times CWB_{jt}$	+			0.767	0.889
				(0.308)	(0.319)
$ADM_{jt} \times CWB^2_{jt}$	−			-1.138	-1.482
				(0.491)	(0.523)
$ADM_{jt} \times CWB_{jt}$	+				0.949
$\times CBNA_{jt}$					(0.493)
$ADM_{jt} \times CWB^2_{jt}$	−				-2.773
$\times CBNA_{jt}$					(1.322)
$Exmar_{jt}$	−		-0.008	-0.008	-0.008
			(0.003)	(0.003)	(0.003)
$UDIFF_{j,t-1}$		1.29	1.331	1.316	1.311
		(0.03)	(0.041)	(0.041)	(0.041)
$UDIFF_{j,t-1}$		-0.302	-0.354	-0.340	-0.336
		(0.031)	(0.041)	(0.041)	(0.041)
Fixed effects		x	x	x	x
N		1926	1311	1311	1311
s.e.r.		0.346	0.357	0.355	0.355

Least squares estimates with panel-corrected standard errors in parentheses. CBNA represents the interaction of Monetary Policy Autonomy and the median central bankers' Career Conservatism, or MPA × CBCC. Model 2 reproduces the fifth column from Table 6.2 as a reference.

8

THE POLITICS OF CENTRAL BANKER APPOINTMENT

> The Treaty does not define price stability, it only says that the ECB should ensure that price stability prevails, but it has not defined what is to be understood by price stability. We did that ourselves you might say.
>
> Wim Duisenberg, *ECB president, to the European Parliament*

So far, I have focused on the link between elite policy makers, the institutions they inhabit, and economic performance. But there is another side to policy making: democratic representation and the transmission of public preferences through elections into public policy. Because there seems to be a tension between democratic control of monetary policy and efficiency, modern central banking is a sore point for democratic theory. Delegation to a relatively conservative, independent central bank lowers inflation but yet sacrifices democratic responsiveness. If there were a one-size-fits-all monetary regime that produced Pareto optimal inflation and unemployment, central banking would be a purely technical issue, but inflation reduction comes at a price – sharper short-run swings in unemployment. The optimal degree of central banker conservatism therefore depends on the people's preferences (Stiglitz, 1998). Where elected governments lose the ability to set even the degree of conservatism of the central bank, the basic chain of democratic responsiveness is broken, and from a democratic perspective, the wrong monetary policy may be adopted.

Many supporters of independent central banks think the solution to this problem is to make the central bank "accountable" to democratic institutions.[1] According to this view, central banks with operational autonomy can still be disciplined for failing to meet democratically determined goals, especially when the goal in question is an inflation target (Buiter, 1999; Issing, 1999; Eijffinger and Hoeberichts, 2002).

But history suggests accountability mechanisms function poorly, if at all. Judging from the European case, the marriage of democracy and central bank independence is an unequal partnership. When ECB officials appear before the European Parliament, the frustration of the sole elected body in the European Union is palpable. Even the way the ECB defines "democratic accountability" as a narrow judgment of whether the ECB achieves the goals it sets for itself ensures the real issues, the choice of goals and their macro-economic consequences, remain beyond debate. Responding in the early days of the European Central Bank to demands for easier interest rate policy, and following a pattern that would persist through a decade of lackluster economic performance, founding chair Wim Duisenberg implacably argued that ECB policy goals were frozen by a treaty the European Parliament could not change. And though the treaty did not define the inflation target itself, he insisted Parliament should have no say on that question. Finally, Duisenberg rebuffed concerns about unemployment by insisting treaty requirements on the topic were irrelevant, even meaningless. (This sparring generally involved Socialist members worried about the real effects of monetary policy; right-wing parliamentarians generally praised hawkish ECB policies. See Box 8.1 for examples.)

As McCallum (1995) notes, if central banks must be independent to do things governments cannot bring themselves to do because of time inconsistent pref-

1 Some defend the legitimacy of central banks, arguing that while these institutions do not embody deliberative or direct democracy, they are consistent with constitutionalism and the common practice of delegating complex policy problems to expert agencies (Moravcsik, 2002; Drazen, 2002). Persuasive up to a point, this defense requires robust accountability mechanisms to ensure delegation remains plausibly democratic and rests heavily on the claim that monetary policy has few distributive consequences and can therefore be judged mainly in terms of its efficiency benefits (Majone, 1998; Stiglitz, 1998). It is little surprise, then, that democratic critics of independent central banks dispute the seriousness of elected governments' monetary myopia and emphasize the tradeoff they perceive between conservative monetary policy and unemployment. Critiques of independent central banks, and the ECB in particular, as undemocratic, unaccountable, or unnecessary can be found in Berman and McNamara (1999), McNamara (2002), and Bowles and White (1994).

Box 8.1. The ECB and Central Bank Accountability

Three exchanges illustrate the nature of early conflicts between ECB officials and the European Parliament; see Jabko (2001) for more.

Hearing before the Committee on Economic and Monetary Affairs of the European Parliament, Brussels, March 5, 2001:

Pervenche Berès (France, Party of European Socialists): [Y]our optimism about ... growth is not necessarily shared, and one wonders how the Central Bank understands its twin role.... Doesn't that mean that we have to reopen the debate on defining the inflation rate which is to be targeted by the Central Bank?

Duisenberg: I wouldn't think so. The Treaty does not define price stability, it only says that the ECB should ensure that price stability prevails, but it has not defined what is to be understood by price stability. We did that ourselves you might say.

Testimony before the Committee on Economic and Monetary Affairs of the European Parliament, Brussels, May 28, 2001:

Robert Goebbels (Luxembourg, Party of European Socialists): Your main mission, we all agree, is to uphold price stability. Article 105 also says that, without prejudice to that objective, the European Central Bank must support the Union's general economic policy. Now, those who drafted the Treaty obviously did not include this as a superfluous addition, but as an invitation to the European Central Bank to do something to work towards Article 2 of the Treaty ensuring high employment ... But up until now, you have never defined the second mission as you understand it, although it was vested in you by the authors of the Treaty.

Duisenberg: We have always maintained – and we still do – that the best contribution that monetary policy can give to fulfill that second task is to maintain price stability.

Hearing before the European Parliament, Brussels, September 27, 1999:

ECB Vice President Christian Noyer: Regarding democratic responsibility, I think that we have undertaken to do what the Treaty requires us to do, which is to ensure price stability. So if we have an inflation rate of less than 2 percent in the medium term, we realise that that is the basis on which we will be judged. Either we succeed in delivering that or we don't, and people can criticise us for not maintaining price stability.

erences, then governments are no help when the central bank fails to implement time consistent policy – it is doubtful the government would discipline a central bank for making the same "mistakes" the government itself would choose to make. In short, the one kind of accountability the ECB offers (the government may chastise the ECB for being too dovish) is simply unnecessary, whereas the sort of accountability that would increase democratic responsiveness (giving the government a say on central bank priorities) is just another name for reduced central bank independence. In practice, meaningful accountability and institutional independence appear incompatible, even antithetical.

But democrats in the age of independent central banks should not lose all hope. Like any policy arena, there is more to choosing monetary policy than is written in the law. Foremost, there are the agents who decide and implement monetary policy. Their preferences vary, can be predicted, and matter for policy outcomes. Despite the legal independence of many modern central banks, democracies therefore retain one avenue of control: appointment power. The elected national governments of Europe select their representatives on the ECB Governing Council – democracy at a distance. Even in the United States, where Congress retains the long disused and dusty power to override the Fed, appointment may be the most important democratic influence on monetary policy.

Given the democratic principles and economic outcomes at stake, it is surprising that there has not been a significant comparative study of how elected governments choose central bankers.[2] This chapter tries to advance our understanding of the democratic control of the economy by linking the preferences of elected governments to the types of central bankers they appoint. I take as my starting point the fact that central bankers' with different career backgrounds tend to choose different monetary policies. Career backgrounds are cues suggesting which prospective central bankers have preferences that meet the government's needs. This leads to a simple hypothesis: *Central banker appointment is partisan, with left-wing governments choosing liberal types of central bankers, and right-wing governments choosing conservative types.* To support this claim, I examine the

2 In contrast, there is work on why governments choose to increase central bank *independence*; see Bernhard (2002), who argues that CBI is a strategic choice of governments to avoiding paying a political price for monetary policy. Bernhard identifies several cases where policy may be controversial, including internally divided coalition governments, and parties that must win elections in diverse federal states all subject to the same central bank. But as Bernhard stresses, CBI does not eliminate politics for monetary policy – independence can still be revoked, and central bankers must still be selected.

appointments of more than 400 different central bankers in 20 rich democracies over the second half of the twentieth century. I show these appointments can be best understood as a partisan phenomenon linking the government's economic priorities and the direction of monetary policy, regardless of the legal independence of the central bank.

What We Know About Central Bank Appointments: Studies of the Fed

The comparative literature tends to assume central bankers are, to a first approximation, no more than uniformly conservative automata, supposing all of the action lies in institutional differences across central banks. Under this assumption, comparative scholars, with a few exceptions (Maxfield, 1997; Hamilton-Hart, 2002), have shown little interest in who runs the central bank. Most of what we know about central banker appointment comes from the study of the Federal Reserve, an institution that has changed little since 1951 or so (Kettl, 1986, and see Chapter 1, note 4). Lacking any institutional variation to explain differences in policy choices made over time, Fed observers long ago abandoned the idea that central bankers were incorruptible, apolitical technocrats maximizing social welfare (see Morris [2000], who presents a comprehensive review). Instead, scholars spent a quarter century debating whether Federal Open Market Committee (FOMC) appointees' policy preferences reliably reflected the preferences of their appointing party, usually taken to be the party of the president. Generally, Republican appointees are expected to be more hawkish than Democratic appointees, because of Republican constituents' greater concern with inflation and Democrats' stronger preoccupation with unemployment (Havrilesky, 1987; Hibbs, 1987).

The best evidence for partisan appointment in the United States comes from Havrilesky (1988, 1994, 1995), Havrilesky and Gildea (1992), Chappell, Havrilesky, and McGregor (1993), and Chappell, McGregor, and Vermilyea (2004*a*,*b*). They find strong econometric evidence that Fed governors' interest rate preferences and voting behavior follow the party appointing them. Grier (1987, 1991) and Caporale and Grier (2000, 1998) counter with evidence of direct Congressional and presidential influence. Still, although Congress has the power to override the Fed, or change the laws governing its operation, appointment power is probably the main avenue through which legislature and executive alike influence the Fed. Overrides are likely very costly, because they would visibly undermine the Fed's credibility as an independent agency. Though they are possible in principle and probably affect Fed decisions on the margin (in the sense of Lohmann [1992] or Weingast and Moran [1983]) the absence of even a precedential veto argues for a greater focus on the routine mechanism of appointment, by which principals can shift the Fed's policies without damaging the underlying institution. But the appointment channel works slowly and uncertainly: Morris (2000) estimates it takes 45 months on average for a new government to fill a majority of FOMC seats with reliable appointees, so the pivotal vote on the FOMC is usually somewhere between the governing party and its predecessors. Of course, not all central banks have long lags between changes in government and replacement of the central bank board. For example, members of the Swedish Riksbank's governing board have four year terms which end shortly after scheduled elections, allowing incoming governments to remake the central bank quickly (Schaling, 1995).

Political scientists' work on the Fed shows broad evidence of partisan selection of central bankers within the unique institutional constraints of the American case. Most of this work focuses on the bargaining relationship between the president, who proposes appointees, and the Senate, which must confirm them. In these models, due to Romer and Rosenthal (1978) and first applied to the separation-of-powers problem by Ferejohn and Shipan (1990), the preferences of appointers and confirmers filter through the voting procedure to jointly produce outcomes. According to this view, there is no presidential or Congressional dominance *per se*, but only interactive influence. Both Chang (1998; 2003) and Morris (2000) articulate separation-of-powers models, and find empirical support for combined President-Senate appointment along partisan lines.[3]

Rational Partisan Appointment of Central Bankers

Based on the experience of the Federal Reserve, the hypothesis that central bankers reflect the preferences of partisan governments seems obvious, even pedestrian. Yet readers more familiar with comparative and theoretical work on central banks may be puzzled by the assumption that central bankers' preferences vary much at all. Some interpret the conventional wisdom in monetary economics as suggesting there is no reason to ever appoint "liberal" central bankers; readers may also have more basic theoretical questions.

3 Morris (2000) also finds support for Congressional influence through the implicit threat of overriding Fed decisions, tempered in his model by the threat of presidential veto. In some sense, all sides of the debate about political influence on the Fed are right about something: both the president and Congress appear to influence appointments and policy.

First, didn't Rogoff (1985) show that the time inconsistency problem could be solved by a conservative, independent central banker? Not unless one oversimplifies his argument. What Rogoff actually showed was that under certain economic assumptions (including, crucially, a perfectly competitive labor market), and given a government with distaste for inflation χ and distaste for unemployment normalized to 1, the government can minimize its losses from inflation and unemployment by choosing a more conservative central banker with distaste for inflation $\chi + \epsilon$, where ϵ is positive and *finite*. This precisely rules out "completely" conservative central bankers: the optimal central banker always has some concern for the real economy. Nor does Rogoff suggest that for two governments with different preferences (say, χ_L and χ_R) there is a common optimal level of central banker conservatism – it is *not* the case that $\chi_L + \epsilon_L = \chi_R + \epsilon_R$. Instead, using Rogoff's model, we can show that government R, more sensitive to inflation than government L, chooses a more conservative central banker than L would choose (that is, the government chooses ϵ_R such that $\chi_R + \epsilon_R > \chi_L + \epsilon_L$; see the Theory Appendix to this chapter).[4] In theory, partisan differences should remain even when all governments try to mitigate the time inconsistency problem by appointing *relatively* conservative monetary agents.[5]

Second, what about the empirical finding that independent central banks offer a free lunch: lower inflation at no real cost (Alesina and Summers, 1993; Grilli, Masciandaro, and Tabellini, 1991)? Drawing on the theoretical and empirical literature on the real costs of central bank nonaccommodation when labor markets are imperfect (Iversen, 1998*a*, 1999; Hall and Franzese, 1998; Cukierman and Lippi, 1999), the foregoing chapters cast considerable doubt on these claims. Moreover, we should be careful to avoid the fallacy of conflating independence and conservatism – even if independence is a free lunch, conservatism may not be. In Chapters 6 and 7 we found central bank conservatism raises unemployment in both mostly decentralized and highly cen-

4 In a related paper, Waller (1992) shows that partisan differences regarding the optimal degree of conservatism of the central banker can also arise from differences in the inflation sensitivity of different sectors of the economy. For example, if some sectors sign rigid nominal wage contracts, while others hire labor at the flexible market rate, parties representing these sectors prefer different levels of ϵ.

5 In this respect, the imperatives of monetary delegation are not so different from any other delegation problem: as usual, a principal is best off selecting an agent with preferences "close" to her own, but with an offset to mitigate the time inconsistency problem (Lupia and McCubbins, 1998).

tralized economies. In these contexts, it would be fully consistent with rational expectations for parties to choose central bankers based on the inflation–unemployment tradeoff.

In sum, there are strong grounds for suspecting left-wing governments will prefer less conservative central bankers. And as long as the central bank has any independence at all – that is, overriding the central bank incurs *some* cost to the government – then governments have an interest in the preferences of its monetary agents.[6]

Even before central bankers make a single monetary decision, observers who know their past careers can predict (albeit imperfectly) whether they will make conservative policy choices. In particular, governments shopping for a new central banker can – and probably do – use career backgrounds as indicators of central bankers' types.[7] Governments seeking very conservative central bankers can look to the financial sector, as Rogoff suggested in his classic paper.[8] To shift the central bank in a dovish direction, governments can appoint career bureaucrats to the monetary policy board, especially bureaucrats without any particular financial expertise. These bureaucratic transplants want to please their political

6 Indeed, Chapter 6 showed that while career conservatism matters more when central banks are more independent, preferences nonetheless makes some difference in inflation performance across the whole range of observed central bank independence; that is, all observed central banks appeared to enjoy *some* independence.

7 The use of career backgrounds as signals of conservatism addresses the concern that governments may not know enough about central bankers' preferences to make delegation to independent agents superior to discretion (Muscatelli, 1995).

8 After showing that governments can maximize utility by appointing relatively conservative monetary agents, Rogoff offered the following speculation about how this might be done when governments are unsure of agent preferences:

> We have assumed that the preferences of the agent appointed to head the central bank can be known with certainty. Clearly, many strategic problems arise when this assumption is relaxed. However, as long as there is some information on the probable preferences of alternative candidates, the basic point of the above analysis is still germane. The model is certainly consistent with the fact that central bankers are typically chosen from conservative elements of the financial community. One incentive that the head of the central bank might have for holding down inflation is that he can thereby improve his standing in the financial community, and thus earn greater remuneration upon returning to the private sector (Rogoff, 1985, 1179–1180).

patrons and are less likely to have strong personal views on monetary policy that could get in the way.

If correct, the hypothesis that parties appoint central bankers by career type has the humbling property that the actors involved in monetary politics have long understood the effects of central banker types, even if scholars paid little attention. Given the rational expectations foundation of the modern view of monetary policy, it is fitting to expect governments to already behave in a manner consistent with our findings. However, we must admit a second possibility. Suppose that careers really do influence central banker preferences, but that governments have even better information about appointee preferences. This information would also help governments recognize off-types, such as liberal financiers or conservative bureaucrats. In this scenario, central bankers' career backgrounds are still correlated with their preferences, and hence with the government's choice of agent, but the government need not rely on this correlation in making appointments. Even in this case, an outside observer lacking private information about appointee preferences can benefit from studying the link between career types and appointing governments. We can use the indirect measure of career types to gain leverage over what governments prefer, even if we cannot observe the mechanism by which governments evaluate appointees. Either way, a correlation between partisanship and career types supports the partisan appointment hypothesis.

Our primary purpose is assessing the link between the partisan ideology of governments and the types of central bankers they appoint, but appointment may result from other causes. For example, countries with larger financial sectors may have more former private bankers on their central bank boards, perhaps because of greater financial sector pressure or simply because the supply of ex-financiers is larger. Likewise, large central bank staffs may produce more governors from within their ranks than smaller central banks. Governments may put more care into their decisions if the central bank is independent, and they may choose central bankers whose level of conservatism either complements or substitutes for the independence of the central bank. Finally, governments may make appointments in reaction to short-run economic concerns, including inflation and unemployment, or in response to economic conditions that make inflation more desirable (high levels of government debt) or less so (high levels of imports).

I will control for the above factors, but it is easy to imagine a broader array of contexts that would influence the pattern of partisan appointment itself. Variables that may interact with partisanship include the state of the economy, the timing of elections, the age of the government, the organization of the labor market, the exchange rate regime, and the independence of the central bank. Future models might address these concerns, but for now I focus narrowly on assessing the unconditional effect of partisanship on central banker appointments.

Data

The outcome of interest is the career composition of central bankers at the time of appointment to the monetary policy authority. "Career composition" refers to the fraction of one's past career spent in each of several categories: private finance, the finance ministry, the central bank staff, other government bureaucrats, economists, and so on. Each career component is an experience score; for example, a finance experience score of 0.3 implies that, prior to appointment to the monetary authority, a central banker spent 30 percent of his career in private banks.

In earlier chapters, I identified two career types leading to conservative policy outcomes (higher real interest rates and lower inflation); these were private finance and the finance ministry. On the other hand, former central bank staffers and other government bureaucrats tended to produce less conservative outcomes. In advanced industrial democracies, the magnitude of these effects was almost identical across the four career types, so in this chapter I simplify matters by combining finance and finance ministry experience into a single conservative experience score, and government and central bank experience into a single liberal score. This yields a three category composition, {Conservative, Liberal, Other}, which will always sum to one.[9]

I collected the career compositions at initial appointment of more than 400 monetary policy makers from twenty industrial democracies appointed in the

9 One might tempted to simplify further to the single variable summary defined by

$$\begin{aligned}\text{Central Banker Career Conservatism} = {} & \\ & \text{Financial Experience} + \text{Finance Ministry Experience} \\ & -\text{Government Experience} - \text{Central Bank Staff Experience},\end{aligned}$$

which could then be analyzed by a single-equation model. But one cannot evade the compositional data problem that easily. CBCC is bounded by -1 and 1 and is trimodal, with peaks at -1, 0, and 1, posing distributional difficulties at least as difficult as those tackled in this chapter and considerably more opaque. Compositional analysis, on the other hand, leads to a model that is closely tied to the structure of the data. See note 15.

years 1945 to 1998.[10] Only central bankers with *de jure* authority to choose or vote on monetary policy are included.[11] These career compositions are the dependent variables in this chapter. Now we must match them to the contemporary values of our explanatory variables.

The key explanatory variable is the partisanship of the government. The best and most precise cross-national time series indicators of partisanship available employ the partisan center of gravity (PCoG) concept (Gross and Sigelman, 1984). PCoG measures report the left-right partisanship of a coalition government as the weighted average of the ideology scores of the parties making up the government. Cusack and Engelhardt (2002) provide partisan center of gravity data for all twenty countries studied here over the period 1945 to 1998. These data include precise election dates, so we can tie each appointment to the characteristics of the appointing government. Cusack and Engelhardt offer several bases for calculating the ideology scores required by PCoG. To minimize the effects of error from any one source, I choose a measure of left-right ideology that consists mainly of averaged expert rankings (Castles and Mair, 1984; Laver and Hunt, 1992; Huber and Inglehart, 1995), but which is supplemented, where expert assessment is unavailable, with party manifesto data (Budge, Klingemann, Volkens, Bara, and Tanabaum, 2001). Fortunately, the results here turn out to be insensitive to the PCoG measure used.

Other variables used as controls include economic variables (inflation, unemployment, and trade openness) and institutional variables (central bank independence and the centralization of wage bargaining). The sources of these data are standard. Finally, I include data on the supply of central bankers of various types; specifically, the fraction of the labor force employed in the financial sector and the size of the central bank staff. For a more detailed discussion of data sources, see the Data Appendix to this chapter. The Data Appendix also includes summary statistics for all variables used in the foregoing analyses.

10 These countries are the usual suspects studied in Chapters 3, 4, and 6: Austria, Australia, Belgium, Denmark, Finland, France, Germany, Ireland, Italy, Japan, the Netherlands, New Zealand, Norway, Portugal, Spain, Sweden, Switzerland, the United Kingdom, and the United States.

11 As in past chapters, I relied on Siklos (2002) and country sources to identify which officials (governors, vice governors, policy board members, and directors) enjoyed the legal right to set monetary policy.

Methods

The appointment data considered here raise many methodological questions, including a few seldom addressed in political economy. Here I discuss the estimation and visualization challenges created by the compositional nature of the dependent variable, sampling concerns, and model specification.

Defining the Sample of Appointments

The central banker biographical dataset includes career histories of all central bankers with monetary policy authority. These include central bank governors and, in some countries, deputy governors, board members, and directors.[12] Moreover, these monetary policy makers may be serving their first term, or may have been reappointed or promoted from a lower position (for example, from board member to governor). Deciding which officials to include in the analysis amounts to answering two questions: First, can we treat appointments to each level within the monetary policy board interchangeably? Second, are appointments and reappointments also interchangeable?

The most important job of central bankers – setting monetary policy – tends to be shared across members of the policy board.[13] Thus it seems likely that governments bear similar factors in mind when appointing governors, deputy governors, board members, and directors: in each case, the government has a chance to move the same policy decision closer to its ideal point. Pooling across these offices thus seems a reasonable way to make the most of the available data. (To the extent that each level draws on a different "supply" of candidates, there may be a fixed effect associated with each level, but we can control for these in a pooled sample.)

A more important distinction is between initial appointments to the monetary board, on one hand, and reappointments and promotions, on the other. For initial appointments, governments likely rely more heavily on career cues

12 Because I focus on new appointments of central bankers by the national government, I exclude those members of the United States Federal Open Market Committee selected by the regional Federal Reserve banks, and the members of the Bundesbank chosen by the German *Länder*.

13 This claim is made by central bankers themselves (Issing, 1999; Meyer, 2004), but even if we choose to be skeptical of self-assessments, we can turn to the work of Chappell, Havrilesky, and McGregor (1993) and Chappell, McGregor, and Vermilyea (2004*a*,*b*), who find that in the United States, at least, the median member's preferences are more important than the governor's.

Box 8.2. Ternary Plots

The first step in data analysis – looking at the data – is often non-trivial for multivariate data, including compositions. Fortunately, there is a convenient graphical representation of three-part compositions known as the ternary plot (Figure 8.1). The ternary plot takes advantage of the fact that the simplex (the space in which the unit constraint holds) of a D-dimensional dataset lies in $D-1$ dimensions, so for a three-part composition, the simplex is a triangular plane (shown at left). Therefore, we can identify any three-part composition as a point in this triangle, which we can plot in two dimensions. The only "trick" to reading a ternary plot is to recognize that the axes are borrowed from three dimensional space. Each of the three axes runs from zero, at the midpoint of a side of the triangle, to one, at the opposing vertex.

to ascertain candidates' policy preferences and shadow principals. In this case, appointers have no guidance from past monetary policy voting behavior, nor have they yet heard rumors about voting, where votes are officially secret. Thus, career effects should show up most strongly in first appointments. On re-appointment and promotion questions, the government and other economic actors can judge agents by their actions and pronouncements as members of the central bank, so career signals are unlikely to be as important in these cases. The decision to reappoint is also complicated by the fact that an existing central banker is a known quantity. The government may reluctantly reappoint less-than-ideal agents to avoid drawing a dud replacement from the candidate pool, especially if the current officeholder enjoys financial market credibility. To keep the questions in this chapter manageable, I focus on situations where a government has already decided (or is compelled by death or retirement) to make a fresh appointment and ask what sort of appointee they will choose.

Visualizing Compositional Data

Because we have three-dimensional compositional data, we can exploit a special graphical display known as a ternary plot to see all the data in just two dimensions (see Box 8.2). The ternary plot to the right of Figure 8.1 shows the appointment data for our twenty country sample. (Note the three sets of gridlines, each running parallel to an axis of the plot.) In fitting a probability model to these data, two constraints on the data are important to observe. Because the data are confined to the simplex, it is clearly inappropriate to assume they

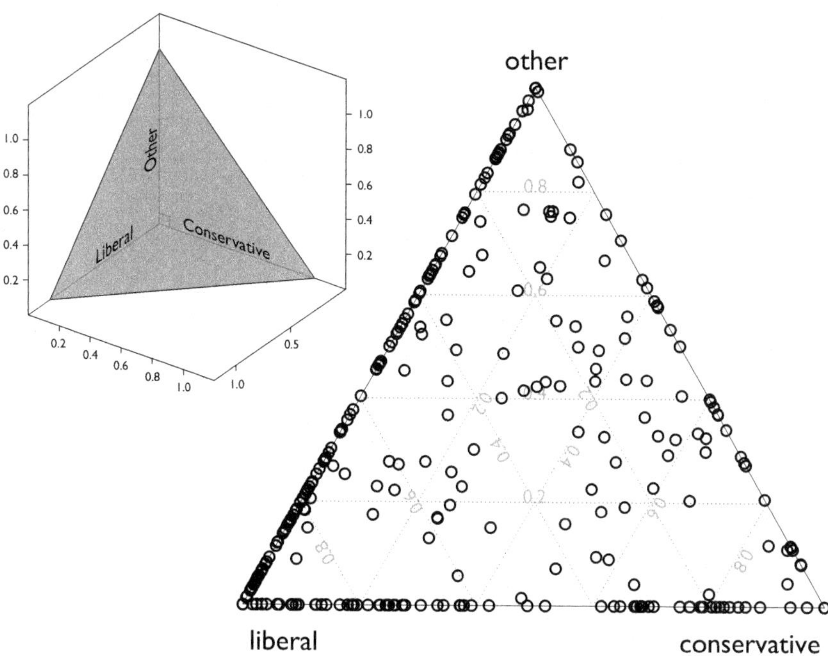

Figure 8.1. *Central banker appointment data plotted on the simplex.* We decompose central bankers' career backgrounds into three categories, based on the effects of those experiences on policy making: "conservative" experience (financial and finance ministry work), "liberal" experience (central bank staff service and other government work), and "other" experience, which is neutral. Because the components of a given career must sum to one, the decomposition of each appointee's background lies in the unit simplex. The left panel shows the simplex in three dimensions (a plane in a three-dimensional space). The right panel gives a two-dimensional representation of the same simplex, and plots on it the characteristics of 411 new appointees to monetary policy boards selected by the governments of twenty advanced democracies over 1945 to 1998. The plot shows most appointees have zero experience in one or more categories.

are spread randomly throughout the three dimensional space shown at the left, as separately-estimated linear models of each career component would require. But even within the simplex, an abnormally large fraction of the data lie on one of the edges of the triangle – that is, most of the compositions contain at least one zero element. This abundance of zeroes requires extra care in estimation.

Finally, note that horizontal movement within the ternary plot is equivalent to movement along the Central Banker Career Conservatism (CBCC) index. That is, the further a central banker's career triplet is to the right on the ternary diagram, the more conservative his monetary policy preferences are expected to be, and vice versa.

Estimation

Many political and economic phenomena are compositional in nature – budget shares, vote shares, the ethnic or religious characteristics of populations, and so on – yet these data are seldom properly modeled. The key characteristic of compositional data is that the sum of the components exactly equals a constraint. Without loss of generality, we can set this constraint to one; hence for a D-part composition $\mathbf{w}$

$$w_1 + \cdots + w_j + \cdots + w_D = 1, \qquad 0 \leq w_j \leq 1. \tag{8.1}$$

It is tempting to model compositional dependent variables with familiar methods (such as equation-by-equation least squares) that fail to recognize this constraint. However, taking this "easy way out" is inefficient and virtually guaranteed to produce impossible fitted values and predictions. A useful model of compositional data must, at a minimum, jointly estimate the components of $\mathbf{w}$ and respect the unit constraint.

Thanks to Aitchison (2003*b*), good methods for compositional data analysis exist. Aitchison's central insight is that logarithms of ratios of compositional data are independent and unbounded, and thus can be jointly modeled using a multivariate distribution. This approach has found wide application in statistics, geology, and other fields. The principal political science applications of compositional data methods have been modeling vote-shares in multiparty elections (Katz and King, 1999) and time-budgets in bureaucratic agencies (Brehm, Gates, and Gomez, 2003).[14]

14 Brehm, Gates, and Gomez (2003) use a Dirichlet model of compositional data, rather than a logratio Normal model. The Dirichlet, a generalization of the Beta distribution,

I use Aitchison's logratio methodology to study the selection of central bankers with different career backgrounds. The composition is made up of the fraction of a central banker's past career spent in each type of career, where I have classified past jobs as leading to either conservative monetary preferences, liberal preferences, or as having no effect. However, there are two complicating features of the career compositions data. The first is that the data contain many zero elements, which logratio methods cannot accommodate. In the Methods Appendix to this chapter, I discuss the various alternatives for dealing with zeroes in compositional data, including zeroes-included compositional data analysis (Aitchison and Kay, 2003), which jointly estimates the probability of a zero and the expected value of a non-zero. The second wrinkle draws on Katz and King (1999), who substitute the more flexible multivariate Student's t distribution for the multivariate Normal distribution typically used to model logratios. Combining these two innovations, I find the data are best fit with a zeroes-included Student's t compositional data model, the likelihood for which is also shown in the Methods Appendix.

Interpreting Results

The usual quantity of interest in compositional models is the expected composition (a D-vector) associated with hypothetical values of the explanatory variables. An appropriate summary of uncertainty is the confidence region around the expected composition. As with most non-linear models, tables of estimated parameters obscure both the quantities of interest and the uncertainty around them, and I relegate these to the Data Appendix. Fortunately, we can use ternary plots to visualize the estimated effect of partisanship on the expected central banker career composition. We can also plot the confidence region around this effect to illustrate the uncertainty of our estimates.

Model Specification

Using a zeroes-included compositional data model entails simultaneous estimation of $2D - 1$ equations for a D-part composition. In our case, the first $D = 3$ equations model the probability of a non-zero in each element of the

is more flexible than the Normal or t-distributions in that it allows multiple modes, but less flexible in that it requires any effect which increases one component to decrease all others. (Brehm, Gates, and Gomez argue the advantages of the Dirichlet may often outweigh the disadvantages.) Like the standard log-normal model, the Dirichlet requires all components be non-zero.

composition, and the remaining $D-1=2$ equations model the logratios of the compositions themselves. Specifically, we need to estimate five quantities: the probabilities (θ_{lib}, θ_{con}, and θ_{oth}) of positive values for each of the three career components, and two logratios ($\mu_{\text{lib/oth}}$ and $\mu_{\text{con/oth}}$) to represent the expected values of the non-zero components. We assume standard functional forms for θ and μ:

$$\theta_{ij} = \frac{1}{1+\exp(-\mathbf{x}_{ij}\beta_j)}, \qquad \mu_{ij} = \mathbf{z}_{ij}\gamma_j. \tag{8.2}$$

This leaves five parameter vectors to estimate: β_{lib}, β_{con}, β_{oth}, $\gamma_{\text{lib/oth}}$ and $\gamma_{\text{con/oth}}$.

As there is little (if any) theoretical justification for excluding any covariates from any of the five equations, I generally assume $\mathbf{X}=\mathbf{Z}$. Adding an extra covariate to the model therefore involves estimating five additional parameters, placing a severe degrees-of-freedom penalty on complex models. As a result, I start with a relatively simple model of partisan appointments, then show the robustness of this baseline specification to serially added controls. Finally, because of data limitations, I do not consider more complex models investigating whether partisan patterns of appointment are themselves contingent on other variables through interactive terms.

Evidence of Partisan Appointment of Central Bankers

The simplest model of partisan central banker appointment I consider regresses each of the five dependent variables of the zeroes-included composition model on the partisan center of gravity and a constant. I first consider using a multivariate Normal distribution for the composition, combined with a Binomial-logit model of zeroes. The estimated parameters from this model are generally correctly signed according to the partisan appointment hypothesis (see Model 1 in Table 8.3 in the Data Appendix). Because all five equations collectively determine the composition of appointments, it is most appropriate to test the contribution of PCoG to the group of equations, rather than to each individually. Therefore, though not all of the five PCoG parameters are significantly different from zero, a likelihood ratio test strongly supports the inclusion of the PCoG variables.

The next step is to relax the assumption of multivariate Normality using a multivariate *t* distribution for the compositional component of the model (the zeroes are still assumed to be Binomially distributed with a logit link). The results of this regression, shown in the Data Appendix (Table 8.3, Model 2), are substantively almost identical to Model 1. However, the wide tails of the *t* distribution are more appropriate for the appointments data, with an estimated degrees of freedom around 8 and a significantly higher log-likelihood than the multivariate Normal model. The multivariate *t* model forms the baseline for all specifications investigated in the remainder of the chapter.[15]

Although the signs of the estimated model are correct, its parameters are difficult to interpret. Following the practice of earlier chapters, I calculate expected values of the outcome variable – which in this case is a triple prediction of the levels of conservative, liberal, and other experience we expect the appointee to have – and show how these expected values depend on the covariates. I consider two running examples: appointment under a fairly left-wing government (with PCoG 1.5 standard deviations below the mean) and appointment under a right-wing government (with PCoG 1.5 standard deviations above the mean).

The ternary plot in Figure 8.2 shows the expected career type of central bankers appointed under partisan governments, as estimated by Model 2. Left governments appoint central bankers with dovish career backgrounds, while right governments appoint central bankers with more conservative career backgrounds. As the confidence regions confirm, the expected values under right and left governments are clearly distinct and appear to lie on an axis of central banker career conservatism running horizontally through the average appointee, who is marked with a +. The difference in the expected career conservatism of the appointed central banker across these two scenarios is 0.315, more than half a standard deviation of the CBCC index.

15 The compositional data model is better than a single equation linear regression model (which might have CBCC as the response) because the assumptions of compositional data models make more sense for the data at hand. Still, a regression of CBCC on the partisan center of gravity returns substantively similar results to the compositional model (standard errors listed in parentheses; all parameters significant at the 99.9% level; equations estimated on 411 observations):

Linear regression:	CBCC =	0.307 × PCoG	−0.264
		(0.094)	(0.032)
Robust regression:	CBCC =	0.321 × PCoG	−0.284
		(0.100)	(0.034)

More conservative governments appoint central bankers with higher CBCC (more conservative and less liberal career background). But the distributional assumptions of this linear regression are plainly heroic. The compositional data models in the main text – which come to substantively similar conclusions – are more reliable.

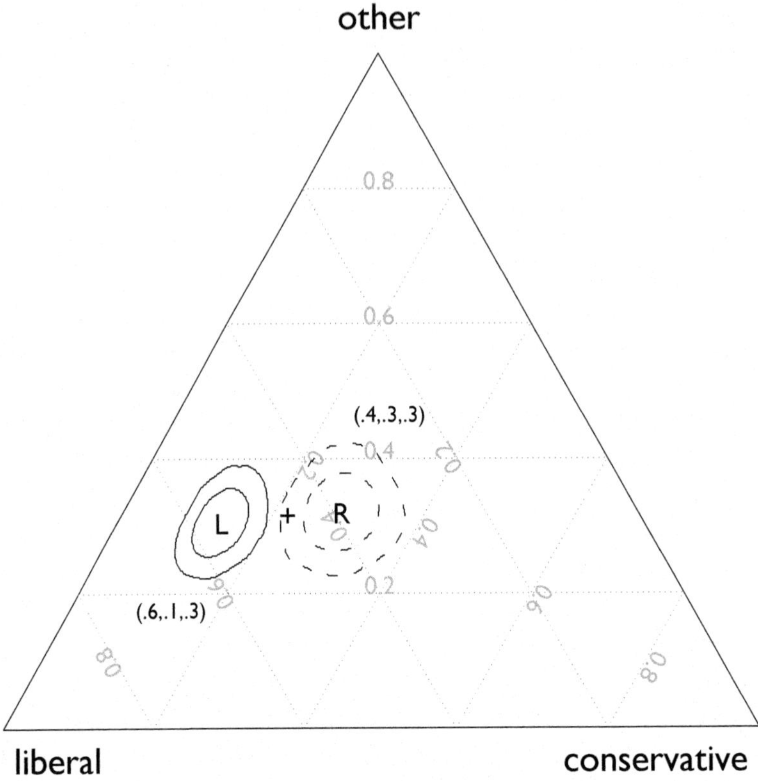

Figure 8.2. *Effect of partisanship on central banker appointment.* The expected career composition of an appointment under a (L)eft wing government (with a partisan center of gravity 1.5 standard deviations below the mean) and under a (R)ight wing government (1.5 s.d. above the mean), with 67 and 95 percent confidence regions, drawn from Model 2. A + marks the mean composition observed in the data.

Chapter 3 estimated the relationship between the median central banker's CBCC score and inflation outcomes; these estimates now quantify the central-banker-appointment–related welfare consequences of a shift from left to right government. Suppose a left-government has selected the median central banker, but is then replaced by a right-wing government, which chooses a new median central banker. The model predicts an 0.315 point increase in the median central banker's CBCC, leading inflation to fall by 0.90 points over a five-year period.

But Chapter 6 showed this inflation reduction may come at a price. In an economy with weak, decentralized labor unions such as the United States, an increase in CBCC of 0.315 also leads to an 0.47 point *increase* in unemployment after five years, as an inflation-wary central bank tends to hobble the economy in order to restrain unions' bargaining power. In decentralized labor markets, governments can gradually manipulate this inflation–unemployment tradeoff through central bank appointments. However, in a moderately centralized labor market, a conservative central bank not only restrains inflation, but also prevents powerful unions from pushing through employment-sapping real wage hikes. In this case, we expect conservative central bank appointments to lower inflation without any real cost.

It is important to remember these partisan effects work through a series of lags: new governments cannot always replace the median central banker quickly, especially if the central bank law makes firing central bankers costly, and once appointed, new central bankers' policy preferences only gradually show up in economic outcomes, because monetary policy also operates at a lag. Thus, the partisan cycles identified here are subtle and staggered compared to the clockwork cycles of classic studies (Hibbs, 1987; Alesina, Roubini, and Cohen, 1997). Nevertheless, central-banker-appointment–induced cycles unfold by a clearly defined mechanism, in contrast to theories of partisan cycles that gloss over the details of policy change.

I employ several alternative specifications to check the robustness of central-banker-mediated partisan effects. First, I include country fixed effects in each of the five equations to soak up any confounding effects of time-invariant institutions.[16] The fixed effects specification is demanding, adding 90 additional parameters to Model 2, but as the left panel of Figure 8.3 shows, the effect of government ideology on central bank appointments is very much the same, though the confidence regions are slightly larger. A similar approach controls for the composition of the board in place the quarter preceding a new appointment. Once again, partisan effects persist when this lag-like control is added to the model (Figure 8.3, middle panel). Finally, the right panel shows that partisan

16 One potential problem with the fixed effects zeroes-included compositional model is the logit specification used in the zeroes functions. Although fixed effects logit is statistically consistent as the number of "periods" (that is, appointments per country) goes to infinity, it is well-known to be inconsistent in the number of units. This should not worry us too much if the degree of bias in small samples is negligible. According to Monte Carlo evidence from Katz (2001), unconditional fixed effects logit is unlikely to introduce much bias even in fairly small samples. However, because the fixed effects specification greedily absorbs degrees of freedom in the five-equation model, I use it primarily as a robustness check.

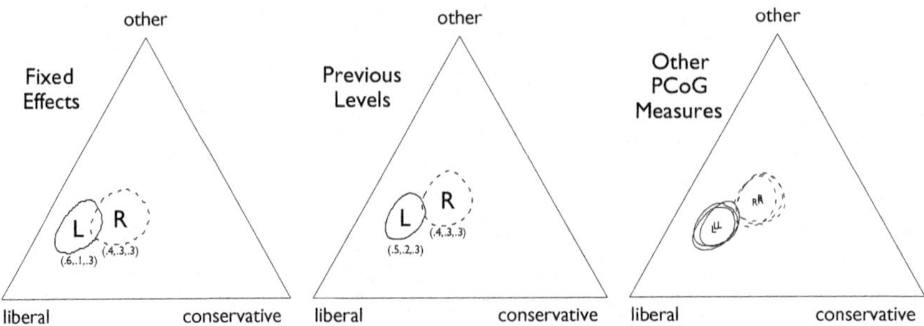

Figure 8.3. *Partisanship of central banker appointment: Robustness, part 1.* Each plot shows the expected career composition of an appointment under a (L)eft wing government (with a center of gravity 1.5 standard deviations below the mean) and under a (R)ight wing government (1.5 s.d. above the mean), with 95 percent confidence regions. Numbers in parentheses mark the {Liberal, Conservative, Other} career composition for appointees of each party. The left plot is drawn from Model 3, which includes fixed effects. The middle plot, summarizing Model 4, controls for the pre-appointment composition of the board. The right plot shows how the estimates of Model 2 vary when rerun with alternative measures of the partisan center of gravity. In all cases, partisan effects on appointments are substantively the same as in Figure 8.2.

appointments are not an artifact of the measure of partisanship chosen; whether we capture PCoG using manifesto data or expert rankings, the estimated partisan effects are so similar they appear as blurry copies of each other. However, because the expert rankings used in Models 1 to 4 arguably incorporate more information than manifestos and yield higher likelihoods, I continue to use this measure of the partisan center of gravity through the rest of the chapter.

These three robustness checks are broadly reassuring, but there are many specific variables missing from the baseline model which might affect appointment. These include central bank independence, recent inflation and unemployment levels, trade openness, government debt, the size of the financial sector, and the size of the central bank. A specification including all these factors at once is impractical, so I add them one-by-one to the model. I find the effect of government ideology – as measured by the expected change in the career conservativism of appointed central bankers – remains unperturbed and significant in every case. This is obvious from a glance at the ropeladder plot to the right of Figure 8.4, but it is worth discussing each specification briefly.

The first new specification test adds a separate fixed effect for each office of appointment (governor, deputy governor, board member, or director). Unsur-

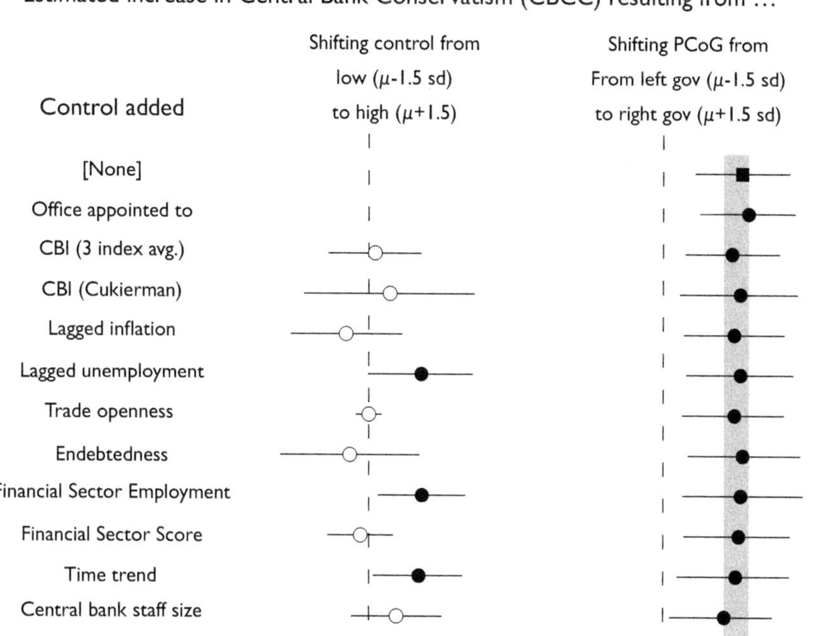

Figure 8.4. *Partisanship of central banker appointment: Robustness, part 2.* Each row presents a different specification, adding to the baseline model the variable listed at the left. To save space, neither the estimated parameters nor the ternary plots of expected values are shown; instead, I plot the first difference in career conservatism (CBCC) for a three standard deviation increase in the control variable (at the left) or partisan center of gravity (at the right). Horizontal bars show 95 percent confidence intervals; the gray box shows the range of point estimates for the partisan effect across all robustness checks. In all cases, partisan effects on appointments are substantively the same as in Figure 8.2.

prisingly, I find some differences in the average composition of appointees to different offices (not shown), but it is unclear whether these differences have any predictive utility. Regardless, the partisan effect is identical to the baseline model.

Next I include CBI, either as measured by Cukierman, Webb, and Neyapti (1992) or as the average of three different indexes. This allows for the possibility that governments choose central bankers to complement the effect of independence by pairing it, as Rogoff recommends, with conservative central bankers. On the other hand, perhaps governments view CBI and central banker conservatism as substitutes, which would produce a negative correlation. It turns out that in this sample there is no effect of CBI on the kinds of central bankers appointed. Once again, the partisan effect persists unchanged.

I also control for various economic conditions – inflation, unemployment, trade openness, and government debt – that might affect government preferences over central bankers, regardless of the government's ideology. Every specification reveals the same partisan pattern of central banker selection. However, the effects of the economic controls are at first blush puzzling. Only unemployment has a significant relationship with the change in appointed central bankers' career conservatism, and this relationship is the reverse of what one might expect: when unemployment is high, governments tend to appoint more conservative central bankers, which is likely to exacerbate unemployment. This perverse correlation turns out to have a mundane explanation: an omitted time trend. Both conservative appointments and unemployment trended upwards over the period studied. With a time trend is added to the model, career conservatism and the lagged unemployment rate are no longer significantly related. We are left to tentatively conclude that neither recent inflation nor recent unemployment rates influence appointment decisions, suggesting governments are not trying to fine tune short-run business cycles through their appointments, but instead are looking at the medium-run or longer.

Next, I add to the model the percentage of all employees working in the financial sector, broadly defined, a variable I call Financial Sector Employment (FSE). As expected, higher FSE correlates with more conservative central bank appointments. However, the interpretation of this results is not straightforward. As I show in the Data Appendix, FSE reflects two phenomena: persistent cross-country differences in financial sector size and a secular increase in financial sector employment in all countries. As with unemployment, FSE may be only spuriously linked to central banker career conservatism through this time trend. I decompose FSE into a time trend and a country intercept, and label the country intercept the Financial Sector Score (FSS; see Data Appendix for details). FSS turns out to have no significant relationship with central banker career conservatism, whereas including a simple time trend recovers the FSE result almost exactly. That is, financial sector employment may be responsible for the shift to more conservative bankers, but so might any other variable trending in a single direction over the last half century. Thus, we cannot firmly conclude that financial sector strength induces more conservative central bank appointments, although we cannot dismiss the possibility either. Fortunately, we do not need to settle this question in order to decide the effect of partisanship. Either way, the partisan effect remains strong and significant.

Finally, one might expect more appointments of former central bank staffers to central bank boards in countries with large central bank staffs. To check for this, I include in the model the natural log of the number of staff at the central bank but find no significant effect on central banker career conservatism. As in every other robustness check, partisan appointment remains significant and little changed from the baseline result.

Conclusion

Though most governments in the industrialized world have given up direct control of the money supply, they have not and cannot give up indirect influence over monetary policy, and through it economic performance, as long as they choose successors to the central bank. This is because central bankers' preferences matter: monetary agents with conservative preferences produce similarly conservative outcomes. Indeed, the more legal independence the central bank enjoys, the more strongly central bankers' preferences influence inflation and unemployment. In a world of independent central banks, the appointment of central bankers is more fraught with economic consequence than ever before.

Monetary delegation is empirically not just a matter of picking the "best" technocrat to run the central bank. Alongside the uncontroversial goal of selecting competent central bankers runs the divisive question of which economic goals these appointees are inclined to pursue. Through their appointments, governments can tip the balance of power in the central bank towards either hawkish or dovish views on inflation. In this chapter, I showed that a clear and robust pattern exists in the appointment of central bankers: left-leaning governments tend to pick central bankers whose career backgrounds foster dovish monetary policy preferences, whereas right-wing governments choose central bankers whose careers identify them as likely inflation hawks. These partisan differences comport with standard monetary policy theory and have significant welfare implications: through their central bank appointments, governments may be able to noticeably alter the course of inflation and, depending on the organization of the labor market, real outcomes like unemployment. In particular, a tradeoff between inflation and unemployment emerges in decentralized economies, pitting the monetary policy appointees of left- and right-wing parties against each other.

Partisan appointment to the central bank board forms an important link in the democratic control of the economy. Voters dissatisfied with the government's economic priorities can vote the government out and expect the new government to change the central bank's goals accordingly. However, this process operates at arm's length, and through a series of lags – voters must wait for an election, a new government may not be able to appoint a new median central banker immediately, and finally, there is the lag between policy and economic performance. Because of the hurdles central bank independence has added, governments can adjust monetary policy not with tweezers but with salad tongs. But against the conventional wisdom that independent central banks are insulated from politics, there remains the stubborn fact that governments still find a way to turn their preferences into policy and thus remain, in the long run, responsible for the actions even of independent central bankers.

Theory Appendix to Chapter 8

In this appendix, I review Rogoff's optimal central banker conservatism result and demonstrate that in the Rogoff model, the optimal central banker is more anti-inflation when the appointing government is more conservative.

Rogoff assumes the economy has a competitive goods market and a distorted labor market, leading to a gap, $y > 0$, between actual and desired employment. The government dislikes excess inflation and excess unemployment and minimizes the loss function

$$\Lambda = y^2 + \chi\pi^2, \tag{8.3}$$

where y is the employment gap and π is the difference between observed inflation and the government's preferred inflation rate. The government then picks an agent to choose the inflation rate on its behalf. The agent's distaste for inflation is proportional to $\chi + \epsilon$. Rogoff shows that the government's loss minimization problem is to choose the level of ϵ that minimizes

$$\Lambda_\epsilon = y + \chi\Pi_\epsilon + \Gamma_\epsilon, \tag{8.4}$$

where Π_ϵ is the loss from inflation and Γ_ϵ the loss from the failure to stabilize output under the central banker defined by ϵ. Rogoff further demonstrates that under his economic assumptions,[17] the loss-minimizing central bank appointment $\epsilon^\star$ satisfies three conditions:

$$\frac{\partial\Lambda}{\partial\epsilon} = \chi\frac{\partial\Pi}{\partial\epsilon} + \frac{\partial\Gamma}{\partial\epsilon}, \tag{8.5}$$

$$\frac{\partial\Gamma}{\partial\epsilon} = 2\left(\frac{\sigma_z^2}{\alpha^2(1+\alpha\omega)^2}\right)\left[\left(\frac{\epsilon}{\alpha^2}\right) / \left(\alpha^{-2}+\chi+\epsilon\right)^3\right], \tag{8.6}$$

17 The key economic assumptions of the Rogoff model are embodied in five equations,

Goods market supply:	$x^s = c + \alpha\bar{k} + (1-\alpha)n + z$
Goods market demand:	$x^d = -\delta[r - \mathrm{E}(\Delta p)] + u$
Labor market supply:	$n^s = \bar{n} + \omega(w-p)$
Labor market demand:	$c + \log(1+\alpha) + \alpha\bar{k} - \alpha n^d + z = w - p$
Demand for money:	$m - p = -\lambda r + \phi x + v$

where x is output, $\bar{k}$ is the (fixed) supply of capital, n is the supply of labor, Δp is inflation, w is the wage level, p is the price level, m is the money supply, r is the real interest rate, c and $\bar{n}$ are constants, and z, u, and v are uncorrelated Normal disturbances. See Rogoff (1985) for derivations of equations 8.6 and 8.7.

$$\frac{\partial \Pi}{\partial \epsilon} = \frac{2\gamma^2/a^2}{(\chi + \epsilon)^3}, \tag{8.7}$$

where σ_z^2 is the variance of a productivity shock, α denotes the return to capital, and ω is the wage elasticity of labor (all three are assumed positive).

It is hard to solve for $\epsilon^\star$ directly, but Rogoff shows that so long as output is suboptimal ($y > 0$), the optimal increment of agent conservatism is bounded such that $0 < \epsilon^\star < \infty$. This appendix investigates the conjecture that conservative governments should rationally select more conservative central bankers than less conservative governments would appoint:

$$\chi_R > \chi_L \Rightarrow \chi_R + \epsilon_R > \chi_L + \epsilon_L. \tag{8.8}$$

To test this conjecture, we need a more explicit representation of $\epsilon^\star$. Eijffinger and Schaling (1995) suggest rearranging the first order condition implied by equation 8.5 to obtain the following equation satisfied at the optimal ϵ:

$$\epsilon = \alpha(1 + \alpha\omega)\frac{y^2}{\sigma_z^2}\frac{\chi\left(\alpha^{-2} + \chi + \epsilon\right)^3}{(\chi + \epsilon)^3} \equiv F(\epsilon). \tag{8.9}$$

For our purposes, y and σ_z^2 are not of particular interest, allowing us to rewrite equation 8.9 as

$$\epsilon = \psi\alpha(1 + \alpha\omega)\frac{\chi\left(\alpha^{-2} + \chi + \epsilon\right)^3}{(\chi + \epsilon)^3} \equiv F(\epsilon) \tag{8.10}$$

where $\psi = y^2/\sigma_z^2$. We assume $\psi > 0$ (that is, there is an employment gap).

Eijffinger and Schaling note that $F(\epsilon)$ is monotonically decreasing in ϵ and that there is a unique solution for ϵ where $F(\epsilon)$ meets the 45° line. To see this, we can restrict attention to $0 < \epsilon < \infty$, because this is where Rogoff showed $\epsilon^\star$ lies. Note that

$$F(0) = \psi\alpha(1 + \alpha\omega)\frac{\left(\alpha^{-2} + \chi\right)^3}{\chi^2} \quad \text{and} \quad \lim_{\epsilon\to\infty} F(\epsilon) = \psi\alpha(1 + \alpha\omega)\chi. \tag{8.11}$$

Recalling that $\alpha > 0$ by assumption, and letting γ be a positive finite number, we see that

$$\frac{\left(\alpha^{-2} + \chi\right)^3}{\chi^2} > \frac{\chi\left(\alpha^{-2} + \chi + \gamma\right)^3}{(\chi + \gamma)^3} > \chi, \tag{8.12}$$

which establishes that $F(\epsilon)$ is monotonically decreasing in ϵ and bounded by $F(0)$ and $\lim_{\epsilon \to \infty} F(\epsilon)$.

Explicitly solving for $\epsilon^{\star}$ is still impractical, but equation 8.10 and the inequalities in 8.12 are amenable to numerical methods, as we seek the unique solution of a bounded, monotonic function with three nuisance parameters. For a given quadruplet $\{\chi, \psi, \alpha, \omega\}$, a one-dimensional grid search for $\epsilon = F(\epsilon)$ within the bounds will converge on $\epsilon^{\star}$ quickly and without fail.

The conjecture given by 8.8 can be restated as the claim that for any given $\{\psi, \alpha, \omega\}$, $\chi + \epsilon$ is increasing in χ. I test this by searching for the solutions for a wide range of $\{\chi, \psi, \alpha, \omega\} \in \mathbb{R}^4_+$. For each parameter, I test 25 values evenly spaced on a logarithmic scale; that is, the sequence defined by $\exp(T)$ for $T \in \{-4.8, -4.4, \ldots, 4.4, 4.8\}$, thereby constituting a full factorial search. In all, I check 15,625 $\{\psi, \alpha, \omega\}$ triplets, in each case calculating the optimal conservatism of the central banker given 25 different levels of government conservatism. In every case, $\chi_R > \chi_L \Rightarrow \chi_R + \epsilon_R > \chi_L + \epsilon_L$ holds. That is, out of 390,625 examples, not one violates the conjecture that more conservative governments can maximize their utility by selecting more conservative central bankers than liberal governments do. While not a formal proof, we can be reasonably certain that under the Rogoff assumptions, the partisanship of governments and the conservatism of optimal central bankers are correlated.

Methods Appendix to Chapter 8

Compositional data present unique challenges for quantitative analysis. In this appendix, I review the principal technique for modeling composition data, as well as its inability to cope with zero-valued components. Because the data at hand are rife with meaningful zeroes, I survey a range of solutions to this problem and explore the best solution, an explicit model of zeroes, in detail.

Aitchison's Model of Compositional Data

A compositional data set consists of an $N \times D$ matrix, $\mathbf{W}$, with ith row denoted $\mathbf{w}_i$. The elements of $\mathbf{W}$ meet the following criteria:

$$w_{i1} + \cdots + w_{iD} = 1, \qquad 0 \leq w_{ij} \leq 1. \tag{8.13}$$

Naïve application of multiple-equation linear regression to these components fails because the fitted values $\widehat{\mathbf{W}}$ must lie in $[0,1]$. But the problems inherent in modeling compositional data run much deeper. The unit sum constraint guarantees a bias towards negative correlations among $\mathbf{w}_i$, which in turn ensures that any modeling strategy assuming the independence of $\mathbf{w}_i$ is inefficient and almost always produces impossible fitted values and predictions.

The most widely used method of analyzing compositional data, due to Aitchison (2003*b*), avoids these problems through the logratio transformation, which turns $\mathbf{W}$ into an $N \times D - 1$ matrix $\mathbf{Y}$ such that

$$\mathbf{y}_{i,\sim D} = \ln(\mathbf{w}_{i,\sim D}/w_{iD}). \tag{8.14}$$

The columns of $\mathbf{Y}$ are independently distributed, but the new matrix retains all the ratio information in $\mathbf{W}$. It is often assumed that $\mathbf{Y}$ is distributed multivariate Normal, $\mathbf{Y} \sim \text{MVN}(\mu, \Sigma)$, in which case we may refer to the compositional data as logratio Normal. Katz and King (1999) consider the multivariate t distribution as a robust alternative. Either way, the logratio transformation allows easy estimation of the quantities of interest (μ and Σ) using standard maximum likelihood techniques; results can be easily transformed back to the unit-sum-restricted composition space, known as the simplex. Note, however, that this approach has an Achilles heel: it cannot be used if any of the elements of $\mathbf{W}$ are zero.

Structural Zeroes in Compositional Data Analysis

Zeros in compositional data come in two flavors: trace zeroes, which are presumed positive but for measurement error (a rock contains small amounts of a chemical compound below the detection limit of the measuring technology), and essential or structural zeroes, which are meaningfully exact (the proportion of a nonsmoker's budget devoted to tobacco). In either case, modeling runs up against the same problem: one cannot take the log of zero. For structural zeroes, this difficulty is especially troubling, because our model cannot handle a true feature of the data. A number of techniques have been proposed to deal with the zero problem.

Option 1: Combine categories until the zeroes disappear. This technique elides the problem but even where feasible often prevents the analyst from answering the research question (Aitchison, 2003*a*). Aitchison also proposes substituting the Box-Cox transformation for the logratio transformation when one component is greater than zero for all observations; this approach likewise depends on the cooperation of the data. Neither approach is usable for the central banker career data.

Option 2: Replace zeroes with some small value and perturb other components accordingly. Most analysts facing trace zeroes choose a replacement strategy, often based on the detection threshold (Aitchison, 2003*b*). At a minimum, replacement risks creating outliers and may induce considerable bias. An improved variant preserves the ratios of known components (Fry, Fry, and McLaren, 2000; Martín-Fernández, Barceló-Vidal, and Pawlowsky-Glahn, 2003). The procedure is simple: in a composition $\mathbf{W}$ with D components, C of which are zero, replace the zeroes with $\delta(C+1)(D-C)/D^2$ and reduce all other components by $w_i\delta C(C+1)/D^2$, $\delta > 0$. Although arbitrary, "zero replacement" is amenable to sensitivity analysis regarding the appropriate level of δ, and Aitchison (2003*b*) recommended it as the then best available approach.

Option 3: Convert interval data to rank data. Bacon-Shone (1992) proposes an intriguing kludge for the zeroes problem: take the entire compositional dataset (of N observations with D components each) and assign each of the $D\times N$ entries a rank based on their relative magnitudes. Rescale the ranks to $(0,1)$ and analyze them using Aitchison's logratio normal methods. For data in $(0,1)$, the ranks approximate (though do not necessarily converge on) the real data as $D \times N$ increases. The statistical properties of this technique remain unclear. Moreover, unless one has reason to believe that the substantive difference between zero and $\epsilon > 0$ is best captured by rank intervals, Bacon-Shone's method is as arbitrary as zero replacement, while abandoning interval information.

Option 4: Impute a latent non-zero value using outside data. Another way around the problem of zeroes is to respecify the model in terms of a latent composition which is always positive and preferably closer to the research question. Katz and King (1999) and Honaker, Katz, and King (2002), who study multiparty election returns, multiply impute the latent party vote of parties that failed to contest a given district (they also impose reasonable restrictions on their imputations, such that imputed vote shares must be smaller than observed positive vote shares in a given district). In contrast to techniques previously listed, this method uses covariates to help fill in zeroes.

Option 5: Estimate a two-stage model, where the first stage generates zeroes. Aitchison and Kay (2003) specify a two-part model for compositional data with zeroes, analogous to the hurdle and zero-inflated models used in the study of counts (Cameron and Trivedi, 1998). Like Katz and King (1999) and Honaker, Katz, and King (2002), this methods uses covariate data, in this case to separate zeroes from non-zero components. A two-part model has several advantages over methods discussed above; crucially, it treats the structural zeroes problem in logratio models as a mismatch of data and distributional assumptions. It is clearly preferable to arbitrary "filling in" because it requires the data analyst to specify how zeroes differ from positive values.

For the central banker experience score data, combining categories does not work, because zeroes are prevalent throughout all substantively interesting partitions. Nor is there any justification for treating experience scores as ranks, or for treating zeroes as missing positives to be imputed (as in electoral data). Although zero replacement is a reasonable first approach, the high proportion of zeroes in the career data make the magnitude (but not the sign) of the results strongly sensitive to the choice of δ.[18] In this case, a two stage model is clearly the best solution.

18 In this analysis, arbitrary choices of different δ's shifted parameter estimates by a factor of two or more, highlighting the importance of sensitivity analysis for zero replacement methods.

Zeroes-Included Compositional Data Analysis

This section outlines Aitchison and Kay's (2003) procedure for modeling zeroes in compositional data. The first step is to model the presence of zeroes in the compositional data matrix. Define an $N \times D$ matrix $\mathbf{U}$. Let $u_{ij} = 0$ whenever $w_{ij} = 0$ and $u_{ij} = 1$ when $w_{ij} > 0$. Now assume that $\mathbf{U}$ is distributed Binomial with probability of a non-zero equal to θ such that

$$\mathbf{u}_i \sim \text{Binomial}(\theta_i) = \prod_{j=1}^{D} \theta_{ij}^{u_{ij}} (1 - \theta_{ij})^{1-u_{ij}}. \tag{8.15}$$

The second step is to model the positive components of $\mathbf{w}_i$ as a single subcomposition with $D_i \leq D$ elements. Define a list of the indices of those non-zero elements, J_i, as the set of all j such that $u_{ij} = 1$. Now form the log ratios of those subcompositions,

$$\mathbf{y}_{i,\sim D_i} = \ln(\mathbf{w}_{i,\sim D_i} / w_{i,D_i}), \tag{8.16}$$

which we assume are distributed multivariate Normal.

It follows that the likelihood for compositional data with zeroes is

$$\mathcal{L}(\theta, \mu, \Sigma | \mathbf{U}, \mathbf{Y}) \propto \prod_{i=1}^{N} p(\mathbf{u}_i | \theta_i) p(\mathbf{y}_{i,\mathrm{J}_i} | \mu_{i,\mathrm{J}_i}, \Sigma_{i,\mathrm{J}_i}). \tag{8.17}$$

We substitute the Binomial for $p(\mathbf{u}_i | \theta)$, and the subcompositional form of the multivariate Normal for $p(\mathbf{y}_{i,\mathrm{J}_i} | \mu_{i,\mathrm{J}_i}, \Sigma_{i,\mathrm{J}_i})$ (see Aitchison [2003a], Sections 2.5, 4.5, 5.7, and 11.7), to obtain:[19]

$$\begin{aligned} \mathcal{L}(\theta, \mu, \Sigma | \mathbf{U}, \mathbf{Y}) \quad \propto \quad & \prod_{i=1}^{N} \prod_{j=1}^{D} \theta_{ij}^{u_{ij}} (1 - \theta_{ij})^{1-u_{ij}} \times \\ & 2\pi^{\frac{D_i - 1}{2}} \left| \mathbf{Q}_{S_i} \Sigma \mathbf{Q}_{S_i}^T \right|^{-\frac{1}{2}} \times \\ & \exp\left\{ -\frac{1}{2} (\mathbf{y}_i - \mathbf{Q}_{S_i} \mu_i)^T (\mathbf{Q}_{S_i} \Sigma \mathbf{Q}_{S_i}^T)^{-1} (\mathbf{y}_i - \mathbf{Q}_{S_i} \mu_i) \right\} \end{aligned}$$

19 See Aitchison (2003*b*) for a full explanation of the relationship between subcompositions and compositions. Here, it is sufficient to note that we may make inferences from subcompositional relationships to the full composition because the ratios of components are invariant to the subcomposition chosen, whereas the covariance matrix is fully determined by the covariance of each two-part subcomposition.

where

$$\begin{aligned}
\mathbf{Q}_{Si} &= \mathbf{F}_{D_i-1,D_i}\mathbf{S}_i\mathbf{F}^T_{D-1,D}\mathbf{H}_D^{-1}, \\
\mathbf{F}_{A-1,A} &\text{ is the identity matrix of rank } A-1, \\
&\qquad \text{with a column of ones appended,} \\
\mathbf{H}_A &\text{ is the sum of the identity matrix of rank } A \\
&\qquad \text{and a matrix of ones, and} \\
\mathbf{S}_i &\text{ is a } D_i \times D \text{ matrix selecting the subcomposition} \\
&\qquad \text{from the composition.}
\end{aligned} \tag{8.18}$$

Note that we treat the final term of the likelihood as equal to one when a single component is unity, rendering the composition moot.

We can maximize this likelihood using the usual numerical methods. The easiest way to interpret the estimated model is to examine expected values of $\mathbf{w}$ drawn from the predictive distribution. It is worth spelling out this procedure, which follows the general approach of King, Tomz, and Wittenberg (2000). Suppose that we model θ and μ as follows:

$$\theta_{ij} = \frac{1}{1+\exp(-\mathbf{x}_{ij}\beta_j)}, \qquad \mu_{ij} = \mathbf{z}_{ij}\gamma_j. \tag{8.19}$$

To obtain a predicted value of the composition, $\widehat{\mathbf{w}}$, for a given counterfactual $\{\mathbf{x}^{\text{hyp}}, \mathbf{z}^{\text{hyp}}\}$ and estimated model parameters $\{\hat{\beta}, \hat{\gamma}, \hat{\Sigma}\}$, we draw the corresponding incidence vector of non-zeroes $\widehat{\mathbf{u}}$ from the Binomial distribution, and the corresponding composition vector $\widehat{\mathbf{w}}'$ from the multivariate Normal. For each component j, if $\hat{u}_j$ is 0, we record $\hat{w}_j$ as 0; if $\hat{u}_j$ is 1, we record $\hat{w}_j = \hat{w}'_j$. For any $\widehat{\mathbf{w}}$ including zeroes, we must finally "close" the composition by dividing each element by the sum of $\widehat{\mathbf{w}}$, ensuring the composition sums, as logically required, to one.[20] We now have a single predicted value of $\widehat{\mathbf{w}}$. To obtain a single expected value, we repeat the procedure many times and average the results.

Once we have collected a large number of expected values, we can summarize the results of a zeroes-included compositional regression by the mean expected composition and confidence regions around that mean. Note that we

20 We may carry out the closure operation here without distorting the estimates because closure of a composition preserves the ratios of the components, and it is the ratios (y's) that are actually modeled.

cannot assume these expected values are distributed multivariate Normal, because they also reflect the contribution of the zeroes function. But because the simulated expected values come from the predictive distribution of the model, with enough simulates we can summarize the confidence regions with arbitrary precision.[21]

Further Refinements

Aitchison and Kay also suggest relaxing the independence of the zeroes function. This produces additional parameters and a substantially more complex likelihood that requires a Markov chain Monte Carlo approach to estimate.

Another logical extension of the zeroes-included composition model is to replace the multivariate Normal distribution with the more robust multivariate t (Katz and King, 1999). All that is required is to substitute the additive logistic form of the multivariate t distribution into equation 8.17, producing the likelihood

$$\mathcal{L}(\theta, \mu, \Sigma, \nu | \mathbf{U}, \mathbf{Y}) \propto \prod_{i=1}^{N} \prod_{j=1}^{D} \theta_{ij}^{u_{ij}} (1 - \theta_{ij})^{1-u_{ij}} \times \frac{\Gamma\left[(\nu + D_i - 1)/2\right] \left|\mathbf{Q}_{S_i} \Sigma \mathbf{Q}_{S_i}^T\right|^{-\frac{1}{2}}}{\Gamma(\nu/2)\nu^{(D_i-1)/2}\pi^{(D_i-1)/2}\prod_{j=1}^{D_i-1} w_{ij}} \times \left\{1 + \frac{1}{\nu}(\mathbf{y}_i - \mathbf{Q}_{S_i}\mu_i)^T(\mathbf{Q}_{S_i}\Sigma\mathbf{Q}_{S_i}^T)^{-1}(\mathbf{y}_i - \mathbf{Q}_{S_i}\mu_i)\right\}^{-(\nu+D_i-1)/2} \tag{8.20}$$

Γ denotes the Gamma function, and ν is the degrees of freedom parameter from the t distribution. (As $\nu \to \infty$, the t approximates the Normal distribution, while for smaller ν, the t has fatter tails than the Normal.) Once again, if a single component is equal to one, absorbing the entire composition, we treat the final two terms of the likelihood as equal to one, because there is no compositional problem to model.

21 A straightforward way to calculate these regions is through bivariate kernel density estimation of the simulated expected values. Provided a small bandwidth is chosen (say, 0.01), the kernel densities should accurately reflect the predictive distribution, and the contours of these densities should be the confidence regions of the quantity of interest. All confidence regions in the main text are estimated in this fashion.

As before, we can maximize this likelihood function using standard numerical techniques. We can also calculate expected values as in the multivariate Normal case, except now we draw from the multivariate-*t* distribution instead of the multivariate Normal.[22]

22 There is some debate over whether the multivariate *t* is worth the extra modeling and interpretative complexity (Tomz, Tucker, and Wittenberg, 2002) or indeed, whether it is ever possible to distinguish *t* regression from Normal regression in practice (Breusch, Robertson, and Welsh, 1997). For our data, the Normal and *t* distribution produce substantively identical results, while the *t* produces a much lower log likelihood and estimates of ν that are "small" (less than ten). Therefore, I primarily use the *t* based composition model, but this choice has little consequence for my substantive findings.

Data Appendix to Chapter 8

Sources and Summaries

Partisan Center of Gravity (PCoG). Cusack and Engelhardt (2002) provide detailed data on the partisan center of gravity for all twenty countries studied over the period 1944 to 1998. For each appointment, I use the PCoG score of the appointing government. Cusack and Engelhardt offer four ways to calculate PCoG: an expert-based ranking (`pjoint`) and three rankings based on party manifestos (`rile`, `myrl2`, and `myrl3`). I primarily use `pjoint`.

Central Bank Independence (CBI). Central bank independence data were taken from Cukierman, Webb, and Neyapti (1992), whose dataset ranges over 1950 to 1989, and supplemented using Maxfield's (1997) coding of the same countries through 1994; this comprises CBI-c. Additional CBI indexes are taken from Grilli, Masciandaro, and Tabellini (1991) and Bade and Parkin (1982); averaged together with CBI-c, these comprise CBI-3.

Inflation (π). Source: IMF International Financial Statistics. Calculated as the percentage change in the consumer price index. If available, the quarterly inflation rate is used; if not, the annual rate covering the time of appointment. In regressions, I use the natural log of inflation, and thus a small number of cases of deflation are omitted.

Unemployment (Unem). Source: OECD Statistical Compendium. If available, the quarterly unemployment rate is used; if not, the annual rate covering the time of appointment.

Imports/GDP (Open). Source: IMF International Financial Statistics. If available, the quarterly figures for total imports and GDP are used; if not, the annual rate covering the time of appointment.

Debt/GDP (Debt). Annual data on gross government debt are taken from the OECD Economic Outlook.

Central Bank Staff (CBS). I am unaware of any available long time series on central bank staff sizes. Instead, I averaged the data for 1991 to 1998 provided by Pringle (1999) for each of the twenty central banks studied and used the natural log of this average as an indicator of staff size, dubbed CBS. High CBS countries include the United States (about 23,000 staffers) and Germany (about 17,000 staffers), both federal systems. Low CBS countries include New Zealand (about 300), Switzerland (about 550) and Ireland (about 600).

Financial Sector Employment (FSE). Financial sector employment data come from the OECD National Accounts and include employment in private banks, insurance companies, and real estate and financial intermediation. Data after 1990 follow the employment categories laid out in ISIC Revision 2. Data from 1990 and before follow the earlier ISIC scheme and were provided by Robert Franzese (Franzese, 2003). FSE is expressed as a percentage of total national employment and shows a strong time trend.

Financial Sector Score (FSS). To purge the trend from the financial sector employment data, for each country I regress FSE on a time variable and an indicator for the post-1990 change in ISIC codes. Table 8.1 summarizes the results of these regressions. In all countries – except Japan, where FSE actually declined over the 1990s – the trend variable explains virtually all of the variance in FSE. The trend is similar across countries, with the financial sector absorbing another 0.25 percent of total employment each year. The constant term in these regressions serves as a simple summary of the relative financial sector importance in each country; this number is referred to as the Financial Sector Score (FSS) in the main text.

Table 8.1. *Financial Sector Scores for twenty OECD countries, 1960 to 2003.*

Countries, in order of financial Sector Score	De-trended Financial Sector Score	Annual Increase in Fin Sect Employment	R^2 from regression of FSE on a time trend
Switzerland	0.071	0.0020	0.94
United States	0.053	0.0029	0.97
Australia	0.040	0.0023	0.98
Canada	0.031	0.0028	0.98
Denmark	0.029	0.0023	0.98
Japan	0.026	0.0007	0.78
France	0.026	0.0025	0.99
Belgium	0.017	0.0008	0.99
Finland	0.017	0.0021	0.99
Portugal	0.015	0.0007	0.99
Norway	0.015	0.0020	0.97
United Kingdom	0.014	0.0031	0.99
Italy	0.013	0.0042	0.97
Germany	0.012	0.0008	0.97
New Zealand	0.003	0.0026	0.98
Spain	-0.001	0.0017	0.99
Austria	-0.004	0.0026	0.96
Sweden	-0.018	0.0033	0.98
Netherlands	-0.033	0.0050	0.98
Ireland	-0.119	0.0060	0.94
Mean	0.010	0.0025	0.97
Standard deviation	0.037	0.0013	0.05

Each row reports results for a single country regression of financial sector employment on a constant (the first column; this is the Financial Sector Score), a time trend (the second column), and an indicator for observations using ISIC version 2 (not shown). The last column shows that trending explains the large majority of variance in each country's financial sector employment, suggesting that each country's fixed effect may be a more appropriate measure of financial sector strength than the annual employment shares.

Table 8.2. *Summary statistics for the central banker appointments dataset.*

Variable	Mean	Std. Dev.	Minimum	Maximum	N
LibExp	0.464	0.402	0.000	1.000	411
ConExp	0.221	0.337	0.000	1.000	411
OthExp	0.315	0.370	0.000	1.000	411
PCoG (`pjoint`)	0.071	0.335	-0.470	0.966	411
PCoG (`myr12`)	-0.012	0.070	-0.226	0.175	410
PCoG (`myr13`)	-0.092	0.495	-1.000	1.000	410
PCoG (`rile`)	-0.023	0.185	-0.573	0.394	410
CBI-c	0.388	0.154	0.090	0.690	389
CBI-3	0.439	0.179	0.141	0.852	399
$\ln \pi_{t-1}$	1.429	0.917	-3.385	3.452	349
Unem_{t-1}	5.977	4.506	0.007	24.500	337
Imports/GDP	0.230	0.117	0.040	0.697	384
Debt/GDP	1.489	1.004	0.111	5.055	250
FSE	0.088	0.037	0.019	0.184	246
FSS	0.017	0.028	-0.119	0.071	343
CBS	7.961	1.298	5.694	10.071	399

Summaries across the available appointments in twenty industrialized democracies. The observations selected for each variable are those for which LibExp, ConExp, OthExp, and PCoG are also available (that is, the observations included in the regressions presented herein).

Table 8.3. *Zeros-included compositional data analysis of central banker appointments.*

Response		Covariates	E(sign)	Model 1	Model 2	Model 3	Model 4
Model of non-zeroes	LibExp > 0	Constant		$1.142^{0.124}$	$1.142^{0.124}$	1.308[a]	$-0.139^{0.389}$
		PCoG	−	$-1.487^{0.343}$	$-1.487^{0.342}$	$-0.691^{0.486}$	$-1.770^{0.371}$
		$ConExp_{pre}$					$1.520^{0.678}$
		$LibExp_{pre}$					$1.980^{0.596}$
	ConExp > 0	Constant		$-0.242^{0.101}$	$-0.242^{0.101}$	−0.440[a]	$-1.050^{0.377}$
		PCoG	+	$0.171^{0.288}$	$0.170^{0.280}$	$0.648^{0.444}$	$-0.208^{0.322}$
		$ConExp_{pre}$					$2.350^{0.645}$
		$LibExp_{pre}$					$0.573^{0.539}$
	OthExp > 0	Constant		$0.482^{0.105}$	$0.482^{0.105}$	0.452[a]	$1.710^{0.402}$
		PCoG		$-0.662^{0.302}$	$-0.662^{0.302}$	$-0.163^{0.434}$	$-0.461^{0.327}$
		$ConExp_{pre}$					$-1.960^{0.653}$
		$LibExp_{pre}$					$-1.500^{0.564}$
Model of composition	$\ln\left(\frac{LibExp}{OthExp}\right)$	Constant		$0.415^{0.128}$	$0.381^{0.124}$	0.497[a]	$-0.443^{0.440}$
		PCoG	−	$-0.390^{0.419}$	$-0.252^{0.419}$	$-0.561^{0.482}$	$-0.147^{0.414}$
		$ConExp_{pre}$					$0.314^{0.775}$
		$LibExp_{pre}$					$1.470^{0.612}$
	$\ln\left(\frac{ConExp}{OthExp}\right)$	Constant		$-0.111^{0.160}$	$-0.112^{0.147}$	0.085[a]	$-0.152^{0.498}$
		PCoG	+	$0.557^{0.471}$	$0.491^{0.446}$	$0.057^{0.495}$	$0.546^{0.445}$
		$ConExp_{pre}$					$0.071^{0.818}$
		$LibExp_{pre}$					$0.007^{0.722}$
		Est. t dfs			$7.779^{2.698}$	$4.730^{1.920}$	$6.900^{3.160}$
Composition Model				Normal	Student's t	Student's t	Student's t
Notes						a,b	b
N				411	411	411	391
ln likelihood				−1414.82	−1066.29	−962.84	−985.80
p-value of LR test				0.000	0.000	0.000	0.000
against model lacking				PCoG	t-dist	f.e.	prev exp

Entries are parameter estimates with superscripted standard errors. Each column reports a five equation model estimated by maximum likelihood. Likelihood ratio tests compare that column's model to a simpler model estimated on the same observations.
a. Includes country fixed effects, weighted averages of which are printed as the constant.
b. Variance-covariance matrix calculated by Gill and King's (2004) generalized inverse method.

9

THE POLITICS OF CENTRAL BANKER TENURE

> Because it isn't maybe as simple as bribery, campaign contributions, and that kind of thing. I think that we've had twenty-five years of the Goldman Sachses of the world ruling the world, and the people like Tim Geithner, when they leave office, the way they make their living... is to go to work for a financial institution for huge sums of money; that people have trouble with getting their minds around the world where that's not the way the world works, and there is maybe a slight quickness to believe the world can't function without Goldman Sachs.
>
> MICHAEL LEWIS*

THE OVERLOOKED EVIDENCE that central banker conservatism affects monetary policy demonstrates that a narrow-minded focus on institutional guarantees of autonomy has crowded out attention to other facets of monetary politics. When distinct or even potentially opposing concepts are gathered under the umbrella of central bank independence, we end up with confused explanations and misguided policy. In this chapter, we turn from central bank independence and central bankers' conservatism to consider two other concepts, central banker turnover and central bank accountability, which have too often been blended with independence. As with conservatism and independence, a sharper distinction between turnover and accountability reveals that politics play a larger than expected role in monetary policy.

Most studies of central banker tenure treat the rate of turnover among monetary policy makers as an epiphenomenon of legal independence or at most, as

* Michael Lewis, a former bond trader and a critic of the financial sector, in a June 1, 2009 lecture delivered to the Hudson Union Society, New York; quoted in Johnson and Kwak (2010, 188).

a behavioral indicator of informal autonomy. But deeper examination suggests popular explanations of central banker tenure are weak, and the link drawn between tenure and independence unwarranted. Moreover, in mistaking tenure for a proxy of independence, we miss another opportunity to investigate the interaction of governments and central bankers.

Despite more than a decade of debate, basic questions about central bank accountability – what it means, who enforces it, and how – remain murky.[1] I argued in Chapter 2 that central bank independence and accountability must be opposing forces, not mutually supportive ones. Otherwise, independence itself will forestall governments' efforts to hold central banks responsible for their policies. Indeed, central bank accountability, first proposed in an era of high central bank independence, low inflation, and widespread prosperity, slunk furtively through its first real test. No central bank was held to account for its failure to foresee the 2008 banking crisis or for mishandling its aftermath, and central bankers like Ben Bernanke still fail to specify any mechanisms of accountability beyond voluntary measures to increase the reporting of central bank activities (Bernanke, 2010).

In this chapter, I offer a new view of central banker turnover which suggests it is quite separate from central bank independence. Indeed, the dismissal of central bankers may form a limited kind of accountability to partisan governments. But as I show in the following, this accountability acts after a delay and may not even apply to central bankers whose shadow principals lie in the financial sector, waiting to offer central bankers who lose their posts the lucrative consolation of private sector employment.

Are Long-Serving Central Bankers More Effective?

Most studies addressing central banker tenure assume that rapid turnover reflects government meddling in monetary policy through the dismissal (or failure to reappoint) conservative central bankers who resist the government. If this were the case, central banker turnover rates might be a correlate of low central bank independence or even a proxy for the actual, behavioral autonomy of central bankers, in contrast to the independence written into the law (Cukierman, 1992). Indeed, low turnover appears to be correlated with low inflation in developed (Cukierman, Webb, and Neyapti, 1992; Cukierman et al., 1993) and

1 Ironically, the meaning of the subsidiary concept of "transparency" is particularly contentious, as shown, for example, in the debate between central bankers Willem Buiter (1999) and Otmar Issing (1999).

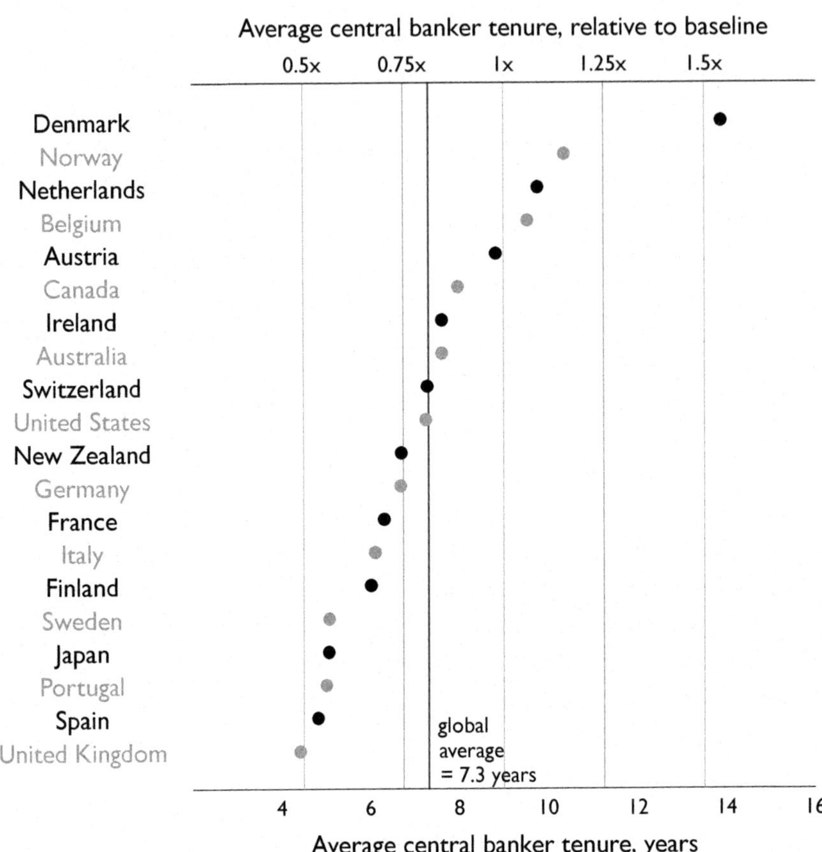

Figure 9.1. *Average empirical central banker tenures by country, 1950 to 2001.* Included in the averages are all members of the central bank with monetary policy authority. Tenure refers to the contiguous time period spent in a position with a monetary policy vote; promotions within the monetary policy board count as a single duration.

Box 9.1. Dot Plots

Figure 9.1 is an example of a dot plot (Cleveland, 1994). The ropeladders used throughout this book are specialized dot plots designed for displaying counterfactuals from regression models, but the generic dot plot is also useful for comparing large amounts of raw data. In this respect, dot plots replace the better known bar and pie charts. Cognitive science research suggests dot plots are easier to read accurately than either of these more traditional methods (Ware, 2004). Dot plots also facilitate comparison across graphics, an almost impossible task for pie charts given limited human capacity to compare thin wedges.

especially developing countries (de Haan and Kooi, 2000; Sturm and de Haan, 2001).

This chapter uses the central banker biographical database to examine how and why central banker tenures end. I define the length of a central banker's tenure as the time an individual spends in continuous appointment to any office with a monetary policy vote. Thus a single central bank tenure may cover several different titles (board member, vice governor, or governor) for central bankers who are promoted or reappointed. The end comes only when the central banker loses monetary policy authority, usually because of retirement, dismissal, non-reappointment, or death.

For comparison with past studies, I first consider country-averaged central banker tenure and its relationship to inflation and legal central bank independence. Average central banker tenure manifestly varies across industrialized countries, as Figure 9.1 shows (Figure 9.1 is a dot plot; see Box 9.1). Average tenures range from a high of nearly fourteen years in Denmark to a low of four and a half years in the United Kingdom. Central bankers in the Federal Reserve and Bundesbank, paradigmatic independent central banks, have only middling tenures, around seven years on average. (In the case of the Fed, this is just half the official term of fourteen years guaranteed to Governors.) To the extent tenure "proxies" independence, it can only be different sense of central bank independence than the usual one.

At first blush, central banker tenure appears to be an important factor behind inflation performance. Figure 9.2 is a scatterplot (with rugs; see Box 9.2) showing the bivariate relationship between tenure and inflation in twenty countries, averaged over a half century. Long tenures appear moderately strongly associated with low inflation ($r = -0.36$), and there are no countries with both long-

Box 9.2. Rug Plots

Scatterplots remain the most useful available display of the joint distribution of two continuous variables. Rugs are an "add-on" for scatterplots showing the marginal distributions of each variable. Figures 9.2, 9.3, and 9.4 incorporate rugs along each axis, allowing us to quickly see where the variable on that axis is densely distributed and where it is sparse. The format of these scatterplots was proposed by Tufte (2001), who recommends replacing axis guidelines with rugs to render every element of the plot a useful display of quantitative information.

serving central bankers and higher-than-average inflation. For comparison, Figure 9.3 shows the relationship between inflation and central bank independence over the same half century. The measure of central bank independence is the widely used Cukierman, Webb, and Neyapti index, and it shows the familiar strong negative association between inflation and independence ($r = -0.44$).

Have we uncovered two separate correlates of inflation? A scatterplot of tenure against independence gives reason for caution (Figure 9.4); they are mildly positively correlated ($r = 0.24$), and regressing inflation on both tenure and central bank independence gives the first indication that the bivariate relationship between inflation and tenure may be spurious (reported coefficients are from robust MM-estimation, with standard errors in parentheses):[2]

$$\begin{aligned} \text{Inflation} = \underset{(1.05)}{8.20} \; \underset{(0.13)}{-0.06} \times \text{Tenure} \; \underset{(1.92)}{-5.89} \times \text{CBI} \\ N = 20, \text{ standard error of the regression} = 1.11 \end{aligned}$$

Controlling for independence, tenure's effect on inflation is no longer remotely significant in the cross-section. We might conclude that the appearance of a bivariate relationship between tenure and inflation is merely an artifact of omitted variable bias, and let the issue of central banker tenure rest. But we should be skeptical of the cross-sectional results: they collate fifty years of variation into simple averages, presume that tenure may affect inflation but not the other way around, and omit any other controls besides central bank independence. While typical of some past studies of central banker tenure, this kind of cross-sectional model simply cannot settle the issue one way or the other.

2 MM-estimates combine the high resistance properties of least trimmed squares with the higher efficiency of traditional robust regression methods (Venables and Ripley, 2002).

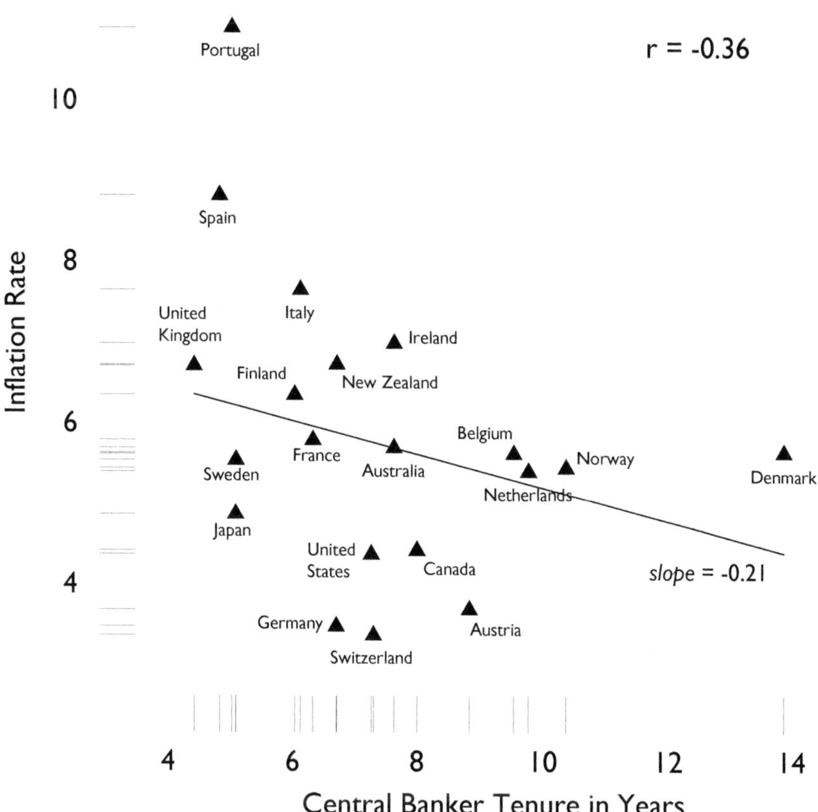

Figure 9.2. *Bivariate relationship between average inflation and average central banker tenure.* Data are averages over 1950 to 2001. All central bankers with monetary policy votes are included in the tenure calculation. Fitted regression line is from a robust and resistant MM-estimator to minimize the influence of outliers.

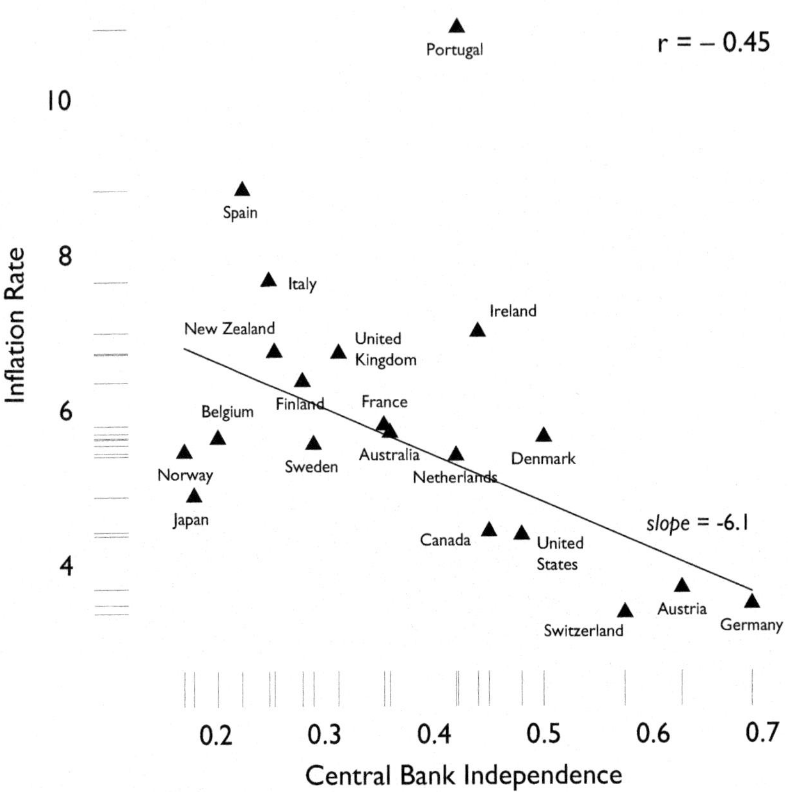

Figure 9.3. *Bivariate relationship between average inflation and central bank independence.* Data are averages over 1950 to 2001. Fitted regression line is from a robust and resistant MM-estimator to minimize the influence of outliers.

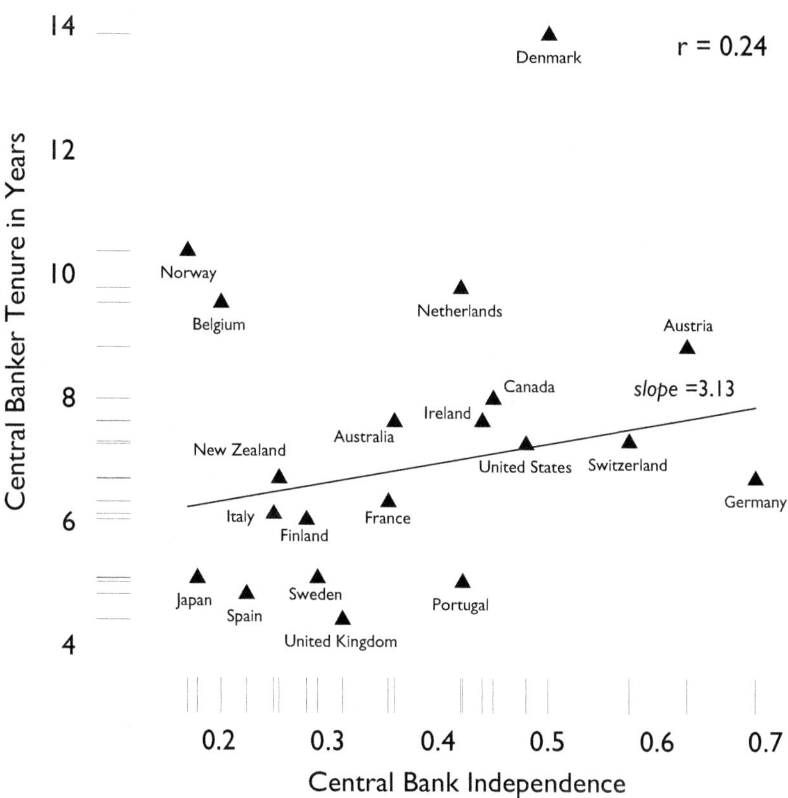

Figure 9.4. *Bivariate relationship between average central banker tenure and central bank independence.* Data are averages over 1950 to 2001. All central bankers with monetary policy votes are included in the tenure calculation. Fitted regression lines from a robust and resistant MM-estimator to minimize the influence of outliers.

Problems with Tenure as a Proxy of Independence

The idea that central bank independence *causes* central bankers to serve longer terms is superficially plausible but shows serious inconsistencies under close examination. To see this, it helps to again consider the government and central banker as principal and agent, each with their own preferences over monetary policy, as is standard in the literature (Barro and Gordon, 1983; Rogoff, 1985).

Independence and tenure need not be correlated. How can we tell whether a principal effectively controls an agent's actions? As Weingast and Moran (1983) argued in the context of Congressional oversight, it is not enough to measure how often the principal punishes or overrides the agent: a lack of vetoes is equally consistent with an independent, untouchable agent, or with a subservient lackey. In the latter case, the threat of punishment or override is enough to insure compliance, leading to effective delegation without the cost of punishment.

In the context of central banking, Lohmann (1992) considered a version of the standard Rogoff model of monetary policy delegation in which the monetary policy agent faces the threat of override if the government is willing to pay some cost. She showed theoretically that conservative central bankers may rationally anticipate and partially accept government wishes, just up to the point at which the government is indifferent between carrying out its threat and accepting the central banker's compromise. Anticipatory behavior makes actual overrides unnecessary, or at least severs the observational link between their rate and their cost. Using the same logic, central bankers facing the threat of veto through dismissal might accept partial accommodation. If Lohmann is right about how central bankers think, governments that must pay different costs to fire central bankers might create different levels of inflation but similar rates of central banker turnover, all else equal.

The difficulties run deeper still: if central bankers are alike in their competence, monetary policy preferences, and willingness to cooperate with government, then the dismissal and replacement of central bankers should have no effect on outcomes. Dismissal can only affect inflation to the extent the dismissed banker's replacement differs from his predecessor – otherwise, dismissal would be a far inferior tool for influencing monetary policy than legislative or executive vetoes. Perhaps the government can find more pliant replacements, but if so, we would expect the obedient, inflationary replacement to have low risk of dismissal, breaking the correlation between inflation and turnover.

To rescue the link between monetary policy outcomes and central banker turnover, we must introduce further heterogeneity among central bankers or among governments, leading to more nuanced hypotheses regarding the link between economic performance and central banker tenures.

High inflation itself may cause rapid central banker turnover. One interpretation of Figure 9.2 is that if a country frequently dismisses its central bankers, inflation rises as a result, leading that country to have both short tenures and high inflation. But suppose instead that central bankers vary in quality (that is, their ability to deliver some combination of low inflation and low unemployment via sound policy judgment) and by luck of the draw, some countries had more competent central bankers over the second half of the twentieth century. An alternative interpretation of the correlation between central banker tenure and inflation follows: unlucky countries had several incompetent central bankers, who produced high inflation and got sacked quickly; lucky countries found skilled central bankers and kept them in office as long as possible. Under this interpretation, the act of *dismissing* central bankers is essential to *lowering* inflation in countries that make unfortunate appointments, but does not explain any interesting cross-sectional variation in behavioral central bank independence.

Of course, because the data underlying these scatterplots are country-level aggregates, the correlations they show could be wholly spurious: the central bankers with short tenures in a given country may have served long after the periods of highest inflation.[3] The ambiguity of Figure 9.2 illustrates a key limitation of past studies of central banker turnover: the use of aggregate data to study the link between inflation and the fates of particular central bankers. By averaging tenures across time and across individuals, we commit the ecological fallacy. Correlations which appear to hold in averaged data may not hold or may even be reversed when we look at the individual data underlying the aggregates (Robinson, 1950). Without individual-level analysis, we simply cannot make reliable inferences about the relationship of central banker tenure to economic performance or central bank independence.

3 Anticipating this argument, Cukierman (1992) performs Granger causality tests purporting to show turnover precedes inflation, not the reverse. Unfortunately, his analysis is cast in terms of five-year averages of turnover rates, rather than at the level of individual central bankers tenures, so there remains some question as to whether his data accurately capture the dynamics of turnover and inflation performance. Moreover, Granger causality tests are not necessarily evidence of actual causality; see Chapter 5, note 14 on page 150.

Given some combinations of central banker and government preferences, dismissing central bankers could *lower* inflation. Like most comparative analyses of monetary policy, work on central banker turnover tends to assume that all central bankers are uniformly conservative, or at least uniformly more conservative than elected governments. But as this book shows, central bankers observably vary in their hawkishness by career-type (Chapter 3), and partisan governments exploit these differences to appoint monetary agents in line with their own preferences (Chapter 8). If central bankers appointed by left-wing governments are less conservative than those appointed by right-wing governments, we could easily imagine incoming right-wing governments dismissing held-over central bankers for being insufficiently conservative, rather than insufficiently dovish. In such cases, short tenures advance the cause of tight monetary policy, turning the conventional wisdom regarding central banker tenure on its head. Again, the essential point is to look to individual level data to distinguish the dismissal of hawks from the dismissal of doves.

The Politics of Central Banker Survival

There is more to central banker turnover than central bank independence, and more to be gleaned from the duration of central bankers' appointments than another measure of this over-used and under-theorized concept. Central bankers' survival in office is the outcome of a *political process* and reflects the concerns of partisan governments with producing not just good macro-economic outcomes, but macro-economic outcomes likely to please their own constituents. When a central banker chooses to end his stint at the central bank voluntarily, the timing of departure may reveal private career ambitions. Understanding the pattern of central banker turnover sheds light not only on the institutional balance of power between central bank and government, but also on the motives of politicians and central bankers intervening in monetary policy.

The concerns of governments. A long-standing proposition holds that left- and right-wing governments differ in their sensitivity to unemployment and inflation (Hibbs, 1987; Alesina and Roubini, 1990). Although all governments would prefer low levels of each, they perceive tradeoffs between the two economic indicators differently: left-wing governments are more concerned with reducing unemployment, and right-wing governments with keeping inflation in check. A simple rationale for this difference in preferences is that voters for left-wing parties tend to face greater risk of unemployment, whereas right-wing voters hold larger stakes in nominal assets, leading their representatives to push macroeconomic policy in opposite directions (Powell and Whitten, 1993).

Chapter 8 argued partisan central banker appointment is widespread among industrial democracies, with right-wing governments picking central bankers whose past careers in finance make them likely hawks, while left-wing governments tend to draft more easily controlled careerists from other parts of the bureaucracy. A similar logic of partisan selection may apply when central bankers come up for reappointment, or more frequently in countries where the government has the power to dismiss central bankers. Combining partisan variation in economic preferences with variation in central banker competence and monetary policy preference leads to three simple hypotheses about the influence of governments on central banker tenure.

First, central bankers who preside over better economic conditions – low inflation and low unemployment – should be kept in office longer by governments than central bankers whose observed performance is poor, all else equal.

Second, given the differing economic goals of right and left governments, right-wing governments should curtail central bankers' tenures more sharply under high inflation than under high unemployment. In contrast, left governments should push out central bankers more quickly under high unemployment than under high inflation.

Third, governments not only can dismiss (or fail to reappoint) central bankers whose actual performance displeases them, but also anticipate the undesired actions of central bankers appointed in the past by partisan rivals. It follows that when there is a change in the partisan composition of government during a central banker's tenure, that tenure should subsequently be shorter the greater the ideological distance between the present and appointing governments.

The concerns of central bankers. Governments are not the only arbiters of central banker tenure – central bankers often voluntarily leave before their terms are up. Anecdotal evidence suggests that former financiers are especially inclined to curtail their service, given the large pay cut associated with leaving the private banking sector.[4] Recall that in Chapter 2, I drew a distinction between two models of career effects on monetary policy. If career effects operate purely

4 Recall from Chapter 2, note 10, the complaints of former Fed Governors Robert C. Holland, who claimed he could not pay his children's tuition bills on a Fed Governor's salary, and Jeffrey M. Bucher, who decried the "financial penalty" he paid to leave the private sector for the Fed. Both served only three years before returning to private employment (Katz, 1992).

through signals from central bankers to financial firms, firms have no reason to delay hiring central bankers who successfully use conservative monetary policy to credibly indicate their appropriateness for leadership of private banks. On the other hand, if banks are shadow principals striking job-for-policy bargains, they would prefer to keep their agents in office as long as they can before dispensing rewards. This leads to a simple test of signaling versus bargaining: central bankers with "places to go," especially financiers and bureaucrats, should have shorter tenures than other central bankers (like economists, who can return to academia at their leisure) to the extent that career signals over policy dominate career bargains.

The constraining effects of institutions? One might reasonably expect central banker tenures to be longer, all else equal, in countries with greater central bank independence. But there are at least three caveats to this hypothesis. First, many of the components of central bank independence have little or nothing to do with the ability of governments to fire central bankers. Second, even where governments' hands are tied during central bankers' terms of office, they generally have latitude to reappoint or replace central bankers when their terms expire, so even in highly independent central banks governments can exert influence over tenures. Third, and most important, central bankers at the mercy of the government may choose to accommodate government wishes, extending their tenure and eliminating the link between tenure and legal independence altogether. For these reasons, I expect to find little systematic relationship between central banker tenure and central bank independence once other factors are taken into account.

Data

To disentangle the effects of legal independence, inflation performance, and government partisanship on central banker's tenures, we need to go beyond scatterplots to specify a multivariate model of tenure. To avoid the ecological fallacy, we need to look deeper than country level aggregates, to the patterns of retention and retirement of individual central bankers. In the rest of this chapter, I exploit the same central banker biographical database used in earlier chapters, now focused on the duration of individual central banking careers in twenty industrialized countries. Summary statistics for the data are displayed in Table 9.2 in the Data Appendix to this chapter.

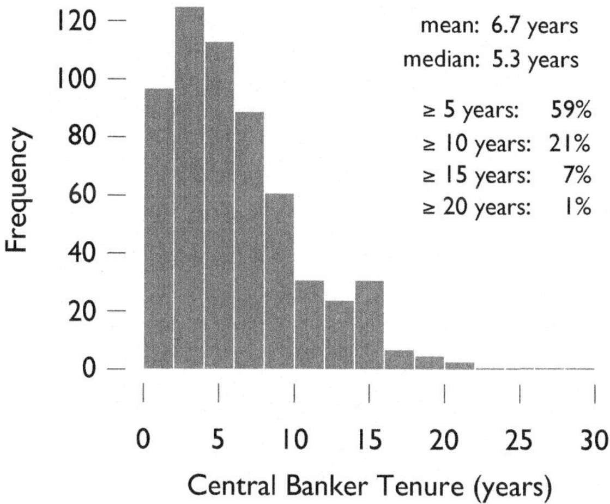

Figure 9.5. *Distribution of observed central banker tenures.* Included are 474 tenures on the monetary policymaking body of twenty advanced industrial central banks, 1950 to 2001. Right-censored tenures are excluded from this histogram but are included in the survival model that follows. Tenures may include consecutive appointments to the same of different positions within the monetary policy board.

Central Banker Tenure. Tenure refers to the length of time between the appointment of the central banker to the monetary policy board (or its equivalent) and the central banker's departure from the central bank. Within that period, the central banker may be officially reappointed or even promoted; the end of a tenure comes only when the official no longer has a position of authority over monetary policy. Tenures of all members with the legal right to vote are included, with the relevant offices by country taken from Siklos (2002). Figure 9.5 summarizes the distribution of central banker tenures. Fully half of central bankers served five years or less, including reappointments and promotions. A small fraction served very long terms, including the post-war record holder, Erik Hoffmeyer, who headed the Bank of Denmark from 1965 to 1994.

Career Experience. Once again, central bankers' career backgrounds up to the date of appointment to the monetary policy authority are recorded as experience scores. Career experience scores are thus time invariant for this chapter's unit of analysis. As usual, these scores measure the fraction of a central banker's career spent, up to a given time, within the financial sector, finance ministry, central bank staff, the rest of the government bureaucracy, the academic field of economics, business, or some other pursuit. Although at any given time the board of a central bank comprises a mixture of career backgrounds, individual central bankers often hail entirely or primarily from one sector. As in past chapters, all career scores for a single individual must logically sum to one, making them compositional variables. When interpreting the effect of career components entered on the right-hand side of regression models, it is important to maintain this constraint (see the Data Appendix to Chapter 3 for details).

Age. The central banker's age is an obvious and important control in any model of central banker tenure; just as obviously, age varies over the course of the career, making it a time-varying covariate. To accommodate age and other time-varying covariates, I follow standard practice and break each tenure into periods, with the period start- and stop-dates marked either at quarters (when economic data changes) or at the exact handover dates between governments (when the partisan composition of the government changes). In each period, I increment the age of the central banker as needed.

Partisan Center of Gravity. To measure the ideological position of governments, I use the partisan center of gravity (PCoG) data collected by Cusack and Engelhardt (2002) over the period 1945 to 1998 for all twenty countries studied here. Partisan center of gravity measures the left-right partisanship of a coalition government as the weighted average of the ideology scores of the parties making up the government (Gross and Sigelman, 1984). Cusack and Engelhardt's data include precise election dates, and I tie each appointment and each subsequent period of a central banker's tenure to the appropriate government, avoiding the error introduced by using quarterly or annual measures of partisanship.[5]

Inflation. I draw data on quarterly changes in the consumer price index from the International Monetary Fund's International Financial Statistics. Where quarterly data are unavailable, I substitute annual rates. Inflation thus enters the analysis as a time-varying covariate changing every three months.

5 Cusack and Engelhardt offer four separate measures of the partisan center of gravity, but they are highly correlated and the choice among them makes little substantive difference. To minimize the effects of error from any one source, I chose `pjoint`, a measure of left-right ideology that consists mainly of averaged expert rankings (Castles and Mair, 1984; Laver and Hunt, 1992; Huber and Inglehart, 1995), but which is supplemented, where expert assessment is unavailable, with party manifesto data (Budge et al., 2001).

Unemployment. I obtain quarterly (and in some cases, annual) unemployment rates from the OECD's Statistical Compendium. Like inflation, unemployment is a time-varying covariate changing every three months.

Central Bank Independence. As in past chapters, I use either Cukierman, Webb, and Neyapti's (1992) index of central bank independence as supplemented by Maxfield (1997), or the three index average of Grilli, Masciandaro, and Tabellini (1991), Bade and Parkin (1982), and Cukierman, Webb, and Neyapti (1992). Finally, as in Chapter 6, I also use a measure of monetary policy autonomy, which I construct from the components of the Cukierman, Webb, and Neyapti index that pertain specifically to the government's powers over monetary policy and personnel.

Complete data on contemporaneous economic conditions, the partisanship of contemporaneous and appointing governments, and central banker careers, ages, and tenures are available for 349 central bankers.

Methods

Central banker tenures are a classic example of lifetime variables marking the passage of time from "birth" to "death" for each observation. Rather than formulate statistical models directly in terms of durations, the usual practice is to model the probability of failure – the *hazard* – as a function of time, $h(t)$. The most popular statistical tool of this kind is the Cox proportional hazards model (Cox, 1972; Box-Steffensmeier and Jones, 2004). This semi-parametric model allows for a flexible, data-driven underlying hazard rate, in turn subject to proportional shifts as a result of covariates. The Cox proportional hazards model can be written as

$$h_i(t) = h_0(t)\exp(\mathbf{x}_i\beta), \tag{9.1}$$

where $h_i(t)$ is the hazard function for individual i and $h_0(t)$ is the baseline hazard function. Covariates $\mathbf{x}$ associated with individual i cause proportional changes in the baseline hazard to create that individual's hazard function.

The Cox model avoids the restrictive distributional assumptions of fully parametric models with minimal efficiency cost. This model is especially appropriate for central banker tenures because of the clumping of retirements and dismissals at yearly intervals, which often mark the end of formal or informal terms at the central bank.

Table 9.1. *Cox proportional hazards estimates of central banker tenure.*

Covariate	Hazard ratio	95% CI lower	upper
Age > 75	5.78	2.28	14.68
70 < Age ≤ 75	3.48	2.32	5.22
65 < Age ≤ 70	2.01	1.24	3.27
Other Government Experience	1.86	0.82	4.23
Abs diff in PCoG, appt party vs. current	1.67	1.24	2.25
Financial Experience	1.40	0.83	2.38
Finance Ministry Experience	1.34	0.71	2.52
Current PCoG × Inflation	1.05	1.00	1.11
Unemployment	1.04	1.00	1.08
Inflation	1.04	1.01	1.07
Current PCoG × Unemployment	0.95	0.89	1.02
Central Bank Staff Experience	0.90	0.62	1.30
Economics Experience	0.87	0.52	1.43
Current Partisan Center of Gravity (PCoG)	0.86	0.41	1.82
N	10,863	349 individuals	
log likelihood	−1229.4	LR test $p < 10^{-9}$	

Entries are hazard ratios (exponentiated coefficients) and their associated 95 percent confidence intervals. Hazard ratios greater than one indicate factors making retirement/dismissal *more* likely. Confidence intervals are calculated using standard errors clustered by country; significant results are those with lower and upper bounds on the same side of 1.00.

Results

The estimated Cox proportional hazards model is presented in Table 9.1, with covariates sorted so that the greatest hazards are listed first and the variables most likely to lengthen tenure at the central bank are listed last. Coefficients have been exponentiated to form hazard ratios, so that values greater than one indicate *increases* in the hazard rate (and hence shorter expected tenures), while values less than one show reductions in the hazard rate (longer tenures). For example, the estimated hazard ratio of 2.01 for being older than 65 years means that crossing the 65 year threshold raises the probability of departure by 101 percent, with a 95 percent confidence interval between 24 and 227 percent.[6] The hazard rate jumps an additional 73 percent when central bankers turn 70, and a further 66 percent past the age of 75, although the last increase is not quite statistically significant.

One result is immediately marked by its absence: central bank independence has dropped out of the model. When included, this variable has a hazard ratio of 0.67 but is far from significant, with a 95 percent confidence interval of 0.21 to 2.15 – that is, central bank independence might reduce the hazard rate by 79 percent, or increase it by 115 percent. Moreover, the inclusion or exclusion of central bank independence has no effect on the substantive or statistical significance of any other estimates. Alternative measures of legal independence – either an average of the three most popular indexes, or a subset of Cukierman, Webb and Neyapti's index focused on the power of governments to interfere with the central bank – produce similar non-findings.[7] Nor do interactive specifications find any role for legal independence in mediating other factors in the model. In sum, central bank independence does little to increase the job tenure of central bankers. Indeed, most central bankers survive to the five year mark, so much of the variation in tenure depends on their ability to be reappointed by the government. In matters of reappointment, governments are usually not constrained by central bank charters.

Central bank independence aside, most of the parameters in the model are significant, and the remainder have the signs expected, even if they are not quite significant by conventional standards. However, interpretation of the interaction terms is complicated. The effect of partisanship of government, for example, works through four parameters, requiring considerable arithmetic simply to get the proportional change in the hazard given a change in the composition of government. A simpler approach is to consider the net effect of each covariate on the hazard rate, accumulated across all the terms in the model.

6 The percentage change in the hazard rate resulting from changing x_j from a to b can be easily calculated as $100 \times \left[\exp(\hat{\beta}_j b) - \exp(\hat{\beta}_j a)\right] / \exp(\hat{\beta}_j a)$, which reduces to $\exp(\hat{\beta}_j) - 100$ when considering an increase in x_j from zero to one.

7 The three index average has a hazard ratio of 0.66 and a 95 percent confidence interval from 0.22 to 1.97, almost identical to the results for the Cukierman, Webb, and Neyapti index. The subset of the Cukierman index most relevant to governments ability to dismiss central bankers has a hazard ratio of 1.34 – which would indicate paradoxically *less* job security – but is similarly insignificant, with a 95 percent interval of 0.40 to 5.42.

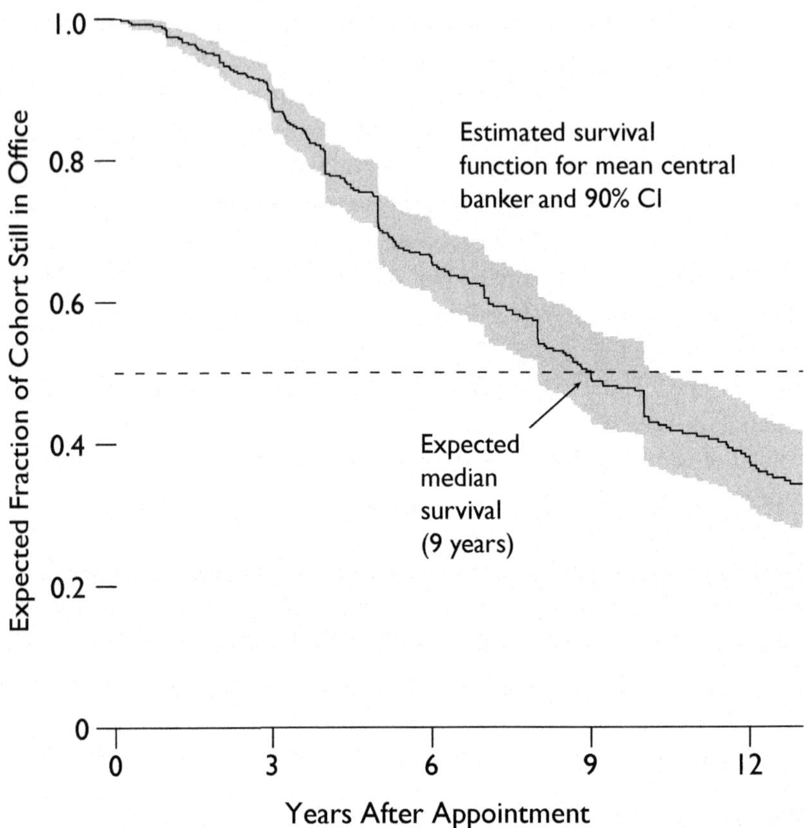

Figure 9.6. *The survival curve for central bankers estimated at the means of the covariates.* The horizontal line marks the point at which half the entering cohort has left the central bank, known as the expected median tenure or halflife. The sharp vertical jumps in the survival curve are clustered at yearly intervals.

Recall that the Cox proportional hazards model estimates a non-parametric baseline hazard function that is proportionally shifted by covariates. This baseline probability of failure, $h(t)$, can be easily transformed into the cumulative probability of survival, $S(t)$.[8] Figure 9.6 shows the cumulative survival function $S(t)$ estimated by our model for a central banker with average characteristics – appointed at age 52.4, presiding over inflation of 5.6 percent, serving under a middle-of-the-road government with partisan center of gravity equal to 0.07, and so on.

Given the roughly linear form of the baseline survival function, we can summarize it in a single number with negligible distortion. The simplest summary available for the Cox proportional hazards model is the expected median survival time, or the period after which only half a cohort with the specified covariates is expected to survive. The median survival time (or halflife) is simply the time at which the cumulative survival function crosses a horizontal line drawn at 0.5, as shown in Figure 9.6. For the average central banker, the median time in office is exactly 9 years, with a 90% confidence interval from 8.0 to 10.3 years.[9] To translate the model implications in easily digested form, I calculate conditional survival functions and expected median tenures, for several hypothetical scenarios. This involves no new estimation or simulation and is merely a different way to present the same information contained in Table 9.1.

I begin by considering the effect of contemporaneous inflation and unemployment rates on the probability of central banker survival. Table 9.1 shows that the base terms for both variables are significant and correctly signed, with higher rates of either of these economic "bads" reducing the probability a central banker will stay in office. The first group of results in Figure 9.7 shows the net effect of inflation and unemployment on median survival for the average central banker. On average, central bankers appear to be punished equally for high inflation and unemployment: a one standard deviation increase in either cuts tenures by 2 years, or roughly 20 percent.

This is striking evidence that governments reward central bankers for their competence and punish them for their failures. A closer look reveals important partisan nuances. The next group of results shows that central bankers working under left-wing governments lose two years of tenure for high unemployment, compared to just one year for high inflation. Right-wing governments

8 The survival function is defined as $S(t) = \exp(-\int_0^t h(s)\mathrm{d}s)$.

9 This seems like a long tenure compared to the observed mean of 6.67 years in this sample, but the sample average is brought down by the much shorter tenures of central bankers appointed near retirement age.

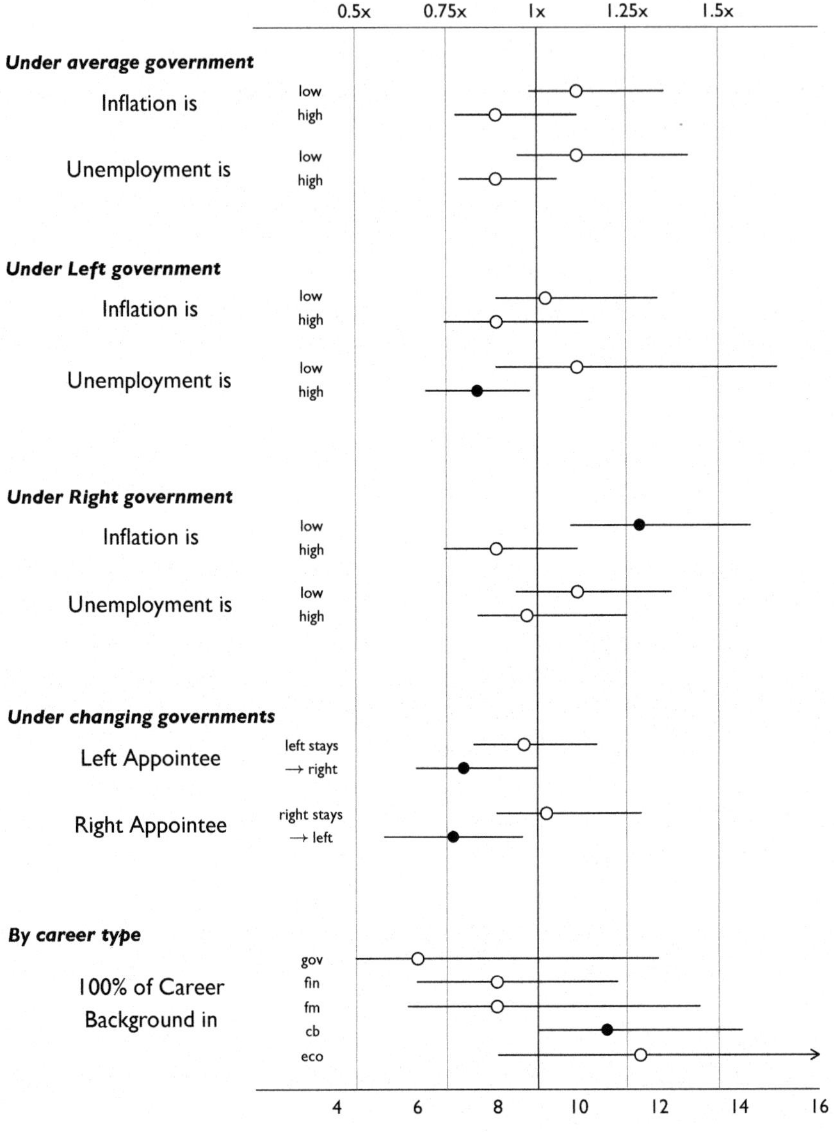
Conditional median central banker tenure, relative to baseline
0.5x
0.75x
1x
1.25x
1.5x
Under average government
Inflation is
low
high
Unemployment is
low
high
Under Left government
Inflation is
low
high
Unemployment is
low
high
Under Right government
Inflation is
low
high
Unemployment is
low
high
Under changing governments
Left Appointee
left stays
→ right
Right Appointee
right stays
→ left
By career type
100% of Career
Background in
gov
fin
fm
cb
eco
4
6
8
10
12
14
16
Conditional median central banker tenure, in years

Figure 9.7. *Determinants of median central banker tenure (facing page).* Each row shows the expected median tenure for a central banker who has average values of all covariates except the one listed at the left. "Low" inflation (or unemployment) refers to inflation (or unemployment) that is one standard deviation below its mean, "high" to inflation (or unemployment) one standard deviation above. "Left" government refers to governments with partisan centers of gravity one standard deviation below the mean; "right" to governments one standard deviation above. The change-in-government scenarios assume that the party or coalition in power either does not change over the central banker's tenure, or that it is replaced by an ideological opposite immediately after the central banker's appointment. 90 percent confidence intervals include uncertainty in the baseline hazard rate and are thus wider than the estimated parameters alone would lead one to expect.

appear to penalize central bankers just one year for high unemployment but a full three years for high inflation. This is exactly what we would expect of partisan governments retaining or replacing central bankers based on whether their past performance advanced the government's economic priorities.

In addition to expecting governments to judge central bankers by their past performance, we expect them to push out monetary policy makers appointed by ideologically opposed predecessors. The third group of results in Figure 9.7 show this is the case. Central bankers serving under their appointing governments expect to serve, all else equal, about nine years, regardless of whether appointed by the left or right. But if the government changes hands to an ideological opponent immediately following the central banker's appointment, the expected tenure of the central banker falls to seven years, even under identical economic conditions. Adding further interactions to distinguish moves to the right from moves to the left shows that parties on each side of the spectrum exact an equal career penalty from held-over central bankers.

Finally, variation in expected tenure across central bankers of differing career backgrounds provides mixed and indirect evidence on whether career-motivated central bankers send costly signals to shadow principals or reach career-for-policy bargains with them. Although none of the differences among career types are statistically significant, their order, at least, fits with our expectations under signalling, as central bankers coming from outside careers in the government or financial sectors may have shorter careers than those who rose up within the central bank or from academic economics. The small and insignificant differences here suggest that the career effects we have uncovered could be a combination of signaling and bargaining, as well as a reflection of pre-existing differences in policy preferences.

Nevertheless, the possibility that financial sector types may actually choose shorter tenures in the central bank – or at least be willing to set policies which shorten their tenures – suggests any incentives created by governments' refusal to appoint wayward central bankers have asymmetric effects, motivating only those central bankers whose shadow principal is the government. Central bankers with patrons in the financial sector can accept the loss of central bank posts with greater equanimity, given the promise of a private sector haven.

Conclusions

Over the last seven chapters, I have shown that partisan governments appoint central bankers of systematically differing career types to achieve partisan economic objectives. Central bankers play to type, pursuing the degree of inflation control and monetary stimulus desired by their shadow principals in the government and financial sector. We now reach the final test, as governments judge the performance of their monetary agents and then dismiss, decline to reappoint, or prompt the resignation of central bankers who fail to live up to partisan goals on inflation and unemployment. Contrary to the mission and conclusions of the central bank independence literature, monetary policy has not become a purely technocratic exercise but remains, at least at key moments, a political and even democratic process, in which partisan governments get to choose central bankers according to partisan preferences and may later deny re-appointment on partisan criteria. But because governments must often wait years to inflict punishments on central bankers who either fail to meet or fail to comply with public objectives for monetary policy, and because these punishments may only sting for central bankers without patrons in the financial sector, central banker turnover likely can only ever provide a limited measure of accountability for central bankers.

Table 9.2. *Summary of data used in the central banker tenure analysis.*

Variable	Mean	Median	Std. Dev.	Min	Max
Central Banker Tenure	6.67	5.33	4.67	0.12	29.99
Financial Experience	0.12	0.00	0.27	0.00	1.00
Finance Ministry Experience	0.10	0.00	0.24	0.00	1.00
Central Bank Staff Experience	0.30	0.00	0.39	0.00	1.00
Other Government Experience	0.18	0.00	0.28	0.00	1.00
Economics Experience	0.10	0.00	0.23	0.00	1.00
Current Age	57.6	57.5	7.8	36.0	78.8
Appointment Age	52.4	52.1	8.8	30.2	79.5
Current Partisan Center of Gravity	0.07	0.00	0.33	-0.47	0.97
Appointing Partisan Center of Gravity	0.07	0.07	0.33	-0.47	0.97
Inflation	5.60	4.54	4.15	0.03	32.01
Unemployment	5.85	5.30	4.09	0.00	24.50
Central Bank Independence	0.40	0.36	0.16	0.09	0.69

Observations with missing data for any of the above variables have been deleted. The data consist of 10,863 periods comprising 474 spells in the central bank on the part of 349 individuals from 20 countries and are right-censored at 2001. For this table only (and not the regression model in this chapter), the data on tenures include only non-censored cases.

10

CONCLUSION

The Dilemma of Discretion

If men were angels, no government would be necessary.
If angels were to govern men, neither external
nor internal controls on government would be necessary.
In framing a government which is to be administered
by men over men, the great difficulty lies in this:
you must first enable the government to control the governed;
and in the next place oblige it to control itself.

JAMES MADISON, *Federalist 51*

It's simple. We own them, we tell them what to do and if the directors don't, we sack them and get people who can.

Swedish Finance Minister ANDERS BORG on nationalized banks*

THE PIECES OF THIS BOOK build up a single encompassing theory: we cannot understand the politics of monetary policy – from the selection of central bankers and central bank institutions to the creation of short run economic outcomes – unless we understand the objectives of the central bank officials who actually make monetary policy. This theory rests on the insight that economic performance results not from institutions or interests alone, but from their interaction across the political economy.

The first part of this book laid out a career theory of monetary policy centered on the idea that past experience (career socialization) and the shadow of

* Borg pointed out this rather direct career incentive to a British peer, who asked how the Swedish government made their newly nationalized banks increase lending (Lord Oakeshott, quoted in Paul Owen and Andrew Sparrow, "London mayor and local election results – live coverage," *The Guardian*, May 4, 2012).

the future (career incentives) lead some central bankers to favor tighter monetary policy, and others to take a easier stance. The stereotypical conservative career type is the former private banker and stands in contrast to the dovish former bureaucrat. Using a comprehensive new database of central bankers' career histories over the last half of the twentieth century, I showed these same career types reprise their roles in different concentrations in central banks across the world, setting the stage for a broadly applicable measure of variation in central banker conservatism.

The career approach explains different facets of monetary policy over a wide array of countries: career effects lie behind individual central bankers' votes and revealed interest rate preferences in the United States, collective interest rate decisions by central bank boards across the rich democracies, and inflation rates around the globe. In a side-by-side comparison, career factors appear at least as important as central bank independence. Moreover, career effects are more robust and portable than central bank independence, explaining behavior in industrialized countries as well as the developing world.

The second part of the book expanded the argument to take institutional context into account. Preferences and institutions belong to the same puzzle, and the effect of each depends on the other. Unfortunately, the preferences of policy making agents and the liberty or constraint bestowed on them by institutions are seldom studied jointly, particularly in central banking. Using career-based measures of central banker conservatism, I showed that conservatism and independence reduce inflation most when they coincide, but much less when only one is present.

I extended the argument to further institutional interactions and looked at the effects of central bank nonaccommodation under different labor market arrangements and partisan governments. This nuanced approach allows us to sort out the effects of monetary policy on the real economy. When labor union are mostly (but not entirely) self-restraining in their wage demands, aggressive nonaccommodation bears an unemployment cost. But where wage bargaining structure produces excessive real wage pressure, central bank nonaccommodation helps keep a lid on inflation without raising unemployment. Finally, partisan governments play a role: left-wing governments lower unemployment in moderately centralized labor markets, where social policy concessions offer an alternative way to mollify labor unions' wage demands.

Finally, in the third part of the book, I turned from the economic performance of political agents to the politics of economic performance. Because different types of central bankers have different effects on inflation and unemployment, partisan governments have preferences over the types of agents they appoint. This connection between partisan governments and central bank appointees ties voters' choices to short-run economic outcomes – central bank independence has weakened the link between elections and monetary policy, but cannot completely sever it. Because every term of office must eventually end, governments have a final chance to hold central bankers accountable through the reappointment process. I find that central bankers are more likely to stay in office when they produce the economic outcomes sought by the party in power. However, the financial sector's role as a shadow principal offering outside employment may limit government's ability to hold central bankers to account through reappointment rewards.

Monetary Policy and Shadow Principals in the United States and Europe

This book's findings have significant implications for the design of real-world macroeconomic institutions. Consider central bank independence, now embraced around the world as a simple "solution" for the problem of inflation. Seducing some supporters with a clever idea backed by tantalizing evidence, while providing powerful financial sector actors with an intellectual mandate for the self-regulation they'd always wanted, the proposal of a few academic economists to solve a specific time-inconsistency problem in monetary policy helped create independent central banks around the globe (Maxfield, 1997; Johnson, 2002). Like many popular economic memes, reformers' preference-free version of central bank independence has proven too simple and too catchy, depriving policy makers and publics of the economic imagination needed to solve any crisis other than a rerun of 1970s-style inflation (Stiglitz, 2012).

A broader perspective, still consistent with the foundational theoretical research on the problem of monetary policy delegation, suggests governments should select legally independent central bankers carefully. Governments should bear in mind that central bankers' preferences determine whether the economy achieves good nominal *and* real outcomes throughout the business cycle, as well as whether the full force of monetary policy and regulation is brought to bear to prevent and combat financial crises. (And outside of crises: to the extent private banks care even more about day-to-day regulatory decisions than interest rate policy, a book parallel to this one but focused on the effects of financial shadow principals on these choice would likely find even *greater* policy effects from central banker careers.)

Although Chapter 8 found strong partisan effects on central bank appointment, not all governments treat this decision as seriously as they should.[1] Some central bankers are plainly too conservative to be a good fit with the elected governments that appointed them and the mass publics to whom they are responsible. And though the definition of "too conservative" depends on the society, it surely includes any central banker who fears inflation more than unemployment in the midst of the deepest debt-deflation spiral since the Great Depression.

There can be no better sign that independent central banks have lost their way than Kenneth Rogoff's quixotic efforts to help central bankers understand that not all monetary policy problems demand a hawkish response. Starting in 2009, Rogoff began advocating "6 percent inflation for at least a couple of years" to "ameliorate the debt bomb and help us work through the deleveraging process."[2] Rogoff built the intellectual case for conservative, independent central bankers; if he thinks central bankers have gone too far to prove their commitment to low inflation, policy makers should pay attention.

Yet even amidst widespread frustration with the pace of economic recovery, Rogoff's proposals have been poorly received by the same central bankers who rely on his theories to justify their legal independence. Indeed, one central banker's response deployed a maximalist version of Rogoff's own argument for credibility in monetary policy (Rogoff, 1985), insisting that "[a]nybody who has been a central banker wouldn't want to see inflation expectations become unhinged," because "[t]he Fed would have to create a recession to get its credibility

1 Barack Obama, for example, neglected to fill vacant seats on the Federal Reserve Board of Governors during the months his party commanded a filibuster-proof majority in the Senate (July 2009 to February 2010), leading to a costly and preventable delay in Obama's economic agenda. Waiting until his Republican opponents could again block nominees cost Obama the chance to appoint Peter Diamond, a Nobel Prize winning economist. Later, Republican Senator David Vitter held up two more Obama nominees for months, claiming they would be "rubber stamps" for Bernanke's "activist policies" against unemployment (Adam Sorenson, "Two more Fed nominees blocked: a missed chance for Obama," *Time*, May 7, 2012, `swampland.time.com/2012/05/07/two-more-fed-nominees-blocked-a-missed-chance-for-obama`). The vacancies remained until May 2012, when controversial derivatives trading losses at J.P. Morgan Chase spurred the Senate into action (John H. Cushman, "Senate confirms 2 nominees to Federal Reserve board," *New York Times*, May 18, 2012, B3).

2 Rich Miller, "U.S. Needs More Inflation to Speed Recovery, Say Mankiw, Rogoff," *Bloomberg*, May 19, 2009.

back."[3] In 2011, with little real hope of influencing the system he once helped create, Rogoff renewed his proposal in stronger terms:

> By far the main problem is a huge overhang of debt that creates headwinds to faster normalisation of post-crisis growth... there is still the option of trying to achieve some modest deleveraging through moderate inflation of, say, 4 to 6 per cent for several years. Any inflation above 2 per cent may seem anathema to those who still remember the anti-inflation wars of the 1970s and 1980s, but a once-in-75-year crisis calls for outside-the-box measures.[4]

Rogoff has the better of this argument: a round of inflation *would* help ameliorate the worst economic recession to hit the globe since the 1930s.[5] Nor is he along among prominent academic economists: Olivier Blanchard (Blanchard, Dell'Ariccia, and Mauro, 2010), Paul Krugman (2012), Michael Woodford (2012), and Joseph Stiglitz (2012) have all made similar proposals. But these

3 Marvin Goodfriend, formerly of the Federal Reserve Bank of Richmond, quoted in Miller, *op cit*. Note that the narrative of credibility at the heart of the original Rogoff formula leads Goodfriend to see all monetary crises through a 1970s lens. It follows that inflationary episodes must end in the same way, with a 1981-style central-bank–engineered recession. But the current crisis differs in many respects: we have debt-deflation, not supply-shock inflation; Rogoff proposes setting expectations for moderate inflation, which would carry only a modest economic cost even if the inflation persisted; and, most obviously, we are already *in* a deep recession – Goodfriend's critique only applies when the economy is close to full employment. His warnings of recession are, of course, painfully redundant.

4 Kenneth Rogoff, "The bullets yet to be fired to stop the crisis," *Financial Times*, August 8, 2011.

5 Even with interest rates skipping along the zero lower bound, there are still many options open to the Federal Reserve and ECB. The easiest is establishing firm expectations for moderate inflation. To make these expectations credible, central banks can take further steps, including financing tax cuts or refundable tax credits through monetary expansion, broadening the purchase of private debt, and establishing nominal GDP targets or floors under long-term interest rates. The canonical source on creative monetary policy at the zero bound is, of course, economics' Ben Bernanke (2000) – leading critics to wonder whether the Federal Reserve's Ben Bernanke is a victim of institutional capture (Ball, 2012; Krugman, 2012). This argument probably gives Bernanke too little credit. Chapter 4 suggests an alternative explanation for the two Bernankes: the chairman cannot dictate to the voting members of the FOMC and may not be able to find the votes among its more conservative members for the very measures he once recommended.

recommendations have so far gone no further than the occasional conference paper or op-ed, in part because the convenient idea of total delegation to an independent central bank now dominates elite discourse on monetary policy.[6] Central bankers brandish this alluring concept to silence – as a matter of economic necessity – any policy discussion about the range of appropriate types of central bankers to appoint or the conditions under which central bankers should be terminated or declined reappointment. Agents empowered and insulated by an intellectual framework are unlikely to question it; resistance must come from political leaders outside central banks. Unfortunately, until governments reconsider their hands-off approach to central banking, there is hardly any payoff to academic debate over when inflation might be good for the economy or even essential to its recovery.

Changing the terms of the broader debate requires focused attention on the role of financial sector shadow principals throughout government. The banking crisis that destroyed Lehman Brothers and prompted rapid banking consolidation had many well-understood causes – the development of financial instruments too complex for counterparties or regulatory officials to understand, optimistic risk ratings applied to these financial innovations, and the massive leveraging of complex, misrated assets by banks that were "too big to fail." But regardless of the origins of the crisis, a clear prescription for its resolution – Sweden's success in negotiating its own banking collapse in 1992 – went unconsidered except by academic economists and a handful of economics-savvy bloggers.[7]

6 As this book went to press, Bernanke announced new quantitative easing measures that would last until the labor market improves (Benyamin Applebaum, "Fed links new aid to jobs recovery in forceful move," *New York Times*, September 14, 2012, A1). This is a welcome step towards nominal GDP targeting, although the mechanism – mainly purchases of mortgage-backed securities from banks – is both weaker and riskier than alternatives focused on consumption. If Chapter 4's arguments are right, the Fed's move suggests growing support for accommodation within the FOMC. Following on the heels of significant movement towards Obama in the 2012 presidential race, the new policy also hints that FOMC hawks decided that stalling intervention no longer made sense: in a second term, Obama could respond to a still-recalcitrant board by appointing new FOMC members more interested in accommodation, following the logic of Alt (1991). And with dwindling chances of a Romney victory, Republican accusations of Federal Reserve meddling in a close election had lost their sting.

7 In the midst of the pivotal month of the financial crisis, the United States' paper of record ran a detailed account of Sweden's success (Carter Dougherty, "Stopping a financial crisis, the Swedish way," *New York Times*, September 23, 2008, C9), but

The Swedish case suggests a state facing a major financial crisis can temporarily nationalize failed or tottering banks, then impose losses on unlucky – or irresponsible – financial sector risk-takers, while keeping the credit channel for the real economy open. Ignoring this success story, governments mostly followed the failed example of Japan, generously recapitalizing the very banks responsible for the crisis and meekly passing by the unique opportunity to impose a new financial regulatory regime until *after* banks regained the economic and political power to fight reform. Instead of a quick, wrenching solution to an existential economic crisis, government after government chose to protect the shadow principals responsible for it, even at the risk of creating a long-term drag on the economy in the form of zombie banks.[8]

Governments' choice to follow the wrong example in response to the financial crisis is depressing, but not truly a puzzle. The revolving door between finance and government regulators, including central banks, made genuine reform irrational and unthinkable. Many of the officials responsible for these choices were financial sector veterans, and giving banks vast, largely unconditional loans preserved the ability of banking shadow principals to reward them later. Bringing the power of regulation down on the banks in their moment of weakness would have conflicted with the socialized beliefs of these financial sector veterans and risked any future bank bonuses they might hope to collect.

In light of career motivations, it is clear that neither widening banking regulation nor breaking up newly-formed megabanks is enough to restore democratic accountability to financial policy making. These are important steps, to be sure, but cannot stand alone: in the past, these very mechanisms were subverted – and will be undermined again – by financial sector shadow principals. Discussing the growing gap between banking executives' compensation and that of elite federal banking regulators, Ferguson and Johnson (2010, 22) bluntly state what reformers are sometimes loathe to admit:

---

only economics bloggers like Berkeley professor Brad DeLong seemed to be listening (J. Bradford DeLong, "Time not for a bailout, but a nationalization," September 26, 2008, delong.typepad.com/sdj/2008/09/time-not-for-a.html).

8 I do not mean to suggest that this alternative course would have been easy. For the United States or other large countries to replicate the Swedish solution would require the rapid mobilization of extensive technical expertise in finance and forensic accounting and the near-instant construction or radical extension of regulatory agencies. What is telling is the absence of any known serious debate in policy circles about whether this sort of financial D-Day could have been implemented – even during the month of September 2008, when in the United States other radical options were on the table.

> Once that gulf reaches a certain point, talk about improving regulation by drafting better, more specific laws, new supervisory agencies, or even campaign finance reform is largely idle. The interest of the regulators in going for gold through the "revolving door" will overwhelm every other consideration.

An agent-centered perspective makes clear that restoring regulators' accountability to the public requires measures prohibiting officials from walking through the revolving door again. Whether reformers delegating monetary policy to independent central banks really thought they were forging a credible commitment, their unbalanced efforts were destined to give power not to independent agents, but to shadow principals. A commitment that constrains only principals is not enough; the loyalty of agents to their assigned task cannot be taken for granted. When the Sirens called, crafty Odysseus bound his hands to the mast – but he stopped his crew's ears with wax *first*.

Banning central bankers and other banking regulators from taking private banking jobs or money after leaving public office is an important step. Salaries and training for financial regulators also need to rise dramatically to replace the state's implicit reliance on the revolving door for both expertise and delayed compensation. In comparison to the staggering cost of financial crises (Reinhart and Rogoff, 2009), this is a negligible price to pay. Finally, countries like the United States should end the practice of including on monetary policy boards members directly selected by private banks – the Board of Governors nominated by the president and confirmed by the Senate should make monetary policy, without vetoes from regional Federal Reserve presidents accountable only to the narrow interests of the banking sector.[9] While there will

9 These are significant changes in policy, but concrete and potentially popular ones. Requiring new central bank appointees to sign contracts renouncing the revolving door is not, after all, very different from ubiquitous non-competition agreements preventing new scienific and engineering hires in private industry from taking intellectual secrets to competitors. In the public sphere, a similar contract would likewise ensure public officials' loyalty to their current employer, the public itself, rather than to a shadow principal. The American public was recently surprised that J.P. Morgan Chase's chief Jamie Dimon, whose bank came under fire for risky trading, supervises his own regulators through a position at the New York Fed (Danielle Kurtzleben, "Calls for Jamie Dimon to leave New York Fed grow louder," *U.S. News and World Report*, May 31, 2012). Just as no one would tolerate an SEC chair simultaneously working at a hedge fund, a fully public membership for bodies like the FOMC satisfies public desire to avoid conflicts of interest in regulatory agencies. (For a similar critique, see Simon

always be a place in central banks for private bankers' expertise, there must be a limit to their influence if governments are to satisfy public demands not just for low inflation, but also low and stable unemployment, and a sound, well-managed financial sector. As this book shows, many countries have been able to achieve good economic outcomes – and especially, good real economic outcomes – without putting private bankers on their monetary policy boards.

If the United States needs to reconsider its selection of financial officials to prevent the next crisis, the European Union and European national governments must face the role preferences play in monetary policy in order to survive the current one. Many governments have already fallen, but much more than governments are at stake. The decades-long pursuit of monetary union came to fruition just as the unquestioning acceptance of central bank independence was at its peak. As a result, the European Central Bank is the most unconstrained of all central banks – without even a countervailing elected fiscal authority – and in practice the most conservative. Yet this institution appears ready to preside over both a preventable recession and the dissolution – or radical shrinkage – of its own currency union.

As critics charged from the beginning, the eurozone is hardly an optimal currency area (De Grauwe, 1993). In response to the 2008 financial crisis, a number of European economies, including Ireland and the countries of the Mediterranean, guaranteed private banking debts and increased Keynesian stimulus, leading to sharp increases in sovereign debt. Before monetary union, countries would have followed these moves with currency depreciation, which would simultaneously increase trade and tourism and erode debt. The European Central Bank, dominated by a German economy that neither wants to inflate nor to subsidize its southern neighbors' spending, has blocked this route, locking the south into a contagious and seemingly inescapable cycle of budget cuts, declining GDP, and growing euro-denominated sovereign debt. The ECB has accelerated this vicious cycle by resisting its natural role as lender of last resort to European governments – instead doubling down on the now-comical claim that price stability is both its only function and its key contribution to resolving the crisis.[10] As noted at the close of Chapter 7, there is even reason to believe

Johnson, "An institutional flaw at the heart of the Federal Reserve," *New York Times*, June 14, 2012, economix.blogs.nytimes.com/2012/06/14/an-institutional-flaw-at-the-heart-of-the-federal-reserve.)

10 ECB head Mario Draghi – a managing director at Goldman Sachs International as recently as 2005 – denies his reponsibility for the real economy in the plainest terms possible: "Are we doing all we can for growth? Our task is not that. Our task is to

the ECB is knowingly keeping interests rates higher than needed to hit its own inflation target as leverage to coerce deeper fiscal austerity.

The ECB's intransigence has forced the European Union into a painful choice. Europe can either abandon the euro experiment, restrict it to a more reasonable area centered on the German economy, or turn control of the euro over to less conservative ECB governors both willing to serve as the lender of last resort and able to tolerate enough inflation to restore the southern economies. European governments have for more than a year postponed this choice through bank bailouts and austerity packages, but ever-sharper electoral rebukes demonstrate that most Europeans find these bargains intolerable. Meanwhile, austerity is deepening the recession everywhere it is tried, and few have the stomach for repeating this game much longer.[11]

The lessons of this book for the euro fiasco are two-fold. First, I have shown that conservative, independent, nonaccommodating central banks can benefit countries in terms of inflation without raising unemployment if they constrain moderately centralized labor markets. Moreover, these benefits are even stronger when they are paired with left-wing governments, playing off central banks' non-accommodation of union wage demands with fiscal policy carrots that widely share the benefits of growth and keep labor happy even under competitive wage bargains. This was the set of interlocking political and economic institutions that helped make the conservative, independent Bundes-

ensure price stability and through this contribute to growth. That's what I think we are delivering" (Robin Emmott, "Draghi, seeking growth, throws crisis ball to governments," *Reuters*, April 25, 2012, uk.reuters.com/article/2012/04/25/uk-ecb-idUKBRE83O0CJ20120425). See also J. Bradford DeLong, "The ECB's battle against central banking," Project Syndicate, October 31, 2011, www.project-syndicate.org/commentary/the-ecb-s-battle-against-central-banking, and John Quiggin, "Euro crisis's enabler: The central bank," *New York Times*, November 8, 2011.

11 As this book went to press, the ECB announced plans to make "unlimited" sterilized purchases of member government bonds, subject to fiscal conditions on participating governments – conditions which may yet prove to be a poison pill. But if governments accept these conditions, the ECB would likely become the lender of last resort for the Eurozone, thus buying time for Europe to find a compromise on monetary and fiscal stimulus (Jack Ewing and Steve Erlander, "Huge step taken by Europe's bank to abate a crisis," *New York Times*, September 6, 2012, A1). However, the move does not guarantee or even suggest a political resolution to the conflict over the appropriate degree of accommodation. Moreover, conditional lending will only extend the ECB's influence over the member countries' fiscal policies, a concern raised in Chapter 7.

bank a widely-heralded economic success. Unfortunately, most of the key ingredients of this recipe were lost in transfering the central banking practices of the Bundesbank to the ECB, which presides over an effectively decentralized Europe-wide labor market with no fiscal policy partner at the European Union level. In this context, a hawkish anti-inflation line carries real economic costs.

This brings us to the second lesson. If the euro project is to survive, the European Central Bank badly needs rethinking. At one level, it needs new, far less inflation-averse governors. But at a deeper institutional level, the problem is that ECB governors only have shadow principals. Structurally, the ECB is designed to ignore the European Parliament, Commission, and Council, but no rules limit the influence of private banks on its members. If this book has shown anything, it is that the complete legal independence of central banks does not create political neutrality, but regulatory capture; Stigler, not Weber. The ECB should face, as the Federal Reserve does, at least the possibility of override by democratically elected officials. (Until the European Union decides who those officials should be, the very idea of ECB "independence" is meaningless – *independence from whom*?) It is unclear whether the euro can or even should survive, but for countries enduring Europe's manmade crisis, the mystique of the central banker as an apolitical technocrat should pass away.

Of course, sweeping policy recommendations are easier to lay out than to implement, especially when they conflict with the personal interests of political incumbents. No one fights recessions with fiscal and monetary austerity because of any notable evidence austerity works. Instead of economies righted by two years of belt-tightening, today's deficit- and inflation-hawks can only point to promised crises of investor confidence and inflation that, like Godot, never actually arrive. These zombie policy solutions dominate the agenda even after manifest failure because of the concentrated interests they benefit. And these policies are adopted, and preserved against whatever limited outcry bad technocratic policy can provoke, by agents conditioned by their past careers – and sometimes even rewarded through their future careers – for so doing. Nevertheless, it is sobering to imagine what may happen if European elites continue to man the barricades against reform of the European Central Bank. Because it has been more important for insiders to pursue a low inflation policy than to prevent widespread immiseration, the political stability of an entire continent is now at risk.

Agent-Centered Political Economy

The immediate purpose of this book is to bring preferences back to the study of central banks, but models of career concerns are useful for the study of delegation broadly. Too often, especially in quantitative tests of institutional hypotheses, political economists neglect to meld an increasingly sophisticated understanding of rules with similarly nuanced examinations of the actors who operate within those constraints.[12] The solution is to introduce the detailed study of agents into institutional political economy. I have shown this in a setting many would consider unpromising for an agent-centered approach. Surprising as it may seem to readers of the central bank independence literature, even modern central banks are subject to manipulation by monetary policy agents, whose preferences are more diverse than the architects of independence assumed.

The revolving door is the very essence of regulatory capture, and career effects and incentives permeate regulatory agencies, courts, and political parties throughout the world. Using career incentives to explore preferences offers an alternative to models which blithely "deduc[e] officials' preferences from the attributes of their agencies, without considering how preferences develop informally and over time" (Schneider, 1993). At the same time, career paths can help researchers sort through relationships among competing principals and organizations using the characteristics of agents themselves. Research along these lines enriches our understanding of what happens within and across institutions by bringing the political actors inhabiting them back to center stage.

Lack of easy-to-use social science methods to study careers is one reason the revolving door hypothesis is seldom rigorously explored. As a tool for capturing career types, measures like experience scores should see wider use in the study of bureaucracy, especially to test whether agencies have been captured by private interests. Studies that do link agents' past careers with their actions in government tend not to take full advantage of the available data, instead using binary or categorical indicators of experience types rather than finer grained measures of experience that distinguish dabblers from careerists. Researchers may fear that creating more detailed records of careers would be more expensive, but the opposite is the case. With careful design and a simple

12 In a call to rectify this imbalance, Katznelson and Weingast argue that "[a]lthough central to accounts of purposive action, preferences remain a relatively primitive category of analysis.... Preferences are foundational for any theory that relies on agency. We know too little about preferences, where they come from or how they are generated" (Katznelson and Weingast, 2005, 2).

coding scheme, recording detailed career data is faster and involves fewer coder judgments than recording binary career types. All that is required is a record of each official's past jobs, with starting and ending dates, and software to tabulate these data.[13] By coding underlying histories in a common format, the analyst can easily to produce experience scores, as well as more complicated variables that weight experience over time or capture contextual relationships.

The tools are important because political economy needs more career-based studies of the bureaucracy: if even central bankers, sober guardians of the economic punch-bowl, have preferences diverse enough to create substantially different economic outcomes, how much more important are differences across agents operating in hotly contested policy areas, harder to observe regulatory arenas, or street-level service provision? What of the differences among agents issuing citations to polluters, signing defense contracts, or regulating public utilities? If, holding constant the preferences and institutional devices of principals, the agents of the central bank make a difference, we are surely missing something important in the empirical study of public policy generally.

Two areas of study in particular illustrate the potential for an agent-centered political economy. The first is the emerging literature on independent electoral management bodies. Before the turn of the twenty-first century, when scholars considered election administration at all, they tended to assume the neutral competence of election agencies (Mozaffar and Schedler, 2002). However, democractization and especially partial democratization across the former communist bloc and Latin America led to a proliferation of independent election commissions. In response came scholarly interest in the ability of these institutions to insulate election administration from the machinations of political parties and other interested actors (López-Pintor, 2000; Mozaffar, 2002; Pastor, 1999). Despite some recognition of the theoretical importance of election agents' own interests (Elklit and Reynolds, 2002), empirical work on election management bodies has focused exclusively on the formal location of these bodies within the bureaucracy (Birch, 2008) and on institutions of appointment and tenure (Hartlyn, McCoy, and Mustillo, 2008), and so far pays no explicit attention to the agents within these institutions. But the example of central banks shows that formal independence means little if the "independent" agents' careers depend on the actors they regulate. Put another way, granting Katherine Harris independent authority over election administration in Florida does not

13 The author's Escore package is one such tool.

insulate election administration from the competing parties if Harris's next career move depends on her standing with party patrons.

Comparative studies of courts have also neglected agents. This is not true of the American literature on courts, as a major strand of the Supreme Court literature emphasizes the role of judicial preferences, countering the traditional view of justices as wise, impartial jurists. Beginning with the "attitudinal model" of Segal and coauthors (Segal and Cover, 1989; Segal and Spaeth, 1993, 2002), work in this mode now encompasses sophisticated accounts of the strategic interaction of judicial and legislative preferences (Epstein and Knight, 1998; Clark, 2011), as well as efforts to trace the evolution of the ideological stance of individual Supreme Court justices over time (Martin and Quinn, 2002). However, most comparative work focuses on institutions alone, and especially on the benefits of independent courts, which various authors argue protect human rights (Powell and Staton, 2009), democracy (Gibler and Randazzo, 2011), and growth-enhancing properties rights (Porta, de Silanes, Pop-Eleches, and Shleifer, 2004). There are exceptions, such as Helmke's (2002; 2005) investigation of Argentinean courts' strategic behavior under democracy and dictatorship, and Maravall (2003), who notes an autonomous and conservative German judiciary helped undermine the Weimar Republic. But in general, the comparative literature on courts would benefit from more attention to judges' preferences and fewer universal assumptions about the effects of their independence.

Career concerns have long been central to the study of public officials motivations, but with the simplifying – and democratically reassuring – axiom that officials primarily seek the continuation of their political careers through re-election, or perhaps election to a higher office. In an era when members of Congress audition to be lobbyists and major presidential candidates seem more interested in winning a cable timeslot than a shot at the White House, career concerns are just as important as ever, but less supportive of democratic representation. Christopher Hayes (2012) takes this concern to its logical end. Focusing on the United States, he paints the disheartening picture of a self-sustaining elite, initially generated by "meritocratic" institutions, that increasingly uses career protections – specifically, an implicit promise that elite actors who produce poor outcomes as public servants "fail upwards" into lucrative private sector jobs – to insulate its members from mass disapproval for policies which protect the interests of the powerful. Hayes argues this system leads to increasingly inequitable outcomes without accountability, eroding public trust in the institutions of governance.

Whether or not Hayes' dystopian vision really describes our present political world is the sort of question agent-oriented political economy can answer. Although this book is about the role agents play in setting monetary policy, it is also part of a general approach investigating the sources of agent preference and the pathways of successful careers in elite institutions. At the micro-level, we need to trace the motivations of elite bureaucrats and other political leaders through the development of their careers, with closer attention to how early career choices affect later career goals. Shih, Adolph, and Liu (2012) provide one example of how this might be done, linking reform-era Chinese leaders' early careers with their later rise to the upper echelons of the party. With career data for many organizations hiding in plain sight, the field is wide open. Where the evidence to test career path arguments is lacking, or the predictions from career tracks ambiguous, agent-centered studies may still point towards ideational clusters or epistemic communities among agents, which scholars could try to link with agents' material interests.

Turning to an agent-centered political economy does not mean leaving institutions behind: agents and institutions are inescapably interdependent. After all, institutions are the force multipliers that make agency important – in a Hobbesian, institution-free world, solitary political actors' efforts are negligible and countervailing. In the case of central banks, a handful of monetary delgates' preferences became supremely important precisely because they enjoyed extraodinary legal independence from other actors. Only institutions make agency matter, but when we ignore the role agents play within institutions, we write the story of political economy in the passive voice.

REFERENCES AND AUTHOR INDEX

The pages of this book citing the works below appear in bold at the end of each entry.

Acemoglu, Daron, Pablo Querubín, Simon Johnson, and James A. Robinson. 2008. "When does policy reform work? The case of central bank independence." *Brookings Papers on Economic Activity* 39(1): 351–417. **147**

Acemoglu, Daron, Simon Johnson, and James A. Robinson. 2002. "Reversal of fortune: Geography and institutions in the making of the modern world income distribution." *Quarterly Journal of Economics* 117(4): 1231–1294. **9**

Acemoglu, Daron, Simon Johnson, and James Robinson. 2004. "Institutions as the fundamental cause of long-run growth." NBER Working Paper 10481. **4**

Achen, Christopher H. 2000. "Why lagged dependent variables can suppress the explanatory power of other independent variables." Presented at the Annual Meeting of the Society for Political Methodology, Los Angeles. **123 and 124**

Adolph, Christopher. 2003. "Visual interpretation and presentation of Monte Carlo results." *The Political Methodologist* 11(2): 31–5. **43**

Adolph, Christopher. 2004. "The dilemma of discretion: Career ambitions and the politics of central banking." Ph.D. Dissertation, Department of Government, Harvard University. **220 and 228**

Ahlquist, John S., and Margaret Levi. 2013. *In the Interests of Others: Provoking Political Activism in Labor Unions.* Princeton: Princeton University Press. **40**

Aitchison, John. 2003*a*. "Compositional data analysis: Where are we and where should we be heading?" Compositional Data Analysis Workshop, October 15–17, Girona, Spain, http://ima.udg.es/Activitats/CoDaWork03. **269**

Aitchison, John. 2003*b*. *The Statistical Analysis of Compositional Data.* Caldwell, NJ: Blackburn Press. **72, 104, 106, 254, 268, 269, and 271**

Aitchison, John, and J. W. Kay. 2003. "Possible solutions of some essential zero problems in compositional data analysis." Compositional Data Analysis Workshop, October 15–17, Girona, Spain, http://ima.udg.es/Activitats/CoDaWork03/. **255, 270, and 271**

Alesina, Alberto. 1987. "Macroeconomic policy in a two-party system as a repeated game." *Quarterly Journal of Economics* 102(3): 651–678. **208**

Alesina, Alberto, and Guido Tabellini. 2007. "Bureaucrats or politicians? Part I: A single policy task." *American Economic Review* 97(1): 169–179. **17**

Alesina, Alberto, and Jeffrey Sachs. 1988. "Political parties and the business cycle in the United States, 1948–1984." *Journal of Money, Credit, and Banking* 20(1): 63–82. **131**

Alesina, Alberto, and Lawrence H. Summers. 1993. "Central bank independence and macroeconomic performance: Some comparative evidence." *Journal of Money, Credit, and Banking* 25(2): 151–162. **5, 29, 184, 208, and 246**

Alesina, Alberto, and Nouriel Roubini. 1990. "Political cycles in OECD economies." NBER Working Paper 3478. **208 and 290**

Alesina, Alberto, Nouriel Roubini, and Gerald Cohen. 1997. *Political Cycles and the Macroeconomy*. Cambridge, MA: MIT Press. **93, 109, 195, 208, 217, 221, 237, 238, and 259**

Allison, Graham T. 1969. "Conceptual models and the Cuban Missile Crisis." *American Political Science Review* 63(3): 689–718. **11 and 13**

Alt, James E. 1991. "Leaning into the wind or ducking out of the storm? U.S. monetary policy in the 1980s." In *Politics and Economics in the Eighties*, ed. Alberto Alesina and Geoffrey Carliner. Chicago: University of Chicago Press. pp. 41–82. **309**

Alt, James E., and John T. Woolley. 1982. "Reaction functions, optimization, and politics: Modelling the political economy of macroeconomic policy." *American Journal of Political Science* 26(4): 709–740. **124**

Alvarez de Cienfuegos, Ignacio Molina. 1999. "Spain: Still the primacy of corporatism?" In *Bureaucratic Élites in Western European States*, ed. Edward C. Page, and Vincent Wright. Oxford: Oxford University Press. pp. 32–54. **35**

Alvarez, R. Michael, Geoffrey Garrett, and Peter Lange. 1991. "Government partisanship, labor organization, and macroeconomic performance." *American Political Science Review* 85(3): 539–546. **208**

Amsden, Alice, and Takashi Hikino. 1994. "Project execution capability, organizational know-how, and conglomerate corporate growth in late industrialization." *Industrial and Corporate Change* 3(1): 111–149. **145**

Armstrong, David, and Irwin Morris. 2003. "Studying central bank independence: Missing data and other methodological issues." Presented at the Annual Meeting of the American Political Science Association, Philadelphia. **190**

Arrow, Kenneth. 1951. *Social Choice and Individual Values*. New York: Wiley. **12**

Åslund, Anders. 1995. *How Russia Became a Market Economy*. Washington, D.C.: Brookings Institution. **148**

Bacon-Shone, John. 1992. "Ranking methods for compositional data." *Applied Statistics* 41(3): 533–537. **269**

Bade, R., and M. Parkin. 1982. "Central bank laws and monetary policy." Department of Economics, University of Western Ontario. **85, 109, 275, and 295**

Ball, Laurence. 1999. "Policy rules for open economies." In *Monetary Policy Rules*, ed. John B. Taylor. Chicago: University of Chicago Press. pp. 127–144. **118**

Ball, Laurence. 2012. "Ben Bernanke and the zero bound." NBER Working Paper

17836. **308**

Banaian, King, and William A. Luksetich. 2001. "Central bank independence, economic freedom, and inflation rates." *Economic Inquiry* 39(1): 149–161. **189**

Banaian, King, R. C. K. Burdekin, and T. D. Willett. 1995. "On the political economy of central bank independence." In *Monetarism and the Methodology of Economics: Essays in Honor of Thomas Mayer*, ed. K. D. Hoover, and S. M. Sheffrin. Aldershott, England: Edward Elgar. pp. 178–197. **190**

Banco de Portugal. Various years. *Relatório do Conselho de Administração*. Lisbon: Tipographia do Banco de Portugal.

Bank of Canada. Various years. *Annual Report of the Governor to the Minister of Finance.*

Banks, Arthur S. 2004. "Cross-national time-series data archive." State University of New York, Binghampton. http://www.databanksinternational.com. **160**

Barofsky, Neil. 2012. *Bailout: An Inside Account of How Washington Abandoned Main Street While Rescuing Wall Street.* New York: Free Press. **35**

Barro, Robert J., and David B. Gordon. 1983. "Rules, discretion and reputation in a model of monetary policy." *Journal of Monetary Economics* 12(1): 101–121. **5, 29, 56, 184, 207, and 288**

Batini, Nicoletta, and Andrew G. Haldane. 1999. "Forward-looking rules for monetary policy." In *Monetary Policy Rules*, ed. John B. Taylor. Chicago: University of Chicago Press. pp. 157–192. **119**

Beck, Nathaniel. 2001. "Time-series cross-section data: What have we learned in the past few years?" *Annual Reviews of Political Science*. pp. 271–293. **166**

Beck, Nathaniel, and Jonathan Katz. 1995. "What to do (and not to do) with time-series cross-section data." *American Political Science Review* 89(3): 634–647. **84, 100, 160, and 218**

Belden, Susan. 1989. "Policy preferences of FOMC members as revealed by dissenting votes." *Journal of Money, Credit, and Banking* 21(4): 432–441. **37 and 128**

Bendor, J., A. Glazer, and T. Hammond. 2001. "Theories of delegation." *Annual Reviews of Political Science* 4: 235–269. **5 and 36**

Berger, Helge, and Ulrich Woitek. 2001. "The German political business cycle: money demand rather than monetary policy." *European Journal of Political Economy* 17(3): 609–631. **30**

Berger, Helge, Jacob de Haan, and Sylvester C.W. Eijffinger. 2001. "Central bank independence: An update of theory and evidence." *Review of Economic Surveys* 15(1): 3–40. **29 and 190**

Berman, Sheri, and Kathleen McNamara. 1999. "Bank on democracy: Why central banks need public oversight." *Foreign Affairs* 78(2): 2–8. **241**

Bernanke, Ben S. 2000. "Japan's slump: A case of self-induced paralysis?" In *Japan's Financial Crisis and Its Parallels to US Experience: Special Report 13*, ed. Adam Posen, and Ryoichi Mikitani. Washington, DC: Peterson Institute for International Economics. **308**

Bernanke, Ben S. 2010. "Central bank independence, transparency, and accountability." Presentation to the Institute for Monetary and Economic Studies International

Conference, Bank of Japan, Tokyo, May 25. **281**

Bernhard, William. 2002. *Banking on Reform: Political Parties and Central Bank Independence in the Industrial Democracies.* Ann Arbor: University of Michigan Press. **243**

Bernstein, Marver H. 1955. *Regulating Business by Independent Commission.* Princeton: Princeton University Press. **11, 13, and 16**

Beyer, Janice M., Prithviraj Chattopadhyay, Elizabeth George, Bill Glick, dt ogilvie, and Dulce Pugliese. 1997. "The selective perception of managers revisited." *The Academy of Management Journal* 40(3): 716–737. **39**

Birch, Sarah. 2008. "Electoral institutions and popular confidence in electoral processes: A cross-national analysis." *Electoral Studies* 27(2): 305–320. **316**

Black, Bernard, Reinier Kraakman, and Anna Tarassova. 2000. "Russian privatization and corporate governance: What went wrong?" *Stanford Law Review* 52: 1731–1808. **148**

Blanchard, Olivier, Giovanni Dell'Ariccia, and Paolo Mauro. 2010. "Rethinking macroeconomic policy." *IMF Staff Position Papers* (February 12). **308**

Blinder, Alan. 1997. "What central bankers could learn from academics – and vice versa." *Journal of Economic Perspectives* 11(2): 3–19. **31**

Blinder, Alan. 1998. *Central Banking in Theory and Practice.* Cambridge, MA: MIT Press. **29**

Blythe, Mark. 2002. *Great Transformations: Economic Ideas and Institutional Change in the Twentieth Century.* Cambridge: Cambridge University Press. **3**

Bodea, Cristina, and Kalina Popova. 2004. "Central banks and exchange rates: Commitments and inflationary performance in Eastern Europe and former Soviet Union." Working Paper, University of Rochester, Department of Political Science. **147**

Bowles, Paul, and G. White. 1994. "Central bank independence: a political economy approach." *Journal of Development Studies* 31(2): 235–264. **37 and 241**

Box-Steffensmeier, Janet M., and Bradford S. Jones. 2004. *Event History Modeling: A Guide for Social Scientists.* Cambridge University Press. **295**

Brans, Marleen, and Annie Hondeghem. 1999. "The senior civil service in Belgium." In *Bureaucratic Élites in Western European States*, ed. Edward C. Page, and Vincent Wright. Oxford: Oxford University Press. pp. 121–146. **35**

Brehm, John, and Scott Gates. 1999. *Working, Shirking, and Sabotage: Bureaucratic Response to a Democratic Public.* Ann Arbor, MI: The University of Michigan Press. **10, 12, and 13**

Brehm, John, Scott Gates, and Brad Gomez. 2003. "Donut shops, speed traps, and paperwork: Supervision and the allocation of time to bureaucratic tasks." In *Politics, Policy, and Organizations: Frontiers in the Scientific Study of Bureaucracy*, ed. George A. Krause, and Kenneth J. Meier. Ann Arbor, MI: University of Michigan Press. pp. 133–159. **254 and 255**

Breusch, T. S., J. C. Robertson, and A. H. Welsh. 1997. "The emperor's new clothes: a critique of the multivariate *t* regression model." *Statistica Neerlandica* 51(3): 269–286. **274**

Brezis, Elise S., and Avi Weiss. 1997. "Conscientious regulation and post-regulatory employment restrictions." *European Journal of Political Economy* 13(3): 517–536. **16**

Brezis, Elise S., Jacob Paroush, and Avi Weiss. 2002. "Red tape: Oiling the hinges of the 'revolving door.'" Working Paper. Department of Economics, Bar-Ilan University, Israel. **16**

Budge, Ian, Hans-Dieter Klingemann, Adreas Volkens, Judith Bara, and Eric Tanabaum. 2001. *Mapping Policy Preferences: Estimates for Parties, Electors, and Governments, 1945–1998.* Oxford: Oxford University Press. **250 and 294**

Buiter, Willem. 1999. "Alice in Euroland." *Journal of Common Market Studies* 37(2): 181–209. **241 and 281**

Burden, Barry C. 2007. *Personal Roots of Representation*. Princeton, NJ: Princeton University Press. **39**

Calmfors, Lars, and John Driffill. 1988. "Bargaining structure, corporatism, and macroeconomic performance." *Economic Policy* 3(6): 14–61. **184 and 207**

Cam, Cindy, and Robert J. Franzese. 2007. *Modeling and Interpreting Interactive Hypotheses in Regression Analysis.* Ann Arbor, MI: University of Michigan Press. **218**

Cameron, A. Colin, and Pravin K. Trivedi. 1998. *Regression Analysis of Count Data.* Cambridge: Cambridge University Press. **270**

Cameron, David. 1984. "Social democracy, corporatism, labor quiescence, and the representation of economic interest in advanced capitalist society." In *Order and Conflict in Contemporary Capitalism*, ed. John Goldthorpe. Oxford: Oxford University Press. pp. 143–178. **207**

Campillo, Marta, and Jeffrey A. Miron. 1997. "Why does inflation differ across countries?" In *Reducing Inflation*, ed. Christina D. Romer, and David H. Romer. Chicago: University of Chicago Press. pp. 335–357. **29, 85, 147, 159, 161, and 168**

Canadian Who's Who. Various years. Toronto: University of Toronto Press.

Canterbery, E. Ray. 1967. "A new look at Federal Open Market voting." *Western Economic Journal* 6: 25–38. **128**

Caporale, Tony, and Kevin B. Grier. 1998. "A political model of monetary policy with application to the real Fed funds rate." *Journal of Law and Economics* 41(2): 409–428. **244**

Caporale, Tony, and Kevin B. Grier. 2000. "Political regime change and the real interest rate." *Journal of Money, Credit and Banking* 32(3): 320–334. **244**

Carey, John. 1994. "Political shirking and the last term problem: Evidence for a party-administered pension system." *Public Choice* 81: 1–22. **33**

Carey, John. 1996. *Term limits and legislative representation.* Cambridge: Cambridge University Press. **33**

Carey, Kevin. 2001. "Testing for stabilizing monetary policy rules: How robust to alternative specifications?" *Topics in Macroeconomics* 1(1). **120, 123, and 124**

Carpenter, Daniel P. 2001. *The Forging of Bureaucratic Autonomy: Reputations, Networks, and Policy Innovation in Executive Agencies, 1862–1928.* Princeton: Princeton University Press. **11, 12, 14, and 24**

Castelnuovo, Efrem. 2003. "Taylor Rules, omitted variables, and interest rate smoothing in the U.S." *Economics Letters* 81(1): 55–59. **120**

Castles, Frank, and Peter Mair. 1984. "Left-right political scales: some expert judgments." *European Journal of Political Research* 12(1): 73–88. **250 and 294**

Centeno, Miguel, and Patricio Silva. 1998. *The Politics of Expertise in Latin America.* New York: St. Martin's Press. **145**

Chang, Kelly H. 1998. "Their people equal their policy: The President, Congress, and appointments to the Federal Reserve." Ph.D. Dissertation, Department of Political Science, Stanford University. **189 and 245**

Chang, Kelly H. 2003. *Appointing Central Bankers: The Politics of Monetary Policy in the United States and the European Monetary Union.* Cambridge: Cambridge University Press. **10, 17, 189, and 245**

Chappell, Henry W., Jr., Thomas Havrilesky, and Rob Roy McGregor. 1993. "Partisan monetary policies: Presidential influence through the power of appointment." *Quarterly Journal of Economics* 108(1): 185–218. **30, 72, 244, and 251**

Chappell, Henry W., Jr., Thomas Havrilesky, and Rob Roy McGregor. 1995. "Policymakers, institutions, and central bank decisions." *Journal of Economics and Business* 47(2): 113–136. **38**

Chappell, Henry W., Jr., Rob Roy McGregor, and Todd Vermilyea. 2004*a*. *Committee Decisions on Monetary Policy: Evidence from Historical Records of the Federal Open Market Committee.* Cambridge, MA: MIT Press. **10, 72, 73, 128, 129, 130, 131, 136, 137, 189, 244, and 251**

Chappell, Henry W., Jr., Rob Roy McGregor, and Todd Vermilyea. 2004*b*. "Majority rule, consensus building, and the power of the chairman: Arthur Burns and the FOMC." *Journal of Money, Credit, and Banking* 36(3): 407–422. **73, 244, and 251**

Che, Y. K. 1995. "Revolving doors and the optimal tolerance for agency collusion." *RAND Journal of Economics* 26(3): 378–397. **16**

Clarida, Richard, Jordi Galí, and Mark Gertler. 1998. "Monetary policy rules in practice: Some international evidence." *European Economic Review* 42: 1033–1067. **118 and 119**

Clarida, Richard, Jordi Galí, and Mark Gertler. 1999. "The science of monetary policy: A New Keynesian perspective." *Journal of Economic Literature* 37(4): 1661–1707. **118 and 119**

Clarida, Richard, Jordi Galí, and Mark Gertler. 2000. "Monetary policy rules and macroeconomic stability: Evidence and some theory." *Quarterly Journal of Economics* 115(1): 147–180. **118, 119, and 120**

Clark, Tom S. 2011. *The Limits of Judicial Independence.* Cambridge: Cambridge University Press. **317**

Clark, William Roberts. 1993. "The sources of central bank independence in developing countries." Presented at the Annual Meeting of the American Political Science Association, Washington, D.C. **145**

Clark, William Roberts, and Mark C. Hallerberg. 2000. "Mobile capital, domestic institutions and electorally induced monetary and fiscal policy." *American Political Science Review* 94(2): 323–346. **4 and 131**

Cleveland, William S. 1994. *The Elements of Graphing Data*. New Jersey: Hobart Press. **283**

Cohen, Jeffrey E. 1986. "The dynamics of the 'revolving door' on the FCC." *American Journal of Political Science* 30(4): 689–708. **13 and 16**

Collier, David, and James Mahoney. 1996. "Insights and pitfalls: Selection bias in qualitative research." *World Politics* 49(1): 56–91. **174**

Cox, D. R. 1972. "Regression models and life tables (with discussion)." *Journal of the Royal Statistical Society B* 50(2): 187–220. **295**

Cukierman, Alex. 1992. *Central Bank Strategy, Credibility, and Independence: Theory and Evidence*. Cambridge, MA: MIT Press. **149, 150, 281, and 289**

Cukierman, Alex. 2002. "Are contemporary central banks transparent about economic models and objectives and what difference does it make?" *Federal Reserve Bank of St. Louis Review* 84(4): 15–35. **31**

Cukierman, Alex, and Francesco Lippi. 1999. "Central bank independence, centralization of wage bargaining, inflation and unemployment: theory and some evidence." *European Economic Review* 43(7): 1395–1434. **22, 182, 184, 185, 189, 210, 219, and 246**

Cukierman, Alex, and Stefan Gerlach. 2003. "The inflation bias revisited: Theory and some international evidence." *The Manchester School* 71(5): 541–565. **29**

Cukierman, Alex, and Steven B. Webb. 1995. "Political influence on the central bank: International evidence." *World Bank Economic Review* 9(3): 397–423. **150**

Cukierman, Alex, Geoffrey P. Miller, and Bilin Neyapti. 2001. "Central bank reform, liberalization and inflation in transition economies – An international perspective." CEPR Discussion Papers 2808. **158 and 189**

Cukierman, Alex, Pantelis Kalaitzidakis, Lawrence H. Summers, and Steven B. Webb. 1993. "Central bank independence, growth, investment, and real rates." *Carnegie-Rochester Conference Series on Public Policy* 39: 95–140. **149, 150, and 281**

Cukierman, Alex, Steven B. Webb, and Bilin Neyapti. 1992. "Measuring the independence of central banks and its effect on policy outcomes." *World Bank Economic Review* 6(3): 353–398. **5, 21, 29, 85, 109, 147, 149, 158, 161, 189, 190, 191, 219, 237, 262, 275, 281, and 295**

Cusack, Thomas R., and Lutz Engelhardt. 2002. "The PGL file collection." Computer File. Wissenschaftszentrum Berlin für Sozialforschung. `http://www.wzb.eu/en/persons/thomas-r-cusack?s=5662`. **21, 93, 250, 275, and 294**

Dargie, Charlotte, and Rachel Locke. 1999. "The British civil service." In *Bureaucratic Élites in Western European States*, ed. Edward C. Page, and Vincent Wright. Oxford: Oxford University Press. pp. 178–204. **35**

David-Barrett, Liz. 2011. "Cabs for hire? Fixing the revolving door between government and business." Transparency International–UK. **35**

Davidson, R., and J. MacKinnon. 1981. "Several tests for model specification in the presence of alternative hypotheses." *Econometrica* 49(3): 781–793. **198**

Dawkins, Richard. 1986. *The Blind Watchmaker*. New York: Norton. **7**

Dearborn, DeWitt C., and Herbert A. Simon. 1958. "Selective perception: A note on the departmental identifications of executives." *Sociometry* 21(2): 140–144. **39**

Debelle, G., and S. Fischer. 1994. "How independent should a central bank be?" In *Goals, Guidelines, and Constraints Facing Monetary Policymakers*, ed. J. Fuhrer. Number 38 *in* "Federal Reserve Bank of Boston Conference Series," Federal Reserve Bank of Boston. **32**

De Grauwe, Paul. 1993. "The political economy of monetary union in Europe." *The World Economy* 16(6): 653–661. **312**

de Haan, Jakob, and Willem Kooi. 2000. "Does central bank independence really matter? New evidence for developing countries using a new indicator." *Journal of Banking and Finance* 24(4): 643–664. **149 and 283**

Desi, E. L. 1971. "Effects of externally mediated rewards on intrinsic motivation." *Journal of Personality and Social Psychology* 18: 105–115. **11 and 12**

Dezalay, Yves, and Bryant G. Garth. 2002. *The Internationalization of Palace Wars: Lawyers, Economists, and the Contest to Transform Latin American States*. Chicago: University of Chicago Press. **145**

Diermeier, Daniel, Michael Keane, and Antonio Merlo. 2005. "A political economy model of Congressional careers." *American Economic Review* 95(1): 347–373. **33**

DiMaggio, Paul J., and Walter W. Powell. 1991. "Introduction." In *The New Institutionalism in Organizational Analysis*, ed. Walter W. Powell, and Paul J. DiMaggio. Chicago: University of Chicago Press. pp. 1–38. **9**

Domínguez, Jorge. 1997. *Technopols: Freeing politics and markets in Latin America in the 1990s*. University Park, PA: Pennsylvania State University Press. **145**

Donahue, John D. 2003. "In-and-outers: Up or down?" In *For the People: Can We Fix Public Service?* ed. John D. Donahue, and Joseph S. Nye. Washington, DC: Brookings Institution Press. pp. 55–71. **33**

Dowding, Keith. 1995. *The Civil Service*. London: Routledge. **36**

Downs, Anthony. 1967. *Inside Bureaucracy*. Boston: Little, Brown. **10 and 11**

Downs, Ian. n.d. "Discipline for some, none, or all? ERM membership and inflation." University of North Carolina, Chappel Hill. **92**

Drazen, Allan. 2000. "The political business cycle after 25 years." In *NBER Macroeconomics Annual*. Cambridge, MA: MIT Press. **208 and 228**

Drazen, Allan. 2001. *Political Economy in Macroeconomics*. Princeton: Princeton University Press. **150**

Drazen, Allan. 2002. "Central bank independence, democracy, and dollarization." *Journal of Applied Economics* 5(1): 1–17. **241**

Ebbinghaus, Bernhard, and Jelle Visser. 2000. *Trade Unions in Western Europe since 1945*. London: Macmillan Reference. **231**

Eckert, Ross D. 1981. "The life cycle of regulatory commissioners." *Journal of Law and Economics* 24(1): 113–120. **15 and 16**

Eijffinger, Sylvester C.W., and Eric Schaling. 1995. "Optimal commitment in an open economy: Credibility vs. flexibility." Discussion Paper 79, Tilburg University, Center for Economic Research. **266**

Eijffinger, Sylvester C.W., and Marco M. Hoeberichts. 2002. "Central bank accountability and transparency: Theory and some evidence." In *International Finance*, Vol. 5. Wiley Blackwell. pp. 73–96. **241**

Eijffinger, Sylvester C.W., and Petra M. Geraats. 2004. "How transparent are central banks?" Cambridge Working Papers in Economics 0411. **73**

Eldredge, Niles, and Stephen Jay Gould. 1972. "Punctuated equilibrium: An alternative to phyletic gradualism." In *Models in Paleobiology*, ed. J. M. Schopf. San Francisco: Freeman Cooper. pp. 82–115. **7**

Elklit, Jørgen, and Andrew Reynolds. 2002. "The impact of election administration on the legitimacy of emerging democracies: A new comparative politics research agenda." *Commonwealth & Comparative Politics* 40(2): 86–119. **316**

Encyclopaedia of Austria. n.d.

English, William B., William R. Nelson, and Brian P. Sack. 2003. "Interpreting the significance of the lagged interest rate in estimated monetary policy rules." *Contributions to Macroeconomics* 3(1). **120**

Epstein, David, and Sharyn O'Halloran. 1996. "Divided government and the design of administrative procedures: A formal model and empirical test." *Journal of Politics* 58(2): 393–417. **37**

Epstein, David, and Sharyn O'Halloran. 1999. *Delegating powers: A transaction cost politics approach to policymaking under separate powers*. Cambridge: Cambridge University Press. **6 and 37**

Epstein, Lee, and Jack Knight. 1998. *The Choices Justices Make*. Washington, DC: CQ Press. **10 and 317**

Ertman, Thomas. 1997. *Birth of the Leviathan : Building States and Regimes in Medieval and Early Modern Europe*. Cambridge: Cambridge University Press. **4**

Evans, Peter. 1995. *Embedded Autonomy: States and Industrial Transformation*. Princeton: Princeton University Press. **145 and 153**

Federal Reserve Bulletin. Various issues.

Ferejohn, John, and Charles Shipan. 1990. "Congressional influence on the bureaucracy." *Journal of Law, Economics, and Organization* 6: 1–43. **129 and 245**

Ferguson, Thomas, and Robert Johnson. 2010. "When wolves cry 'wolf': Systemic financial crises and the myth of the Danaid Jar." INET Inaugural Conference. King's College, Cambridge University. **35 and 310**

Finer, Herman. 1941. "Administrative responsibility in democratic government." *Public Administration Review* 7(4): 335–350. **11**

Franzese, Robert J. 1999. "Partially independent central banks, politically responsive governments, and inflation." *American Journal of Political Science* 43(3): 681–706. **189, 190, and 217**

Franzese, Robert J. 2001. "Monetary policy and wage/price bargaining: Macro-institutional interactions in the traded, public, and sheltered sectors." In *Varieties of Capitalism: The Institutional Foundations of Comparative Advantage*, ed. Peter Hall, and David Soskice. Oxford: Oxford University Press. pp. 104–144. **187 and 210**

Franzese, Robert J. 2002. "Strategic Interactions of Monetary Policymakers and Wage/Price Bargainers: A Review with Implications for the European Common-

Currency Area." *Empirica: Journal of Applied Economics and Economic Policy* 28(4). **187 and 210**

Franzese, Robert J. 2003. "Multiple hands on the wheel: Empirically modeling partial delegation and shared policy control in the open and institutionalized economy." *Political Analysis* 11(4): 445–474. **183, 189, and 276**

Frey, Bruno S. 1997. *Not Just For the Money: An Economic Theory of Personal Motivation.* Brookfield: Edward Elgar. **12**

Fry, Jane M., Tim R. L. Fry, and Keith R. McLaren. 2000. "Compositional data analysis and zeros in micro data." *Applied Economics* 32(8): 953–959. **269**

Fry, Maxwell, DeAnne Julius, Lavan Mahadeva, Sandra Roger, and Gabriel Sterne. 2000. "Key issues in the choice of monetary policy framework." In *Monetary Frameworks in a Global Context*, ed. Lavan Mahadeva, and Gabriel Sterne. London: Routledge. pp. 1–216. **110, 128, 154, and 181**

Fudenberg, Drew, David M. Kreps, and Eric S. Maskin. 1990. "Repeated games with long-run and short-run players." *Review of Economic Studies* 57(4): 555–573. **18 and 66**

Geddes, Barbara. 1990. "How the cases you choose affect the answers you get: Selection bias in comparative politics." *Political Analysis* 2: 131–150. **174**

Gibbons, Robert, and Kevin J. Murphy. 1992. "Optimal incentive contracts in the presence of career concerns: Theory and evidence." *Journal of Political Economy* 100(3): 468–505. **17 and 55**

Gibler, Douglas M., and Kirk A. Randazzo. 2011. "Testing the effects of independent judiciaries on the likelihood of democratic backsliding." *American Journal of Political Science* 55(3): 696–709. **317**

Gildea, John. 1990. "Explaining FOMC members' votes." In *The Political Economy of American Monetary Policy*, ed. Thomas Mayer. Cambridge: Cambridge University Press. pp. 211–227. **128**

Gill, Jeff, and Gary King. 2004. "What to do when your Hessian is not invertible: Alternatives to model respecification in nonlinear estimation." *Sociological Methods and Research* 32(4): 1–34. **279**

Golden, Marissa Martino. 2000. *What Motivates Bureaucrats? Politics and Administration during the Reagan Years.* New York: Columbia University Press. **10, 11, 13, and 14**

Goodman, John B. 1992. *Monetary Sovereignty: The Politics of Central Banking in Western Europe.* Ithaca, NY: Cornell University Press. **14 and 73**

Gormley, William T., Jr. 1979. "A test of the revolving door hypothesis at the FCC." *American Journal of Political Science* 23(4): 665–683. **16**

Gould, David M., and Mary S. Rosenbaum. 1998. "Latin American central banking: Have reforms made a difference?" *Federal Reserve Bank of Dallas In Depth* (Jun). **147**

Gowa, Joanne. 1988. "Public goods and political institutions: Trade and monetary policy processes in the United States." *International Organization* 42(1): 15–32. **88 and 145**

Greider, William. 1987. *Secrets of the Temple.* Simon & Schuster. **20 and 129**

Grier, Kevin B. 1987. "Presidential elections and Federal Reserve policy: An empirical test." *Southern Ecoonomic Journal* 54(2): 474–486. **131 and 244**

Grier, Kevin B. 1989. "On the existence of a political monetary cycle." *American Journal of Political Science* 33(2): 376–389. **131**

Grier, Kevin B. 1991. "Congressional influence on U.S. monetary policy: An empirical test." *Journal of Monetary Economics* 28(2): 201–220. **131 and 244**

Grier, Kevin B. 1996. "Congressional oversight committee influence on U.S. monetary policy revisited." *Journal of Monetary Economics* 38(3): 571–579. **131**

Grilli, Vittorio, Donato Masciandaro, and Guido Tabellini. 1991. "Political and monetary institutions and public financial policies in the industrial countries." *Economic Policy* pp. 341–392. **5, 29, 85, 109, 127, 184, 189, 208, 246, 275, and 295**

Gross, Donald A., and Lee Sigelman. 1984. "Comparing party systems: A multidimensional approach." *Comparative Politics* 16(4): 463–479. **250 and 294**

Grossman, Gene, and Elhanan Helpman. 2001. *Special Interest Politics.* Cambridge, MA: MIT Press. **213**

Gunz, Hugh P., and Michael Jalland. 1996. "Managerial careers and business strategies." *Academy of Management Review* 21(3): 718–756. **39**

Haggard, Stephan, Sylvia Maxfield, and Ben Ross Schneider. 1997. "Theories of business and business-state relations." In *Business and the State in Developing Countries*, ed. Sylvia Maxfield, and Ben Ross Schneider. Ithaca, NY: Cornell University Press. pp. 36–60. **145 and 153**

Hall, Peter A. 1989. *The Political Power of Economic Ideas: Keynesianism Across Nations.* Princeton: Princeton University Press. **3**

Hall, Peter A. 1986. *Governing the Economy: The Politics of State Intervention in Britain and France.* Oxford: Oxford University Press. **102**

Hall, Peter A., and David Soskice. 2001. "An introduction to varieties of capitalism." In *Varieties of Capitalism: The Institutional Foundations of Comparative Advantage*, ed. Peter A. Hall, and David Soskice. Oxford: Oxford University Press. pp. 1–70. **4 and 210**

Hall, Peter A., and Robert J. Franzese. 1998. "Mixed signals: Central bank independence, co-ordinated wage bargaining, and European Monetary Union." *International Organization* 52(3): 505–536. **22, 182, 184, 185, 189, 210, 219, and 246**

Hambrick, Donald C., and Phyllis A. Mason. 1984. "Upper echelons: The organization as a reflection of its top managers." *Academy of Management Review* 9(2): 193–206. **39**

Hamilton-Hart, Natasha. 2002. *Asian States, Asian Bankers: Central Banking in Southeast Asia.* Ithaca, NY: Cornell University Press. **244**

Hartlyn, Jonathan, Jennifer McCoy, and Thomas M. Mustillo. 2008. "Electoral governance matters: Explaining the quality of elections in contemporary Latin America." *Comparative Political Studies* 41(4/5): 73–98. **316**

Hassel, Anke, and Bernhard Ebbinghaus. 2000. "From means to ends: Linking wage policy moderation and social policy reform." In *Social Pacts in Europe – New Dynamics*, ed. Giuseppe Fajertag, and Philippe Pochet. Brussels: European Trade Union Institute. pp. 61–84. **212**

Havrilesky, Thomas M. 1987. "A partisanship theory of fiscal and monetary policy." *Journal of Money, Credit and Banking* 19(3): 308–325. **131 and 244**

Havrilesky, Thomas M. 1988. "Monetary policy signaling from the administration to the Federal Reserve." *Journal of Money, Credit and Banking* 20(1): 83–101. **244**

Havrilesky, Thomas M. 1994. "Outside influences on monetary policy: A summary of recent findings." *Contemporary Economic Policy* 12(1): 46–51. **244**

Havrilesky, Thomas M. 1995. *The Pressures on American Monetary Policy.* 2nd ed. Boston: Kluwer. **244**

Havrilesky, Thomas M., and John A. Gildea. 1991*a*. "The policy preferences of FOMC members as revealed by dissenting votes: Comment." *Journal of Money, Credit and Banking* 23(1): 130–138. **37 and 128**

Havrilesky, Thomas M., and John A. Gildea. 1991*b*. "Screening FOMC members for their biases and dependability." *Economics & Politics* 3(2): 139–150. **128**

Havrilesky, Thomas M., and John A. Gildea. 1992. "Reliable and unreliable partisan appointees to the Board of Governors." *Public Choice* 73(4): 397–417. **128, 131, 132, and 244**

Havrilesky, Thomas M., and Robert Schweitzer. 1990. "A theory of FOMC dissent voting with evidence from the time series." In *The Political Economy of American Monetary Policy*, ed. Thomas Mayer. Cambridge: Cambridge University Press. pp. 197–210. **128**

Hayes, Christopher. 2012. *Twilight of the Elites: America after Meritocracy.* New York: Crown Publishers. **317**

Heclo, Hugh. 1988. "The in-and-outer system: A critical assessment." *Political Science Quarterly* 103(1): 37–56. **33**

Helmke, Gretchen. 2002. "The logic of strategic defection: Court-executive relations in Argentina under dictatorship and democracy." *American Political Science Review* 96(2): 305–320. **317**

Helmke, Gretchen. 2005. *Courts Under Constraints: Judges, Generals, and Presidents in Argentina.* Cambridge: Cambridge University Press. **317**

Hennessy, Elizabeth. 1999. *Flemings Who's Who in Central Banking.* London: Central Banking Publications.

Hennessy, Elizabeth, and Yvonne Messenger. 2001. *Flemings Who's Who in Central Banking, 2002.* London: Central Banking Publications.

Hetzel, Robert L. 2000. "The Taylor Rule: Is it a useful guide to understanding monetary policy?" *Federal Reserve Bank of Richmond Economic Quarterly* 86(2): 1–33. **118**

Heyes, Anthony G. 2003. "Expert advice and regulatory complexity." *Journal of Regulatory Economics* 24(2): 119–133. **15 and 16**

Hibbs, Douglas A. 1987. *The American Political Economy.* Cambridge, MA: Harvard University Press. **131, 208, 244, 259, and 290**

Hitt, Michael A., and Beverly B. Tyler. 1991. "Strategic decision models: Integrating different perspectives." *Strategic Management Journal* 12(5): 327–351. **39**

Ho, Karen. 2009. *Liquidated: An Ethnography of Wall Street.* Durham, NC: Duke University Press. **39**

Hollingsworth, J. Rogers, and Robert Boyer. 1997. *Contemporary Capitalism: The Embeddedness of Institutions*. Cambridge: Cambridge University Press. **4**

Hölmstrom, Bengt. 1999. "Managerial incentive problems: A dynamic perspective." *Review of Economic Studies* 66(1): 169–182. **17 and 55**

Honaker, James, Jonathan N. Katz, and Gary King. 2002. "A fast, easy, and efficient estimator for multiparty election data." *Political Analysis* 10(1): 84–100. **270**

Hoover, Kevin. 2001. *Causality in Macroeconomics*. Cambridge: Cambridge University Press. **150**

Huber, John D., and Ronald Inglehart. 1995. "Expert interpretations of party space and party locations in 42 societies." *Party Politics* 1(1): 73–111. **250 and 294**

Huber, John D., and Charles R. Shipan. 2002. *Deliberate Discretion? The Institutional Foundations of Bureaucratic Autonomy*. Cambridge: Cambridge University Press. **4, 6, and 36**

Imai, Kosuke, and Gary King. 2004. "Did illegal overseas absentee ballots decide the 2000 U.S. presidential election?" *Perspectives on Politics* 2(3): 537–549. **18**

Issing, Otmar. 1999. "The Eurosystem: Transparent and accountable, or 'Willem in Euroland'?" *Journal of Common Market Studies* 37(3): 503–519. **241, 251, and 281**

Iversen, Torben. 1998*a*. "Wage bargaining, central bank independence, and the real effects of money." *International Organization* 52(3): 31–62. **22, 185, and 246**

Iversen, Torben. 1998*b*. "Wage bargaining, hard money, and economic performance: Theory and evidence for organized market economies." *British Journal of Political Science* 28(1): 31–62. **185**

Iversen, Torben. 1999. *Contested Economic Institutions: The Politics of Macroeconomics and Wage Bargaining in Advanced Democracies*. Cambridge: Cambridge University Press. **22, 182, 184, 185, 189, 191, 196, 197, 206, 210, 220, 231, 237, and 246**

Jabko, Nicolas. 2001. "Expertise et politique à l'âge de l'euro: La Banque Centrale Européenne sur le terrain de la démocratie." *Revue Française de Science Politique* 51(6): 903–931. **242**

Jácome, Luis I. 2001. "Legal central bank independence and inflation in Latin America during the 1990s." IMF Working Paper 01/212. **147**

Janssens, Valery. 1997. *De beheerders van ons geld: Negentien gouverneurs van de Nationale Bank van België*. Lannoo.

Jensen, Hanne Nexø, and Tim Knudson. 1999. "Senior officials in the Danish central administration: From bureaucrats to policy professionals and managers." In *Bureaucratic Élites in Western European States*, ed. Edward C. Page, and Vincent Wright. Oxford: Oxford University Press. pp. 229–248. **35**

Johnson, Juliet. 1999. "Misguided autonomy: Central bank independence and the Russian transition." In *The Self-Restraining State: Power and Accountability in New Democracies*, ed. Andreas Schedler, Larry Diamond, and Marc F. Plattner. London: Lynne Rienner. pp. 293–311. **148**

Johnson, Juliet. 2000. *A Fistful of Rubles: The Rise and Fall of the Russian Banking System*. Ithaca, NY: Cornell University Press. **144, 148, and 149**

Johnson, Juliet. 2002. "Agents of transformation: The role of the West in Post-Communist central bank development." In *Studies in Public Policy*. Number 361. Glasgow: Centre for the Study of Public Policy, University of Strathclyde. **39, 146, 149, and 306**

Johnson, Simon, and James Kwak. 2010. *13 Bankers*. Pantheon. **2, 34, and 280**

Judd, John P., and Glenn D. Rudebusch. 1998. "Taylor's Rule and the Fed: 1970–1997." *Federal Reserve Bank of San Francisco Economic Review* (3): 3–16. **32, 118, and 119**

Kapstein, Ethan Barnaby. 1992. "Between power and purpose: Central bankers and the politics of regulatory convergence." *International Organization* 46(1): 265–287. **39**

Katz, Bernard S. 1992. *Biographical Dictionary of the Board of Governors of the Federal Reserve*. New York: Greenwood Press. **38 and 291**

Katzenstein, Peter. 1985. *Small States in World Markets*. Ithaca: Cornell University Press. **207**

Katz, Ethan. 2001. "Bias in conditional and unconditional fixed effects logit estimation." *Political Analysis* 9(4): 379–384. **259**

Katz, Jonathan N., and Gary King. 1999. "A statistical model for multiparty electoral data." *American Political Science Review* 93(1): 15–32. **254, 255, 268, 270, and 273**

Katznelson, Ira. 2003. "Periodization and preferences: Reflections on purposive action in comparative historical social science." In *Comparative Historical Analysis in the Social Sciences*, ed. James Mahoney, and Dietrich Rueschmeyer. Cambridge: Cambridge University Press. **6**

Katznelson, Ira, and Barry R. Weingast. 2005. "Intersections between historical and rational choice institutionalism." In *Preferences and Situations: Points of Intersection Between Historical and Rational Choice Institutionalism*, ed. Ira Katznelson and Barry R. Weingast. New York: Russell Sage Foundation. pp. 1–24. **315**

Kaufman, Herbert. 1960. *The Forest Ranger*. Baltimore: Johns Hopkins University Press. **11, 13, and 39**

Keele, Luke J., and Nathan J. Kelly. 2006. "Dynamic models for dynamic theories: the ins and outs of LDVs." *Political Analysis* 14(2): 186–205. **166**

Kettl, Donald F. 1986. *Leadership at the Fed*. New Haven: Yale University Press. **10, 131, and 244**

Kim, Paul S. 1988. *Japan's Civil Service System*. New York: Greenwood Press. **36**

King, Gary, Michael Tomz, and Jason Wittenberg. 2000. "Making the most of statistical analyses: Interpretation and presentation." *American Journal of Political Science* 44(2): 341–355. **194, 218, and 272**

King, Gary, Robert O. Keohane, and Sidney Verba. 1994. *Designing Social Inquiry*. Princeton: Princeton University Press. **174**

Knight, Jack. 1992. *Institutions and Social Conflict*. Cambridge: Cambridge University Press. **4 and 6**

Koh, B. C. 1989. *Japan's Administrative Elite*. Berkeley: University of California Press. **36**

Krause, George A. 1994. "Federal Reserve policy decision making: Political and bureaucratic influences." *American Journal of Political Science* 38(1): 124–144. **129**

Kreile, M. 1978. "West Germany: The dynamics of expansion." In *Between Power and Plenty*, ed. Peter Katzenstein. Madison: University of Wisconsin Press. pp. 191–224. **102**

Krugman, Paul. 2012. *End this Depression Now!* New York: W. W. Norton. **308**

Kydland, Finn E., and Edward C. Prescott. 1977. "Rules rather than discretion: The inconsistency of optimal plans." *Journal of Political Economy* 85(3): 473–491. **5, 29, 184, and 207**

Laffont, Jean-Jacques, and David Martimort. 2002. *The Theory of Incentives: The Principal-Agent Model.* Princeton: Princeton University Press. **5**

Laffont, Jean-Jacques, and Jean Tirole. 1993. *A Theory of Incentives in Procurement and Regulation.* Cambridge, MA: MIT Press. **16**

Lane, Philip R. 1997. "Inflation in open economies." *Journal of International Economics* 42(3–4): 327–347. **85, 168, and 192**

Lange, Peter, and Geoffrey Garrett. 1985. "The politics of growth: Strategic interaction and economic performance in the advanced industrial democracies, 1974–1980." *Journal of Politics* 47(3): 257–274. **206 and 208**

Lansing, Kevin J. 2002. "Real-time estimation of trend output and the illusion of interest rate smoothing." *Federal Reserve Bank of San Fransisco Economic Review* pp. 17–34. **120**

Laver, Michael, and Kenneth A. Shepsle. 1996. *Making and Breaking Governments: Cabinet and Legislature in Parliamentary Democracies.* Cambridge: Cambridge University Press. **4**

Laver, Michael, and W. Ben Hunt. 1992. *Policy and Party Competition.* New York: Routledge. **250 and 294**

Letwin, William. 1981. *Law and Economic Policy in America: The Evolution of the Sherman Antitrust Act.* Chicago: University of Chicago Press. **7**

Levi, Margaret. 2005. "Inducing preferences within organizations: The case of unions." In *Preferences and Situations: Points of Intersection between Historical and Rational Choice Institutionalism*, ed. Ira Katznelson, and Barry R. Weingast. New York: Russell Sage Foundation. pp. 219–246. **40**

Levin, Andrew, Volker Wieland, and John C. Williams. 1999. "Robustness of simple monetary policy rules under model uncertainty." In *Monetary Policy Rules*, ed. John B. Taylor. Chicago: University of Chicago Press. pp. 263–299. **118, 119, and 120**

Levine, R., and D. Renelt. 1992. "A sensitivity analysis of cross-country growth regressions." *American Economic Review* 82(4): 942–63. **92**

Liso, Josep M., Teresa Balaguer, and Montserrat Soler. 1996. *El sector bancario europeo: panorama y tendencias.* Collección estudios e informes Barcelona: La Caixa – Caja de Ahorros y Pensiones de Barcelona.

Little, Roderick J. A., and Donald B. Rubin. 1987. *Statistical Analysis with Missing Data.* New York: J. Wiley & Sons. **83**

Lohmann, Susanne. 1992. "Optimal commitment in monetary policy: Credibility versus flexibility." *American Economic Review* 82(1): 273–286. **29, 37, 56, 150, 190, 245, and 288**

Lohmann, Susanne. 1998*a*. "Federalism and central bank independence: The politics of German monetary policy, 1957–92." *World Politics* 50(3): 401–446. **37**

Lohmann, Susanne. 1998*b*. "Institutional checks and balances and the political control of the money supply." *Oxford Economic Papers* 50(3): 360–377. **37**

López-Pintor, Rafael. 2000. *Electoral Management Bodies as Institutions of Governance.* United Nations Development Programme, Bureau for Development Policy. **316**

Lupia, Arthur, and Mathew D. McCubbins. 1998. *The Democratic Dilemma.* Cambridge: Cambridge University Press. **246**

Majone, Giandomenico. 1998. "Europe's 'democratic deficit': The question of standards." *European Law Journal* 4(1): 5–28. **241**

Makkai, T., and John Braithwaite. 1992. "In and out of the revolving door: Making sense of regulatory capture." *Journal of Public Policy* 12(1): 61–78. **16**

Mander, Benedict. Various issues. *Central Bank Insider.* London: Central Banking Publications.

Mangano, G. 1998. "Measuring central bank independence: A tale of subjectivity and of its consequences." *Oxford Economic Papers* 50(3): 468–492. **190**

Maravall, José María. 2003. "The rule of law as a political weapon." In *Democracy and the Rule of Law*, ed. José María Maravall, and Adam Przeworski. Cambridge: Cambridge University Press. pp. 261–301. **317**

March, James. 1997. "Administrative practice, organizational theory and political philosophy: Ruminations on the reflections of John Gaus." *PS: Political Science & Politics* 30(4): 689–698. **6**

Martin, Andrew D., and Kevin M. Quinn. 2002. "Dynamic ideal point estimation via Markov chain Monte Carlo for the U.S. Supreme Court, 1953–1999." *Political Analysis* 10(2): 134–153. **10 and 317**

Martín-Fernández, J. A., C. Barceló-Vidal, and V. Pawlowsky-Glahn. 2003. "Dealing with zeros and missing values in compositional data sets using nonparametric imputation." *Mathematical Geology* 35(3):253–278. **269**

Mas, Ignacio. 1995. "Central bank independence: A critical view from a developing country perspective." *World Development* 23(10): 1639–1652. **144 and 151**

Maxfield, Sylvia. 1994. "Financial incentives and central bank authority in industrializing nations." *World Politics* 46(4): 556–588. **144**

Maxfield, Sylvia. 1997. *Gatekeepers of Growth: The International Political Economy of Central Banking in Developing Countries.* Princeton: Princeton University Press. **5, 21, 85, 109, 144, 158, 237, 244, 275, 295, and 306**

Mayhew, David R. 1974. *Congress: The Electoral Connection.* New Haven: Yale University Press. **33**

Mayntz, R., and H. U. Derlien. 1989. "Party patronage and politicization of the West German administrative elite 1970–87 – Toward Hybridization?" *Governance* 2(4): 384–404. **36**

McCallum, Bennett T. 1995. "Two fallacies concerning central bank independence." *American Economic Review* 85(2): 207–211. **29, 30, 190, and 241**

McCallum, Bennett T. 1999. "Recent developments in the analysis of monetary policy rules." Homer Jones Memorial Lecture, University of Missouri, St. Louis. **39**

McCallum, Bennett T., and Edward Nelson. 1999. "Performance of operational policy rules in an estimated semiclassical structural model." In *Monetary Policy Rules*, ed. John B. Taylor. Chicago: University of Chicago Press. pp. 15–45. **118**

McCubbins, Mathew D., and Thomas Schwartz. 1984. "Congressional oversight overlooked: Police patrols versus fire alarms." *American Journal of Political Science* 28(1): 165–179. **36**

McCubbins, Mathew D., Roger Noll, and Barry Weingast. 1987. "Administrative procedures as instruments of political control." *Journal of Law, Economics, and Organization* 3(2): 243–277. **6**

McNamara, Kathleen R. 1998. *The Currency of Ideas: Monetary Politics in the European Union.* Ithaca, NY: Cornell University Press. **5**

McNamara, Kathleen R. 2002. "Rational fictions: Central bank independence and the social logic of delegation." *West European Politics* 25(1): 47–76. **241**

Meier, Kenneth J., and George A. Krause. 2003*a*. "Conclusion: An agenda for the scientific study of bureaucracy." In *Politics, Policy, and Organizations: Frontiers in the Scientific Study of Bureaucracy*, ed. George A. Krause, and Kenneth J. Meier. Ann Arbor, MI: University of Michigan Press. pp. 292–307. **6**

Meier, Kenneth J., and George A. Krause. 2003*b*. "The scientific study of bureaucracy: An overview." In *Politics, Policy, and Organizations: Frontiers in the Scientific Study of Bureaucracy*, ed. George A. Krause, and Kenneth J. Meier. Ann Arbor, MI: University of Michigan Press. pp. 1–19. **5**

Meier, Kenneth J., and Lloyd G. Nigro. 1976. "Representative bureaucracy and policy preferences." *Public Administration Review* 36(4): 458–469. **13, 39, and 40**

Melone, Nancy Paule. 1994. "Reasoning in the executive suite: The influence of role/experience-based expertise on decision processes of corporate executives." *Organization Science* 5(3): 438–455. **39**

Meltzer, Allan H. 2003. *A History of the Federal Reserve: Volume 1: 1913–1951.* Chicago: University of Chiacgo Press. **5**

Meyer, Laurence H. 2004. *A Term at the Fed: An Insider's View.* HarperBusiness. **12, 129, 130, and 251**

Miles, Rufus. 1978. "The origin and meaning of Miles' Law." *Public Administration Review* 38(5): 399–403. **13**

Moravcsik, Andrew. 2002. "In defence of the 'democratic deficit': Reassessing legitimacy in the European Union." *Journal of Common Market Studies* 40(4): 603–624. **241**

Morris, Irwin L. 2000. *Congress, the President, and the Federal Reserve.* Ann Arbor, MI: The University of Michigan Press. **17, 37, 244, and 245**

Morris, Irwin L. 2004. "Review of Kelly Chang, *Appointing Central Bankers*." *Perspectives on Politics* 2(2): 369–370. **189**

Mosley, Layna. 2003. *Global Capital and National Governments*. Cambridge: Cambridge University Press. **144**

Mozaffar, Shaheen. 2002. "Patterns of electoral governance in Africa's emerging democracies." *International Political Science Review* 23(1): 85–101. **316**

Mozaffar, Shaheen, and Andreas Schedler. 2002. "The comparative study of electoral governance: Introduction." *International Political Science Review* 23(1): 5–27. **316**

Muscatelli, Anton. 1995. "Delegation versus optimal contracts: Do we really need conservative central bankers?" Working Paper, University of Glasgow. **247**

Naka, Kura. 1980. *Kokkai giin no kōsei to henka*. [The Change and Structure of Diet Membership.] Tokyo: K. K. Seiji jōhō Sentaa. **36**

Newey, Whitney K., and Kenneth D. West. 1987. "A simple, positive semi-definite, heteroskedasticity and autocorrelation consistent covariance matrix." *Econometrica* 55(3): 703–708. **124**

Niskanen, William A., Jr. 1971. *Bureaucracy and Representative Government*. Chicago: Aldine Atherton. **11, 12, and 131**

Nordhaus, William D. 1975. "The political business cycle." *Review of Economic Studies* 42(2): 169–190. **131**

North, Douglass C. 1990. *Institutions, Institutional Change, and Economic Performance*. Cambridge: Cambridge University Press. **3, 4, and 9**

Obstfeld, Maurice, and Kenneth Rogoff. 1995. "The mirage of fixed exchange rates." *Journal of Economic Perspectives* 9(4): 73–96. **92**

O Grande Livro dos Portugueses. 1991. Lisbon: Circulo de Leitores.

Olson, Mancur. 1965. *The Logic of Collective Action*. Cambridge, MA: Harvard University Press. **145**

Olson, Mancur. 1982. *The Rise and Decline of Nations*. New Haven: Yale University Press. **184 and 207**

Orphanides, Athanasios. 1999. "The quest for prosperity without inflation." Working Paper, Board of Governors of the Federal Reserve System. **118 and 119**

Orphanides, Athanasios. 2001. "Monetary policy rules based on real time data." *American Economic Review* 91(4): 964–985. **119**

Orren, Karen, and Stephen Skowronek. 1994. "Beyond the iconography of order: notes for a 'new' institutionalism." In *The Dynamics of American Politics: Approaches and Interpretations*, ed. Lawrence C. Dodd, and Calvin Jillson. Boulder, CO: Westview. pp. 311–332. **9**

O Século XX Português. 2000. Lisbon: Texto Editora.

Padayachee, Vishnu. 2000. "Independence in an era of globalisation: Central banking in developing countries." *International Review of Applied Economics* 14(4): 495–500. **37**

Page, Edward C., and Vincent Wright. 1999. "Introduction." In *Bureaucratic Élites in Western European States*, ed. Edward C. Page, and Vincent Wright. Oxford: Oxford University Press. pp. 1–12. **36**

Pastor, Robert A. 1999. "The role of electoral administration in democratic transitions: Implications for policy and research." *Democratization* 6(4): 1–27. **316**

Peltzman, Sam. 1976. "Towards a more general theory of regulation." *Journal of Law* *and Economics* 19(2): 211–240. **13 and 16**

Persson, Torsten, and Guido Tabellini. 2000. *Political Economics: Explaining Economic Policy*. Cambridge, MA: MIT Press. **29 and 150**

Pesaran, H., and A. Deaton. 1978. "Testing non-nested nonlinear regression models." *Econometrica* 46(3): 677–694. **198**

Peters, B. Guy. 1981. "The problem of bureaucratic government." *Journal of Politics* 43(1): 56–82. **31**

Peters, B. Guy. 1997. "Bureaucrats and political appointees in European democracies: Who's who and does it make any difference?" In *Modern Systems of Government: Exploring the Roles of Bureaucrats and Politicians*, ed. Ali Farazmand. Thousand Oaks, CA: Sage Publishing. pp. 232–254. **36**

Pierre, Jon, and Peter Ehn. 1999. "The welfare state managers: Senior civil servants in Sweden." In *Bureaucratic Élites in Western European States*, ed. Edward C. Page, and Vincent Wright. Oxford: Oxford University Press. pp. 249–265. **35**

Pierson, Paul. 2004. *Politics in Time: History, Institutions, and Social Analysis*. Princeton: Princeton University Press. **7**

Pluym, Walter. 1995. *L'Hôtel du Gouverneur de la Banque Nationale de Belgique*. Pandora.

Pochet, Philippe, and Giuseppe Fajertag. 2000. "A new era for social pacts in Europe." In *Social Pacts in Europe – New Dynamics*, ed. Giuseppe Fajertag, and Philippe Pochet. Brussels: European Trade Union Institute. pp. 9–40. **212**

Poole, Keith T., and Howard Rosenthal. 1997. *Congress: A Political-Economic History of Roll Call Voting*. Oxford: Oxford University Press. **10**

Porta, Rafael La, Florencio Lopez de Silanes, Cristian Pop-Eleches, and Andrei Shleifer. 2004. "Judicial checks and balances." *Journal of Political Economy* 112(2): 445–470. **317**

Posen, Adam. 1995. "Declarations are not enough: Financial sector sources of central bank independence." In *NBER Macroeconomics Annual*. Cambridge, MA: MIT Press. **37 and 189**

Posen, Adam. 1998. "Central bank independence and disinflationary credibility: A missing link?" *Oxford Economic Papers* 50(3): 335–359. **144**

Powell, Emilia Justyna, and Jeffrey K. Staton. 2009. "Domestic judicial institutions and human rights treaty violation." *International Studies Quarterly* 53(1): 149–174. **317**

Powell, G. Bingham, Jr., and Guy D. Whitten. 1993. "A cross-national analysis of economic voting: taking account of the political context." *American Journal of Political Science* 37(2): 391–414. **131 and 291**

Pringle, Robert. 1999. *The Morgan Stanley Dean Witter Central Bank Directory*. London: Central Banking Publications. **275**

Przeworski, Adam, and Michael Wallerstein. 1982. "The structure of class conflict in democratic capitalist societies." *American Political Science Review* 76(2): 215–238. **208**

Putnam, Robert D. 1976. *The Comparative Study of Political Elites*. Englewood Cliffs, NJ: Prentice-Hall, Inc. **40**

***Quien es Quien en España*.** Various years.

Qui Est Qui en France. Various years. Paris: Editions Jacques Lafitte.

Ramseyer, J. Mark, and Frances McCall Rosenbluth. 1993. *Japan's Political Marketplace*. Cambridge, MA: Harvard University Press. **36**

Reinhart, Carmen M., and Kenneth S. Rogoff. 2009. *This Time is Different: Eight centuries of financial folly*. Princeton: Princeton University Press. **311**

Rhodes, Martin. 2001. "The political economy of social pacts: Competitive corporatism and European welfare reform." In *The New Politics of Welfare*, ed. Paul Pierson. Oxford: Oxford University Press. pp. 165–194. **212**

Robinson, William S. 1950. "Ecological correlations and the behavior of individuals." *American Sociological Review* 15(3): 351–357. **289**

Rogoff, Kenneth. 1985. "The optimal degree of commitment to an intermediate monetary target." *Quarterly Journal of Economics* 100(4): 1169–1188. **5, 28, 29, 37, 56, 184, 207, 246, 247, 265, 288, and 307**

Rogoff, Kenneth. 1990. "Equilibrium political budget cycles." *American Economic Review* 80(1): 21–36. **150**

Rogoff, Kenneth, and Anne Sibert. 1988. "Elections and macroeconomic policy cycles." *Review of Economic Studies* 55(1): 1–16. **150**

Romer, David. 1993. "Openness and inflation: Theory and evidence." *Quarterly Journal of Economics* 108(4): 869–903. **85, 168, and 192**

Romer, Thomas, and Howard Rosenthal. 1978. "Political resource allocation, controlled agendas, and the status quo." *Public Choice* 33(4): 27–44. **129 and 245**

Roselli, Alessandro. 1987. "Notes on the contributors." In *Money and the Economy: Central Bankers' Views*, ed. Pierluigi Ciocca. New York: St. Martin's Press. pp. 313–324.

Rosman, Andrew, Michael Lubatkin, and Hugh O'Neill. 1994. "Rigidity in decision behaviors: A within-subject test of information acquisition using strategic and financial informational cue." *Academy of Management Journal* 37(4): 1017–1033. **39**

Rotemberg, Julio J., and Michael Woodford. 1999. "Interest rate rules in an estimated sticky price model." In *Monetary Policy Rules*, ed. John B. Taylor. Chicago: University of Chicago Press. pp. 1–14. **118**

Rothenberg, Lawrence S., and Mitchell S. Sanders. 2000. "Severing the electoral connection: Shirking in the contemporary Congress." *American Journal of Political Science* 44(2): 316–325. **33**

Rouban, Luc. 1999. "The senior civil service in France." In *Bureaucratic Élites in Western European States*, ed. Edward C. Page, and Vincent Wright. Oxford: Oxford University Press. pp. 65–89. **35**

Rudebusch, Glenn D. 2001. "Is the Fed too timid? Monetary policy in an uncertain world." *Review of Economics and Statistics* 83(2): 203–217. **120**

Rudebusch, Glenn D. 2002. "Term structure evidence on interest rate smoothing and monetary policy inertia." *Journal of Monetary Economics* 49(6): 1161–1187. **120**

Rudebusch, Glenn D., and Lars E. O. Svensson. 1999. "Policy rules for inflation targeting." In *Monetary Policy Rules*, ed. John B. Taylor. Chicago: University of Chicago Press. pp. 203–246. **118 and 119**

Salant, D. J. 1995. "Behind the revolving door: A new view of public utility regulation." *RAND Journal of Economics* 26(3): 362–377. **16**

Santoni, G. J. 1986. "The effects of inflation on commercial banks." *Federal Reserve Bank of St. Louis Review* (March): 15–26. **41**

Schaling, Eric. 1995. *Institutions and Monetary Policy.* Aldershot, UK: Edward Elgar. **245**

Scheve, Kenneth. 2002. "Nominal asset ownership and individual macroeconomic priorities." Department of Political Science, Yale University. **39**

Scheve, Kenneth. 2004. "Public inflation aversion and the political economy of macroeconomic policymaking." *International Organization* 58(1): 1–34. **39**

Schlesinger, Joseph. 1966. *Ambition in Politics: Political Careers in the United States.* Chicago: Rand McNally. **33**

Schneider, Ben Ross. 1993. "The career connection: A comparative analysis of bureaucratic preferences and insulation." *Comparative Politics* 25(3): 331–350. **16, 35, and 315**

Schneider, Ben Ross. 1998. "The material bases of technocracy: Investor confidence and neoliberalism in Latin America." In *The Politics of Expertise in Latin America*, ed. Miguel Centeno, and Patricio Silva. New York: St. Martin's Press. pp. 77–95. **145**

Segal, Jeffrey A., and Albert Cover. 1989. "Ideological values and the votes of U.S. Supreme Court Justices." *American Political Science Review* 83(2): 557–565. **10 and 317**

Segal, Jeffrey A., and Harold J. Spaeth. 1993. *The Supreme Court and the Attitudinal Model.* Cambridge: Cambridge University Press. **10, 40, and 317**

Segal, Jeffrey A., and Harold J. Spaeth. 2002. *The Supreme Court and the Attitudinal Model Revisited.* Cambridge: Cambridge University Press. **10 and 317**

Shepsle, Kenneth A., and Barry R. Weingast. 1981. "Structure-induced equilibrium and legislative choice." *Public Choice* 37(3): 503–519. **4**

Shih, Victor C. 2009. *Factions and Finance in China: Elite Conflict and Inflation.* Cambridge University Press. **152**

Shih, Victor C., Christopher Adolph, and Mingxing Liu. 2012. "Getting ahead in the Communist Party: Explaining the advancement of Central Committee members in China." *American Political Science Review* 106(1): 166–187. **318**

Siklos, Pierre L. 2002. *The Changing Face of Central Banking: Evolutionary Trends Since World War II.* Cambridge: Cambridge University Press. **31, 73, 110, 118, 122, 128, 154, 181, 250, and 293**

Skocpol, Theda. 1979. *States and Social Revolutions: A Comparative Analysis of France, Russia and China.* Cambridge: Cambridge University Press. **4**

Skocpol, Theda. 1995. *Protecting Soldiers and Mothers: The Political Origins of Social Policy in the United States.* Cambridge, MA: The Belknap Press of the Harvard University Press. **24**

Skowronek, Stephen. 1982. *Building a New American State: The Expansion of National Administrative Capacities.* Cambridge: Cambridge University Press. **4**

Smets, Frank. 2002. "Output gap uncertainty: Does it matter for the Taylor rule?"

Empirical Economics 27(1): 113–129. **120 and 122**

Soskice, David. 1990. "Wage determination: The changing role of institutions in advanced industrialized countries." *Oxford Review of Economic Policy* 6(4): 36–61. **187**

Soskice, David, Robert Bates, and David Epstein. 1992. "Ambition and constraint: The stabilizing role of institutions." *Journal of Law, Economics, and Organization* 8(3): 547–560. **17**

Spencer, David E. 2004. "Output gap uncertainty and monetary policy during the 1970s." *Topics in Macroeconomics* 4(1). **120**

Spiller, Pablo T. 1990. "Politicians, interest groups and regulators: A multiple-principals agency theory of regulation (Or: Let them be bribed)." *Journal of Law and Economics* 33(1): 65–97. **15 and 16**

Stigler, George J. 1971. "The theory of economic regulation." *The Bell Journal of Economics and Management Science* 2(1): 3–21. **11, 13, and 16**

Stigler, George J. 1987. *The Theory of Price*. 4th ed. New York: Macmillan. **205**

Stiglitz, Joseph E. 1998. "Central banking in a democratic society." *De Economist (Netherlands)* 146(2): 199–226. **240 and 241**

Stiglitz, Joseph E. 2002. *Globalization and its Discontents*. New York: Norton. **37**

Stiglitz, Joseph E. 2012. *The Price of Inequality*. New York: Norton. **306 and 308**

Stovel, Katherine, Michael Savage, and Peter Bearman. 1996. "Ascription into achievement: Models of career systems at Lloyds Bank, 1890–1970." *American Journal of Sociology* 102(2): 358–399. **71**

Streeck, Wolfgang, and Kathleen Thelen. 2005. "Institutional change in advanced political economies." In *Beyond Continuity: Explorations in the Dynamics of Advanced Political Economies*, ed. Wolfgang Streeck, and Kathleen Thelen. Oxford: Oxford University Press. pp. 1–39. **7**

Sturm, Jan-Egbert, and Jakob de Haan. 2001. "Inflation in developing countries: Does central bank independence matter? New evidence based on a new dataset." CESifo Working Paper Series 511. **149, 159, and 283**

Surico, Paolo. 2003. "U.S. monetary policy rules: The case for asymmetric preferences." Royal Economic Society Annual Conference, Number 199. **122**

Svensson, Lars E. O. 2003. "What is wrong with Taylor Rules? Using judgment in monetary policy through targeting rules." *Journal of Economic Literature* 41(2): 426–477. **118**

Svensson, Lars E. O. 1997. "Inflation forecast targeting: Implementing and monitoring inflation targets." *European Economic Review* 41(6): 1111–1146. **31**

Swenson, Peter. 1991. "Bringing capital back in, or Social Democracy reconsidered: Employer power, cross-class alliances, and centralization of industrial relations in Denmark and Sweden." *World Politics* 43(4): 513–544. **4**

Tate, C. Neal, and Roger Handberg. 1991. "Time binding and theory building in personal attribute models of Supreme Court voting behavior, 1916–88." *American Journal of Political Science* 35(2): 460–480. **40**

Taylor, John B. 1993. "Discretion versus policy rules in practice." *Carnegie-Rochester Conference Series on Public Policy* 39(1): 195–214. **118, 121, and 124**

Taylor, John B. 1999*a*. "A historical analysis of monetary policy rules." In *Monetary Policy Rules*, ed. John B. Taylor. Chicago: University of Chicago Press. pp. 319–340. **118 and 119**

Taylor, John B. 1999*b*. "Introduction." In *Monetary Policy Rules*, ed. John B. Taylor. Chicago: University of Chicago Press. pp. 1–14. **118 and 119**

Taylor, John B. 1999*c*. "The robustness and efficiency of monetary policy rules as guidelines for the interest rate setting by the European Central Bank." *Journal of Monetary Economics* 43(3): 655–679. **119**

Temple, Jonathan. 1998. "Central bank independence and inflation: Good news and bad news." *Economics Letters* 61(2): 215–219. **160, 174, and 189**

Temple, Jonathan. 2002. "Openness, inflation, and the Phillips curve: A puzzle." *Journal of Money, Credit, and Banking* 34(2): 450–468. **168**

The Japan Biographical Encyclopedia & Who's Who, 1964–65. n.d. 3rd edition. Tokyo: Rengo Press.

The Japan Who's Who. n.d. Tokyo: Tokyo News Service.

Thelen, Kathleen. 1999. "Historical institutionalism in comparative politics." *Annual Review of Political Science* 2: 369–404. **9**

Thelen, Kathleen. 2004. *How Institutions Evolve: The Political Economy of Skills in Germany, Britain, the United States, and Japan*. Cambridge: Cambridge University Press. **4, 6, and 7**

Tirole, Jean. 1994. "The internal organization of government." *Oxford Economic Papers* 46(1): 1–29. **55**

Toma, Mark. 1982. "Inflationary bias of the Federal Reserve System: A bureaucratic perspective." *Journal of Monetary Economics* 10(2): 163–190. **13**

Tomz, Michael, Joshua A. Tucker, and Jason Wittenberg. 2002. "An easy and accurate regression model for multiparty electoral data." *Political Analysis* 10(1): 66–83. **274**

Tootell, Geoffrey M.B. 1996. "Appointment procedures and FOMC voting behavior." *Southern Economic Journal* 63(1): 191–204. **131**

Treisman, Daniel. 2000. "Decentralization and inflation: Commitment, collective action, or continuity?" *American Political Science Review* 94(4): 837–858. **37**

Tsebelis, George. 2002. *Veto Players: How Political Institutions Work*. Princeton: Princeton University Press. **4**

Tufte, Edward R. 2001. *The Visual Display of Quantitative Information*. 2nd edition. Graphics Press. **284**

Valdés, Juan Gabriel. 1995. *Pinochet's Economists: The Chicago School in Chile*. Cambridge: Cambridge University Press. **145**

van der Meer, Fritz M., and Jos C.S. Raadschelders. 1999. "The senior civil service in the Netherlands: A quest for unity." In *Bureaucratic Élites in Western European States*, ed. Edward C. Page, and Vincent Wright. Oxford: Oxford University Press. pp. 205–228. **35**

van Maanen, John, and Edgar H. Schein. 1979. "Towards a theory of organizational socialization." *Research in Organizational Behavior* 1: 209–264. **39**

Vem Är Det: Svensk biografisk handbok. Various years. Stockholm: P.A. Norstedt & Söner.

Venables, W.N., and B.D. Ripley. 2002. *Modern Applied Statistics with* S. 4th edition. New York: Springer-Verlag. **284**

von Furstenberg, George M., and Michael K. Ulan. 1998. *Learning from the World's Best Central Bankers: Principles and Policies for Subduing Inflation.* Boston: Kluwer Academic Publishers.

Waller, Christopher J. 1992. "The choice of a conservative central banker in a multi-sector economy." *American Economic Review* 82(4): 1006–1012. **246**

Walsh, Carl E. 2003. *Monetary Theory and Policy.* 2nd edition. Cambridge, MA: MIT Press. **32**

Ware, Colin. 2004. *Information Visualization.* 2nd edition. Morgan Kaufman. **283**

Weber, Max. 1946. *From Max Weber: Essays in Sociology.* New York: Oxford University Press. **11 and 12**

Weingast, Barry, and Mark Moran. 1983. "Bureaucratic discretion or Congressional control? Regulatory policymaking by the Federal Trade Commission." *Journal of Political Economy* 91(5): 765–800. **36, 245, and 288**

Weir, Stuart, and David Beetham. 1999. *Political Power and Democratic Control in Britain.* London: Routledge. **31**

Wer Ist Wer in Österreich. 1953. Vienna: Verlag "Wer Ist Wer in Österreich."

Western, Bruce. 1995. "Concepts and suggestions for robust regression analysis." *American Journal of Political Science* 39(3): 786–817. **92**

Who's Who. Various years. London: A. & C. Black.

Who's Who in America. Various years. Chicago: Marquis Who's Who.

Who's Who in Austria. n.d.

Who's Who in Canada. Various years. Toronto: International Press Limited.

Who's Who in Japan, 1984-85. 1984. Hong Kong: International Culture Institute.

Who's Who in New Zealand. Various years. Wellington, New Zealand: Reed.

Who's Who in Spain. n.d.

Who's Who in Switzerland. n.d.

Who Was Who. Various years. London: A. & C. Black.

Who Was Who in America. Various years. Chicago: Marquis Who's Who.

Wilson, James Q. 1991. *Bureaucracy.* Basic Books. **10, 13, and 39**

Woodford, Michael. 2003. *Interest and Prices: Foundation of a Theory of Monetary Policy.* Princeton: Princeton University Press. **118**

Woodford, Michael. 2012. "Methods of policy accommodation at the interest-rate lower bound." Presented at the Annual Economic Symposium of the Federal Reserve Bank of Kansas City, Jackson Hole, WY, August 31. **308**

Woodward, Bob. 2000. *Maestro.* New York: Simon & Schuster. **10**

Woolley, John T. 1984. *Monetary Politics: The Federal Reserve and the Politics of Monetary Policy.* Cambridge: Cambridge University Press. **37 and 129**

Zysman, John. 1994. "How institutions create historically rooted trajectories of growth." *Industrial and Corporate Change* 3(1): 243–283. **4**

SUBJECT INDEX

For an author index see the references, which include page number back-references in bold following each work cited.

ABOUT THE TYPE, FIGURES, AND DATA

THIS BOOK WAS TYPESET BY THE AUTHOR using XeTeX, a powerful new implementation of the TeX typesetting system. The text is set in Bembo Book; titles, figures, and captions in Gill Sans; computer code in Inconsolata; text boxes in Archer; and Greek symbols in Porson. Most of the figures were produced in R and Adobe Illustrator. Many graphics, including the ropeladder plots for model exploration and robustness analysis, the lineplots for assessing evolution of time series variables, and the scatterplots with detailed marginal distributions, were produced using the `tile` package for R. The latest version of this package is available from `chrisadolph.com`, where the original data collected for this study and other replication materials, including the `Escore` package for career data processing, can also be found.

Other Books in the Series *(continued from page iii)*

Robert Bates, *When Things Fell Apart: State Failure in Late-Century Africa*
Mark Beissinger, *Nationalist Mobilization and the Collapse of the Soviet State*
Nancy Bermeo, ed., *Unemployment in the New Europe*
Carles Boix, *Democracy and Redistribution*
Carles Boix, *Political Parties, Growth, and Equality: Conservative and Social Democratic Economic Strategies in the World Economy*
Catherine Boone, *Merchant Capital and the Roots of State Power in Senegal, 1930–1985*
Catherine Boone, *Political Topographies of the African State: Territorial Authority and Institutional Change*
Michael Bratton, Robert Mattes, and E. Gyimah-Boadi, *Public Opinion, Democracy, and Market Reform in Africa*
Michael Bratton and Nicolas van de Walle, *Democratic Experiments in Africa: Regime Transitions in Comparative Perspective*
Valerie Bunce, *Leaving Socialism and Leaving the State: The End of Yugoslavia, the Soviet Union, and Czechoslovakia*
Daniele Caramani, *The Nationalization of Politics: The Formation of National Electorates and Party Systems in Europe*
John M. Carey, *Legislative Voting and Accountability*
Kanchan Chandra, *Why Ethnic Parties Succeed: Patronage and Ethnic Headcounts in India*
Eric C. C. Chang, Mark Andreas Kayser, Drew A. Linzer, and Ronald Rogowski, *Electoral Systems and the Balance of Consumer-Producer Power*
José Antonio Cheibub, *Presidentialism, Parliamentarism, and Democracy*
Ruth Berins Collier, *Paths toward Democracy: The Working Class and Elites in Western Europe and South America*
Pepper D. Culpepper, *Quiet Politics and Business Power: Corporate Control in Europe and Japan*
Rafaela M. Dancygier, *Immigration and Conflict in Europe*
Christian Davenport, *State Repression and the Domestic Democratic Peace*
Donatella della Porta, *Social Movements, Political Violence, and the State*
Alberto Diaz-Cayeros, *Federalism, Fiscal Authority, and Centralization in Latin America*
Thad Dunning, *Crude Democracy: Natural Resource Wealth and Political Regimes*
Gerald Easter, *Reconstructing the State: Personal Networks and Elite Identity*

Margarita Estevez-Abe, *Welfare and Capitalism in Postwar Japan: Party, Bureaucracy, and Business*

Henry Farrell, *The Political Economy of Trust: Institutions, Interests, and Inter-Firm Cooperation in Italy and Germany*

Karen E. Ferree, *Framing the Race in South Africa: The Political Origins of Racial Census Elections*

M. Steven Fish, *Democracy Derailed in Russia: The Failure of Open Politics*

Robert F. Franzese, *Macroeconomic Policies of Developed Democracies*

Roberto Franzosi, *The Puzzle of Strikes: Class and State Strategies in Postwar Italy*

Timothy Frye, *Building States and Markets After Communism: The Perils of Polarized Democracy*

Geoffrey Garrett, *Partisan Politics in the Global Economy*

Scott Gehlbach, *Representation through Taxation: Revenue, Politics, and Development in Postcommunist States*

Edward L. Gibson, *Boundary Control: Subnational Authoritarianism in Federal Democracies*

Jane R. Gingrich, *Making Markets in the Welfare State: The Politics of Varying Market Reforms*

Miriam Golden, *Heroic Defeats: The Politics of Job Loss*

Jeff Goodwin, *No Other Way Out: States and Revolutionary Movements*

Merilee Serrill Grindle, *Changing the State*

Anna Grzymala-Busse, *Rebuilding Leviathan: Party Competition and State Exploitation in Post-Communist Democracies*

Anna Grzymala-Busse, *Redeeming the Communist Past: The Regeneration of Communist Parties in East Central Europe*

Frances Hagopian, *Traditional Politics and Regime Change in Brazil*

Henry E. Hale, *The Foundations of Ethnic Politics: Separatism of States and Nations in Eurasia and the World*

Mark Hallerberg, Rolf Ranier Strauch, and Jürgen von Hagen, *Fiscal Governance in Europe*

Stephen E. Hanson, *Post-Imperial Democracies: Ideology and Party Formation in Third Republic France, Weimar Germany, and Post-Soviet Russia*

Silja Häusermann, *The Politics of Welfare State Reform in Continental Europe: Modernization in Hard Times*

Gretchen Helmke, *Courts Under Constraints: Judges, Generals, and Presidents in Argentina*

Yoshiko Herrera, *Imagined Economies: The Sources of Russian Regionalism*

J. Rogers Hollingsworth and Robert Boyer, eds., *Contemporary Capitalism: The Embeddedness of Institutions*
John D. Huber and Charles R. Shipan, *Deliberate Discretion? The Institutional Foundations of Bureaucratic Autonomy*
Ellen Immergut, *Health Politics: Interests and Institutions in Western Europe*
Torben Iversen, *Capitalism, Democracy, and Welfare*
Torben Iversen, *Contested Economic Institutions*
Torben Iversen, Jonas Pontussen, and David Soskice, eds., *Unions, Employers, and Central Banks: Macroeconomic Coordination and Institutional Change in Social Market Economies*
Thomas Janoski and Alexander M. Hicks, eds., *The Comparative Political Economy of the Welfare State*
Joseph Jupille, *Procedural Politics: Issues, Influence, and Institutional Choice in the European Union*
Stathis Kalyvas, *The Logic of Violence in Civil War*
David C. Kang, *Crony Capitalism: Corruption and Capitalism in South Korea and the Philippines*
Stephen B. Kaplan, *Globalization and Austerity Politics in Latin America*
Junko Kato, *Regressive Taxation and the Welfare State*
Orit Kedar, *Voting for Policy, Not Parties: How Voters Compensate for Power Sharing*
Robert O. Keohane and Helen B. Milner, eds., *Internationalization and Domestic Politics*
Herbert Kitschelt, *The Transformation of European Social Democracy*
Herbert Kitschelt, Kirk A. Hawkins, Juan Pablo Luna, Guillermo Rosas, and Elizabeth J. Zechmeister, *Latin American Party Systems*
Herbert Kitschelt, Peter Lange, Gary Marks, and John D. Stephens, eds., *Continuity and Change in Contemporary Capitalism*
Herbert Kitschelt, Zdenka Mansfeldova, Radek Markowski, and Gabor Toka, *Post-Communist Party Systems*
David Knoke, Franz Urban Pappi, Jeffrey Broadbent, and Yutaka Tsujinaka, eds., *Comparing Policy Networks*
Allan Kornberg and Harold D. Clarke, *Citizens and Community: Political Support in a Representative Democracy*
Amie Kreppel, *The European Parliament and the Supranational Party System*
David D. Laitin, *Language Repertoires and State Construction in Africa*
Fabrice E. Lehoucq and Ivan Molina, *Stuffing the Ballot Box: Fraud, Electoral Reform, and Democratization in Costa Rica*

Mark Irving Lichbach and Alan S. Zuckerman, eds., *Comparative Politics: Rationality, Culture, and Structure, 2nd Edition*

Evan Lieberman, *Race and Regionalism in the Politics of Taxation in Brazil and South Africa*

Pauline Jones Luong, *Institutional Change and Political Continuity in Post-Soviet Central Asia*

Pauline Jones Luong and Erika Weinthal, *Oil Is Not a Curse: Ownership Structure and Institutions in Soviet Successor States*

Julia Lynch, *Age in the Welfare State: The Origins of Social Spending on Pensioners, Workers, and Children*

Doug McAdam, John McCarthy, and Mayer Zald, eds., *Comparative Perspectives on Social Movements*

Lauren M. MacLean, *Informal Institutions and Citizenship in Rural Africa: Risk and Reciprocity in Ghana and Côte d'Ivoire*

Beatriz Magaloni, *Voting for Autocracy: Hegemonic Party Survival and Its Demise in Mexico*

James Mahoney, *Colonialism and Postcolonial Development: Spanish America in Comparative Perspective*

James Mahoney and Dietrich Rueschemeyer, eds., *Historical Analysis and the Social Sciences*

Scott Mainwaring and Matthew Soberg Shugart, eds., *Presidentialism and Democracy in Latin America*

Isabela Mares, *The Politics of Social Risk: Business and Welfare State Development*

Isabela Mares, *Taxation, Wage Bargaining, and Unemployment*

Cathie Jo Martin and Duane Swank, *The Political Construction of Business Interests: Coordination, Growth, and Equality*

Anthony W. Marx, *Making Race, Making Nations: A Comparison of South Africa, the United States, and Brazil*

Bonnie M. Meguid, *Party Competition between Unequals: Strategies and Electoral Fortunes in Western Europe*

Joel S. Migdal, *State in Society: Studying How States and Societies Constitute One Another*

Joel S. Migdal, Atul Kohli, and Vivienne Shue, eds., *State Power and Social Forces: Domination and Transformation in the Third World*

Scott Morgenstern and Benito Nacif, eds., *Legislative Politics in Latin America*

Layna Mosley, *Global Capital and National Governments*

Layna Mosley, *Labor Rights and Multinational Production*

Wolfgang C. Müller and Kaare Strøm, *Policy, Office, or Votes?*

CPSIA information can be obtained
at www.ICGtesting.com
Printed in the USA
LVOW01s2048200716
497106LV00003B/27/P

9 781107 567092